Lecture Notes in Computer Science

T0250669

Commenced Publication in 1973
Founding and Former Series Editors:
Gerhard Goos, Juris Hartmanis, and Jan van Leeuwen

Antti Valmari (Ed.)

Model Checking Software

13th International SPIN Workshop
Vienna, Austria, March 30 – April 1, 2006
Proceedings

 Springer

Volume Editor

Antti Valmari
Tampere University of Technology
Institute of Software Systems
PO Box 553, 33101 Tampere, Finland
E-mail: antti.valmari@tut.fi

Library of Congress Control Number: 2006922236

CR Subject Classification (1998): F.3, D.2.4, D.3.1, D.2

LNCS Sublibrary: SL 1 – Theoretical Computer Science and General Issues

ISSN   0302-9743
ISBN-10   3-540-33102-6 Springer Berlin Heidelberg New York
ISBN-13   978-3-540-33102-5 Springer Berlin Heidelberg New York

Springer is a part of Springer Science+Business Media

springer.com

© Springer-Verlag Berlin Heidelberg 2006
Printed in Germany

Typesetting: Camera-ready by author, data conversion by Scientific Publishing Services, Chennai, India
Printed on acid-free paper   SPIN: 11691617   06/3142   5 4 3 2 1 0

Preface

The name "SPIN" refers both to a workshop on model checking and to a famous model checking tool. The SPIN workshop is an annual forum for practitioners and researchers interested in state space-based techniques for the validation and analysis of software and hardware systems, including communication protocols. It focuses on techniques based on explicit representations of state spaces, as implemented in the SPIN model checker or other tools, and techniques based on a combination of explicit representations with other representations. The SPIN model checker has proven to be particularly suited for the analysis of concurrent asynchronous systems. The workshop aims to encourage interaction and exchange of ideas with all related areas in software engineering. To promote interaction even further, many SPIN workshops have been held in conjunction with other meetings.

The 13th International SPIN Workshop on Model Checking of Software was held in Vienna, Austria, co-located with the European Joint Conferences on Theory and Practice of Software (ETAPS) 2006. The earlier SPIN workshops were held in Montreal, Canada (1995); Rutgers University, USA (1996); Twente University, The Netherlands (1997); ENST, Paris, France (1998); Trento, Italy (1999); Toulouse, France (1999); Stanford University, USA (2000); Toronto, Canada (2001); Grenoble, France (2002); Portland, Oregon, USA (2003); Barcelona, Spain (2004); and San Francisco, USA (2005). The proceedings of the Trento and Toulouse workshops were published together in Springer's *Lecture Notes in Computer Science* volume 1680. From then on, each SPIN proceedings has been published as an individual LNCS volume.

SPIN 2006 attracted 44 submissions, of which 5 were short tool presentations and 7 were co-authored by a member of the Program Committee. The submissions were distributed to Program Committee members for reviewing. They reviewed the papers either personally or delegated them to sub-reviewers. The sub-reviewers are listed on page VIII. Each paper received three reviews, and in one case an additional fourth review was obtained.

Submissions whose reviews were neither overwhelmingly positive nor overwhelmingly negative were discussed by the Program Committee members. Most discussions led to a consensus on the fate of the paper. In the few cases where a disagreement remained to the end, the decision followed the opinion of the majority of the Program Committee members who had participated in the processing of that submission. All accepted papers had in the end more support (scores 4 and 5) than objection (scores 2, 1 and 0), and no rejected paper had more support than objection. Program committee members who had co-authored a submission, or for some other reason declared a conflict with it, were excluded from all information regarding its processing.

The Program Committee chose 19 submissions to be presented in the workshop and included in the proceedings. Of these, three were short tool presentations and four were co-authored by a member of the PC.

After processing the submitted papers, the Program Committee invited Roope Kaivola (Intel Corporation, USA) to give a keynote talk on the verification of microprocessors at Intel, and Stefan Edelkamp (Universität Dortmund, Germany) to give a tutorial on directed model checking.

The submission deadline of SPIN 2006 was set quite late, to position it reasonably relative to the submission deadlines of other conferences in the field. As a consequence, the Program Committee had to work in an unusually short period of time, perhaps the shortest in the recent history of SPIN. That the full number of reviews was obtained for each submission is a small miracle. I am grateful to every member of the Program Committee for their efficient and excellent work!

In addition to the Program Committee, the help of the SPIN Steering Committee, and in particular its chair, Pierre Wolper (Université de Liège, Belgium), was extremely important for the success of the paper selection process. On the practical side, the OCS Online Conference Service (originally developed by METAFrame) maintained by Martin Karusseit and Markus Bajohr at the University of Dortmund proved once again very helpful in various stages of the paper selection procedure. And, of course, without the hard work of local organizers there would not have been any workshop — our thanks to Jens Knoop, Andreas Krall, and their team.

January 2006   Antti Valmari
                                                        Program Chair
                                                          SPIN 2006

Organization

SPIN 2006 was the 13th International SPIN Workshop on Model Checking of Software. It was held in Vienna, Austria, March 30–April 1, 2006. It was one of the satellite events of ETAPS 2006, The European Joint Conferences on Theory and Practice of Software. On behalf of ETAPS, Jens Knoop and Andreas Krall (Vienna University of Technology) took care of the practical organization of SPIN 2006 and other satellite events.

Advisory Committee

Gerard Holzmann
Amir Pnueli

Steering Committee

Thomas Ball	Susanne Graf	Moshe Vardi
Patrice Godefroid	Stefan Leue	Pierre Wolper (Chair)

Program Committee

Jonathan Billington (University of South Australia)
Bernard Boigelot (University of Liège, Belgium)
Dragan Bošnački (Eindhoven University of Technology, The Netherlands)
Dennis Dams (Bell Labs, USA)
Stefan Edelkamp (University of Dortmund, Germany)
Cormac Flanagan (University of California at Santa Cruz, USA)
Gerard Holzmann (NASA/JPL, USA)
Roope Kaivola (Intel, USA)
Lars M. Kristensen (University of Aarhus, Denmark)
Stefan Leue (University of Konstanz, Germany)
Laurent Mounier (Verimag, France)
Wojciech Penczek (Polish Academy of Sciences, Poland)
Bill Roscoe (University of Oxford, UK)
Theo Ruys (University of Twente, The Netherlands)
Stefan Schwoon (University of Stuttgart, Germany)
Scott Stoller (SUNY at Stony Brook, USA)
Antti Valmari (Tampere University of Technology, Finland) (Chair)
Willem Visser (NASA Ames, USA)

Additional Referees

Aljazzar, Husain
Andova, Suzana
Bednarczyk, Marek
Bingham, Jesse
Borzyszkowski, Andrzej
Bultan, Tevfik
Conway, Christopher
Esser, Robert
Gallasch, Guy Edward
Ghughal, Rajnish
Goel, Amit
Graf, Susanne

Groce, Alex
Han, Bing
Hermanns, Holger
Ioustinova, Natalia
Jabbar, Shahid
Janowski, Pawel
Joshi, Rajeev
Kellomäki, Timo
Lluch Lafuente, Alberto
Namjoshi, Kedar
Narasimhan, Naren
Niewiadomski, Artur

Orzechowski, Maciej
Paczkowski, Pawel
Ştefănescu, Alin
Stegantova, Evghenia
Szreter, Maciej
Wei, Wei
Westergaard, Michael
Wozna, Bozena
Yang, Ping
Zhang, Dezhuang

Table of Contents

Applications

Assume–Guarantee

Partial Order Reduction

Tool Demonstrations

Large-Scale Directed Model Checking LTL

Stefan Edelkamp and Shahid Jabbar

University of Dortmund,
Otto-Hahn Straße 14
{stefan.edelkamp, shahid.jabbar}@cs.uni-dortmund.de

Abstract. To analyze larger models for explicit-state model checking, *directed model checking* applies error-guided search, *external model checking* uses secondary storage media, and *distributed model checking* exploits parallel exploration on multiple processors.

In this paper we propose an external, distributed and directed on-the-fly model checking algorithm to check general LTL properties in the model checker SPIN. Previous attempts are restricted to checking safety properties. The worst-case I/O complexity is bounded by $O(sort(|\mathcal{F}||\mathcal{R}|)/p + l \cdot scan(|\mathcal{F}||\mathcal{S}|))$, where $\mathcal{S}$ and $\mathcal{R}$ are the sets of visited states and transitions in the synchronized product of the Büchi automata for the model and the property specification, $\mathcal{F}$ is the number of accepting states, l is the length of the shortest counterexample, and p is the number of processors. The algorithm we propose returns minimal lasso-shaped counterexamples and includes refinements for property-driven exploration.

1 Introduction

The core limitation to the exploration of systems are bounded main memory resources. Relying on virtual memory slows down the exploration due to excessive page faults. External algorithms [31] exploit hard disk space and organize the access to secondary memory. Originally designed for explicit graphs, external search algorithms have shown considerably good performances in the large-scale breadth-first and guided exploration of games [22, 12] and in the analysis of model checking problems [24][1].

the idea of external model checking was introduced in A Directed explicit-state model checking [13] enhances the error-reporting capabilities of model checkers. The application of guided search for checking liveness properties is restricted to the reduction of trails [14].

Distributed explicit state model checking [9, 25] uses several processors working in parallel to enhance the exploration of larger models.

---

[1] An anonymous referee has pointed us to the work of Roscoe: *Model Checking CSP* in *A Classical Mind, Essays in Honour of C.A.R. Hoare*, Prentice-Hall 1994, which also introduces to the idea of external model checking for the FDR system. Unfortunately, we haven't been able to access the reference.

A. Valmari (Ed.): SPIN 2006, LNCS 3925, pp. 1–18, 2006.

In [18] we have given a first report on combining directed, parallel and external explicit-state model checking to enhance the search for minimal counterexamples for safety errors. Under certain assumptions on the distribution of the applied hash function and the number of file pointers we showed that the approach uses linear, i.e., $O(scan(|\mathcal{S}| + |\mathcal{R}|))$ I/Os. In a sequential setting, for safety explicit-state model checking state-space graphs with bounded locality we arrive at $O(sort(|\mathcal{R}|) + scan(|\mathcal{S}|))$ I/Os, which is optimal [12].

The goal of this work is to extend this work to the exploration for checking liveness properties. The main challenge for distributed and external on-the-fly model checking is that the depth-first traversal of the global state space graph as used in *Nested-DFS* (an on-the-fly variant of Tarjan's algorithm [35]) is not efficient. All attempts to solve this problem via variants of breadth-first search [7, 4, 9] arrive at a time complexity that is non-linear in the size of the model. The approach we propose in this paper is based on a translation procedure of liveness problems into safety problems [32]. The translation approach has the advantage that the underlying algorithm design to detect safety errors has not to be changed. More crucially, the approach includes a rich state description which allows to express lower bounds for cost-optimal guided search. To enhance the exploration, we additionally exploit the *never-claim* automaton structure of the temporal property to be satisfied.

The paper is structured as follows. First we briefly review explicit-state LTL model checking using Büchi automata. Then we consider distributed model checking together with its limits and possibilities. Afterwards we introduce to external model checking safety properties and delayed duplication detection. We first consider breadth-first implicit graph search. Next we turn to the guided search, recalling the algorithm *External A**. The upcoming section points out the problems in externalizing standard DFS model checking algorithms. This leads to the proposed approach for I/O efficient parallel external model checking. We provide monotone heuristics for optimal counterexample search and give empirical data for checking LTL formulae in an external and parallel variant of the SPIN model checker. Finally, we draw conclusions and indicate further research avenues.

2   Explicit-State Model Checking

In automata-based model checking, both the model to be analyzed and the specification to be checked are modeled as non-deterministic *Büchi automata*. Syntactically, Büchi automata are ordinary automata. For accepting *infinite words*, or *runs*, a different acceptance condition is applied. Let ρ be a run and $inf(\rho)$ be the set of states reached infinitely often in ρ, then a Büchi automaton accepts, if the intersection between $inf(\rho)$ and the set of final states F is not empty.

2.1   Automata-Based LTL Model Checking

The desired property of the system is specified in some form of temporal logic. We briefly introduce *linear temporal logic (LTL)*. A path in model $\mathcal{M}$ is a sequence of states $\pi = S_0, S_1, \ldots$ and π^i denotes the suffix of π starting at S_i. LTL formulae have the form "Always f", where f is a *path formula*. If p is an atomic proposition then p is a path formula. If f and g are path formulae so are $\neg f, f \vee g, f \wedge g, \mathbf{X} \; f, \mathbf{F} \; f, \mathbf{G} \; f$, and $f \; \mathbf{U} \; g$.

Transforming the model and the specification into Büchi automata assumes that systems can be modeled by automata, and that the LTL formula can be transformed into an equivalent Büchi automaton. The converse is not always possible, since Büchi automata are clearly more expressive than LTL expressions [36]. Checking correctness is reduced to checking language emptiness. More formally, the model checking procedure validates that a model represented by an automaton $\mathcal{M}$ satisfies its specification represented by an automaton $\mathcal{S}$. The task is to verify if $\mathcal{L}(\mathcal{M}) \subseteq \mathcal{L}(\mathcal{S})$. In words: the *language accepted by the model is included in that of the specification*. We have $\mathcal{L}(\mathcal{M}) \subseteq \mathcal{L}(\mathcal{S})$ if and only if $\mathcal{L}(\mathcal{M}) \cap \overline{\mathcal{L}(\mathcal{S})} = \emptyset$. In practice, checking language emptiness is more efficient than checking language inclusion. Büchi automata are closed under intersection and complementation [8], so that there exists an automaton that accepts $\overline{\mathcal{L}(\mathcal{S})}$ and an automata that accepts $\mathcal{L}(\mathcal{M}) \cap \overline{\mathcal{L}(\mathcal{S})}$. It is possible to complement Büchi automaton equivalent to an LTL formula, *but* the worst-case running time of such a construction is double-exponential in the size of the formula. Therefore, in practice one constructs the *never-claim* automaton for negation of the LTL formula, avoiding complementation.

The product is *synchronous*, that is each transition in one automaton implies one in the other. The property automaton is non-deterministic, such that both the successor generation and the temporal formula representation may introduce branching to the overall exploration. The construction assumes that all states in the model are accepting. If arbitrary Büchi automata are intersected, *extended acceptance conditions* are required [11].

For *checking emptiness* we have to check that the automaton accepts no word. *Accepting runs* are present in the automaton if the strongly connected components (SCCs) reachable from the initial state contain at least one accepting state. In this case, a reachable cycle contains at least one accepting state. Checking language emptiness corresponds to the validation that no such cycle exists.

2.2 Tarjan's Algorithm

For finding accepting cycles, we analyze the state space graph structure; more precisely, the strongly connected components, SCCs for short. An algorithm to compute all such components of a graph in linear time is Tarjan's algorithm [35]. The algorithm is divided into four stages. In the first stage, a DFS starting at the initial state computes the discovery and finishing times $t_d(u)$ and $t_f(u)$ for each visited state u, which corresponds to the time, when node u is entered and left. The second stage computes the inverse of the graph. In the third stage, a series of DFSs considers the nodes in order of decreasing t_f-value. The fourth and last stage outputs the nodes of each tree in the DFS forest of the third stage as a strongly connected component.

2.3 Nested DFS

On-the-fly model checking is an efficient way to perform model checking. It computes the global state transition graph during the construction of the intersection. The advantage is that only a part of the state space is constructed, which is needed in order to check the desired property.

For checking the synchronous product graph of the model and the specification for accepting cycles on-the-fly, *nested-depth-first search* has been proposed [17]. It explores the state space in a depth-first manner, stores visited states in a visited list, marks states which are on the current search stack, and invokes a secondary DFS starting at accepting states after they have been fully explored in the primary DFS. The secondary DFS explores states already visited by the primary search but not by any secondary search; states visited by the second search are *flagged* and if a state is found on the stack of first search, an accepting cycle is found. Typical implementations use 2 bits per state, one for marking, one for flagging. As with Tarjan's algorithm its worst-case is linear in the size of the intersected state transition graph, but it is capable of reporting counter-examples before the entire state space has been seen.

Property-driven or *improved nested-depth-first search* [3, 25] partitions the never-claim into SCCs. The main observation is that cycles in the state transition graph of the intersection of the system $\mathcal{M}$ and the never-claim automaton $\mathcal{N}$ is accepting only if the corresponding cycle in $\mathcal{N}$ is accepting. Therefore, these approaches use Tarjan's algorithm to analyze never-claim. An SCC in $\mathcal{N}$ is called *non-accepting* if none of its states is accepting; *fully-accepting*, if each cycle formed by states of the SCC is accepting, and *partially-accepting*, otherwise. Improved nested DFS partitions the never-claim into SCCs and applies secondary search only in case of partially accepting cycles.

3   Distributed Model Checking LTL

Liveness property validation based on DFS appears to be an inappropriate choice for distributed model checking. For distributed model checking the core reason is that in contrast to BFS, DFS appears to be inherently sequential [29]. Different attempts have been suggested to allow an efficient parallelization for model checking liveness. Unfortunately, none of the approaches guarantee a linear time complexity.

3.1 Breadth-First LTL Model Checking

A line of research tries to avoid *nested depth-first search* by studying variants of breadth-first search [5, 4, 7]. The approach presented in [5, 4] invokes a secondary search for detecting cycles from BFS *backward edges*, i.e., transitions encountered in the overall state space that link states in larger, together with (already explored) states in smaller depth. Those backward edges may potentially spawn cycles and are searched individually. If no accepting cycle is found the depth bound is increased. The number of backward edges is reduced by similar observations as in improved nested depth-first search. The worst case time complexity is $O(|\mathcal{R}| \cdot (|\mathcal{S}| + |\mathcal{R}|))$. The approach allows *on-the-fly* model checking and is compatible with a limited form of partial order reduction. In [7], instead of backward edges, predecessor acceptance is chosen for an $O(|\mathcal{R}|^2 + |\mathcal{S}|)$ algorithm.

3.2 Explicit Fair Cycle Detection

In [9], the symbolic OWCTY[2] algorithm [15] is converted into an explicit one. Similar to Tarjan's algorithm, the approach computes the entire reachability set before extracting the cycle. Unlike Tarjan's algorithm, the order of the exploration does not matter. Next, a loop alternates between a *reachability* and *elimination phase* unless a fixpoint is reached. In the first phase, fair states are checked if they can be reached again. In the second phase, states with a determined fair status are eliminated from the search. The worst case number of iterations is bounded by the diameter d of the search space. The explicit state conversion of the approach runs in $O(d \cdot (|\mathcal{R}| + |\mathcal{S}|))$ time and has been exploited to perform distributed model checking. Cycle extraction for counter-example generation runs in linear time.

4   External Model Checking Safety

I/O-efficient model checking algorithms explicitly manage the memory hierarchy and can lead to substantial speedups compared to caching and pre-fetching heuristics of the underlying operating system, since they are more informed to predict and adjust future memory access.

The standard model for comparing the performance of external algorithms consists of a single processor, a small internal memory that can hold up to M data items, and an unlimited secondary memory. The size of the input problem (in terms of the number of records) is abbreviated by N. Moreover, the *block size* B governs the bandwidth of memory transfers. It is often convenient to refer to these parameters in terms of blocks, so we define $m = M/B$ and $n = N/B$. It is usually assumed that at the beginning of the algorithm, the input data is stored in contiguous blocks on external memory, and the same must hold for the output. Only the number of block reads and writes are counted, computations in internal memory do not incur any cost. The single disk model for external algorithms has been invented by [2]. An extension of the model considers D disks that can be accessed simultaneously. When using multiple disks in parallel, the technique of *disk striping* can be employed to essentially increase the block size by a factor of D. Successive blocks are distributed across different disks.

It is convenient to express the complexity of external-memory algorithms using a number of frequently occurring primitive operations. The simplest operation is *scanning*, which means reading a stream of records stored consecutively on

---

[2] Acronym for *One Way to Catch them Young*.

secondary memory. In this case, it is trivial to exploit disk- and block-parallelism. The number of I/Os is $scan(N) = \Theta(\frac{N}{DB}) = \Theta(\frac{n}{D})$. Another important operation is external *sorting*. The proposed algorithms fall into two categories: those based on the *merging* paradigm, and those based on the *distribution* paradigm. The algorithms' complexity is $sort(N) = \Theta(\frac{N}{DB} \log_{M/B} \frac{N}{B}) = \Theta(\frac{n}{D} \log_m n)$.

4.1   External BFS

Recall the standard internal-memory BFS algorithm: it visits each node $v \in V$ of the input problem graph G in a one-by-one fashion, as stored in a FIFO queue. After a node v is extracted, its adjacency list (the sets of neighbors in G) is examined, and those of them that haven't been visited so far are inserted into the queue in turn. In external search the internal queue is substituted with a file. Naively running the standard internal-BFS algorithm in the same way in external memory will result in $\Theta(|\mathcal{S}|)$ I/Os for unstructured accesses to the adjacency lists, and $\Theta(|\mathcal{R}|)$ I/Os for finding out whether neighboring nodes have already been visited. The explicit external graph algorithm of [27] improves on the latter complexity for the case of undirected graphs, in which duplicates are constrained to be located in adjacent levels. After the preprocessing step the graph is stored in adjacency-list representation, it generating the multi-set of neighbors for each BFS-level followed by a duplicate elimination phase. Duplicate elimination is realized via external sorting followed by an external scan. External BFS requires $O(|\mathcal{S}| + sort(|\mathcal{R}|))$ time, where $O(|\mathcal{S}|)$ is due to the external representation of the graph and the initial reconfiguration time to enable efficient successor generation.

   An implicit variant of the above algorithm algorithm [27] for explicit BFS-search in implicit graphs has been coined to the term *delayed duplicate detection* for *frontier search* [21]. It assumes an undirected search graph. The algorithm maintains BFS layers on disk. Layer $L(i-1)$ is scanned and the set of successors are put into a buffer of size close to the main memory capacity. If the buffer becomes full, internal sorting followed by a duplicate elimination scanning phase generates a sorted duplicate-free state sequence in the buffer that is flushed to disk. The outcome of this phase are k sorted files. In the next step, *external merging* is applied to unify the files into $L(i)$ by a simultaneous scan. The size of the output files is chosen such that a single pass suffices. Duplicates are eliminated. Since the files were sorted, the complexity is given by the scanning time of all files. One also has to eliminate $L(i-1)$ and $L(i-2)$ from $L(i)$ to avoid re-computations; that is, nodes extracted from the external queue are not immediately deleted, but kept until after the layer has been completely generated and sorted, at which point duplicates can be eliminated using a parallel scan. The process is repeated until $L(i-1)$ becomes empty, or the goal has been found. The total execution time is $O(sort(|\mathcal{R}|) + scan(|\mathcal{S}|))$ I/Os. The I/O optimality of External BFS is based on the work of [1], who gave a matching lower bound for external sorting.

   External BFS has been successfully applied to fully explore the 15-Puzzle using 1.4 terabytes of hard disk in about three weeks [22]. The algorithm shares similarities with the internal *frontier search* algorithms [23] that were used for solving multiple sequence alignment problem, an idea that goes back to Hirschberg [16].

4.2 External A*

External A* [12] maintains the search space on disk. The priority queue data structure is represented as a list of buckets. In the course of the algorithm, each bucket $L(i,j)$ will contain all states u with path length $g(u) = i$ and heuristic estimate $h(u) = j$. We will later discuss how such estimates can be derived in real-time minimum-cost reachability analysis. As same states have same heuristic estimates, it is easy to restrict duplicate detection to buckets of the same h-value. By an assumed undirected, unweighted state space problem graph structure, we can restrict aspirants for duplicate detection further. If all duplicates of a state with g-value i are removed with respect to the levels i, $i-1$ and $i-2$, then no duplicate state will remain for the entire search process. For breadth-first-search in explicit graphs, this is in fact the algorithm of [27]. We consider each bucket as a different file that has an individual internal buffer. A bucket is *active* if some of its states are currently expanded or generated. If a buffer becomes full, then it is flushed to disk.

Since External A* simulates A* and changes only the order of elements to be expanded that have the same f-value, completeness and optimality are inherited from the properties of A*. The I/O complexity for External A* in an implicit unweighted and undirected graph with monotone estimates is bounded by $O(sort(|\mathcal{R}|) + scan(|\mathcal{S}|))$, where $|\mathcal{S}|$ and $|\mathcal{R}|$ are the number of nodes and edges in the explored subgraph of the state space problem graph. It has been shown [12] that the lower bound for the delayed duplicate detection is $\Omega(sort(|\mathcal{S}|))$ I/Os.

Parallel External A* [18] is a parallel variant of External A* based on queues of working requests. In the exploration stage, each processor flushes the successors with a particular g and h value to an individual file. It has its own hash table and eliminates some duplicates already in main memory. If the output buffer exceeds memory capacity the processor writes the hash table to disk. In a first sorting stage, it sorts its own files. The number of file pointers needed is restricted by the number of flushed buffers. In the distribution stage, a single processor distributes all states in the pre-sorted files into different files according to the hash value's range. As all input files are sorted this is a mere scan. In the second sorting stage, processors externally sort the partially sorted files to find further duplicates. The output of this phase are sorted and partitioned buffers. Using the hash index as the sorting key the concatenation of files is totally sorted.

5 Problems with Externalizing DFS

External depth-first search relies on an external stack data structure. The search stack is small compared to the overall search but in the worst-case it can become large. For an external stack, the buffer is just an internal memory array of $2B$ elements that at any time contains the $k < 2B$ elements most recently inserted.

We assume that the stack content is bounded by at most N elements. A *pop* operation incurs no I/O, except for the case where the buffer has run empty, where $O(1)$ I/O to retrieve a block of B elements is sufficient. A *push* operation incurs no I/O, except for the case where the buffer has run full, where $O(1)$ I/O is to retrieve a block of B elements is needed. Insertion and deletion take $1/B$ I/Os in the amortized sense.

The I/O complexity for external DFS for explicit (possible directed) graphs has been shown to be $O(|\mathcal{S}| + |\mathcal{S}|/M \cdot scan(|\mathcal{R}|))$ [10]. There are $|\mathcal{S}|/M$ stages where the internal buffer for the visited state set becomes full, in which case it is flushed and duplicates are eliminated from the external adjacency list representation by a file scan. Visited successors in the unexplored adjacency lists are marked not to be generated again, such that all states in the internal visited list can be eliminated for good. As with External BFS in explicit graphs, value $O(|\mathcal{S}|)$ I/Os is due to the unstructured access to the external adjacency list. Computing SCCs in explicit graphs has the same I/O complexity as DFS, i.e. $O(|\mathcal{S}| + |\mathcal{S}|/M \cdot scan(|\mathcal{R}|))$ I/Os. For implicit graphs as generated for model checking liveness, no access to an external adjacency list is needed, so that the world should look better. Dropping the term of $O(|\mathcal{S}|)$ I/O as with External BFS, however, is a challenge. The major problem for external DFS exploration in implicit graphs is that unseen adjacencies cannot been modeled and there is no time for performing delayed duplicate detection. For implicit graphs this is not available, as we cannot access the search graph that we have not seen so far.

6   Large-Scale Model Checking Liveness

We decided to build our external model checker on top of the *liveness as safety model checking* approach [32]. It proposes to convert a liveness model checking problem into a safety model checking problem by roughly doubling the state vector size and *guessing* the seed of a fairness cycle. More precisely, the proposed extension stores with the current state s a previously seen state s' together with two flags *start-cycle* and *closed-cycle*. The first flag is set to prevent future overwriting of the stored state. The second flag indicates that a second occurrence of s' has been found. Unless the seed of the cycle has not been guessed s equals s'. The initial state is spawned to two states, one attached to (*false,false*) and the other attached to *true,false*). If $\mathcal{S}$ and $\mathcal{R}$ are the set of states and the set of transitions of the synchronous product of the model and the (never-claim) specification, then $\mathcal{S}$ is searched at most $|\mathcal{S}|$ times, yielding a time complexity of $O(|\mathcal{S}| \cdot (|\mathcal{S}| + |\mathcal{R}|))$.

The most important observation is that based on this extension the exploration algorithms themselves have not (or only in a minor way) to be changed. For example, in [32] the authors show how to extend models using so-called observers and applying the same model checker. In [33] the authors showed that for fairness constraints of the form $\mathbf{F}p$ we have that

$$\rho = (S_1 \ldots S_{l-1})(S_l \ldots S_{k-1})^\omega$$

is a run in the state space $\mathcal{S}$ if and only if

$$\rho' = (S_0, S_0, 0, 0) \ldots (S_{l-1}, S_{l-1}, 0, 0)((S_l, S_l, 1, 0) \ldots (S_{k-1}, S_l, 1, 0))^\omega (S_l, S_l, 1, 1)$$

is a run in the extended state space $\mathcal{S}'$.

As this construction does not yet record Büchi automaton acceptance conditions for explicit-state model checking, as suggested by [32], we work with a slightly different state description. State pairs in the first phase are called *primary* states, states pairs in the secondary phase are called *sencondary* states. We drop Boolean variables completely as we distinguish primary from secondary states by comparing the state vectors of the state pair. Moreover, we spawn secondary children only at accepting primary states.

Without any heuristic the algorithm executes external breadth-first search, where each iteration can actually be seen as a snapshot in *bounded automata-based model checking*. Bounded model checking [6] uses a propositional SAT solver for the symbolic exploration of model checking problems. It exploits the SATPLAN exploration idea of [20] using a rising search horizon k to generate Boolean formulae encoding the overall exploration problem up the BFS-level k. In bounded automata-based model checking we use a similar approach, but without using BDDs nor SAT-formulae. To avoid traversing the full state space in Tarjan's algorithm, we analyze the cross product graph up to some threshold depth value k. If we find a counter-example already in depth k we terminate, otherwise we increase k. The bounded semantics for this strategy are the same as in BMC [6]: $\pi \models_k^i p$ if and only if $p \in L(p(i))$, $\pi \models_k^i \neg p$ if and only if $p \notin L(p(i))$, $\pi \models_k^i f \wedge g$ if and only if $\pi \models_k^i f$ and $\pi \models_k^i g$, $\pi \models_k^i f \vee g$ if and only if $\pi \models_k^i f$ or $\pi \models_k^i g$, $\pi \models_k^i \mathbf{G}f$ *is always false*, $\pi \models_k^i \mathbf{F}f$ if and only if $\exists j, i \leq j \leq k : \pi \models_k^j f$, $\pi \models_k^i \mathbf{X}f$ if and only if $i < k$ and $\pi \models_k^{i+1} f$, and $\pi \models_k^i f\mathbf{U}g$ if and only if $\exists j, i \leq j \leq k : \pi \models_k^j g$ and $\forall n, i \leq n < j : \pi \models_k^n f$.

Theorem 1. *For problem graphs the external BFS LTL model checking algorithm finds the shortest counterexample with an accepting seed state. Its I/O complexity is $O(\text{sort}(|\mathcal{F}||\mathcal{R}|) + l \cdot \text{scan}(|\mathcal{F}||\mathcal{S}|))$, where l is the length of the shortest counterexample.*

Proof. Since each state is expanded at most once, all sortings can be done in time $O(sort(|\mathcal{F}||\mathcal{R}|))$ I/Os. Filtering, evaluating, and merging are all available in scanning time of the buckets in consideration. The I/O complexity for predecessor elimination depends on the number of buckets that are referred to during file subtraction/reduction. The number of buckets is bounded by the number of layers and thus the length of the shortest counterexample. Consequently, the I/O complexity for large-scale LTL model checking is bounded by $O(sort(|\mathcal{F}||\mathcal{R}|) + l \cdot scan(|\mathcal{F}||\mathcal{S}|))$ I/Os.

6.1   Heuristics for Safety Model Checking

For defining heuristics for safety model checking, we assume that the global state space is generated based on the asynchronous compositions of local state spaces

$\mathcal{P}_i$, $i \in \{1, \dots, n\}$, called processes. In other words, each global system state is partitioned into n local states. The state of a local process $\mathcal{P}_i$ is called its *program counter*, $i \in \{1, \dots, n\}$, pc_i for short.

The *FSM distance heuristic* is defined as the sum for each $\mathcal{P}_i$ of the distance between the local state of $\mathcal{P}_i$ in s and the local state of $\mathcal{P}_i$ in s', i.e.,

$$H_m(s, s') = \sum_{i=1}^{n} D_i(pc_i(s), pc_i(s')),$$

where $D_i(pc_i(s), pc_i(s'))$ denotes the shortest path from $pc_i(s)$ to $pc_i(s')$ in the automaton representation of $\mathcal{P}_i$. The values for D_i are computed prior to the search.

6.2   Trail-Directed Heuristics

The FSM distance heuristic assumes that both states s and s' are known to the exploration module. It has mainly been used in *trail-directed search*, where a counter-example to an existing error state is to be shortened. It has also been applied to the verification of liveness properties where the prefix path to the start of the cycle and the accepting cycle itself are shortened in sequence. For this case the distance in the never-claim automaton $\mathcal{N}$ is included as follows

$$H'_m(s, s') = \max \left\{ H_M(s, s'), D_\mathcal{N}(pc_\mathcal{N}(s), pc_\mathcal{N}(s')) \right\}.$$

As the product of different processes is asynchronous, it is not difficult to see [26] that the FSM distance is *monotone*, i.e., $H_m(s) - H_m(s') \leq 1$ for each pair (s, s') with s' being the direct successor of s. Monotone heuristics guarantee the optimality of counterexample paths in heuristic search exploration algorithms like A* [28]. It is also not difficult to see that the maximum of two monotone heuristics is monotone. Hence, $H'_m(s, s')$ is also a monotone heuristic for shortening liveness trails.

6.3   Heuristic for LTL Properties

In the extended search space $\mathcal{S}'$ we search for shortest lasso-shaped counterexamples, without knowing the start of the cycle beforehand. We used the monotone heuristic

$$H_a(s) = \min_{s' \in F_\mathcal{N}} \left\{ D_\mathcal{N}(pc_\mathcal{N}(s), pc_\mathcal{N}(s')) \right\}$$

for finding accepting states in the original search space.

States in the extended search are abbreviated by tuples (s, s'), with s recording the start state of the cycle s' being the current search state. If we reach an accepting state, we immediately switch to secondary search. Therefore, we observe two distinct cases: primary search, accepting state not yet reached, secondary search, accepting state once found. The state $s = s'$ reached in secondary search is the goal. As it is a successor of a secondary state, we can distinguish the situation from reaching such a state for the first time.

For all $e = (s, s')$ in the extended search space $\mathcal{S}'$, let $H_a(e) = H_a(s)$ and $H_M(e) = H_M(s, s')$. Now we are ready to define a heuristic for liveness

$$H(e) = \begin{cases} H_a(s) & \text{if } s = s' \\ H'_M(s, s') & \text{if } s \neq s' \end{cases} \tag{1}$$

Lemma 1. *Let $h^*(e)$ be the shortest lasso-shaped counterexample with an accepting seed state starting at e. Then $H(e)$ is a lower bound on $h^*(e)$.*

Proof. As each counterexample has to contain at least one accepting state in the never-claim, for primary states e we have that $H = H_a(e)$ is a lower bound. For secondary states $e = (s, s')$, we have

$$H(e) = H'_M(s, s') = \max\{H_M(s, s'), D_\mathcal{N}(pc_\mathcal{N}(s), pc_\mathcal{N}(s'))\},$$

a lower bound to close the cycle and the lasso in total.

Lemma 2. *The estimator H is monotone, i.e., $H(e) - H(e') \leq 1$ for all successor states e' of e.*

Proof. Consistency is a local property. As both H_a and H'_M are monotone [26] and only one of them is true at a time, the only thing we have to show that H is monotone are the transitions between the different cases. The only problematic situation is the transition in case of reaching an accepting state. Here we have that a predecessor e with an evaluation of $H(e) = H_a(e) = 0$ spawns successors e' with evaluation values of $H_M(e') > 0$. However, this incurs no problem as $H(e) - H(e') \leq 1$ still preserves monotonicity.

The gap between H_M and H_a at accepting states may indicate that there is some option for applying an improved search estimate.

The next result shows that, given a monotone heuristic estimate, our approach terminates with an minimal-length counterexample where the lasso seed is accepting. If one allows seed states also to be non-accepting, there are potentially shorter counterexamples. This is possible if the accepting state is reachable only via a non-accepting seed. In this case the path from the seed to the accepting state would appear twice in the corresponding counterexample found in our algorithm starting the secondary search from an accepting seed state. Note that this subtlety does not effect completeness, a lasso with accepting seed exists if and only if an lasso with an accepting cycle exists.

7   External Guided Exploration

The model checking algorithm for directed external LTL search is an extension External A* and traverse the bucket file list along growing $f = g + h$ diagonals. In each external state we store (packed) original state vector pairs (s, s') with $s = s'$.

Figure 1 (left) depicts a prototypical execution of the guided exploration. For primary nodes (illustrated using two white half circles), we apply the heuristic

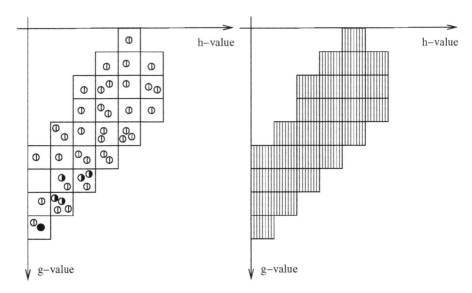

Fig. 1. Directed model checking LTL (left), distribution among several processors (right)

H_a, while for secondary nodes (illustrated using cycles half white/half black) we apply the estimate H_m. Once a terminal state with $s = s'$ (illustrated using two black half circles) is reached we have found an accepting cycle.

Figure 1 (right) illustrates how to perform parallel exploration[3]. The internal work for exploration a bucket is uniformly distributed among the set of available processors, that individually expand and sort individual files as described above.

Theorem 2. *For problem graphs the external, parallel and guided LTL model checking algorithm finds the shortest counterexample with an accepting seed state. Its I/O complexity is $O(\text{sort}(|\mathcal{F}||\mathcal{R}|)/p + l \cdot \text{scan}(|\mathcal{F}||\mathcal{S}|))$, where l is the length of the shortest counterexample.*

Proof. The proof is analogous to Theorem 1. Additionally, the parallelism divides the sorting efforts.

The main advantage of directed search is that the set of expanded states $\mathcal{S}$ (and subsequently $\mathcal{R}$) is smaller than with blind search.

The solution path is reconstructed by backward chaining starting with the final state. There are two main options. Either for a state in depth g we intersect the set of possible predecessors with the buckets of depth $g - 1$. Any state that is in the intersection is reachable on an optimal solution path, so that we can recur. As generating the predecessor state can be problematic in software model

---

[3] For a full treatment of the parallel execution of External A* we refer the reader to [19]. As the paper is not printed yet, the reviewers can obtain a copy of the work at http://ls5-www.cs.uni-dortmund.de/~jabbar/vmcai06.pdf

checking domains, we may store with each state its predecessor on a shortest path, doubling the required disk space. The time complexity is bounded by the scanning time of at most l buckets in consideration and surely in $O(scan(|\mathcal{F}||\mathcal{S}|))$.

8   Experiments

We implemented external LTL property validation on top of our experimental model checker IO-HSF-SPIN [18], the recent extension the directed model checking SPIN-derivate HSF-SPIN. The inputs are Promela-files and the output is a trail file in SPIN's format. The Promela language scope of IO-HSF-SPIN is not as large as in SPIN[4] as it lacks some features like fully dynamic process creation and embedded c-code, but sufficiently strong even for larger models that we have in our benchmark set.

As with its ancestors, in IO-HSF-SPIN Promela models are compiled into self-contained model checking units. The experiments for single-processor were conducted on a Pentium-4 PC, 3 GHz with 2 gigabytes of main memory and 180 gigabytes of hard disk. We exploit disk parallelism by RAID 0 using two hard disk. For multi-processor experiments we chose a Sun Enterprise System with four 750 MHz processors working with 8 gigabyte RAM and 30 gigabyte shared hard disk space. In this case, we worked with a single hard disk, so that no form of disk parallelism was exploited.

We choose a small internal buffer size for buffered reading and writing consisting of only 1,997 states. We applied internal (hash table based) and external (delayed) duplicate detection within the next bucket to expand. Duplicate elimination with respect to visited states in previous buckets is not done. This reduces the number of scans to linear-time complexity by the cost of some redundant states. The heuristic we applied takes a combination of H_a (for primary search) and H_M (for secondary search).

When comparing to SPIN it should be noted that this model checker was invoked with partial order reduction. Actually, as indicated by [26], partial order reduction preserves completeness but not optimality. It may lead to non-optimal counterexamples.

In our first set of experiments we use an elevator simulation protocol[5]. Table 1 shows the exploration results. We denote the number of expanded states, the number of states inserted to the hash table, the CPU time consumed and the length of the counterexample obtained. The sizes of the counterexamples are divided into the prefix and cycle length.

We compare the results of the exploration of External BFS and External A* as implemented in IO-HSF-SPIN with Nested-DFS as implemented in SPIN, Distribution 4.2. Due to the statistic information provided by SPIN instead of the number of expanded and inserted states, we give the number of stored states and explored transitions[6]. SPIN and IO-HSF-SPIN return counterexamples that

---

[4] The SPIN code we started with was SPIN 3.4.

[5] Derived from `www.inf.ethz.ch/personal/biere/teaching/mctools/elsim.html`

[6] The counterexamples are produced with the options -t -p.

Table 1. LTL Model Checking with External A*, External BFS and Internal Nested DFS for 2-Elevator protocol

I/O-HSF-SPIN	Expanded	Inserted	Time	Length
External A*	2,090,933	2,275,778	1m18s	67 + 34
External BFS	2,642,575	2,827,073	2m3.96s	67 + 34
SPIN 4.2	Transition	Stored	Time	Length
Nested DFS	33,900	11,149	0m0.064s	109 + 100

Table 2. LTL Model Checking with External A*, External BFS and Internal Nested DFS for SGC protocol

I/O-HSF-SPIN	Expanded	Inserted	Time	Length
External A*	178	369	0m1.318s	15 + 5
External BFS	1,343	1,427	0m0.787s	15 + 5
SPIN 4.2	Transition	Stored	Time	Length
Nested DFS	155,963	8,500	1m47s	18 + 5

start at accepting states[7]. We observe that SPIN's counterexamples are in general longer than the ones in IO-HSF-SPIN[8].

From the results of our first experiments we do not see a large gain of External A* compared to External BFS in the number of expanded and inserted states. The established counterexample lengths match. In the time, however, we see that External A* is considerably faster. There a different reason for the difference in ratios for the number of expansions and CPU time. First, as there are less buckets in External BFS (one for every layer) compared to External A*, there are more I/Os needed for external sorting. The other reason is that the number of generated nodes that fall into the buckets that are not considered for expansion (with counterexample length larger than the optimum) are larger for External BFS.

SPIN's exploration is remarkably good, as it requires only 6 milliseconds for generating an optimized trail. The number of stored nodes for Nested-DFS is much smaller as compared to blind BFS and A* LTL property search. The established counterexample is longer.

In the second experiment we take a larger protocol, as used in [37], a Promela model of a procedure with related processes. In Table 2 we see an opposite behavior as compared to the previous experiment. External search performed a much smaller number of expansions than internal iterated Nested DFS. The

---

[7] Without the predefined bound on the search depth, SPIN tends to find very long counterexamples, e.g. with 9998 steps. We therefore chose an iterative depth-first search strategy -i for SPIN. As this option may be caught in a depth anomaly [26] we also checked option -DREACH, which should return optimal traces. However, the results we obtained with this setting were not better than with -i.

[8] This is not neccessarily due to their non-optimality, but probably relying on a different measurement for steps, as SPIN is likely to put some additional increment on synchronized never-claim transitions.

reason is that iterative improvement strategy takes a long time to decrease the counterexample length to a feasible low number. The behavior of External BFS compared to External A* is also opposite to the above. Now the number of expansion is smaller in External A* is much smaller due to its good guidance, but External BFS CPU time is superior. The reason for this is that the distribution of the heuristic estimate is fine-grained such that many internal buckets have to be allocated but never used.

In the third set of experiments we choose the scalable Dining Philosophers protocol with 64 philosophers. The LTL property we checked for was

```
[]  (philosopher[1]@eat -> <>  philosopher[2]@eat)
```

realizing the *response* property that always if the first philosopher eats, so does the second. Table 3 shows our results. Coincidently, the number of expanded nodes for guided and unguided external search match. The number of inserted nodes is, however, smaller for External BFS. We explain this behavior by absence of external duplicate removal for unexplored buckets. In agreement with this argument, External BFS took more time to perform external delayed duplicate detection. SPIN, unfortunately, ran out of memory. It found counterexample in very large depth, but was unable to shorten the trail. Even provided with a depth bound of 300 it was unable to terminate its iterated improvement strategy, due to the limits of main memory, which in our case was 2 gigabytes. Manually adapting the search depth to the optimum of 212 allowed SPIN to complete its exploration finding a counterexample with a acceptance cycle seed at depth 207.

For distributed execution on the multi-processor machine we again choose the Dining Philosopher example (see Table 4), now scaled to 128 philosophers. First, we note that disk space consumption is considerably large. The single processor version could not finish its exploration. One file for the set generated states became larger than 2 gigabytes and was killed by the operating system.

Table 3. LTL Model Checking with External A*, External BFS and Internal Nested DFS for 64-Dining Philosopher

I/O-HSF-SPIN	Expanded	Inserted	Time	Length
External A*	2,298	127,813	0m6.108s	196 + 2
External BFS	2,298	47,118	0m13.549s	196 + 2
SPIN 4.2	Transition	Stored	Time	Length
Nested DFS	-out-of-mem-	-out-of-mem-	–	–

Table 4. LTL Model Checking with External A* for 128-Dining Philosopher

I/O-HSF-SPIN	Time	Secondary Memory	Length
1 processor	–	–	–
2 processors	5m53.96s	4.7 gigabytes	388 + 2
3 processors	4m7.13s	5.28 gigabytes	388 + 2

The reason that the multi-processor versions could finalize their implementation, is early duplicate detection in intermediate files. The length of the produced counterexamples match and the observed speed-up is noticeable.

9   Conclusion

In this work we have combined directed, external and parallel approaches to compute optimal counterexamples for LTL properties in explicit-state model checking. The I/O complexity of $O(sort(|\mathcal{F}||\mathcal{R}|)/p + l \cdot scan(|\mathcal{F}||\mathcal{S}|))$ is a drastic improvement to simulating DFS as done for computing strongly connected components in explicit graphs with Tarjan's algorithm, as it avoids unstructured access to the adjacency lists. Different to *NestedDFS* the approach provides an optimality guarantee on the length of the counterexample.

The search space is generated using state pairs of active and cycle seed state, which supports the design of monotone LTL heuristics for directed model checking. Primary and secondary search states are examined together in one common file. The underlying exploration algorithm extends External A* to allow accepting cycles to be found. As with External A*, the approach can be effectively be parallelized. Duplicate detection is delayed. Up to synchronization mechanism for work distribution, no communication between the individual processes is needed, which in large problems allows almost linear speed-ups in a distributed environment.

With this research, we hope to have pushed the limits of practical model checking where the internal memory does not limit the number of realistic models that can be verified. With our support of pause-and-resume the size of the secondary storage can be resized without harming the correctness of the model checking process. Combining this with our approach presented in [19] on parallel external guided safety model checking, we now put our focus on larger industrial-sized models, which means targeting towards state spaces requiring terrabytes of storage.

A challenge for future research will be to reduce the (sequential) time complexity to $O(sort(|\mathcal{R}|) + scan(|\mathcal{S}|))$ as for safety model checking.

Acknowledgments. The work is supported by *Deutsche Forschungsgemeinschaft* (DFG) in the projects *Heuristic Search* (Ed 74/3) and *Directed Model Checking* (Ed 74/2).

References

1. A. Aggarwal and J. S. Vitter. Complexity of sorting and related problems. In *International Colloquim on Automata, Languages and Programming (ICALP)*, number 267 in LNCS, pages 467–478, 1987.
2. A. Aggarwal and J. S. Vitter. The input/output complexity of sorting and related problems. *Journal of the ACM*, 31(9):1116–1127, 1988.
3. J. Barnat, L. Brim, and I. Cerna. Property driven distribution of nested DFS. In *International Workshop on Verification and Computational Logic (VCL)*, pages 1–10, 2002.

4. J. Barnat, L. Brim, and J. Chaloupka. Parallel breadth-first search LTL model checking. In *International Conference on Automated Software Engineering (ASE)*, pages 106–115, 2003.
5. J. Barnat, L. Brim, and J. Chaloupka. From distribution memory cycle detection to parallel model checking. *Electronic Notes in Theoretical Computer Science*, 133:21–39, 2005.
6. A. Biere, A. Cimatti, E. Clarke, O. Strichman, and Y. Zhu. Bounded model checking. In *Advances in Computers (volume 58)*. Academic Press, 2003.
7. L. Brim and I. Cerna. Accepting predecessors are better than back edges in distributed LTL model-checking. In *Formal methods in Computer-Aided Design (FMCAD)*, pages 352–366, 2004.
8. J. R. Buchi. On a decision method in restricted second order arithmetic. In *Conference on Logic, Methodology, and Philosophy of Science*, pages 1–11, 1962.
9. I. Cerna and R. Palanek. Distributed explicit fair cycle detection. In *Model Checking Software (SPIN)*, pages 49–73, 2003.
10. Y.-J. Chiang, M. T. Goodrich, E. F. Grove, R. Tamasia, D. E. Vengroff, and J. S. Vitter. External memory graph algorithms. In *Symposium on Discrete Algorithms (SODA)*, pages 139–149, 1995.
11. E. Clarke, O. Grumberg, and D. Peled. *Model Checking*. MIT Press, 2000.
12. S. Edelkamp, S. Jabbar, and S. Schroedl. External A*. In *German Conference on Artificial Intelligence (KI)*, pages 226–240, 2004.
13. S. Edelkamp, S. Leue, and A. Lluch-Lafuente. Directed explicit-state model checking in the validation of communication protocols. *International Journal on Software Tools for Technology*, 5(2-3):247–267, 2004.
14. S. Edelkamp, S. Leue, and A. Lluch-Lafuente. Partial order reduction and trail improvement in directed model checking. *International Journal on Software Tools for Technology*, 6(4):277–301, 2004.
15. K. Fisler, R. Fraer, G. Kamhi, Y. Vardi, and Y. Ynag. Is there a best symbolic cycle detection algorithm. In *TACAS*, pages 420–434, 2001.
16. D. S. Hirschberg. A linear space algorithm for computing common subsequences. *Communications of the ACM*, 18(6):341–343, 1975.
17. G. J. Holzmann, D. Peled, and M. Yannakakis. On nested depth first search. *The SPIN Verification System*, pages 23–32, 1972.
18. S. Jabbar and S. Edelkamp. I/O efficient directed model checking. In *Conference on Verification, Model Checking and Abstract Interpretation (VMCAI)*, pages 313–329, 2005.
19. S. Jabbar and S. Edelkamp. Parallel external directed model checking with linear I/O. In *Conference on Verification, Model Checking and Abstract Interpretation (VMCAI)*, pages 237–251, 2006.
20. H. Kautz and B. Selman. Pushing the envelope: Planning propositional logic, and stochastic search. In *AAAI*, pages 1194–1201, 1996.
21. R. E. Korf. Best-first frontier search with delayed duplicate detection. In *AAAI*, pages 650–657, 2004.
22. R. E. Korf and P. Schultze. Large-scale parallel breadth-first search. In *AAAI*, 2005.
23. R. E. Korf and W. Zhang. Divide-and-conquer frontier search applied to optimal sequence allignment. In *AAAI*, pages 910–916, 2000.
24. L. Kristensen and T. Mailund. Path finding with the sweep-line method using external storage. In *International Conference on Formal Engineering Methods (ICFEM)*, pages 319–337, 2003.

25. A. Lluch-Lafuente. Simplified distributed ltl model checking by localizing cycles. Technical report, Institute of Computer Science, University of Freiburg, 2002.
26. A. Lluch-Lafuente. *Directed Search for the Verification of Communication Protocols*. PhD thesis, Institute of Computer Science, University of Freiburg, 2003.
27. K. Munagala and A. Ranade. I/O-complexity of graph algorithms. In *Symposium on Discrete Algorithms (SODA)*, pages 87–88, 2001.
28. J. Pearl. *Heuristics*. Addison-Wesley, 1985.
29. J. H. Reif. Depth-first search is inherently sequential. *Information Processing Letters*, 20:229–234, 1985.
30. S. Safra. On the complexity of omega-automata. In *Annual Symposium on Foundations of Computer Science*, pages 319–237. IEEE Computer Society, 1998.
31. P. Sanders, U. Meyer, and J. F. Sibeyn. *Algorithms for Memory Hierarchies*. Springer, 2002.
32. V. Schuppan and A. Biere. From distribution memory cycle detection to parallel model checking. *International Journal on Software Tools for Technology Transfer*, 5(2–3).
33. V. Schuppan and A. Biere. Liveness checking as safety checking for infinite state spaces. page To Appear, 2005.
34. A. P. Sistla, M. Y. Vardi, and P. Wolper. The complementation problem for Buchi automata with applications to temporal logic. *Theoretical Computer Science*, 49(2–3):217–237, 1983.
35. R. Tarjan. Depth-first search and linear graph algorithms. *SIAM Journal of Computing*, (1):146–160, 1972.
36. P. Wolper. Temporal logic can be more expressive. *Information and Control*, 56:72–99, 1983.
37. W. Zhang. Model checking operator procedures. In *Workshop on Model Checking Software (SPIN)*, pages 200–215, 1999.

Directed Model Checking with Distance-Preserving Abstractions

Klaus Dräger[1], Bernd Finkbeiner[1,2], and Andreas Podelski[2]

[1] Universität des Saarlandes, Saarbrücken, Germany
[2] Max-Planck-Institut für Informatik, Saarbrücken, Germany

Abstract. In directed model checking, the traversal of the state space is guided by an estimate of the distance from the current state to the nearest error state. This paper presents a *distance-preserving abstraction* for concurrent systems that allows one to compute an interesting estimate of the error distance without hitting the state explosion problem. Our experiments show a dramatic reduction both in the number of states explored by the model checker and in the total runtime.

1 Introduction

The number of states of a concurrent system is exponential in the number of its components. This fundamental *state explosion* problem raises a complexity-theoretic barrier for all algorithmic methods based on state space traversal. As a consequence, it will always be interesting to investigate new approaches to circumvent the problem at least in particular situations. *Directed model checking* is one such approach that has received a lot of attention recently [1, 2, 4, 7, 10, 13, 17, 20]. The idea is to automatically compute an estimate of the *error distance*, which is the minimal number of steps between a given state and some error state. The state space traversal is then guided ("directed") by the estimate. In some situations, the benefit obtained from the guidance drastically outweighs the cost of the computation of the estimate; for success stories, we refer to [1, 2, 4, 7, 10, 13, 17, 20].

When we apply directed model checking to concurrent systems, the basic research question is: how can one compute an interesting estimate of the error distance without hitting the state explosion problem?

A natural idea is to compute an appropriate abstraction of the concurrent system and to base the estimate of the error distance between *concrete* states on the error distance between corresponding *abstract* states. We must make clear, however, what appropriate here means. We are not in a setting where the state space traversal is performed over abstract states and where the abstraction of a state aims at preserving the reachability vs. non-reachability of an error state. Instead, the state space traversal is performed over concrete states and the abstraction of a state aims at preserving the distance to an error state (we call it a "distance-preserving abstraction").

The contribution of this paper is a distance-preserving abstraction for concurrent systems that allows one to compute an interesting estimate of the error distance without hitting the state explosion problem. The definition of the

A. Valmari (Ed.): SPIN 2006, LNCS 3925, pp. 19–34, 2006.

abstraction originates from insights into the interplay between the impact of an action-based synchronization mechanism on the error distance in concurrent systems on the one hand and the use of estimated error distances during the state space traversal on the other hand.

We have implemented the directed model checking method with the distance-preserving abstraction. Our experiments indicate the usefulness of the estimate for a number of concurrent systems. We obtain a significant reduction both in the number of states explored and in the total running time, compared to directed model checking with an already existing estimate function that does not take into account synchronization.

2 Preliminaries

2.1 Notation

We verify safety properties over concurrent finite-state systems that are given as a finite set of processes $\mathcal{P}$. A *process* is a tuple $(\Sigma, Q, Q^0, Q^e, \rightarrow)$ where Σ is a finite *alphabet* of *observable actions*, Q is a finite set of states including the initial states $Q^0 \subseteq Q$ and error states $Q^e \subseteq Q$, and $\rightarrow \subseteq Q \times (\Sigma \cup \{\tau\}) \times Q$ is a transition relation, where τ represents an unobservable internal action not in Σ. A transition $(p, a, p') \in \rightarrow$ is denoted by $p \xrightarrow{a} p'$.

An error occurs if all processes are in one of their error states Q^e. Often, one of the processes acts as the monitor for the safety property, in which case all other processes have the trivial error condition $Q^e = Q$.

The *error distance* $d_P(q) \in \mathbb{N} \cup \{\infty\}$ of a state q in a process P is the length of a shortest path from q to an error state (or ∞ if no such path exists).

We use a simple model of process synchronization where each observable action is shared by exactly two processes in $\mathcal{P}$. Consider a pair of processes $P_i = (\Sigma_i, Q_i, Q_i^0, Q_i^e, \rightarrow_i)$, $i = 1, 2$. The *parallel composition*

$$P_1 \| P_2 = (\Sigma_1 \cup \Sigma_2, Q_1 \times Q_2, Q_1^0 \times Q_2^0, Q_1^e \times Q_2^e, \rightarrow)$$

synchronizes the two processes on their common action symbols $(\Sigma_1 \cap \Sigma_2)$:

$$(p, q) \xrightarrow{a} (p', q') \text{ iff } \begin{cases} p \xrightarrow{a}_1 p', q = q', \text{ and } a \in (\Sigma_1 \setminus \Sigma_2) \cup \{\tau\} \\ p = p', q \xrightarrow{a}_2 q', \text{ and } a \in (\Sigma_2 \setminus \Sigma_1) \cup \{\tau\} \\ p \xrightarrow{c}_1 p', q \xrightarrow{c}_2 q' \text{ for some } c \in \Sigma_1 \cap \Sigma_2, \text{ and } a = \tau. \end{cases}$$

Since parallel composition is associative and commutative, we do not distinguish systems that are composed from the same set of processes by parallel composition in different orders. We denote the parallel composition of a set of processes $\mathcal{P} = \{P_1, \ldots, P_k\}$ by $\|_{P \in \mathcal{P}} P = P_1 \| \ldots \| P_k$.

2.2 Directed Model Checking

Model checking can be implemented as an instance of the expanding search algorithm for directed graphs, shown in Figure 1. The algorithm maintains an *open list* of visited but not yet expanded states and a *closed list* of states that

---

Algorithm: EXPANDINGSEARCH

Input   : Initial Node q_0 of directed graph G
Output: **true** if a goal node is reachable from q_0, **false** otherwise
/* Initialization */
Open := (s);
Closed := ();
while $Open \neq ()$ **do**
   $q := Open.pop()$;
   if $goal(q)$ **then return true**;
   $Closed.insert(q)$;
   foreach $successor$ q' of q **do**
      if q' not in $Open$ or $Closed$ **then**
         $Open.insert(q')$;
   end
end
return false;

Fig. 1. Algorithm EXPANDINGSEARCH decides reachability of a goal node from the initial node of a directed graph, using lists Open and Closed

have been expanded. In each step, a state is chosen from the open list, expanded (i.e. all its successors that were not yet visited get added to the open list), and moved to the closed list. Organizing the open list as a FIFO queue results in a breadth-first traversal of the state space, while a LIFO stack results in a depth-first traversal.

In *directed* model checking [4], the open list is organized as a priority queue ordered by a function $h(q)$, which indicates the desirability of exploring a state q, usually based on an estimate $f(q)$ of $d_P(q)$. The best-known directed traversal algorithms are best-first traversal, where $h(q) = f(q)$, and A*, where $h(q)$ is the sum of $f(q)$ and the length of the shortest (currently known) path from an initial state to q. The advantage of A* is that it finds *shortest* error traces if the estimate function is *admissible*, which means it never overestimates $d_P(q)$. Typically, best-first traversal is faster than A*.

An even stronger property than admissibility is *consistency*. An estimate function f is *consistent* if, for every state q and every successor q' of q, $f(q) \leq f(q') + 1$. Consistent estimate functions improve the performance of the A* algorithm, because it is never necessary to *reopen* states. In general, a state q has to be put back on the open list if it is encountered again on a shorter path from the initial state. If the estimate function is consistent, we always find the shortest path first. Every consistent estimate is also admissible [16].

Our estimate function is based on an abstraction of the system. We define the abstraction of a process as the quotient with respect to an equivalence relation on the states. The *quotient* of a process $P = (\Sigma, Q, Q^0, Q^e, \rightarrow)$ *with respect to* an equivalence relation $\sim \subseteq Q \times Q$ is the process $P/\sim = (\Sigma, Q/\sim, Q^0/\sim, \{[q^e]_\sim \mid q^e \in Q^e\}, \Rightarrow)$, with

$$[p]_\sim \stackrel{a}{\Rightarrow} [q]_\sim \text{ iff } p' \stackrel{a}{\rightarrow} q' \text{ for some } p' \sim p, q' \sim q,$$

where $[q]_\sim$ denotes the equivalence class of a state $q \in Q$ with respect to $\sim$, and $Q/\sim = \{[q]_\sim \mid q \in Q\}$ denotes the quotient set. Every abstraction $P/\sim$ induces a consistent estimate function $f(q) = d_{P/\sim}([q]_\sim)$ of $d_P(q)$ [16].

3   Computing the Abstract System

Our estimate function is based on an abstraction of the system, which we compute in a preprocessing step before the model checking begins. To avoid constructing the full state space of the parallel product of all processes, we compute the abstraction incrementally: each composition of two processes is directly followed by an abstraction step.

Algorithm ABSTRACTSYSTEM, shown in Figure 2, describes this "compose-and-abstract" loop. For now, we ignore the question how the abstraction of a process is computed (we discuss algorithm ABSTRACTPROCESS in Section 4) as well as the question in which order the processes are composed: algorithm ABSTRACTSYSTEM is parameterized by the *composition strategy*, a function S that selects a pair of two different processes from a set of processes. We discuss the composition strategy in Section 5.

Algorithm ABSTRACTSYSTEM maintains a set of processes $\mathcal{P}'$, which is initially equal to the given set of processes $\mathcal{P}$ and is eventually reduced to the

---

Algorithm: ABSTRACTSYSTEM

Input   : concrete system, given as a finite set of processes $\mathcal{P} = \{P_1, \ldots, P_n\}$

Output: • abstract system, given as process A
         • mapping from concrete to abstract states:
            $\alpha : \prod_{P \in \mathcal{P}} Q_P \rightarrow (Q_A \cup \{\bot\})$

/* Initialization */
$\mathcal{P}' := \mathcal{P}$;
for $i = 1, \ldots, n$ **do** $\alpha_{P_i}(q_1, \ldots, q_n) = q_i$;

/* "Compose-and-abstract" loop */
while $|\mathcal{P}'| > 1$ **do**
     $(P, P') := S(\mathcal{P}')$;
     $(C, \gamma) := $ ABSTRACTPROCESS$(P\|P')$;
     $\mathcal{P}' := \mathcal{P}' \cup \{C\} \setminus \{P, P'\}$;
     $\alpha_C(q) := \begin{cases} \bot & \text{if } \alpha_P(q) = \bot \text{ or } \alpha_{P'}(q) = \bot \\ \gamma(\alpha_P(q), \alpha_{P'}(q)) & \text{otherwise}; \end{cases}$

end

$A := $ the remaining member of $\mathcal{P}'$;
return A, α_A;

Fig. 2. Algorithm ABSTRACTSYSTEM computes an abstract system for a given concrete system

singleton set $\{A\}$, where the process A represents the abstract system. Associated with each process P' in $\mathcal{P}'$ is the function $\alpha_{P'} : \prod_{P \in \mathcal{P}} Q_P \to (Q_{P'} \cup \{\bot\})$, which maps each concrete state q either to its abstraction in process P' or to $\bot$. The result $\alpha_{P'}(q) = \bot$ indicates that q is *irrelevant*, i.e., either q is not reachable from the initial states or the error states are not reachable from q. For the processes in $\mathcal{P}$, α_P is initialized with the projection to the respective component of the product states.

In each iteration of the "compose-and-abstract" loop, two processes P and P' are selected from the current set $\mathcal{P}'$ by the composition strategy S. Their parallel composition $P \| P'$ is first computed explicitly and then immediately abstracted by ABSTRACTPROCESS to process C. In the new process set $\mathcal{P}'$, process C replaces P and P'. Associated with C is the new mapping α_C, which combines the mapping from the states of $P \| P'$ to the states of C (which is provided by ABSTRACTPROCESS) with the mappings associated with P and P'.

The results of ABSTRACTSYSTEM are the abstract process A and the function α, which maps concrete states to abstract states or $\bot$. From these we derive the estimate function

$$f(q) = \begin{cases} \infty & \text{if } \alpha(q) = \bot \\ d_A(\alpha(q)) & \text{otherwise.} \end{cases}$$

Since the mapping α induces an equivalence on the states of the concrete system $(p \sim q \Leftrightarrow \alpha(p) = \alpha(q))$, this estimate function is consistent for any choice of a process abstraction and composition strategy.

4   Computing Abstract Processes

How can we ensure that the error distance of the *abstract* state provides a good estimate for the error distance of the *concrete* state? A natural idea is to use one state in the abstraction as a representative for each set of concrete states with the same error distance. While this preserves the error distance in the immediate abstraction, it changes the *synchronization behavior* of the process. This, in turn, changes the error distance in the next iteration of the "compose-and-abstract" loop, when the abstracted process is composed with some other process. The straightforward solution of this problem, to identify only bisimilar states and thus preserve the synchronization behavior of the process, generally does not sufficiently reduce the state space.

Our approach draws from both ideas. We fix a bound N on the maximal number of states in the abstraction. Within this bound, our first priority is to ensure that only states with the same error distance are identified, and our second priority is to preserve the synchronization behavior.

Algorithm ABSTRACTPROCESS is shown in Figure 3. As part of the initialization, ABSTRACTPROCESS prunes irrelevant states. Process P' contains only states that are both reachable and have paths to some error state. The computation of the equivalence relation $\sim$ starts with the equivalence that identifies two states iff they have the same error distance. During the entire run of the algorithm, we only

---

Algorithm: ABSTRACTPROCESS

Input   : concrete process $P = (\Sigma, Q, Q^0, Q^e, \rightarrow)$

Output: • abstract process A,

   • mapping from concrete to abstract states:
      $\alpha : Q \rightarrow (Q_A \cup \{\bot\})$

/* Initialization */
$Q' := \{q \in Q \mid d_P(q) < \infty \text{ and } q \text{ reachable from } Q^0\};$
$P' := (\Sigma, Q', Q^0 \cap Q', Q^e \cap Q', \rightarrow \cap (Q' \times (\Sigma \cup \{\tau\}) \times Q'));$
$\sim := \{(q, q') \in Q' \times Q' \mid \min(d_P(q), N-1) = \min(d_P(q'), N-1)\};$
$K := |Q'/\sim|;$
for $i = 0, \ldots, K-1$ **do**
   $B_i := \{q \in Q' \mid \min(d_P(q), N-1) = i\};$
   $R_i := \sim \cap (B_i \times B_i) ;$
end

/* Refinement loop */
repeat
   $\sim' := \sim;$
   for $i = 0, \ldots, K-1$ **do**
      $R_i^* := \{(q, q') \in R_i \mid \forall a \; \{[r]_\sim \mid q \xrightarrow{a} r\} = \{[r']_\sim \mid q' \xrightarrow{a} r'\}\};$
      if $|Q'/(R_1 \cup \cdots \cup R_i^* \cup \cdots \cup R_K)| \leq N$ **then**
         $R_i \; := \; R_i^*;$
         $\sim \; := \; \bigcup_{i=0}^{K-1} R_i;$
   end
until $\sim \; = \; \sim'$;

$A := P'/\sim;$
$\alpha(q) := \begin{cases} [q]_\sim & \text{if } q \in Q' \\ \bot & \text{otherwise;} \end{cases}$
return $A, \alpha;$

Fig. 3. Algorithm ABSTRACTPROCESS computes an abstract process for a given concrete process

consider refinements of this equivalence. We therefore partition the states into buckets $B_0, \ldots, B_{N-1}$ according to their error distance and consider a separate equivalence relation $R_i = \sim \cap (B_i \times B_i), i = 1, \ldots, N-1$, on each bucket.

The subsequent loop refines $\sim$ until a fixpoint is reached. For each relation R_i, we tentatively split the equivalence classes in R_i according to the equivalence classes of their successors in $\sim$. If the refined equivalence R_i^* does not increase the total number of equivalence classes beyond the bound N, we refine $\sim$ according to R_i^*. The buckets are considered in the order of increasing error distance, starting with B_0. This choice is based on the intuition that paths from states with high error distance traverse states with lower error distance on their way to the error state. Inaccuracies introduced for states with high error distance are therefore likely to affect fewer states than inaccuracies introduced for states with low error distance.

When the fixpoint is reached (after at most N iterations of the refinement loop), the abstraction is computed as the quotient $P'/\sim$. The function α maps each relevant concrete state q to its equivalence class $[q]_\sim$.

Experiments. To evaluate this approach experimentally, we compare ABSTRACT-PROCESS to an alternative solution that considers buckets with high error distance first. The advantage of ABSTRACTPROCESS is especially clear in systems with long error paths, such as the Towers of Hanoi example described in Section 6. Figure 4 is based on data from the Towers of Hanoi benchmark with three disks. The graph shows the average difference between estimated and actual error distance over all states with the same actual error distance in percent of the actual error distance. The estimate obtained with ABSTRACTPROCESS is significantly more accurate than the estimate obtained by considering buckets with high error distance first. Both estimate functions have an area around the error states with perfect precision, but the area of the estimate

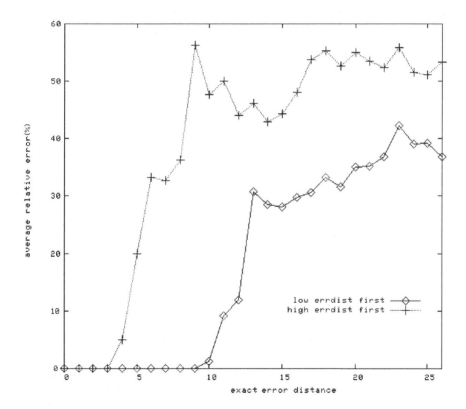

Fig. 4. Comparison of algorithm ABSTRACTPROCESS with an alternative solution that considers buckets with high error distance first. The graph shows the average difference between estimated and actual error distance over all states with the same actual error distance in percent of the actual error distance. (Data from the Towers of Hanoi benchmark with three disks and a bound of 40 states.)

obtained with ABSTRACTPROCESS is twice as large, resulting in a perfectly informed estimate at error distance 9, where the alternative solution already reaches its peak imprecision of 57%.

5   The Composition Strategy

Algorithm ABSTRACTPROCESS is guaranteed to preserve the error distance in the immediate abstraction, but may cause changes to the error distance once the abstract process is composed with further processes. The goal of the composition strategy is to minimize the resulting inaccuracy by choosing a pair of processes such that the error distance in their parallel composition provides a good estimate of the error distance in the completely composed system.

A first observation is that in processes with trivial error condition $Q^e = Q$, the local error distance is 0 for all states. We therefore only consider pairs of processes where at least one process has a non-trivial error condition. Among these, we choose a pair such that their joint actions occur close to error states. The result of this strategy is that we build an area close to the error states where no synchronization is necessary to reach the error. Within this area, the local

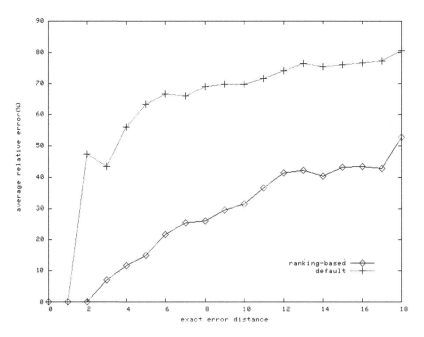

Fig. 5. Comparison of the ranking-based composition strategy with the default strategy, which composes processes in the order in which they are defined. The graph shows the average difference between estimated and actual error distance over all states with the same actual error distance in percent of the actual error distance. (Data from the Arbiter Tree benchmark with eight processes and a bound of 20 states.)

error distance accurately reflects the error distance in the completely composed system.

To implement this strategy, we introduce a ranking on the actions

$$r(P, a) = \min\{d_P(q) \mid q \in Q, \exists q' \in Q : q' \xrightarrow{a} q\}.$$

A low ranking indicates that the action may be taken in close proximity of the error. We associate with each pair (P_1, P_2) of two different processes the weight

$$\min\{\max\{r(P_1, a), r(P_2, a)\} \mid a \in \Sigma_1 \cap \Sigma_2\}$$

and choose a pair of processes that minimizes this weight.

Experiments. We compare the described ranking-based strategy with the default strategy that composes processes in the order in which they are defined. The advantage of the ranking-based strategy is especially clear in systems where only few processes have a non-trivial error condition. Figure 5 is based on data from the Arbiter Tree benchmark (see Section 6) with eight processes, where only two out of the eight processes have non-trivial error conditions. The graph shows the average difference between estimated and actual error distance over all states with the same actual error distance in percent of the actual error distance. The ranking-based strategy results in an estimate function that is roughly twice as accurate as the estimate function resulting from the default strategy.

6   Experiments

Our collection of benchmarks contains standard examples for distributed systems (Arbiter Tree, Towers of Hanoi), randomly generated systems, and industrial case studies. We have implemented our algorithms in an experimental version of the model checker UPPAAL [14].

We evaluate our estimate function both for best-first traversal (Table 1) and for A* (Table 2). For each benchmark, the tables show the running time, the number of explored states, and the length of the discovered error trace. We compare our estimate function with two different bounds ($N50$ and $N100$) to randomized depth-first traversal (rDF) and directed model checking with the FSM estimate function [7] (FSM).

Our experiments were carried out on an Intel Xeon 3.06 Ghz system with 4 GByte of RAM. For all experiments, we set a time limit of 30 minutes. In the case of rDF, the table shows the average runtime over three runs. For some benchmarks, some but not all of these runs hit our time limit. These runs were added into the runtime average with the 30-minute timeout as their runtime.

Arbiter Tree. The Arbiter Tree [19] establishes mutual exclusion between 2^k client processes. The processes are arranged in a binary tree of height k, where each leaf node is a client and each internal node is an arbiter that ensures mutual exclusion between its two children, passes requests and releases upward, and

Table 1. Experimental Results: Comparison of best-first traversal using our estimate function for two different bounds ($N50$ and $N100$) to best-first traversal using the FSM estimate function (FSM) and to randomized depth-first traversal (rDF)

Exp	explored states				seconds				trace length			
	rDF	FSM	$N50$	$N100$	rDF	FSM	$N50$	$N100$	rDF	FSM	$N50$	$N100$
A2	85	54	53	46	0.01	0.01	0.06	0.10	46	45	37	25
A3	6878	420	174	187	0.05	0.05	0.24	0.56	323	183	79	43
A4	1994	1.3e5	1.5e5	10633	0.06	1.01	3.16	2.78	429	1003	509	157
A5	***	9.9e5	7619	10673	1198	12.48	5.66	26.73	***	5213	3869	1151
A6	*	**	4.3e5	5.2e5	**	**	62.30	196.9	*	**	2.0e5	55535
H4	3027	4996	1283	711	0.03	0.05	0.07	0.09	573	761	181	125
H5	52417	57600	6497	6368	0.24	0.24	0.13	0.18	5528	3705	381	405
H6	3.1e5	5.0e5	1.1e5	63403	1.39	1.92	0.65	0.53	31225	26605	1445	1317
H7	1.5e6	4.5e6	7.4e5	7.5e5	7.50	20.37	4.09	4.32	2.3e5	2.0e5	3377	3177
H8	2.9e7	1.6e7	8.6e6	4.5e6	336.2	132.3	60.61	29.34	1.8e6	1.5e6	12073	6705
R5	5840	4177	697	443	0.04	0.04	0.05	0.06	936	154	62	64
R6	71098	19903	395	363	0.32	0.11	0.07	0.10	858	97	43	41
R7	3.1e5	83582	6656	8199	1.42	0.32	0.12	0.17	1040	81	56	50
R8	1.5e6	2.7e5	2.2e5	1.2e5	9.13	1.01	1.32	0.87	1453	138	58	59
R9	***	***	2.9e5	4.9e5	336.3	80.43	2.05	3.64	***	***	77	80
R10	***	***	***	2.6e5	496.3	71.83	38.87	2.20	***	***	***	122
M1	23894	31927	19063	12780	0.54	0.45	0.35	0.23	926	1349	129	74
M2	1.6e5	2.0e5	46545	46337	2.19	2.92	0.74	0.86	3717	7695	131	190
M3	68313	1.7e5	64522	42414	0.92	2.34	0.99	0.80	3589	5690	119	92
M4	2.0e5	5.8e5	1.7e5	1.3e5	2.71	7.34	2.49	1.86	14415	25819	146	105
N1	43655	42931	27275	1660	1.56	1.62	1.02	0.15	985	1803	187	194
N2	1.7e5	2.6e5	1.0e5	67168	5.61	9.43	3.55	2.16	4611	9279	218	138
N3	1.7e5	1.3e5	1.4e5	81804	5.85	4.96	4.99	2.69	3794	11656	178	130
N4	1.0e6	1.5e6	4.8e5	3.8e5	34.71	51.10	17.91	11.07	17851	41986	234	169
C1	25122	19263	871	810	0.24	0.24	0.30	0.49	1087	1442	188	191
C2	65275	68070	1600	2620	0.56	0.59	0.40	1.03	886	2032	203	206
C3	86439	97733	2481	2760	0.74	0.82	0.47	1.14	786	1663	204	198
C4	8.5e5	9.8e5	22223	25206	6.52	6.90	0.91	1.83	1680	5419	247	297
C5	8.3e6	8.8e6	1.6e5	1.6e5	66.41	66.85	2.90	3.97	1900	14163	322	350
C6	***	**	1.7e6	1.2e6	1181	**	18.32	14.87	***	**	480	404
C7	*	**	1.3e7	1.3e7	*	**	156.1	162.4	*	**	913	672
C8	*	**	1.4e7	1.2e7	*	**	163.0	155.3	*	**	1305	2210
C9	*	**	**	3.6e7	*	**	**	1046	*	**	**	1020

* timeout; ** out of memory; *** timeout on some instances

passes grants downward. One additional process handles the requests of the root node by immediately sending a grant upon receiving a request and then waiting for the release. The benchmarks A2 – A6 contain arbiter trees of height 2 – 6, with an exponentially growing number of processes (A2 has 8 processes, A6 has 128). We specified mutual exclusion for one particular pair of client processes and introduced a fault in the form of an incorrect client that erroneously sends *several* release signals when done.

Table 2. Experimental results: Comparison of A* traversal using our estimate function for two different bounds ($N50$ and $N100$) to A* traversal using the FSM estimate function (FSM)

Exp	explored states			seconds			trace length
	FSM	$N50$	$N100$	FSM	$N50$	$N100$	
A2	498	215	46	0.02	0.06	0.10	25
A3	81883	32106	20658	0.41	0.48	0.73	35
H4	6289	3876	3348	0.06	0.08	0.10	105
H5	67202	52348	48361	0.29	0.32	0.36	229
H6	627669	540286	516242	2.46	2.80	2.82	481
H7	5.8e6	5.4e6	5.3e6	27.08	32.29	31.48	989
R5	35784	4642	2392	0.15	0.06	0.08	27
R6	174589	6047	4295	0.69	0.07	0.12	22
R7	764727	14037	12083	3.30	0.16	0.20	27
R8	2.1e6	98420	60322	12.94	0.67	0.52	23
R9	**	93806	70578	125.95	0.71	0.69	25
R10	**	271935	279693	88.46	2.22	2.47	25
M1	50147	25103	23917	0.79	0.52	0.48	50
M2	223034	100513	94426	3.30	1.82	1.82	51
M3	231357	130747	129269	3.42	2.43	2.51	53
M4	971736	561599	516178	13.99	10.57	9.54	54
N1	99840	56550	52564	5.59	3.44	3.03	50
N2	446465	238369	218351	25.30	14.86	13.21	53
N3	473117	286506	257530	27.04	17.86	15.23	53
N4	2.0e6	1.2e6	1.1e6	117.43	74.83	70.88	56
C1	35768	13863	13455	0.37	0.42	0.62	55
C2	110593	38483	36888	0.99	0.76	1.37	55
C3	144199	44730	42366	1.27	0.91	1.54	55
C4	1.4e6	368813	354091	11.23	4.30	5.05	56
C5	1.3e7	2.8e6	2.7e6	116.28	29.60	29.97	57
C6	*	2.8e7	2.7e7	*	377.77	364.15	57

* (**) out of memory (on some instances)

The error in a tree with 128 processes is found in approx. 1 minute using a bound of 50 states. Because not all processes contribute to reaching an error state, this low bound already produces a well-informed heuristic. Using the higher bound of 100 states is expensive: since in this benchmark the length of the shortest error path is only linear in the height of the tree, computing the estimate involves composing a large number of processes with few and therefore large buckets. The more accurate estimate produced by $N100$ does, however, lead to shorter error traces.

The Towers of Hanoi. Benchmarks H4 – H8 model the standard problem of moving a stack of differently sized disks from one of three columns to another, with the constraints that the disks may only be moved one at a time and a disk may never be stacked on top of a smaller disk. We modeled the problem with one process for each disk. A disk can at any time send a request upwards in the hierarchy of smaller disks to check whether itself and a target column is clear of smaller disks. If it gets an "ok" signal, it moves from its current column to the target column. To find a trace that leads to the target configuration we specify the target configuration as the error condition. In this benchmark, the length of the shortest error path grows exponentially with the number of processes. This explains why the bound $N100$ performs significantly better than the bound $N50$ in the largest benchmark H8.

Randomly Generated Systems. We obtained a further suite of benchmarks by randomly generating systems of processes. The parameters of the construction are the number of processes, the minimum and maximum number of states of the processes, and the seed for the random number generator (the Mersenne Twister [15]). Excluded from the benchmarks are systems with no error paths and systems that contain independent subsystems, i.e., systems where the process graph, with edges between processes that have shared actions, is not connected.

Benchmarks R5 – R10 each consist of 15 different randomly generated systems, with the size ranging from 5 (R5) to 10 (R10) processes. We set the number of actions to twice the number of processes, the minimum/maximum size to 3/10, and averaged the results over the 15 systems for each size. The only method besides our estimate function that also finds the error in all systems with 10 processes is rDF, which, however, takes significantly more time.

A* is usually much more expensive than best-first traversal. In this benchmark, however, A* results in a much more focused traversal, as the number of visited states shows. As a result, A* even becomes faster than best-first traversal.

Industrial Examples. Henning Dierks provided us with a collection of UPPAAL benchmarks from two industrial case studies: A real-time mutual exclusion protocol in a distributed system with asynchronous communication [3] (benchmarks M1 – M4 and N1 – N4) and a tramway controller from the UniForM project [11] (C1 – C9). The two case studies add real-time constraints and integer variables to the discrete setting of the other benchmarks: the faults in both case studies are introduced as erroneous time bounds. Even though our implementation is not yet optimized for this type of system (in the computation of the estimate, we simply ignore the clocks and use a flat representation of the integer values as discrete states), the directed model checker performs remarkably well, solving several benchmarks that were previously out of UPPAAL's reach.

7   Related Work

Several researchers have investigated techniques to guide the model checker. Typically, the guidance is application-specific and must be provided by the user. For example, Behrmann et al [1] describe UPPAAL case studies in which a dramatic reduction of the state space was achieved by a user-provided estimate of the error distance. Bloem et al [2] use *hints* in the form of assertions on the primary inputs and state variables of the model: the transition relation can then be underapproximated (by ignoring transitions out of states that violate the hint) or overapproximated (by allowing any transition from a state that violates the hint). Similarly, Kaltenbach and Misra [10] use hints in the form of *regular expressions* over the actions of the program.

Directed model checking with an automatically computed estimate of the error distance has been pioneered by Edelkamp, Leue, and Lluch-Lafuente with the tool HSF-SPIN [6]. In addition to several simpler heuristics for safety and liveness properties (including deadlock-detection), HSF-SPIN implements the FSM heuristic [7]. The FSM heuristic approximates the error distance by the maximum (or, alternatively, the sum) of the error distances in individual processes and is a significant improvement over program-independent estimates like the Hamming-distance [20]. The drawback of the FSM heuristic is that it ignores the synchronization between the processes. It is therefore less useful when searching for errors that require a complex interaction between multiple processes.

Similar to our approach, the *pattern databases* of Qian and Nymeyer [17] and the *abstraction databases* by Edelkamp and Lluch-Lafuente [5] also make use of an abstraction of the system. The error distances in the abstract state space are stored in a table, from which they are read off during the traversal of the concrete state space. Our abstraction technique extends these methods: while both pattern databases and abstraction databases assume that a particular abstraction function is chosen beforehand, we automatically compute an abstraction function that aims at preserving the error distance.

Related to our incremental abstraction technique is the *Incremental Composition and Reduction (ICR) Method* [18], which reduces the partially composed system after each composition of two processes to an observationally equivalent process. Since ICR maintains an accurate representation of the behavior of the partially composed system (which often requires more states than the completely composed system), ICR is only feasible if the user provides additional constraints on the process interaction [8]. By contrast, our method, which only maintains an approximate representation of the behavior, is fully automatic.

In very recent work, Kupferschmid et al [12] investigate using an estimate function from AI planning for directed model checking. The estimate is based on a relaxation of the system in which every state variable, once it has obtained a value, keeps that value forever. Because Kupferschmid et al's estimate function is computed on-the-fly, it can be used in systems with infinite data types (such as unbounded integers), which are currently out of our scope. On the other hand, our precomputed abstraction reflects the process synchronization more accurately, which leads to much better performance in systems with complex process interaction, such as the Towers of Hanoi benchmark (see Section 6). There is obvious potential in a combination of the two approaches, which we plan to explore in future work.

An important complement to directed model checking with estimates of the error distance are structural heuristics as implemented in the Java PathFinder [9]. These heuristics exploit the program structure for example by maximizing thread interleavings and code coverage.

8   Conclusion

Abstraction has always been considered a key in fighting the state explosion problem. Here, we have given a new twist to abstraction. We traverse abstract states in order to compute an estimate of the error distance, and then traverse concrete states in order to find an error path. The quality of an abstraction is not determined by a Boolean value ("does the abstraction preserve the reachability of an error state by the initial state?"). It is rather determined by the ratio between the estimated and the actual error distance.

While we are still in the beginning of the systematic design of such abstractions, this paper has made an initial contribution. It presents a distance-preserving abstraction for concurrent systems that allows one to compute an interesting estimate of the error distance without hitting the state explosion problem. As detailed in the paper, the definition of the abstraction originates from insights into the interplay between the impact of an action-based synchronization mechanism on the error distance in concurrent systems on the one hand and the use of estimated error distances during the state space traversal on the other hand.

We have implemented the resulting directed model checking method, and we have led a series of experiments that indicate the usefulness of an estimate that takes into account synchronization.

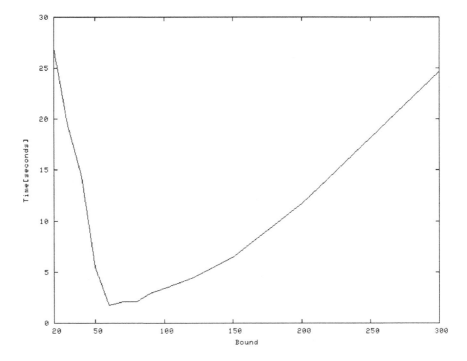

Fig. 6. Running time of the directed model checker for different bounds on the abstract state space. (Data from a randomly generated system with eight processes.)

With abstraction, one always encounters a tradeoff between cost and precision. A potential advantage of our abstraction method is that it is parameterized (by the size of the abstract state space), and that one can fine-tune the parameter (and thus the accuracy of the abstraction). To demonstrate the tradeoff on an example, we took a randomly generated system with eight processes and changed the parameter gradually. Figure 6 shows the corresponding running times. Initially, the runtime decreases with a increasing parameter. After the sweet spot in the tradeoff is reached (in the region between 60 and 80), the runtime increases with increasing parameter. More experience is needed in order to provide systematic ways to choose the parameter.

Acknowledgements. We thank Gerd Behrmann and Henning Dierks for fruitful discussions on heuristics in UPPAAL. Gerd Behrmann helped us with the UP-PAAL source code and Henning Dierks provided us with interesting UPPAAL benchmarks from industrial case studies.

References

1. G. Behrmann, A. Fehnker, T. Hune, K. G. Larsen, P. Pettersson, and J. Romijn. Efficient guiding towards cost-optimality in uppaal. In T. Margaria and W. Yi, editors, *Proceedings of TACAS'01*, number 2031 in Lecture Notes in Computer Science, pages 174–188. Springer-Verlag, 2001.
2. R. Bloem, K. Ravi, and F. Somenzi. Symbolic guided search for CTL model checking. In *Design Automation Conference*, pages 29–34, 2000.
3. H. Dierks. Comparing model checking and logical reasoning for real-time systems. *Formal Aspects of Computing*, 16(2):104–120, 2004.
4. S. Edelkamp, S. Leue, and A. Lluch-Lafuente. Directed explicit-state model checking in the validation of communication protocols. *Software Tools for Technology Transfer*, 2003.
5. S. Edelkamp and A. Lluch-Lafuente. Abstraction databases in theory and model checking. In *Proc. ICAPS Workshop on Connecting Planning Theory with Practice, June 2004*.
6. S. Edelkamp, A. Lluch-Lafuente, and S. Leue. Directed explicit model checking with hsf-spin. In M. B. Dwyer, editor, *Proceedings of SPIN'01*, volume 2057 of *Lecture Notes in Computer Science*, pages 57–79. Springer-Verlag, 2001.
7. S. Edelkamp, A. Lluch-Lafuente, and S. Leue. Trail-directed model checking. *Electr. Notes Theor. Comput. Sci.*, 55(3), 2001.
8. S. Graf, B. Steffen, and G. Lüttgen. Compositional minimization of finite state systems using interface specifications. *Formal Aspects of Computing*, 8:607–616, September 1996.
9. A. Groce and W. Visser. Heuristics for model checking Java programs. In *Proceedings of SPIN'02*, Lecture Notes in Computer Science 2318, pages 242–245. Springer-Verlag, 2002.
10. M. Kaltenbach and J. Misra. A theory of hints in model checking. In B. K. Aichernig and T. Maibaum, editors, *Formal Methods at the Crossroads: From Panacea to Foundational Support*, number 2757 in Lecture Notes in Computer Science, pages 423–438. Springer-Verlag, 2003.

11. B. Krieg-Brückner, J. Peleska, E.-R. Olderog, and A. Baer. The UniForM workbench, a universal development environment for formal methods. In J. Wing, J. Woodcock, and J. Davies, editors, *FM'99 – Formal Methods: World Congress on Formal Methods in the Development of Computing Systems*, number 1709 in Lecture Notes in Computer Science, 1999.
12. S. Kupferschmid, J. Hoffmann, H. Dierks, and G. Behrmann. Adapting an AI planning heuristic for directed model checking. Proceedings of SPIN'06 (this volume).
13. A. L. Lafuente. *Directed Search for the Verification of Communication Protocols.* PhD thesis, Institute of Computer Science, University of Freiburg, June 2003.
14. K. Larsen, P. Petterson, and Wang Yi. Uppaal in a nutshell. *STTT – International Journal on Software Tools for Technology Transfer*, 1(1+2):134–152, Dec. 1997.
15. M. Matsumoto and T. Nishimura. Mersenne Twister: A 623-dimensionally equidistributed uniform pseudo-random number generator. *ACM Transactions on Modeling and Computer Simulation*, 8(1):3–30, 1998.
16. J. Pearl. *Heuristics.* Morgan Kaufmann, San Francisco, CA, 1983.
17. K. Qian and A. Nymeyer. Guided invariant model checking based on abstraction and symbolic pattern databases. In K. Jensen and A. Podelski, editors, *Proceedings of TACAS'04*, number 2988 in Lecture Notes in Computer Science, pages 497–511, 2004.
18. K. K. Sabnani, A. M. Lapone, and M. Ü. Uyar. An algorithmic procedure for checking safety properties of protocols. *IEEE Trans. Commun.*, 37(9):940–948, September 1989.
19. C. Seitz. Ideas about arbiters. *Lambda*, pages 10–14, 1980.
20. C. H. Yang and D. L. Dill. Validation with guided search of the state space. In *Design Automation Conference*, pages 599–604, 1998.

Adapting an AI Planning Heuristic for Directed Model Checking*

Sebastian Kupferschmid[1], Jörg Hoffmann[2], Henning Dierks[3],
and Gerd Behrmann[4]

[1] University of Freiburg, Germany
kupfersc@informatik.uni-freiburg.de
[2] Max Planck Institute for CS, Saarbrücken, Germany
hoffmann@mpi-inf.mpg.de
[3] OFFIS, Germany
dierks@offis.de
[4] Aalborg University, Denmark
behrmann@cs.aau.dk

Abstract. There is a growing body of work on directed model checking, which improves the falsification of safety properties by providing heuristic functions that can guide the search *quickly* towards *short* error paths. Techniques of this kind have also been made very successful in the area of AI Planning. Our main technical contribution is the adaptation of the most successful heuristic function from AI Planning to the model checking context, yielding a new heuristic for directed model checking. The heuristic is based on solving an abstracted problem in every search state. We adapt the abstraction and its solution to networks of communicating automata annotated with (constraints and effects on) integer variables. Since our ultimate goal in this research is to also take into account clock variables, as used in timed automata, our techniques are implemented inside UP-PAAL. We run experiments in some toy benchmarks for timed automata, and in two timed automata case studies originating from an industrial project. Compared to both blind search and some previously proposed heuristic functions, we consistently obtain significant, sometimes dramatic, search space reductions, resulting in likewise strong reductions of runtime and memory requirements.

1 Introduction

When model checking safety properties, the ultimate goal is to prove the absence of error states. However, to do so one has to explore the entire state space of the application under consideration. It is therefore essential to use an efficient representation and implementation of that state space. Prominent examples of such implementations are the SPIN (e.g. [1]) and UPPAAL (e.g. [2]) tools. SPIN handles the Promela language, describing systems of communicating processes. UPPAAL handles networks of extended timed automata, which is a formalism with less complex communication than

---

* This work was partly supported by the German Research Council (DFG) as part of the Transregional Collaborative Research Center "Automatic Verification and Analysis of Complex Systems" (SFB/TR 14 AVACS). See http://www.avacs.org/ for more information.

A. Valmari (Ed.): SPIN 2006, LNCS 3925, pp. 35–52, 2006.

Promela, but where the processes can be annotated with real-valued clock variables. Both languages also feature integer variables.

Enumerating the entire state space is often not feasible in practise. A potentially much easier task is to only try to *detect* error states, i.e., to *falsify* the safety property. An error may be found by exploring only a small fraction of the search space. Algorithms that are good at detecting errors can be used for debugging purposes. They can even be good for proving an application error-free, because they can be used to handle the intermediate iterations in the abstraction refinement life cycle, i.e. those iterations in which spurious error states exist.

There are two main issues to be addressed: first, the *search space size*, i.e. the number of search states that need to be considered before the error state is found; and second, the length of the detected *path* to the error state. The search space size determines the scalability of the search. Short error paths are preferred for debugging; in abstraction refinement, they provide better information about what aspects of the abstraction should be refined. Ideally, one wants an *optimal*, i.e. a shortest possible, path to an error.

Both search space size and error path length can be addressed by the *order* in that the search states are explored. One defines a *heuristic function* h, a function that maps states to integers, estimating the state's distance to the nearest error state. The search then gives a preference to states with lower h value. There are many different ways of doing the latter, of which we consider the wide-spread methods A^* search and *greedy search*. In the former, search nodes s are explored by increasing value of $c(s) + h(s)$ where $c(s)$ is the length of the search path on that s was reached. If h is *admissible*, i.e., if it never overestimates the real distance to the nearest error state, then A^* is guaranteed to return an optimal error path. In greedy search, search nodes are explored by increasing value of $h(s)$. This gives no guarantee on the length of the detected error path, but tends to explore less search states in practise.

The application of heuristic search to model checking was pioneered a few years ago by Edelkamp et al [3,4], christening this research direction *directed model checking*, and inspiring various other approaches of this sort, e.g. [5,6,7]. The main difference between all the approaches is how they define and compute the heuristic function: *How does one estimate the distance to an error state?* Different definitions make all the difference because no heuristic can work well in *all* examples, and the best one can hope to do is to define a range of heuristics that cover (work well in) an as large as possible range of examples.

Edelkamp et al [3,4] work in the context of SPIN. They propose to base the distance estimation on the graph-distances within each single process. For process i, let $d(i)$ be the distance of i's start location to its target location, when ignoring all edge guards (if there is no target location, set $d(i) := 0$). Then an admissible heuristic function, called d^L, is defined as $max_i d(i)$, and a non-admissible heuristic function, called d^U, is defined as $\sum_i d(i)$. We implemented these heuristic functions in UPPAAL, taking the $d(i)$ to be the graph distances in the individual automata.

Note that d^L and d^U are rather crude approximations of the system semantics. They completely ignore communication and integer variables. Our main contribution in this paper is an approximation technique that does *not* do that. The approximation is more costly – i.e., computing the heuristic function takes more runtime than what is needed for d^L and d^U – but, as we will see, this often pays off in terms of much smaller search spaces. We obtain our approximation by adapting the most successful heuristic method [8, 9] from the area of AI Planning, where heuristic search has been overwhelmingly successful in the past decade, in particular winning all the planning competitions (e.g. [9, 10, 11]).

The heuristic method is based on what AI people call a *relaxation*, which is the same as the model checking term *abstraction*: an over-approximation. The abstraction technique used is, however, quite different from what one usually uses in model checking, due to the very different way of *using* the abstracted task. Namely, the heuristic values are generated by solving the abstract problem in every search state, and taking the length of the abstract solution as the distance estimate. To be able to solve the abstract problem in every search state, of course the abstraction has to be very coarse. In our particular case, the abstraction assumes that *every state variable, once it has obtained a value, keeps that value forever.* Which means, in the abstraction the "value" of any variable at any time point is not a member but a subset of the variable's domain. The subsets grow monotonically as abstract transitions are taken. We prove that, like in the planning context, solving the abstract problem optimally, i.e., finding an optimal abstract error path, and thereby computing an admissible heuristic function, is still **NP**-hard, even if the addressed formalism allows only parallel automata with communication. For parallel automata with communication and integer variables, we define two polynomial-time methods for approximating the length of an optimal abstract error path. We call the resulting heuristic functions h^L and h^U. The former is a lower bound on the length of an optimal abstract error path, the latter is an upper bound on that length; h^L is admissible, h^U is not.

Our heuristics are implemented inside the UPPAAL system, since our goal in this research is to speed up model checking of (networks of extended) timed automata. Ultimately, of course, we want to develop heuristics that also take into account the clock variables. We are currently investigating that direction; it is highly non-trivial in our context due to the nature of our abstraction. Since timed transitions are continuous, the value subset of a clock x will be $[0, \infty)$ as soon as one reaches a location without an invariant limiting x; we discuss this in more detail below. As said, so far we can offer heuristics that take into account communication and integer variables. To the best of our knowledge, no similar heuristics were developed in any other area of model checking (the differences to the existing other heuristics are outlined in the related work section).

In the standard versions of UPPAAL, the search order can be fixed to either depth-first (DF) or breadth-first (BF).[1] We test our implementation in networks of extended timed automata. We consider a few toy examples, and two realistic case studies coming from an industrial project. We evaluate the performance of different UPPAAL configurations finding optimal error paths, and of UPPAAL configurations finding (possibly) sub-optimal error paths. The former are BF, and A^* with h^L or d^L; the latter are randomised DF, and greedy search with h^L, h^U, d^L, and d^U (remember that d^L and d^U

---

[1] There is also a version doing heuristic search [12], but for that the user has to provide the heuristic function manually, in difference to our fully-automatic technology. Note that a successful manual heuristic specification requires inside knowledge on the side of the user, and careful tuning.

were defined by Edelkamp et al [4]). Of the optimal configurations, BF and A^* with d^L perform roughly similarly except in the toy examples; A^* with h^L brings a moderate runtime advantage, but much smaller search spaces, enabling success in one more example due to the lower memory usage. For the (potentially) sub-optimal configurations, our results are much stronger. While the d^L and d^U search orders bring hardly any advantage over DF in our industrial case studies, both h^L and h^U yield dramatic search space reductions, and with that better runtimes and the ability to solve more examples. At the same time, the error paths found with h^L and h^U are orders of magnitude shorter than those found with DF, d^L, and d^U.

The next section briefly gives our notations. Sections 3 and 4 formally define the abstraction used, and the algorithms computing the heuristic functions, respectively. Section 5 describes our empirical results, Section 6 discusses related work. Section 7 closes the paper. Most proofs are replaced in the text by short proof sketches; the full proofs are available in a technical report [13].

2   Notations

We assume the reader is roughly familiar with timed automata and their commonly used extensions. We give a brief description of the particular formalism treated in our current implementation. We use (a slight variation of) the terminology and notation given by Behrmann et al [14].

We treat networks of timed automata with binary synchronisation and integer variables. For the sake of presentation herein, we restrict atomic expressions over integer variables to variables, variable increments/decrements, or constants. That is, we allow only comparisons like $v \leq v'$ or $v = c$, and assignments like $v := v'$, $v := c$ or $v := v \pm 1$. Our implementation in fact deals with arbitrary linear expressions over the variables; for the sake of readability, we omit these and only explain the extensions in the text. As mentioned earlier, the heuristic function so far completely ignores the clock variables (the reasons for this are explained in Section 3.2). We therefore don't give formal notations for these variables. Our notations are as follows. The timed automata share a set A of actions, and a set V of integer variables. Each $v \in V$ has a domain $dom(v)$. Each automaton i has a location set $L(i)$, a start location $l^0(i)$, and a set of edges $E(i)$. Each edge is annotated with an action $a \in A$, with a guard g, and with an *effect* f. The guard is a conjunction of conditions of the form $x \bowtie y$ where $x, y \in \mathbb{Z} \cup V$ and $\bowtie \in \{<, \leq, =, \geq, >, \neq\}$. The effect is a list of assignments of the form $v := v'$, $v := c$ or $v := v \pm 1$, where $v, v' \in V$ and $c \in \mathbb{Z}$. Each variable v occurs on the left hand side of at most one such assignment. The semantics are defined as obvious. Transitions are asynchronous and triggered by an edge annotated with a special void action, or synchronous and triggered by two edges with inverse actions.

The safety properties we can verify take the form of (negated) edge guards plus location vectors, i.e., our implementation can check whether there exists a reachable state in that the automata are in specified locations, and that satisfies a conjunction of conditions $x \bowtie y$. We call the former the *target locations*, and the latter the *target formula*. A path of transitions is called a *solution* if it leads from the start state to a state complying with target locations and target formula.

3 Abstraction

We introduce the abstraction method, called *monotonicity abstraction*, underlying our implemented heuristic function. We first give a high-level description of the abstraction in a generic way, then we define it as currently used in the context of networks of automata.

Before we start, let us remark that the monotonicity abstraction was first invented in AI Planning for a formalism called STRIPS, under the name "ignoring delete lists" [8]. In STRIPS, the "delete lists" are effect instructions that make a boolean variable FALSE. This simplifies the problem because, in STRIPS, variables are only ever required to be TRUE. The monotonicity abstraction we describe below is a generalisation of this abstraction approach. We remark that the generalisation is *not* published in the AI Planning literature; it is, in spirit, somewhat similar to the framework presented in [15].

3.1 The Monotonicity Abstraction

The abstraction is based on the simplifying assumption that *every state variable, once it obtained a value, keeps that value forever*. The value of a variable is no longer an element, but a *subset* of its domain. That subset grows monotonically over transition applications – hence the name of the abstraction.

In a little more detail, in general a transition system (a planning task, a system of timed automata, a piece of program code, etc.) can be viewed as given by a set of state variables, a set of transition rules, a start state, and a target formula. The transition rules have a guard – a formula out of some class of valid (non-temporal) formulas – and an effect – an instruction how the variable values change when the rule is applied. States are value assignments to the variables, the target formula is a valid formula. A solution is a path of transitions that, when applied to the start state, ends in a state that satisfies the target formula.

Under the monotonicity abstraction, the semantics of a transition system as above are changed as follows. States now map each variable to a subset of its domain. The start assignment contains the single value assigned by the start state. A formula evaluates to TRUE in a state if there *exists* a variable value vector in the state so that the formula evaluates to TRUE when inserting these values. Executing an effect instruction becomes a *set union* operation, where the new value of each variable x is its old value (a domain subset) plus the new value assigned by the effect. If the effect outcome depends on variables, then all possible value vectors for these variables are used, each yielding a value for x.

E.g., say we have one integer variable v, and one transition with guard $v = 0$ and effect $v := v + 1$. The start state is $v = 0$, and the target formula is $v = 2$. Obviously, there is no solution. There is, however, a solution in the abstraction. The start assignment is $\{0\}$. After one transition, this becomes $\{0, 1\}$. Since the transition guard is abstracted to $\exists c \in s(v) : c = 0$, the transition can be applied a second time, and we get the state $\{0, 1, 2\}$: the new values obtained for v are 1 (inserting 0 into the effect right hand side) and 2 (inserting 1). In this state the abstract target formula, taking the form $\exists c \in s(v) : c = 2$, evaluates to TRUE.

It is not difficult to see that the monotonicity abstraction induces an over-approxima-tion of the real transition system: every solution path in the real system corresponds to a solution path in the abstract system. We will state this formally below, for our abstrac-tion of timed automata. In many cases, deciding solution existence is a polynomial-time problem under the abstraction, making it feasible to solve the abstract problem in every search state.[2]

3.2   The Monotonicity Abstraction in Timed Automata

Before we give our definitions, consider at a higher level of abstraction what happens if we apply the above abstraction to a system of timed automata. Under the abstraction, each automaton will (potentially) be in several locations in a state. The integer variables will have several possible values in a state. The clock variables will only accumulate new values. Transitions will be applicable as soon as one of the possible value vectors satisfies the guard.

Thinking a little more about the clocks, one sees that they are likely to trivialise very quickly under the abstraction. The reason for that are the *timed* transitions: as time passes, the clocks accumulate all the passing time points. After waiting from time point u to time point $u + d$, the new clock value subsets contain the entire interval $[u, u + d]$. So in a location with invariant I, the clock value subsets immediately gather all values up to the upper bound specified by I. Now, all clock values are 0 initially. Since time passes continually, therefore the clock value subsets will always have the form $[0, max]$ (where max is the latest time point yet reached), containing no information other than max. As soon as a location with empty invariant is reached, max will become infinite, i.e., the clock value subsets will be the entire time line.

For the above, reasoning about clock values under the abstraction is not likely to contribute useful information, unless additional techniques are used. We outline an idea for such additional techniques in Section 7. For now, we ignore the clocks altogether (inside the heuristic function). While this is undesirable, as said our empirical results demonstrate that taking (abstract) account of automaton locations, synchronisation, and integer variables can yield useful search guidance.

Our definitions are straightforward and read as follows. We denote abstract con-structs with a superscribed $+$ to indicate the additivity of the abstraction. An abstract state s^+ assigns each automaton i a location subset $s^+(i) \subseteq L(i)$. Each integer vari-able v is assigned a value set $s^+(v) \subseteq dom(v)$. Formulas (conjunctions of conditions) are abstract by, "locally", existentially quantifying the variables *in each condition sep-arately*. E.g. a formula $v \bowtie_1 v' \wedge v \bowtie_2 c$ is abstracted to $\exists c_1 \in s^+(v), c_1' \in s^+(v') : c_1 \bowtie_1 c_1' \wedge \exists c_2 \in s^+(v) : c_2 \bowtie_2 c$. That is, we allow achievement of each condition in separate. When, "globally", quantifying the variables over the entire formula, one gets an **NP**-complete constraint problem, so there is no way around making further ab-stractions. We chose to do local quantification mainly because it is very simple and can be implemented efficiently. Also, it comes in handy also for linear arithmetic. When

---

[2] Under certain conditions, checking satisfaction of a formula becomes **NP**-hard in the abstrac-tion, due to the additional existential quantification. In particular, this is the case in our context of timed automata. We make an additional simplification to get around this, see the explanation below.

allowing linear arithmetic between integer variables, checking even a single condition $\exists \bar{x} : f(\bar{x}) = c$ is **NP**-hard. This isn't usually a problem since the number of variables in the expressions ($f(\bar{x})$) is typically small, up to four maybe.[3] However, the total number of variables in a *conjunction* of expressions can become quite big. So it is convenient to address the single expressions in separate.

An assignment $v := c$ results in $s^+(v) := s^+(v) \cup \{c\}$. An assignment $v := v'$ results in $s^+(v) := s^+(v) \cup s^+(v')$. An assignment $v := v + 1$ results in $s^+(v) := s^+(v) \cup \{c + 1 \mid c \in s^+(v)\}$, $v := v - 1$ results in $s^+(v) := s^+(v) \cup \{c - 1 \mid c \in s^+(v)\}$. Values not contained in $dom(v)$ are removed from the result. An asynchronous transition of automaton i from location l to l' is enabled if $l \in s^+(i)$, and the respective abstract edge guard holds in s^+. The effect assignments are executed as above, and $s^+(i) := s^+(i) \cup \{l'\}$ is set. A synchronous transition of automaton i from location $l(i)$ to $l'(i)$, and of automaton j from location $l(j)$ to $l'(j)$, is enabled if $l(i) \in s^+(i)$, $l(j) \in s^+(j)$, and both respective abstract edge guards hold in s^+. The effect assignments are executed as above, and $s^+(i) := s^+(i) \cup \{l'(i)\}$ as well as $s^+(j) := s^+(j) \cup \{l'(j)\}$ are set.

When the start state is s_0, s_0^+ is given by $s_0^+(i) = \{s_0(i)\}$, and $s_0^+(v) = \{s_0(v)\}$. A path of successively enabled transitions from s_0 is a *abstract solution* if it ends in a state s^+ in which the abstract target formula holds.

Proposition 1. *Given a network of timed automata with binary synchronisation and integer variables, a start state, target locations, and a target formula. If $t_1, \ldots, t_n$ is a solution then $t_1, \ldots, t_n$ is also an abstract solution.*

Proof Sketch: The variable values achieved by $t_1, \ldots, t_n$ in the abstraction subsume the values achieved in reality. ∎

By Proposition 1, every solution in the real search space is also contained in the abstract search space. So the length of an optimal abstract solution is an admissible heuristic function. We will come back to this below.

Consider Figure 1 as an example. The top automaton needs to go through repeated circles. More precisely, if the bottom automaton has n locations, then the real solution takes $2(n - 1)$ steps, half of which are synchronized between both automata. However, an abstract solution can be obtained in only n steps: the top automaton goes to the right once, and can then go to the left n times in sequence since its right location remains in the reached location subset.

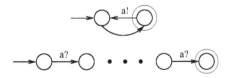

Fig. 1. A simple example where h^L and h^U deliver bad heuristic values

---

[3] Also, one can handle the expressions in an incremental way, see Section 4.

We can decide in polynomial time if there exists an abstract solution or not.

Theorem 1. *Let TASolEx$^+$ denote the following problem. Given a network of timed automata with binary synchronisation and integer variables, a start state, target locations, and a target formula. Is there a abstract solution?*

TASolEx$^+$ is in **P**.

Proof: A polynomial solution algorithm is described in Section 4.   ∎

The polynomial solution algorithm forms the basis of our heuristic functions: for a heuristic function, what we want to know is not primarily if there is an abstract solution, but what the *length* of an abstract solution is (if there is one). Abstract solutions may contain arbitrarily many useless transitions, and we want to know what an *optimal* abstract solution is. We call the length of such a solution, for a state s, $h^+(s)$. Unfortunately, computing h^+ is still hard.

Proposition 2. *Let TASolMin$^+$ denote the following problem. Given a network of timed automata with binary synchronisation, a start state, a target formula, and an integer b. Is there an abstract solution of length at most b?*

TASolMin$^+$ is **NP**-*hard.*

Proof Sketch: By a straightforward reduction of 3SAT, using one automaton per clause and variable.   ∎

Note that *one does not even need integer variables* in the proof to Proposition 2. The desired admissible heuristic function h^+, based on our abstraction, can not be computed efficiently. So, in practise, we will have to *approximate h^+*. We introduce two approximation techniques in the next section, one computing a lower bound, and one computing an upper bound. Both are implemented as heuristic functions inside UPPAAL.

4   Approximating h^+

Our heuristic functions map search states to integers. For each state s during search, we are facing the following situation. We are given a network of timed automata, target locations, and a target formula. The start state is s. We want to approximate the length of an optimal abstract solution.

Both approximations are based on a forward-chaining algorithm that generalises algorithms proposed in the context of numeric planning [16]. The algorithm is a forward fixpoint computation. It determines in polynomial time if there is a abstract solution, by building a data structure called *abstract transition graph*, short *ATG*. The ATG is a layered graph encoding reachability information. Pseudo-code is given in Figure 2.

The ATG is a sequence of location sets $L_k(i)$ and of variable value sets $V_k(v)$: the graph *layers*. The algorithm builds these in an incremental way, so that their contents increase monotonically over k. Satisfaction of a formula, and enabled transitions, are defined in the obvious manner analogous to abstract states. In each iteration of the algorithm, for every enabled transition the respective new values are put into the sets. For the example from Figure 1, if the top automaton has locations t_1 (left) and t_2 (right),

$k := 0$, $L_0(i) := \{s(i)\}$ for all i, $V_0(v) := \{s(v)\}$ for all v
while target locations are not in L_k, or V_k does not model abstract target formula **do**
  $L_{k+1}(i) := L_k(i)$ for all i, $V_{k+1}(v) := V_k(v)$ for all v
  for all transitions t enabled by L_k and V_k **do**
    $L_{k+1}(i) := L_{k+1}(i) \cup \{l(i)'\}$ where t goes to $l(i)'$ in automaton i
    if t synchronously also goes to $l(j)'$ in automaton j **then**
      $L_{k+1}(j) := L_{k+1}(j) \cup \{l(j)'\}$
    endif
    if $v := c$ is an effect of t **then** $V_{k+1}(v) := V_{k+1}(v) \cup \{c\}$ **endif**
    if $v := v'$ is an effect of t **then** $V_{k+1}(v) := V_{k+1}(v) \cup V_k(v')$ **endif**
    if $v := v + 1$ is an effect of t **then** $V_{k+1}(v) := [min(V_k(v)), \infty]$ **endif**
    if $v := v - 1$ is an effect of t **then** $V_{k+1}(v) := [-\infty, max(V_k(v))]$ **endif**
  endfor
  if $L_{k+1}(i) = L_k(i)$ for all i, and $V_{k+1}(v) = V_k(v)$ for all v **then**
    $minlayer := \infty$, stop
  endif
  $k := k + 1$
endwhile
$minlayer := k$

Fig. 2. Building an abstract transition graph (ATG)

and the bottom automaton has locations $b_1, \ldots, b_n$ (from left to right), then $L_0(top) = \{t_1\}$, $L_0(bottom) = \{b_1\}$, $L_1(top) = \{t_1, t_2\}$, and $L_1(bottom) = \{b_1\}$; for $2 \le k \le n$, we get $L_k(top) = \{t_1, t_2\}$ and $L_k(bottom) = \{b_1, \ldots, b_k\}$. In $L_n(bottom)$ we have the target location and the algorithm stops.

The treatment of $v := v + 1$ and $v := v - 1$ effects is slightly more complicated, using a sort of "shortcut" to avoid the repeated incremental increasing (decreasing) of a variable up to (down to) a needed value n (which could take a number of iterations exponential in the representation of n). Setting a border of a $V_k(v)$ interval to ∞ is interpreted as telling us that arbitrarily high/low values can now be reached for v, by applying the respective effect.

It is important to note that the $V_k(v)$ sets can always be represented using only a number of values polynomial in the size of the input task, i.e. one does not need to explicitly enumerate all values in the reachable interval. If one of the bounds is infinite, one just records that plus the value at which the continuous region ends. In more detail, one can represent $V_k(v)$ by an ordered list of possible values, plus a marker at the lowest and highest value, indicating if or if not below/above the bound there is an infinite region inside $V_k(v)$. The values in the explicitly stored list can originate from $v := c$ assignments only, so their number is bounded by the number of such assignments in the input. It should be self-explanatory how this representation corresponds to the pseudo-code given in Figure 2. The representation of each $L_k(i)$ and $V_k(v)$ is polynomial. Satisfaction of an abstract formula in L_k and V_k can be tested in polynomial time processing the – at most binary – single conditions in the formula in turn; a condition on variables v and v' can be tested by, at most, processing the product of $V_k(v)$ and $V_k(v')$. Finally, after a polynomial number of iterations, L_k and V_k will not change anymore, or reach the respective full sets of locations/values. So altogether the algorithm terminates in polynomial time. It encodes admissible reachability information.

Lemma 1. *Given a network of timed automata with binary synchronisation and integer variables, a start state, target locations, and a target formula. If there is an abstract solution of length n, then the algorithm in Figure 2 stops successfully in an iteration $minlayer \leq n$.*

Proof Sketch: When building the ATG without stopping criteria, the abstract solution $t_1, \ldots, t_n$ is a sub-sequence of the ATG, i.e., t_k is enabled by L_{k-1} and V_{k-1}. The effects of t_k are over-approximated and contained in L_k and V_k. ∎

In particular, if the ATG terminates unsuccessfully, then there is no abstract solution. It is easy to see that, if the targets are reached in layer $minlayer$, then an abstract solution can be constructed as the sequence, for $k = 0, \ldots, minlayer - 1$, of all transitions enabled by L_k and V_k. So altogether the ATG is a polynomial procedure deciding existence of an abstract solution, and Theorem 1 follows.

Extending the ATG to deal with linear arithmetic over the integer variables does not require a lot of deep thought, but results in rather unreadable algorithm specifications. As said, testing $\exists \bar{x} : f(\bar{x}) = c$ is **NP**-hard for linear expressions $f(\bar{x})$, but the number of variables in $\bar{x}$ is typically small. Our main algorithmic trick to deal with the expressions efficiently is an *incremental* computation. If, at some point during building the ATG, we want to know whether $\exists \bar{x} : f(\bar{x}) = c$ is true based on the current value subsets (V_k), then we can refer back to the last time we asked that same question, and just take account of how the value subsets have changed since then. In fact, we just keep a flag at each expression occuring in the input, saying if or if not the expression can be satisfied yet. Every time the value subset of a variable occuring in the expression changes (grows), we see whether that change serves to satisfy the expression; if so, we set the flag. Checking guard satisfaction in the ATG then simply means to refer to the flags. Similarly, one can deal with linear expression effect right hand sides, $v := f(\bar{x})$. We just enumerate the set of value tuples for $\bar{x}$, referring back to the previous version of that set. Typically, just one or two variables in $f(\bar{x})$ have gathered new values since the last evaluation of $f(\bar{x})$. It suffices to enumerate these changes and extend the old tuple set correspondingly. The only thing that becomes complicated is the "infinity shortcut" used in Figure 2 to encode arbitrarily many applications of simple increments (and decrements) of the form $v := v + 1$ ($v := v - 1$). If, for example, the effect is $v := v + v'$ where $V_{k-1}(v') = \{2, 5\}$, then the "shortcut" would have to be $V_{k+1}(v) := V_k(v) \cup \{c + 2a + 5b \mid c \in V_k(v), a, b \in \mathbb{N}\}$. Obviously, this gets quite complicated for general effects $v := f(\bar{x})$, so we did not implement a shortcut there and always just insert the new values that can be reached with a *single* step, paying the prize of multiple ATG layers for multiple effect applications; usually this is benign. Note that the incremental approach can be implemented for (almost) arbitrarily complicated expressions, not only linear ones.

Let us focus again on how to approximate h^+. As said, we compute a lower bound as well as an upper bound. We call the lower bound h^L, and the upper bound h^U. By Proposition 1, a lower bound on h^+ is the $minlayer$ value determined by the ATG algorithm. We set $h^L(s)$ to that value as computed by the ATG for s. Regarding an upper bound, note that, with the above, the number of all transitions enabled at layers $k = 0, \ldots, minlayer - 1$ provides such a bound. However, this bound is likely to be far too generous, counting transitions that are reachable but not needed to achieve the

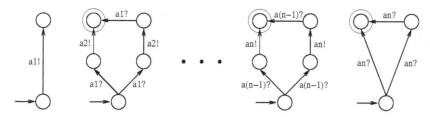

Fig. 3. A simple example where h^L and h^U deliver the precise error state distance

targets. We therefore use a more involved method to determine our upper bound h^U. The method basically selects, at each layer $k = 0, \ldots, minlayer - 1$, a *subset* of the enabled transitions, so that the sequence of the selected transitions is still an abstract solution. This is done by a backward-chaining procedure on the ATG. For space reasons, and since the details are not overly important here, we don't describe the procedure in detail and refer to the TR [13]. The selected abstract solution is not necessarily optimal, and we set h^U to its length. Both h^U and h^L have the value ∞ in case there is no abstract solution (implying with Proposition 1 that there is no real solution either).

Figure 3 gives another example. In the start state, all automata are in the bottom location. The error state is to reach the top left locations. In each automaton except the first one, one has two choices, one of which leads into a dead end (a state from which the error can not be reached), since the required communication signal won't be available anymore. Built for the start state, each layer k of the ATG corresponds exactly to the locations that can be reached within k steps – in particular, the top left location in the kth automaton from the left. So $minlayer = n$, and $h^L = h^U = n$ is the precise error state distance. If, during search, a wrong decision was made in automaton i, then the top left location in i does not appear in the ATG, and the heuristic value is ∞. So all dead ends are excluded from the search space. In contrast, $d^L = 2$ and $d^U = 2n - 1$ for the start state, and no dead ends are detected. Another example where h^L and h^U are precise is, e.g., a situation that requires (only) to repeatedly increment an integer variable. Intuitively, h^L and h^U are good at detecting long sequences of transitions that build upon each other to achieve some target, and at finding out that such a sequence is not available. What they are *not* good at is to see that *the same thing has to be done multiple times*[4] – under the monotonicity abstraction, everything needs to be done at most once. A bad situation was given earlier in Figure 1, where the top automaton needs to go through repeated circles, while h^L and h^U act as if a single circle is sufficient.

5   Results

We ran experiments on an Intel Xeon 3.06 Ghz system with 4 GByte of RAM. As said, our configurations finding optimal error paths are UPPAAL's standard BF, and A^* search with h^L or d^L. Our sub-optimal configurations are UPPAAL's standard randomised DF, short *rDF* (which is by far the most efficient standard method across many examples, including ours), and greedy search with any of h^L, h^U, d^L, and d^U.

---

[4] When repeatedly incrementing a variable, every increment has a *different* effect.

Table 1. Experimental results for the sub-optimal configurations rDF, greedy search with h^L, and greedy search with h^U. Abbreviations: a number of automata, c number of clocks, v number of variables, t runtime in seconds, S search space size (number of visited states, "e+x" means $\cdot 10^x$), M peak memory used in MByte ("G" GByte), l length of detected error path ("K" thousand). Dashes indicate out of memory.

Exp	a	c	v	t rDF	h^L	h^U	S rDF	h^L	h^U	M rDF	h^L	h^U	l rDF	h^L	h^U
F_5^A	5	5	1	0.0	0.0	0.0	526	27	34	3	1	1	161	9	9
F_{10}^A	10	10	1	0.4	0.0	0.0	6371	42	54	7	1	1	1096	9	9
F_{15}^A	15	15	1	1.3	0.0	0.0	20010	57	74	10	1	1	2356	9	9
F_5^B	5	5	1	0.0	0.0	0.0	356	612	74	2	1	1	114	13	18
F_{10}^B	10	10	1	0.5	0.8	0.0	7885	55866	274	7	11	1	1363	29	33
F_{15}^B	15	15	1	3.8	40.3	0.0	58793	1.5e+6	599	18	75	1	6956	367	48
F_5^C	5	5	2	0.0	0.0	0.0	63	22	23	1	1	1	23	7	7
F_{10}^C	10	10	2	0.0	0.0	0.0	205	37	38	1	1	1	37	7	7
F_{15}^C	15	15	2	0.0	0.0	0.0	692	52	53	1	1	1	83	7	7
M_1	3	4	11	0.8	0.1	0.2	29607	5656	14679	7	1	9	1072	169	120
M_2	4	4	13	3.1	0.3	0.8	118341	30742	67398	10	11	11	3875	431	142
M_3	4	4	13	2.8	0.2	0.8	102883	18431	75976	9	10	11	3727	231	158
M_4	5	4	15	12.7	0.8	2.5	543238	76785	230466	22	13	16	15K	731	185
N_1	3	7	11	1.9	0.5	0.8	41218	16335	25577	7	10	10	1116	396	157
N_2	4	7	13	9.3	2.4	3.8	199631	88537	134444	13	13	13	4775	990	241
N_3	4	7	13	8.4	0.6	4.0	195886	28889	143969	12	11	13	3938	324	228
N_4	5	7	15	40.9	5.1	19.2	878706	240366	758167	39	20	31	18K	1671	282
C_1	5	3	12	0.8	0.2	0.2	25219	2339	3021	7	9	10	1056	95	87
C_2	6	3	14	1.0	0.3	0.5	65388	5090	7484	8	10	10	875	86	100
C_3	6	3	15	1.1	0.5	0.6	85940	6681	8259	10	10	10	760	109	101
C_4	7	3	17	8.4	2.5	3.8	892327	40147	65781	43	11	13	1644	125	140
C_5	8	3	19	72.4	13.2	16.7	8.0e+6	237600	333692	295	21	23	2425	393	218
C_6	9	3	21	–	10.1	94.7	–	207845	8.7e+6	–	20	223	–	309	1000
C_7	10	3	23	–	169	836	–	2.7e+7	9.2e+7	–	595	2.1G	–	1506	4630
C_8	10	3	24	–	14.5	932	–	331733	9.8e+7	–	23	2.3G	–	686	16K
C_9	10	3	25	–	1198	–	–	1.3e+8	–	–	2.5G	–	–	18K	–

In the sub-optimal configurations, we use a *bitstate hashing* technique. This is a table with N entries, containing heuristic values, indexed by hash values of search states. Initially all table entries are empty. If the table entry for a new search state already contains a value, then that value is returned. Otherwise, the heuristic value is computed and stored in the table. This is a greedy method to bound the number of calls of the heuristic computation. After some limited experimentation, we set N to 256,000 in the reported experiments.[5]

---

[5] For very small values of N, around 10,000, we observed many "outliers", i.e., examples where search took several orders of magnitude shorter or longer when using the bitstate hashing. For larger N values, the behaviour becomes more stable, and most of the time gives a speedup factor of around 2 to 10 in our examples.

Table 2. Experimental results for greedy search with d^L and d^U. Abbreviations as in Table 1.

Exp	a	c	v	t d^L	d^U	S d^L	d^U	M d^L	d^U	l d^L	d^U
F_5^A	5	5	1	0.0	0.0	80	80	1	1	21	21
F_{10}^A	10	10	1	0.0	0.0	130	130	1	1	21	21
F_{15}^A	15	15	1	0.0	0.0	180	180	1	1	21	21
F_5^B	5	5	1	0.0	0.0	1300	23	1	1	58	7
F_{10}^B	10	10	1	24.7	0.0	1.5e+6	38	81	1	42K	7
F_{15}^B	15	15	1	37.2	0.0	1.5e+6	53	277	1	112K	7
M_1	3	4	11	0.4	0.5	31927	39288	10	10	1349	1695
M_2	4	4	13	2.8	40.0	203051	3.4e+6	17	150	7695	183K
M_3	4	4	13	2.2	1.5	174655	130580	14	14	5690	5412
M_4	5	4	15	6.8	65.7	579494	6.0e+6	33	445	25K	668K
N_1	3	7	11	1.6	1.3	42931	36858	10	10	1803	1601
N_2	4	7	13	9.1	124	264930	5.1e+6	20	289	9279	366K
N_3	4	7	13	4.8	77.4	134798	2.6e+6	19	218	11K	127K
N_4	5	7	15	49.4	181	1.5e+6	6.7e+6	74	234	41K	127K
C_1	5	3	12	0.2	0.2	19263	19628	10	10	977	987
C_2	6	3	14	0.5	0.4	68070	60618	12	12	1501	830
C_3	6	3	15	0.7	0.6	97733	86474	14	14	1238	856
C_4	7	3	17	6.3	5.6	979581	854090	47	45	4510	1906
C_5	8	3	19	61.7	58.6	8.8e+6	8.3e+6	306	306	12K	8943
C_6	9	3	21	–	–	–	–	–	–	–	–

The tool executable and our benchmark examples are available for download from http://www.informatik.uni-freiburg.de/~kupfersc/spin/. The data for the sub-optimal configurations are in Table 1 (rDF, h^L, and h^U) and Table 2 (d^L and d^U). The data for the optimal configurations are in Table 3. Below, we first explain the examples used, then we discuss the results.

We use three variants of the Fischer protocol for mutual exclusion. The examples are "F_i^X" in the tables, where X is A, B, or C, and i is the number of parallel automata. The error condition is that at least two of the automata are in a certain location simultaneously. We made the error possible by weakening one of the temporal conditions in the automata (from ">" to "≥"). The variants differ in the way they encode the error condition. Variant A adds additional automata with synchronisation. Variant B selects and specifies two of the automata for the error condition. Variant C introduces a variable specifying the number of automata in the error location.

The other examples in the tables are from two more realistic case studies. Examples "M_i" and "N_i", $i = 1, \ldots, 4$, come from a study called "Mutual Exclusion". This study models a real-time protocol to ensure mutual exclusion of states in a distributed system via asynchronous communication. The protocol is described in full detail in [17]. By increasing an upper time bound in the model we got a flawed specification that we transformed into its timed automata semantics by applying various abstractions techniques. The resulting models do not have many automata but a non-trivial amount of clocks and variables.

Table 3. Experimental results for our optimal configurations, i.e., BF, A^* search with h^L, and A^* search with d^L. Abbreviations as in Table 1, na means not applicable.

Exp	a	c	v	t BF	h^L	d^L	S BF	h^L	d^L	M BF	h^L	d^L	l
F_5^A	5	5	1	0.0	0.0	0.0	1467	207	1457	6	1	1	9
F_{10}^A	10	10	1	0.5	0.0	0.6	37942	2022	37922	8	1	8	9
F_{15}^A	15	15	1	7.8	0.3	7.8	348827	9187	348797	31	10	32	9
F_5^B	5	5	1	0.0	0.0	0.0	362	138	242	1	1	1	7
F_{10}^B	10	10	1	0.0	0.0	0.0	5422	1768	2352	1	1	1	7
F_{15}^B	15	15	1	0.6	0.2	0.2	34307	8648	10437	7	11	6	7
F_5^C	5	5	2	0.0	0.0	na	362	130	na	1	1	na	7
F_{10}^C	10	10	2	0.0	0.0	na	5442	755	na	1	1	na	7
F_{15}^C	15	15	2	0.6	0.0	na	34307	2255	na	7	1	na	7
M_1	3	4	11	0.8	0.3	0.8	50001	24035	50147	7	7	7	50
M_2	4	4	13	3.1	1.4	3.4	223662	101253	223034	11	10	10	51
M_3	4	4	13	3.3	1.6	3.4	234587	115008	231357	11	10	10	53
M_4	5	4	15	13.6	6.4	14.5	990513	468127	971736	29	22	25	54
N_1	3	7	11	5.2	3.2	5.6	100183	59573	99840	9	9	8	50
N_2	4	7	13	25.6	15.1	25.5	442556	273235	446465	18	15	15	53
N_3	4	7	13	26.4	16.7	27.2	476622	301963	473117	17	15	15	53
N_4	5	7	15	120	77.4	119	2.0e+6	1.3e+6	2.0e+6	65	39	45	56
C_1	5	3	12	0.3	0.7	0.3	35325	17570	35768	7	9	7	55
C_2	6	3	14	0.9	1.7	1.0	109583	46495	110593	10	12	10	55
C_3	6	3	15	1.2	2.1	1.3	143013	53081	144199	11	13	11	55
C_4	7	3	17	10.8	16.9	12.2	1.4e+6	451755	1.4e+6	78	49	51	56
C_5	8	3	19	114	128	123	1.2e+7	3.4e+6	1.2e+7	574	322	377	57
C_6	9	3	21	–	1328	–	–	3.2e+7	–	–	2.7G	–	57

Examples "C_i", $i = 1, \ldots, 9$, come from a case study called "Single-tracked Line Segment". This study stems from an industrial project partner of the UniForM-project [18] and the problem is to design a distributed real-time controller for a segment of tracks where trams share a piece of track. A distributed controller was modeled in terms of PLC-Automata [17, 18], an automata-like notation for real-time programs. The PLC-Automata were translated into timed automata with the tool Moby/RT [19]. The property to be checked requires that never both directions are given permission to enter the shared segment simultaneously. This property is ensured by 3 PLC-Automata of the whole controller. We injected an error by manipulating a delay such that the asynchronous communication between these automata is faulty. In Moby/RT abstractions are offered for the translation into the timed automata. The given set of PLC-Automata had eight input variables and we constructed nine models with decreasing size by abstracting more and more of these inputs.

The results in Tables 1 and 2 clearly demonstrate the potential of our heuristic functions. Consider Table 1 first. Except in F_i^B (where h^L behaves very badly), and F_i^C (where no approach needs any time), the heuristic searches consistently find the error paths much faster. Due to the reduced search space size and memory requirements, they can solve more of the large C_i examples. At the same time, they find *much*, by orders of magnitude, shorter error paths in *all* cases. In F_i^B, h^L does worse than h^U because its heuristic value does not improve if only one of the two target automata moves closer to its destination: the ATG becomes shorter only if both get closer. The somewhat odd behaviour of h^L in C_8, where search is a lot faster than in C_9, is an outlier caused by the bitstate hashing (outliers suggest a direction for future work discussed in Section 7).

Considering Table 2, we observe that, using d^L and d^U in greedy search, except in the Fischer variants the search space sizes and runtimes one gets are similar to that of rDF, in most cases somewhat worse. The error paths are longer (up to two orders of magnitude) than those found by rDF, except in Fischer variant A. The heuristics can't handle Fischer variant C – the target condition is not expressed in terms of target *locations* – which is, for that reason, left out of the table. In variant B, similarly to h^L, d^L fails quickly. In variant A, due to the construction both d^L and d^U are constantly 1, and the search spaces are identical to those of a non-randomised DF.

The results for the optimal configurations, Table 3, demonstrate that h^L also has some potential to improve the finding of optimal error paths, if to a lesser extent than in the sub-optimal setting. A^* with h^L has the smallest search spaces in all cases, and the best runtimes in all cases except the large C_i examples, *of which it can solve more than the other configurations due to the lower memory requirements*. The d^L heuristic, on the other hand, most of the time yields performance very similar to that of BF. None of the configurations could solve C_7, C_8, or C_9.

6   Related Work

The published approaches to directed model-checking all differ from ours either in that the heuristic has to be provided by the user, or in that the heuristic is based on a very different kind of reasoning.

Bloem et al [20] describe a mechanism how to model check ECTL and ACTL formulas. The method computes least and greatest fixpoints by under and over approximations based on *hints* provided by the user. Apart from relying on the user, this method differs from ours in that it can treat more general formulas, and does not do a heuristic search. Behrmann et al [12] have studied *priced* timed automata. Transitions are labelled with prices, and a heuristic estimates the remaining costs. Behrmann et al achieved good results in an application for which they hand-coded the heuristic; they don't provide an automatic computation.

Yang and Dill [21] use Hamming distance to drive a heuristic search. This is generally a much cruder approximation than our ATG-based heuristics (with the advantage of taking much less time to compute). We implemented the Hamming distance heuristic in UPPAAL, and found it to not work well in our examples: roughly similar to d^L and d^U in the Fischer examples, by far the worst heuristic (much worse runtime results) in the M_i, N_i, and C_i examples. Groce and Visser [6] introduce two heuristics, inspired by the area of testing, for model checking Java programs. The heuristics do not try to target an error formula but instead drive the search to cover yet unexplored branches in the program. Edelkamp et al [4] introduced heuristics to improve error detection with SPIN. As discussed earlier, we implemented these heuristics (d^L and d^U) in UPPAAL and found them to not work very well in our context. Qian and Nymeyer [7] introduced the use of "pattern database" heuristics based on abstractions generated by ignoring some of the state variables. This is a very different abstraction technique than ours, which keeps all variables, and, instead, simplifies their semantics.

In parallel to ours, related work is done by Dräger et al [5]. A paper is submitted to this same conference. The two pieces of work are conducted (and submitted) separately because, like in the works listed above, *the techniques used to generate the heuristic functions are fundamentally different.* While we approach from an AI Planning perspective, Dräger et al modify established abstraction methods from Verification. While we developed combined treatments of communication and integer variables, their focus so far is (almost) exclusively on finding good approximations of communication, particularly of cyclic patterns. Treating integer variables in Dräger et al's approach appears non-trivial, and has not yet been done. Their approximation works by, in a pre-process, iteratively "merging" a pair of automata, i.e., by computing their product and then merging locations until there are at most N locations left, where N is an input parameter. The resulting heuristic has, in difference to ours, no trouble with the communication structure depicted in Figure 1 (Section 4) – however, when merging locations one runs the risk to lose the distinction between dead ends and non dead ends in Figure 3. Indeed, in that example, UPPAAL excels with our heuristics but doesn't scale with Dräger et al's; in Towers of Hanoi – an example containing excessively many repetitions in its solution – the picture is exactly inverse. As more realistic examples, we shared the M_i, N_i, and C_i benchmarks. While these have communication structures more like Figure 1, they also rely heavily on integer variables. The results for the two different heuristics are roughly comparable. There are advantages for h^L in the M_i and N_i benchmarks, and advantages for Dräger et al's heuristic in the C_i benchmarks except C_6, C_7, and C_8. Investigating combinations of the two approaches – e.g., using our approach to treat integers in Dräger et al's approach – is future work.

7   Conclusion

We have introduced methods for automatically generating two heuristic guidance functions in UPPAAL. We have shown the functions' potential for yielding more reliable finding of error states, by reducing the number of search states that need to be considered, as well as guiding the search to short error paths.

The most pressing research topic right now is how to take clock variables into account in the heuristic computation. As said, a straightforward treatment is very unlikely to yield any useful information. We think there is hope in, when building the ATG, distinguishing between the clock value subsets that can be reached *at the individual automaton locations.* Due to location invariants restricting the passage of time, the intervals possible at individual locations are more restricted than the "global" reachable interval. Particularly, constraints on how one clock value can change due to a transition often transfer to all other clocks as well since for them time elapses in the same way. (As a simple example, if one steps from l to l' and $x \leq 5$ is an invariant for l', then we know that the maximum reachable value for any clock is at most 5 larger than it was in l.) In a similar fashion, we hope to make the treatment of integer variables more informed by distinguishing between the value subsets that can be reached at individual locations.

In the long term, we want to explore the following two directions. First, the "outliers" – instances solved in extremely short time – observed with very small hash tables in bitstate hashing suggest that *randomised local search with restarts* might be suitable. Such methods do gradient descents on the search space surface, with random perturbations, until either a solution is reached or a termination criterion (e.g. path length bound exceeded) holds, and a restart is made. We take the existence of outliers to indicate that there is a good enough chance for such gradient descents to find shallow solutions. Second, we believe there is hope in generating heuristic functions based on *predicate abstractions*: these could take the clocks into account very naturally.

References

1. Holzmann, G.: The Spin Model Checker - Primer and Reference Manual. Addison-Wesley (2003)
2. Behrmann, G., Bengtsson, J., David, A., Larsen, K.G., Pettersson, P., Yi., W.: UPPAAL implementation secrets. In: Proceedings of the 7th International Symposium on Formal Techniques in Real-Time and Fault Tolerant Systems. (2002)
3. Edelkamp, S., Lluch-Lafuente, A., Leue, S.: Directed explicit model checking with hsf-spin. In: Proc. of the 8th International SPIN Workshop on Model Checking of Software (SPIN'2001). (2001) 57–79
4. Edelkamp, S., Lluch-Lafuente, A., Leue, S.: Directed explicit-state model checking in the validation of communication protocols. International Journal on Software Tools for Technology (2004)
5. Dräger, K., Finkbeiner, B., Podelski, A.: Directed model checking with distance-preserving abstractions. In: 13th International SPIN Workshop on Model Checking of Software (SPIN'2006). (2006)
6. Groce, A., Visser, W.: Model checking Java programs using structural heuristics. In: Proceedings of the 2002 ACM SIGSOFT international symposium on Software testing and analysis, New York, NY, USA, ACM Press (2002) 12–21
7. Qian, K., Nymeyer, A.: Guided invariant model checking based on abstraction and symbolic pattern databases. In: 10th International Conference on Tools and Algorithms for the Construction and Analysis of Systems (TACAS-04), Berlin, Heidelberg, Springer-Verlag (2004) 497–511
8. Bonet, B., Geffner, H.: Planning as heuristic search. Artificial Intelligence **129**(1–2) (2001) 5–33
9. Hoffmann, J., Nebel, B.: The FF planning system: Fast plan generation through heuristic search. Journal of Artificial Intelligence Research **14** (2001) 253–302
10. Gerevini, A., Saetti, A., Serina, I.: Planning through stochastic local search and temporal action graphs. Journal of Artificial Intelligence Research **20** (2003) 239–290
11. Wah, B., Chen, Y.: Subgoal partitioning and global search for solving temporal planning problems in mixed space. International Journal of Artificial Intelligence Tools **13**(4) (2004) 767–790
12. Behrmann, G., Fehnker, A.: Efficient guiding towards cost-optimality in UPPAAL. In: Proceedings of the 7th International Conference on Tools and Algorithms for the Construction and Analysis of Systems, London, UK, Springer-Verlag (2001) 174–188
13. Kupferschmid, S., Hoffmann, J., Dierks, H., Behrmann, G.: Adapting an AI planning heuristic for directed model checking. Technical Report 222, Albert-Ludwigs-Universität Freiburg, Institut für Informatik, Freiburg, Germany (2006) available at http://www.informatik.uni-freiburg.de/tr/2006/Report222/.

14. Behrmann, G., David, A., Larsen, K.G.: A tutorial on UPPAAL (2005) Department of Computer Science, Aalborg University, Denmark.
15. Edelkamp, S.: Generalizing the relaxed planning heuristic to non-linear tasks. In Biundo, S., Frühwirth, T., Palm, G., eds.: KI-04: Advances in Artificial Intelligence, Ulm, Germany, Springer-Verlag (2004) 198–212
16. Hoffmann, J.: The Metric-FF planning system: Translating "ignoring delete lists" to numeric state variables. Journal of Artificial Intelligence Research 20 (2003) 291–341
17. Dierks, H.: Comparing model-checking and logical reasoning for real-time systems. Formal Aspects of Computing 16(2) (2004) 104–120
18. Krieg-Brückner, B., Peleska, J., Olderog, E.R., Baer, A.: The UniForM Workbench, a universal development environment for formal methods. In Wing, J.M., Woodcock, J., Davies, J., eds.: FM'99 – Formal Methods. Volume 1709 of LNCS., Springer (1999) 1186–1205
19. Olderog, E.R., Dierks, H.: Moby/RT: A tool for specification and verification of real-time systems. Journal of Universal Computer Science 9(2) (2003) 88–105
20. Bloem, R., Ravi, K., Somenzi, F.: Symbolic guided search for CTL model checking. In: Proceedings of the 37th conference on Design automation, New York, NY, USA, ACM Press (2000) 29–34
21. Yang, C.H., Dill, D.L.: Validation with guided search of the state space. In: Proceedings of the 35th annual conference on Design automation, New York, NY, USA, ACM Press (1998) 599–604

Larger Automata and Less Work
for LTL Model Checking

Jaco Geldenhuys[1] and Henri Hansen[2]

[1] Department of Computer Science, Stellenbosch University,
Private Bag X1, 7602 Matieland, South Africa
jaco@cs.sun.ac.za
[2] Institute of Software Systems, Tampere University of Technology,
PO Box 553, FI-33101 Tampere, Finland
hansen@cs.tut.fi

Abstract. Many different automata and algorithms have been investigated in the context of automata-theoretic LTL model checking. This
article compares the behaviour of two variations on the widely used Büchi
automaton, namely (i) a Büchi automaton where states are labelled with
atomic propositions and transitions are unlabelled, and (ii) a form of testing automaton that can only observe changes in state propositions and
makes use of special livelock acceptance states. We describe how these
variations can be generated from standard Büchi automata, and outline
an SCC-based algorithm for verification with testing automata.

The variations are compared to standard automata in experiments
with both random and human-generated Kripke structures and LTL$_{-X}$
formulas, using SCC-based algorithms as well as a recent, improved version of the classic nested search algorithm. The results show that SCC-
based algorithms outperform their nested search counterpart, but that
the biggest improvements come from using the variant automata.

Much work has been done on the generation of small automata, but
small automata do not necessarily lead to small products when combined
with the system being verified. We investigate the underlying factors for
the superior performance of the new variations.

1 Introduction

The automata-theoretic approach to model checking is based on the correspondence between temporal logic, automata and formal languages. Checking that a
system S complies with a temporal logic correctness formula entails the application of two algorithms: the first to translate a formula ϕ to an ω-automaton
(on infinite words), and the second to determine whether the intersection of this
automaton and a similar automaton derived directly from S accepts only the
empty language. It comes as no surprise that since this approach was first proposed, the use of many different kinds of automata has been investigated, and
several variations on the two algorithms have been proposed; some of this work
is mentioned in Section 2.

A. Valmari (Ed.): SPIN 2006, LNCS 3925, pp. 53–70, 2006.

It is probably accurate to say that most of the research in this field is based on Büchi automata with propositional formulas on transitions. We shall refer to this standard form as *transition-labelled*. In this work we study two variations on this theme. First, in Section 3, we consider Büchi automata where the states carry propositional formulas and the transitions are unlabelled — we shall refer to these as *state-labelled* Büchi automata. The second form, the so-called *testing automaton* described in Section 4, is a modification that accommodates stuttering in a more natural way. In addition to the standard acceptance states, testing automata also feature *livelock accepting* states.

The work on testing automata is based on the results of [21]. There the authors defined another, slightly more complicated form of testing automaton and showed that they are more often deteministic than state-labelled Büchi automata. We extend this work in two important ways: we show how to construct our form of testing automata and provide an SCC-based algorithm for on-the-fly verification with them.

In Section 5, we compare the amount work required for on-the-fly verification using two different algorithms for transition- and state-labelled Büchi automata and our new algorithm for testing automata. It turns out that, in our experiments, the new variations were considerably more efficient in terms of the number of states and transitions they explore. An important part of the contribution of this paper comes in Section 6, where we discuss exactly how and when the differences in performance occur and attempt to explain why this is so. Our conclusions are presented in Section 7.

2   Background and Related Work

The connection between temporal logic and formal languages has been a topic of research since the 1960's [3, 23, 26]; a short but excellent overview of the development of this work and its relation to model checking is [25, Section 1.3]. The potential benefits of an automata-theoretic approach to model checking was first pointed out by Wolper in [35], and Wolper, Vardi, and Sistla in [36].

Our definitions of Kripke structures and Büchi automata are standard but, for the sake of later work, we state them explicitly. From here on we use $\mathcal{P}$ to denote a finite set of atomic propositions.

A *Kripke structure* [24] over $\mathcal{P}$ is a tuple $M = (S, I, L, R)$ where S is a finite set of states, $I \subseteq S$ is the set of initial states, $L : S \to 2^{\mathcal{P}}$ is a labelling function that maps each state s to the set of atomic propositions that are true in s, and $R \subseteq S \times S$ is the transition relation. We assume that R is total. An *execution path* or *run* of M is an infinite sequence of states $r = s_1 s_2 s_3 \ldots \in S^{\omega}$ such that $s_1 \in I$ and $(s_i, s_{i+1}) \in R$ for all $i \geq 1$.

A *Büchi automaton* [4] over an alphabet K is a tuple $A = (S, I, R, F)$ where S is a finite set of states, $I \subseteq S$ is the set of initial states, $R \subseteq S \times 2^K \times S$ is the transition relation, and $F \subseteq S$ is a set of acceptance states. Because sets of symbols of the alphabet appear on the transitions, we shall refer to this form as a *transition-labelled Büchi automaton (TLBA)*.

Each word accepted by A is an infinite sequence of symbols from K. A *run* of the automaton over a word $w = k_1 k_2 \ldots \in K^\omega$ is an infinite sequence of states $r = s_1 s_2 \ldots \in S^\omega$ such that $s_1 \in I$ and for all $i \geq 1$ there exists a $K_i \subseteq K$ such that $k_i \in K_i$ and $(s_i, K_i, s_{i+1}) \in R$. The set of states that occur infinitely often in run r is denoted by $inf(r)$ (and clearly $inf(r) \subseteq S$), and the run is *accepting* if and only if $inf(r) \cap F \neq \emptyset$.

When Büchi automata are used for verification we shall use $K = 2^\mathcal{P}$. This is interpreted in such a way that if f is a propositional logic formula over $\mathcal{P}$, and $P = \{P_1, \ldots, P_n\} \subseteq 2^\mathcal{P}$ is the set of all models of f (in other words, $P_i \in P$ if and only if $P_i \models f$), then we use (s, f, s') and (s, P, s') interchangeably as members of R.

2.1   Construction of Büchi Automata

An early algorithm for converting LTL formulas to Büchi automata was described by Vardi and Wolper in [34], but unfortunately it always produced automata with $2^{\mathcal{O}(n)}$ states, where n is the number of subformulas of the LTL formula. A more practical algorithm is [18], on which many later improvements are based. The basic idea is a two-step approach that first translates the input formula to a generalized Büchi automaton, which is then turned into a (standard) Büchi automaton using the flag construction due to Choueka [5].

A general class of improvements is based on rewriting rules to simplify the LTL formula before any automaton is constructed, and several ad hoc heuristics have been proposed to simplify the final automaton. Several groups have proposed improvements based on different procedures for computing covering sets [9, 28], while others have concentrated on reducing the final automaton using *simulations* [12, 13, 14, 20, 29].

Gastin and Oddoux have investigated the use of *very weak alternating automata* as an intermediate form to improve both the size of the final Büchi automata and the speed of their generation [16]; this approach is not especially relevant to our work, but we shall make use of their tool for our experiments.

2.2   Verification with Büchi Automata

A Kripke structure M satisfies a specification ϕ if all its executions are allowed by the specification. This is equivalent to checking that none of M's executions satisfy $\neg\phi$. The automata-theoretic approach therefore consists of constructing a Büchi automaton $A_{\neg\phi}$, computing its product with M, and checking that it is empty, in other words, checking that no execution of M violates ϕ. Although it is possible to first express M itself as a Büchi automaton, the product of M and $A_{\neg\phi}$ can be defined more directly as follows.

Let $\mathcal{F} = \{\text{propositional formulas over } \mathcal{P}\}$, and let $M = (S_M, I_M, L_M, R_M)$ be a Kripke structure over $\mathcal{P}$, and $A_{\neg\phi} = (S_A, I_A, R_A, F_A)$ a TLBA over $2^\mathcal{P}$. Then the product of M and $A_{\neg\phi}$, denoted $M \parallel A_{\neg\phi}$, is a triple (S, R, I), where

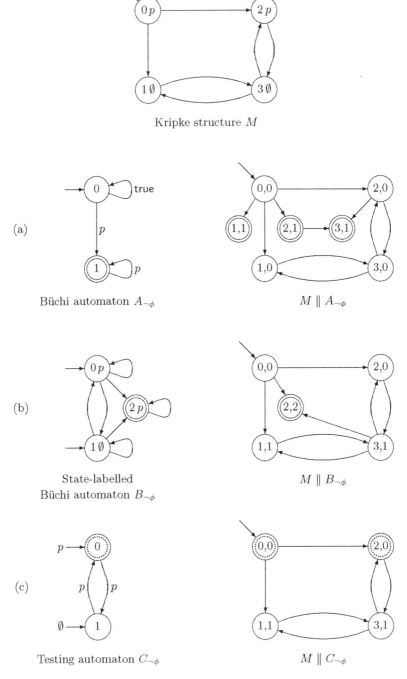

Fig. 1. Examples of automata and products for verifying $\phi = \Box\Diamond\neg p$

- $S = S_M \times S_A$ is the set of states,
- $R \subseteq S \times S$ is the transition relation where $((s,a),(s',a')) \in R$ if and only if $(s,s') \in R_M \wedge \exists f \in \mathcal{F} : (a,f,a') \in R_A \wedge L_M(s) \models f$, and
- $I \subseteq I_M \times I_A$ is the set of initial states.

A run of the product is an infinite sequence of states $(s_1,a_1)(s_2,a_2)\ldots$ such that $(s_1,a_1) \in I$ and $((s_i,a_i),(s_{i+1},a_{i+1})) \in R$ for all $i \geq 1$. A counterexample for ϕ in the product is a run such that $a_1 a_2 \ldots$ is an accepting run of $A_{\neg\phi}$.

An example of a Kripke structure, Büchi automaton, and their product is shown in Figure 1. Each state of the Kripke structure (at the top of the figure) is numbered and labelled with the set of atomic propositions that hold in the state. In this example, $\mathcal{P} = \{p\}$. The initial state is indicated by the sourceless arrow that points to the top left state. The accepting state of the Büchi automaton, shown in (a), is indicated by a double circle. The states of the product are labeled with (*Kripke state, Büchi state*) pairs and those state where the Büchi automaton is in an accepting state is similarly indicated by a double circle.

Arguably the most popular on-the-fly algorithm for computing the product automaton and detecting accepting cycles is a nested depth-first search algorithm first proposed by Courcoubetis, Vardi, Wolper and Yannakasis in 1990 [6]. Subsequent improvements [15, 19, 22, 27] has not only made it compatible with partial-order methods, but has also led to a significant reduction in the number of states and transitions it needs to explore. The core algorithm has also been adapted for use with generalized Büchi automata [32] and heuristic search [2, 11]. Recent work has looked again at the use of strongly connected component (SCC) algorithms for both standard and generalized Büchi automata [7, 8, 17, 27]; the algorithm we describe in Section 4.2 is based on one such.

3   State-Labelled Büchi Automata

A *state-labelled Büchi automaton (SLBA)* over an alphabet K is a tuple $B = (S, I, U, R, F)$ where S is a finite set of states, $I \subseteq S$ is the set of initial states, $U : S \rightarrow K$ maps each state to a symbol of the alphabet, $R \subseteq S \times S$ is the transition relation, and $F \subseteq S$ is a set of acceptance states.

A *run* of the automaton over a word $w = k_1 k_2 \ldots \in K^\omega$ is an infinite sequence of states $r = s_1 s_2 \ldots \in S^\omega$ such that $s_1 \in I$ and $(s_i, s_{i+1}) \in R$ and $U(s_i) = k_i$ for all $i \geq 1$. As for TLBAs, a run r is *accepting* if and only if $inf(r) \cap F \neq \emptyset$.

3.1   Construction of State-Labelled Büchi Automata

The conversion from a TLBA to an SLBA is straightforward. Given a TLBA $A = (S_A, I_A, R_A, F_A)$ over K, the equivalent SLBA is $B = (S_B, I_B, U_B, R_B, F_B)$ where

- $S_B = S_A \times K$, $I_B = I_A \times K$, $F_B = F_A \times K$,
- U_B maps each state to its second component, so that $U_B((s,k)) = k$, and
- R_B is such that $((s_1,k_1),(s_2,k_2)) \in R_B$ if and only if $(s_1,k,s_2) \in R_A$ for some $k \in 2^K$, and $k_2 \in k$, and k_1 is any element of K.

Some states of B may not be reachable from an initial state and can be eliminated. Isomorphic copies of subautomata of B can also be removed using an algorithm such as partition refinement. Other, more intricate optimizations are also possible but we do not focus on them here.

3.2   Verification with State-Labelled Büchi Automata

Let $M = (S_M, I_M, L_M, R_M)$ be a Kripke structure over $\mathcal{P}$, and let $B_{\neg\phi} = (S_B, I_B, U_B, R_B, F_B)$ be an SLBA over $K = 2^{\mathcal{P}}$. Then the product of M and $B_{\neg\phi}$, denoted $M \parallel B_{\neg\phi}$, is a triple (S, R, I), where

- $S = S_M \times S_B$ is the set of states,
- $R \subseteq S \times S$ is the transition relation where $((s, b), (s', b')) \in R$ if and only if $(s, s') \in R_M \wedge (b, b') \in R_B \wedge L_M(s') = U_B(b')$, and
- $I \subseteq I_M \times I_B$ are initial states where $(s, b) \in I$ if and only if $L_M(s) = U_B(b)$.

A run of the product is an infinite sequence of states $(s_1, b_1)(s_2, b_2)\ldots$ such that $(s_1, b_1) \in I$ and $((s_i, b_i), (s_{i+1}, b_{i+1})) \in R$ for each $i \geq 1$. A counterexample for ϕ in the product is a run such that $b_1 b_2 \ldots$ is an accepting run of $B_{\neg\phi}$. Exactly the same algorithms used for TLBAs can be used for SLBAs.

We refer once again to Figure 1 for examples of an SLBA and its product with a Kripke structure. The notation should be clear; it corresponds to what was discussed before for the TLBA. It may seem that the difference between a TLBA and the equivalent SLBA is merely a matter of notation that carries no benefit. However, the product shown in (b) is already an early indication that this is not so: $M \parallel B_{\neg\phi}$ has two states and two transitions fewer than $M \parallel A_{\neg\phi}$.

4   Testing Automata

A *testing automaton* (*TA*) over an alphabet K is a tuple $C = (S, I, U, R, F, G)$ where S is a finite set of states, $I \subseteq S$ is the set of initial states, $U : I \to K$ maps each initial state to a symbol of the alphabet, $R \subseteq S \times K \times S$ is the transition relation, $F \subseteq S$ is a set of Büchi acceptance states, and $G \subseteq S$ is a set of livelock acceptance states.

A *run* of the testing automaton C over a word $w = k_1 k_2 \ldots \in K^{\omega}$ is only defined when $K = 2^{\mathcal{P}}$. In such a case, it is an infinite sequence of states $r = s_1 s_2 \ldots \in S^{\omega}$ such that $s_1 \in I$ and $U(s_1) = k_1$, and for all $i \geq 1$ either

1. $k_i \neq k_{i+1}$ and $(s_i, k_i \oplus k_{i+1}, s_{i+1}) \in R$, or
2. $k_i = k_{i+1}$ and $s_i = s_{i+1}$.

Here $\oplus$ denotes the symmetric difference operator on sets. A run r over a word $w = k_1 k_2 \ldots$ is *accepting* if and only if either

1. $inf(r) \cap F \neq \emptyset$ and $|inf(w)| > 1$, or
2. $\exists n : (s_n \in G) \wedge (\forall i > n : s_i = s_n \wedge k_i = k_n)$.

This general formulation of testing automata allows transitions of the form $(s, \emptyset, s')$, but since they do not add any expressive power to an automaton and are undesirable in the context of verification, we restrict our attention to automata without such transitions. However, we do not forbid them, as they are useful for the conversion algorithm outlined in the next section.

Informally speaking, a TA is an SLBA that, whenever the Kripke structure executes a stuttering transition, executes a null transition (stays in the same state). Its transitions are not labelled with propositions or formulas, but with "change sets", so that it only observes changes in atomic propositions. In addition to Büchi acceptance states, TAs also have livelock acceptance states. A run is accepted if and only if

1. it visits at least one Büchi acceptance state infinitely often and includes an infinite number of non-stuttering transitions (the $|inf(w)| > 1$ condition), or
2. it reaches a livelock acceptance state and from that point on contains only stuttering transitions.

4.1   Construction of Testing Automata

The conversion from SLBA to TA is a two-step process. Given an SLBA $B = (S_B, I_B, U_B, R_B, F_B)$ over alphabet K, we first construct an *intermediate* TA $C = (S_C, I_C, U_C, R_C, F_C, G_C)$ such that

- $S_C = S_B$, $I_C = I_B$, $F_C = F_B$, and $G_C = \emptyset$,
- $U_C(s) = U_B(s)$ for all $s \in I_C$, and
- $(s_1, k, s_2) \in R_C$ if and only if $(s_1, s_2) \in R_B$ and $k = U_B(s_1) \oplus U_B(s_2)$.

In the second step, C is converted to its final form by computing the maximal strongly stuttering-connected components, where stuttering-connected means that every state of the component can reach every other state via a sequence of zero or more transitions of the form $(s, \emptyset, s')$. Those components that are non-trivial (in other words, consists of at least two states or a single state with a self-loop) and contain at least one Büchi accepting state, are added state-by-state to the livelock acceptance states G_C. Then, every stuttering transition $(s, \emptyset, s')$ is removed. If s' is a member of I_C or G_C, we add s to the same set (and define $U_C(s) = U_C(s')$ when $s' \in I_C$). Finally we remove all unreachable states and transitions from the automaton.

Note that this construction can be carried out with any Büchi automaton, but it is only meaningful if the original property is expressible without the use of the next-state operator. It is not required, however, that the Büchi automaton itself exhibits no stuttering [21], only that the property is insensitive to stuttering. This ensures that the language accepted by the automaton remains the same.

As in the case of SLBAs, various further optimizations are possible, but we do not want to discuss them here. However, it is important to note one technical aspect that also applies to TLBAs and SLBAs, but which is especially important for TAs. The set of atomic propositions $\mathcal{P}$ may contain propositions that are never referenced by the automaton in question. For the purposes of efficient verification, such propositions should be removed from $\mathcal{P}$; they cannot influence the outcome of the verification and may lead to unnecessary work.

4.2 Verification with Testing Automata

Let $M = (S_M, I_M, L_M, R_M)$ be a Kripke structure over $\mathcal{P}$, and let $C_{\neg\phi} = (S_C, I_C, U_C, R_C, F_C, G_C)$ be a TA over $2^{\mathcal{P}}$. Then the product of M and $C_{\neg\phi}$, denoted $M \parallel C_{\neg\phi}$, is a triple (S, R, I), where

- $S = S_M \times S_C$ is the set of states,
- $R \subseteq S \times S$ is the transition relation where $((s, c), (s', c')) \in R$ if and only if either
  1. $(s, s') \in R_M \wedge (c, L_M(s) \oplus L_M(s'), c') \in R_A$, or
  2. $(s, s') \in R_M \wedge c = c' \wedge L_M(s) = L_M(s')$, and
- $I \subseteq I_M \times I_C$ are initial states where $(s, c) \in I$ if and only if $L_M(s) = U_C(c)$.

A run of the product is an infinite sequence of states $(s_1, c_1)(s_2, c_2) \ldots$ such that $(s_1, c_1) \in I$ and $((s_i, c_i), (s_{i+1}, c_{i+1})) \in R$ for each $i \geq 1$. A counterexample for ϕ in the product is a run such that $c_1 c_2 \ldots$ is an accepting run of $C_{\neg\phi}$.

As before, an example of a TA and its product with a Kripke structure can be found in Figure 1. Those states in part (c) of the picture where the TA (or the TA component of the product) is in a livelock accepting state have been marked with a dotted circle; in this particular example, the TA has no Büchi acceptance states, so that $F_C = \emptyset$ and $G_C = \{0\}$. The U_C labels are shown on the left of the TA at the source of the arrows to the initial states.

The same algorithms that are used for verification with TLBAs and SLBAs can be used with a TA to detect those violations that involve Büchi acceptance states. Also, in [21, 33] the authors propose a one-pass algorithm to detect violations involving the livelock acceptance states of the TA. Unfortunately, it is not possible to merge these into a single one-pass algorithm: while the first usually relies on a depth-first exploration of the product automaton, the key to the second algorithm is that transitions are explored in a specific, non-depth-first order. One solution is of course to first run the one algorithm, and then the other, but this is wasteful since any information that the first algorithm could conceivably gather is lost when it terminates. Moreover, a single one-pass algorithm has distinct advantages. For software model checking it is often expensive to generate transitions (which may involve steps such as garbage collection or heap canonization). Furthermore, if each state is visited only once, partial order reduction is simplified and there is no need to "remember" reductions made during a previous visit.

We now describe a new one-pass algorithm which is based on the LTL model checking algorithm in [17] (which, in turn, is based on Tarjan's algorithm for SCC detection [30]). The new algorithm detects both Büchi and livelock violations. While the algorithm works entirely reliably for Büchi violations, it does, in certain cases, fail to report an existent livelock violation. However, these circumstances are exceptional; for example, during the random experiments we present in the next section, this happened in only 2 out of 93560 ($= 0.00214\%$) cases.

First, we review the Tarjan-based algorithm in [17], a recursive version of which called TARJAN is shown in Figure 2. The algorithm explores the product of a Kripke structure and a TLBA A (or SLBA B) and therefore does not take

0 **for** each $i \in I$ **do if** $colour[i] = $ WHITE **then** TARJAN(i)

TARJAN(s)	UPDATE(s, t)
1 $colour[s] \leftarrow$ GREY	11 $low[s] \leftarrow \min(low[s], low[t])$
2 $dfnr[s] \leftarrow low[s] \leftarrow n$; INC(n)	12 **if** $low[s] \leq dfnr[A.\text{TOP}]$ **then**
3 $S.\text{PUSH}(s)$	13 **report violation**
4 **if** $accept[s]$ **then** $A.\text{PUSH}(s)$	
5 **for** each successor t of s **do**	SCC(s)
6 $c \leftarrow colour[t]$	14 **repeat**
7 **if** $c = $ WHITE **then** TARJAN(s)	15 $x \leftarrow S.\text{POP}$
8 **if** $c \neq $ BLACK **then** UPDATE(s, t)	16 $colour[x] \leftarrow$ BLACK
9 **if** $A.\text{TOP} = s$ **then** $x \leftarrow A.\text{POP}$	17 **until** $x = s$
10 **if** $low[s] = dfnr[s]$ **then** SCC(s)	

Fig. 2. The Tarjan-based algorithm presented in [17]

stuttering transitions into account. For every product state $s = (k, b)$ the Boolean predicate $accept[s]$ is true if and only if the Büchi component b is accepting; if, in other words, $b \in F_A$ (or $b \in F_B$). The algorithm is identical to Tarjan's classic algorithm, except for its use of an additional stack A where the accepting product states that appear on the depth-first search path are stored. Line 4 inserts such a state when it is first explored, and line 9 removes it once it has been fully explored. The test in lines 12 and 13 reports a violation as soon as a transition "closes" an SCC containing an accepting state. TARJAN uses colours to classify states; initially all states are unexplored and coloured WHITE. As the product automaton is explored, fully explored states are coloured BLACK, and states that are still on the depth-first stack or the component stack S, GREY. In the classic presentation of Tarjan's algorithm [1], this classification is made with Boolean flags, but it is trivial to see that the methods are equivalent.

Our new algorithm appears in Figure 3, and is called TARJAN$^+$. It operates on the product of a Kripke structure and a TA C. Given two product states $s = (k, c)$ and $s' = (k', c')$, the predicate $stutter(s, s')$ is true if and only if $c = c'$, in other words, $s \to s'$ is a stuttering transition. Predicate $accept[s]$ is true if and only if c is a Büchi acceptance state $(c \in F_C)$, and predicate $livelock[s]$ is true if and only if c is livelock accepting $(c \in G_C)$. The three abbreviated conditions that appear in lines 2b, 4a, and 13a are defined as follows:

$$C_1(p, s) \equiv livelock[s] \wedge (p = \perp \vee \neg stutter(p \to s))$$
$$C_2(s, t) \equiv accept[s] \wedge \neg stutter(s \to t)$$
$$C_3(s, t) \equiv livelock[s] \wedge stutter(s \to t)$$

The first change from TARJAN to TARJAN$^+$ is moving lines 4 and 9 of TARJAN into the **for**-loop in line 5; in the new algorithm the lines are labeled 4a and 9a. Although it is less efficient, this change clearly has no effect on the correctness of TARJAN. However, in the new algorithm the condition in line 4 has also been strengthened so that a Büchi acceptance state is only placed on stack A for certain transitions: it is present when the next transition explored is non-stuttering,

0   **for** each $i \in I$ **do if** $colour[i] = $ WHITE **then** TARJAN$^+(\bot, i)$

TARJAN$^+(p, s)$		UPDATE$^+(c, s, t)$

TARJAN$^+(p, s)$

1   $colour[s] \leftarrow$ GREY
2   $dfnr[s] \leftarrow low[s] \leftarrow n$; INC(n)
2a $liveset[s] \leftarrow \emptyset$
2b **if** $C_1(p, s)$ **then** L.PUSH(s)
3   S.PUSH(s)
5   **for** each successor t of s **do**
4a   **if** $C_2(s, t)$ **then** A.PUSH(s)
6       $c \leftarrow colour[t]$
7   **if** $c = $ WHITE **then** TARJAN$^+(s, t)$
8   **if** $c \neq $ BLACK **then** UPDATE$^+(c, s, t)$
9a   **if** A.TOP $= s$ **then** $x \leftarrow A$.POP
9b **if** L.TOP $= s$ **then** $x \leftarrow L$.POP
9c $colour[s] \leftarrow$ BLUE
10 **if** $low[s] = dfnr[s]$ **then** SCC(s)

UPDATE$^+(c, s, t)$

11 $low[s] \leftarrow \min(low[s], low[t])$
12 **if** $low[s] \leq dfnr[A$.TOP$]$ **then**
13   **report violation**
13a **if** $C_3(s, t)$ **then** ADDLINKS(c, s, t)

ADDLINKS(c, s, t)

18 **for** each $u \in liveset[t] \cup \{t\}$ **do**
19   **if** $colour[u] \neq $ GREY **then**
20   **continue** at line 18
21   **if** $dfnr[u] \geq dfnr[L$.TOP$]$
22          $\wedge\ (u \neq t \vee c \neq $ WHITE$)$ **then**
23   **report violation**
24      $liveset[s] \leftarrow liveset[s] \cup \{u\}$

Fig. 3. The new algorithm used in this paper

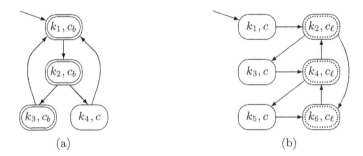

(a)   (b)

Fig. 4. Illustrative state graphs for the new algorithm

and absent when it is stuttering. This avoids the erroneous reporting of cycles that contain only stuttering transitions. Consider, for example, Figure 4(a): if $c_b \in F_C$, then states (k_1, c_b), (k_2, c_b), and (k_3, c_b) are all Büchi accepting. However, none of the states are placed on A when exploring the stuttering transitions between them, and the cycle $(k_1, c_b) \to (k_2, c_b) \to (k_3, c_b) \to (k_1, c_b)$ is therefore correctly ignored. The non-stuttering $(k_2, c_b) \to (k_4, c)$ transition satisfies C_2, and state (k_2, c_b) *is* placed on stack A before exploring it; the ensuing cycle is subsequently correctly reported as a violation.

The second change from TARJAN to TARJAN$^+$ involves the colouring of states. With the addition of line 9c, TARJAN$^+$ further distinguish those states that are currently on the depth-first stack from those that are only present in S, by colouring the latter BLUE. Once again, the detection of Büchi accepting cycles is not affected, since that part of the code (lines 7 and 8) is only concerned with the non-WHITE or non-BLACK status of states.

The last change is the introduction of the L stack and the *liveset*[ ] attribute of states. Stack L is analogous to stack A in storing the livelock acceptance states that appear on the current depth-first search path. However, an important difference is that states reached via stuttering transitions are not stored. (Only states that satisfy C_1 are pushed onto L.) For each livelock accepting state s, attribute *liveset*[s] stores the set of all other states that can be reached via already-explored stuttering transitions. For those states s' that are not livelock accepting, *liveset*[s'] = $\emptyset$. When a stuttering transition $s \rightarrow t$ is explored and state s is livelock accepting (condition C_3 in line 13a), the contents of *liveset*[t] is propagated back to s by procedure ADDLINKS. In addition, if t or some element of *liveset*[t] lies on the depth-first stack at or above the top entry of L, a livelock violation is reported (lines 21–23). (The only exception is the case where s is the direct depth-first tree parent of t, in line 22.) This is correct by the following reasoning:

1. s is livelock accepting (since $s \rightarrow t$ satisfies C_3),
2. s can reach some $u \in$ *liveset*[t] via stuttering transitions,
3. u lies at or below s on the depth-first stack (s is the top-most state on the depth-first stack and *colour*[u] = GREY), and
4. the depth-first stack transitions from u to s are stuttering, since otherwise stack L would contain an entry such that $dfnr[u] < dfnr[L.\text{TOP}] \leq dfnr[s]$.

As mentioned above, the algorithm may in certain cases fail to detect a livelock violation. An example of this is shown in Figure 4(b). Suppose that $G_C = \{c_\ell\}$, so that (k_2, c_ℓ), (k_4, c_ℓ), and (k_6, c_ℓ) are the livelock accepting states. If the stuttering transitions $(k_4, c_\ell) \rightarrow (k_2, c_\ell)$ and $(k_2, c_\ell) \rightarrow (k_6, c_\ell)$ are explored after the non-stuttering transitions in their respective states, then the valid livelock violation $(k_2, c_\ell) \rightarrow (k_6, c_\ell) \rightarrow (k_4, c_\ell) \rightarrow (k_2, c_\ell)$ is not reported. This happens because transition $(k_6, c_\ell) \rightarrow (k_4, c_\ell)$ is explored before $(k_4, c_\ell) \rightarrow (k_2, c_\ell)$, and therefore the fact that state (k_6, c_ℓ) can reach (k_2, c_ℓ) via stuttering transitions is never recorded.

Consequently, when TARJAN[+] fails to report a violation, it is necessary to run the livelock detection algorithm of [21, 33] before we can claim that a Kripke structure satisfies an LTL formula, using our approach. This may appear to nullify the advantages of a single one-pass algorithm we extolled before. In practise it means that the new algorithm may be more efficient at detecting violations, but less efficient when it comes to checking that there are none.

5   Experimental Results

Table 1 shows the outcome of experiments performed to measure the effect of using SLBAs and TAs instead of TLBAs. The procedure described in [31] was used to generate 480 random 100-state Kripke structures and 360 random LTL formulas. An additional 130 formulas were taken from the literature (mostly from [13, 10, 29]), and all formulas were negated. After the elimination of stuttering-sensitive formulas and duplicates, the remaining 261 formulas were

Table 1. Comparison of automata on random graphs and random & real formulas

Automata	TLBA		SLBA		TA	
Ave.		5.56 17.33		30.89 584.87	16.94 310.43	
Max.		53 314		389 18196	193 10944	

States & transitions	TLBA				SLBA				TA	
	SE		TARJAN		SE		TARJAN		TARJAN+	
All Ave.	30.3	96.2	25.2	80.1	18.6	37.2	17.6	35.2	21.1	43.7
Max.	3342	29404	2533	18250	1154	10184	1103	10041	1294	11284
Viol. Ave.	33.3	105.9	27.3	85.2	20.4	33.8	19.2	31.4	20.0	31.0
Max.	3342	29404	1652	18250	966	5888	613	3831	442	2045

Normalized	TLBA				SLBA				TA	
	SE		TARJAN		SE		TARJAN		TARJAN+	
All Ave.	51.1	19.3	38.0	15.8	33.6	8.6	32.5	8.0	57.8	11.8
Max.	1550.0	2800.0	1250.0	2400.0	360.0	700.0	340.0	700.0	200.0	200.0
Viol. Ave.	13.7	7.6	11.3	6.6	9.8	4.9	9.3	4.7	9.5	4.5
Max.	1033.3	1305.3	537.5	700.0	220.0	255.1	200.0	250.0	131.1	107.5

Percentages	TLBA				SLBA				TA	
	SE		TARJAN		SE		TARJAN		TARJAN+	
All Best	0.0	0.0	3.1	1.5	0.0	0.0	4.5	2.9	10.3	11.4
1/Best	55.7	66.5	70.2	68.5	40.5	43.4	47.9	47.8	29.0	49.9
Viol. Best	0.0	0.0	4.1	2.0	0.0	0.0	3.7	2.5	13.7	15.1
1/Best	56.8	60.3	65.1	62.9	23.0	26.0	30.5	30.4	38.7	38.3

converted to Büchi automata using the LTL2BA program [16], and SLBAs and TAs were constructed as described in previous sections. For TLBAs and SLBAs we used the Schwoon and Esparza modification of the CPVW algorithm [27] (shown in the "SE" column), and the Tarjan-based algorithm from [17] (shown in the "TARJAN" column). For TAs the modified Tarjan algorithm we mentioned in the previous section was used (shown in the "TARJAN+" column). Even though the Kripke structures are quite small (100 states) compared to realistic models, they are large enough for our purposes. Experiments with larger Kripke structures (still random) yielded similar results.

Every cell of the table contains two numbers, the first refers to the number of states and the second to the number of transitions. The first part of the table labelled "Automata" shows the average and maximum sizes of the TLBAs, SLBAs, and TAs. From TLBA to SLBA there is roughly a 6-fold increase in the number of states and a 34-fold increase in the number of transitions. The average size of a TA is about half that of an SLBA. The next part of the table, "States & transitions" shows the average and maximum number of states and transitions explored, first in all runs, and then in only those runs where a violation was found. Unfortunately, these numbers are somewhat misleading, since large and small products carry equal weight. Therefore, the next part of the table, "Normalized", describes the same runs, but with the numbers of each run expressed as a percentage of the size of the product of the Kripke structure and the TA. The last part of the table labelled "Percentages" indicates in what percentage of runs each automaton/algorithm pair did better than any of the others (the "Best" row), or no worse than any of the others (the "1/Best" row). Note that the figures in the TA/TARJAN$^+$ column include the number of states and transitions explored by both the TARJAN$^+$ algorithm and the livelock detection algorithm [21, 33] that is run when TARJAN$^+$ finds no violation.

We have consciously decided to report only the number of states and transitions, and not the number of bytes and milliseconds consumed by our implementations. This protects the results (to some extent) against the influence of various optimizations, implementation tricks, and the central processor and memory architecture. We generally find that the number of states gives a reliable indication of the memory required, and, similarly, the number of transitions a reliable indication of the time consumption.

When we compare only the TLBA/TARJAN and TA/TARJAN$^+$ combinations, in the case that a violation was detected, the TAs achieved a 26.7% reduction in the average number of states, and a 63.6% reduction in the average number of transitions. For the worst-case performance, TA/TARJAN$^+$ reduced the states and transitions by a factor of 3.7 and 8.9, respectively. When it comes to all runs (now including those where no violation was detected), the reduction is 16.3% and 45.4% for the average states and transitions, with factors of 2.0 and 1.6 for the worst-case states and transitions.

However, the results contain some apparent contradictions: despite the fact that the TLBA/SE combination has the highest average and worst-case numbers, it is still one of the best algorithms in more than half the cases. Conversely, the SLBA/TARJAN combination which explores the lowest average number of states in all runs, only explores the unique, least number of states in 3.7% of those runs. The cause of this phenomenon is of course the different distribution of costs for the different combinations.

It is difficult to say which of the algorithms is "best": for a single run one may use the TLBA/TARJAN combination and know that the probability is less than 0.35 that another combination can explore fewer states. Invariably, however, more than one run of a system is required and, in that case, the SLBA/TARJAN combination explores the fewest number of states and transitions, *on average*. On the other hand, the worst-case of the TA/TARJAN$^+$ combination looks more promising and it is more often the fastest ($\geq 11.4\%$ of cases) and most memory-efficient ($\geq 10.3\%$ of cases) choice.

The amount of work needed by the TLBA in the worst case is so much bigger that it tilts the averages heavily in favour of the SLBA and the TA. This, we believe, justifies the conclusion that the variants are, in fact, superior in performance to the TLBA.

Experience has shown that measurements with random Kripke structures are often over-optimistic since the "shape" of random and real state spaces can differ significantly. We would have liked to present experimental results for actual state spaces, but that approach has its own pitfalls. It is easy to find examples where one combination fares exceptionally well, while the others founder. Also, each state space should be verified against a variety of LTL properties to yield robust results. For now we have to leave this project as future work.

6   A Closer Look: Why Less Is More?

The results show that it is not so much the size of the automaton itself that counts, but rather the size of the product of Kripke structure and automaton. In the negative case—when there is no violation—all states and transitions of the product need to be explored, and, in the case of our new algorithm, it is done twice. We therefore investigated the relationship between the formulas and the size of the resulting products by devising classes of formulas of increasing length and calculating the size of the product with a set of random Kripke structures.

For the set of experiments we used 100 random 1000-state Kripke structures with a varying number of transitions. We constructed the TLBAs, SLBAs and TAs for the formulas we describe below and calculated their products with the Kripke structures. Table 2 shows the average number of states and transitions obtained in each case. The first column gives the formula class and n. The "E" formulas were of the form

$$E(n) = \bigwedge_{i=1}^{n} \Diamond p_i,$$

and the "U" and "R" were of the form

$$U(n) = (\cdots (p_1 \cup p2) \cup \cdots) \cup p_n \quad \text{and} \quad R(n) = \bigwedge_{i=1}^{n} (\Box \Diamond p_i \vee \Diamond \Box p_{i+1}).$$

The simplest, $E(n)$ formulas resulted in products with the same number of states for all the automata, while the TAs produced a somewhat smaller number of transitions. The two more complicated classes result in differences that increase with the length of the formula.

Table 2. Growth of state spaces

	TLBA		SLBA		TA	
E(1)	1999.90	9126.84	1999.90	9126.84	1999.86	7730.18
E(2)	3999.68	23690.54	3999.68	23690.54	3999.62	19057.17
E(3)	7999.24	62119.04	7999.24	62119.04	7999.24	49853.79
E(4)	15998.36	164327.68	15998.36	164327.68	15998.36	134019.09
E(5)	31996.61	437872.53	31996.61	437872.53	31996.61	363967.54
U(1)	1188.75	5195.20	1145.54	5095.67	1151.85	4473.37
U(2)	3082.19	20936.82	2266.81	14020.64	2266.76	10772.02
U(3)	8702.22	92692.54	6185.00	66821.92	6233.29	47379.99
U(4)	22162.49	373415.82	15286.18	266001.99	15257.98	187339.66
U(5)	53471.09	1432869.88	35175.60	980114.68	34998.03	703055.77
R(1)	3619.32	17790.64	3326.13	16635.44	3647.73	15555.14
R(2)	9674.17	49992.48	8195.00	43328.05	8115.63	34584.78
R(3)	26620.67	150150.63	20492.62	117661.40	20113.34	88977.67
R(4)	72449.32	460101.94	51041.64	328031.95	50019.04	239408.10
R(5)	194741.06	1447741.57	127220.17	951739.06	124600.22	675327.73

We experimented with other classes as well, but were unable to find any where the TLBA products are smaller. There were classes where the results were similar to the E formulas, including

$$U_2(n) = p_1 U(p_2 U(\cdots p_{n-1} U p_n) \cdots),$$

$$C_1(n) = \bigvee_{i=1}^{n} \square \lozenge p_i \quad \text{and} \quad C_2(n) = \bigwedge_{i=1}^{n} \square \lozenge p_i.$$

Other classes performed much like the U and R formulas, for example

$$Q(n) = \bigwedge_{i=1}^{n} (\lozenge p_i \vee \square p_{i+1}) \quad \text{and} \quad S(n) = \bigvee_{i=1}^{n} \square p_i.$$

The smaller products have very little, if anything, to do with the livelock acceptance states of the testing automata, since the state-labelled automata result in products that are just as small. So the question remains, why do the SLBAs and TAs produce smaller products? We cannot give a definitive answer, but we believe that there are two important factors:

Firstly, an SLBA makes a finer distinction between different states, in the sense that the state of the SLBA contains more information about the state of the product than is the case for the TLBA. Undoubtably the TLBA is a more dense representation of the property than the equivalent SLBA. In other words, in the product several Kripke states may be paired with the same TLBA state, but because the automaton will later have to distinguish between the states, extra work needs to be performed.

Secondly, and partly because of the first reason, the TLBA is, in a sense, more nondeterministic and therefore, on average, more of its transitions are enabled in a given state. In [28] the authors suggest that more deterministic, rather than smaller automata result in smaller products, and to some extent, the generation of the SLBA removes some of the nondeterminism.

The sometimes significantly smaller number of transitions in the products of TAs can be explained, at least in part, by the fact that they have no stuttering transitions and therefore cannot cause a multiplication of stuttering steps of the Kripke structure. The theoretical results in [21], which state that testing automata are more often deterministic, do not, however explain anything at all in these findings, since the SLBA and TA products have almost exactly the same number of states.

The size of the product is not an accurate measure of performance when there actually is a violation. It might be the case that a counterexample is found relatively early on in a bigger product. This may be due to two factors. Firstly, the decision of which transitions to explore first in the on-the-fly algorithm may play a crucial role. An endless variety of heuristics and shufflings of transitions are possible and we currently know of no definitive way to decide which is best. Secondly, the counterexamples themselves may have different properties. The SLBA- or TA-induced product may be smaller but contain only relatively few, lengthy and complicated counterexamples, whereas the product arising from a TLBA may be big but have more shallow and simple counterexamples. One open question is exactly what the relative contribution of the two phenomena in different circumstances is.

7 Conclusions

We have investigated two alternatives to the standard (transition-labelled) form of Büchi automata, namely state-labelled Büchi automata and testing automata, described the conversion from the standard form to the variant forms, and sketched our current (SCC-based) algorithm for verification with testing automata. Even though the differences between the automata may appear to be merely a matter of notation, our experimental results suggest that there are real benefits to be had from using the variant forms.

To explain the improved performance of the variants, we considered simple classes of LTL_{-X} formulas and compared the products of a set of random Kripke structures with the transition-labelled and state-labelled Büchi automata and testing automata. Despite the fact that the variant automata are invariably much larger, the resulting product automata are invariably smaller. In the case of testing automata, the number of transitions is clearly smaller and grows at a much slower rate than is the case for the other two automata.

Two factors that play a role in this phenomenon are (1) that SLBAs and TAs make finer distinctions among states, and (2) that they are more often deterministic than standard Büchi automata. This concurs with the work in [28], where the authors focused on the standard form.

Our research perhaps raises more questions than it answers. By no means do we wish to discourage further work on the reduction of Büchi automata or other ω-automata; rather our results point to the need to further investigate the factors that lead to improved performance. Other lines of future research include the characterization of LTL_{-X} properties for which the SLBAs and TAs do better, and an extension of these results to generalized Büchi automata and alternating automata.

Acknowledgments. The work of H. Hansen was supported by the Nokia Foundation.

References

1. A. V. Aho, J. E. Hopcroft, & J. D. Ullman. *The Design and Analysis of Computer Algorithms*. Addison-Wesley, 1974.
2. L. Brim, I. Černá, M. Nečesal. Randomization helps in LTL model checking. In *Proc. Joint Intl. Worksh. Process Alg. and Probabilistic Methods, Performance Modeling and Verif.*, LNCS #2165, pp. 105–119, Sept 2001.
3. J. R. Büchi. Weak second-order arithmetic and finite automata. *Zeitschrift für mathematische Logik und Grundlagen der Math.* 6, pp. 66–92, 1960.

4. J. R. Büchi. On a decision method in restricted second-order arithmetic. In *Proc. 1960 Intl. Congr. Logic, Method and Philosophy of Science*, pp. 1–11, Stanford Univ. Press, Jun 1962.
5. Y. Choueka. Theories of automata on ω-tapes: a simplified approach. *Journal Computer and System Sciences* 8, pp. 117–141, 1974.
6. C. Courcoubetis, M. Y. Vardi, P. Wolper, M. Yannakakis. Memory-efficient algorithms for the verification of temporal properties. In *CAV'90*, LNCS #531, pp. 233–242, Jun 1990. Journal version: *Formal Methods in System Design* 1(2/3), pp. 275–288, Oct 1992.
7. J.-M. Couvreur. On-the-fly verification of linear temporal logic. In *Proc. World Congr. Formal Methods in the Development of Computing Systems (FM'99)*, LNCS #1708, pp. 253–271, Sept 1999.
8. J.-M. Couvreur. On-the-fly emptiness checks for generalized Büchi automata. In *Proc. 12th Intl. SPIN Worksh. on Model Checking Software*, LNCS #1708, pp. 999–999, Aug 2005.
9. M. Daniele, F. Giunchiglia, M. Y. Vardi. Improved automata generation for linear time temporal logic. In *CAV'99*, LNCS #1633, pp. 249–260, Jul 1999.
10. M. B. Dwyer, G. S. Avrunin, & J. C. Corbett. Property specification patterns for finite-state verification. In *Proc. 2nd ACM Worksh. Formal Methods in Software Practice*, pp. 7–15, Mar 1998.
11. S. Edelkamp, S. Leue, A. Lluch Lafuente. Directed explicit-state model checking in the validation of communication protocols. Technical Report 161, Institut für Informatik, Albert-Ludwigs-Universität Freiburg, Oct 2001.
12. K. Etessami. A hierarchy of polinomial-time computable simulations for automata. In *CONCUR'02*, LNCS #2421, pp. 131–144, Aug 2002.
13. K. Etessami, G. J. Holzmann. Optimizing Büchi automata. In *CONCUR'00*, LNCS #1877, pp. 154–167, Aug 2000.
14. C. Fritz. Constructing Büchi automata from linear temporal logic using simulation relations for alternating Büchi automata. In *Proc. 8th Intl. Conf. Implementations and Application of Automata*, LNCS #2759, pp. 35–48, Jul 2003.
15. P. Gastin, P. Moro, M. Zeitoun. Minimization of counterexamples in SPIN. In *Proc. 11th Intl. SPIN Worksh. Model Checking Software*, LNCS #2989, pp. 92–108, Apr 2004.
16. P. Gastin, D. Oddoux. Fast LTL to Büchi automata translation. In *CAV'01*, LNCS #2102, pp. 53–65, Jul 2001.
17. J. Geldenhuys, A. Valmari. Tarjan's algorithm makes on-the-fly LTL verification more efficient. In *TACAS'04*, LNCS #2988, pp. 205–219, Mar–Apr 2004. Journal version: *Theor. Computer Science* 345(1), pages 60-82, Nov 2005.
18. R. Gerth, D. Peled, M. Y. Vardi, P. Wolper. Simple on-the-fly automatic verification of linear temporal logic. In *Proc. 15th IFIP Symp. Protocol Spec., Testing, and Verif.*, pp. 3–18, Jun 1995.
19. P. Godefroid, G. J. Holzmann. On the verification of temporal properties. In *Proc. 13th IFIP Symp. Protocol Spec., Testing, and Verif.*, pp. 109–124, May 1993.
20. S. Gurumurthy, R. Bloem, F. Somenzi. Fair simulation minimization. In *CAV'02*, LNCS #2404, pp. 610–624, Jul 2004.
21. H. Hansen, W. Penczek, A. Valmari. Stuttering-insensitive automata for on-the-fly detection of livelock properties. In *Proc. 7th Intl. ERCIM Worksh. Formal Methods for Industrial Critical Systems*, pp. 185–200, Jul 2002. Also published in Elec. Notes in Theor. Computer Science 66(2), Elsevier Science, Dec 2002.
22. G. J. Holzmann, D. Peled, M. Yannakakis. On nested depth first search. In *Proc. 2nd SPIN Worksh.*, Held Aug 1996, DIMACS Series No. 32, pp. 23–32, 1997.

23. J. A. W. Kamp. *Tense Logic and the Theory of Linear Order.* PhD thesis, Univ. of California, 1968.
24. S. A. Kripke. Semantical analysis of modal logic I, normal propositional calculi. *Zeitschrift für mathematische Logik und Grundlagen der Math* 9, pp. 67–96, 1963.
25. R. P. Kurshan. *Computer-aided Verification of Coordinating Processes: The Automata-theoretic Approach.* Princeton Univ. Press, 1994.
26. M. O. Rabin. Decidability of second-order theories and automata on infinite trees. *Trans. of the American Mathemathical Society* 141, pp. 1–35, 1969.
27. S. Schwoon, J. Esparza. A note on on-the-fly verification algorithms. In *TACAS'05*, LNCS #3440, pp. 174–190, Mar 2005.
28. R. Sebastiani, S. Tonetta. "More Deterministic" vs "Smaller" Büchi Automata for Efficient LTL Model Checking *Correct Hardware Design and Verif. Methods*, LNCS #2860, pp. 126–140, 2003.
29. F. Somenzi, R. Bloem. Efficient Büchi automata from LTL formulae. In *CAV'00*, LNCS #1855, pp. 248–267, Jun 2000.
30. R. E. Tarjan. Depth-first search and linear graph algorithms. *SIAM Journal of Computing* 1(2), pp. 146–160, Jun 1972.
31. H. Tauriainen. A randomized testbench for algorithms translating linear temporal logic formulae In *Proc. Worksh. Concurrency, Specifications, and Programming*, pp. 251–262, Sept 1999.
32. H. Tauriainen. Nested emptiness search for generalized Büchi automata. Technical Report HUT–TCS–A79, Laboratory for Theoretical Computer Science, Helsinki Univ. of Technology, Jul 2003.
33. A. Valmari. On-the-fly verification with stubborn sets. In *CAV'93*, LNCS #697, pp. 397–308, Jun 1993.
34. M. Y. Vardi, P. Wolper. An automata-theoretic approach to automatic program verification. In *Proc. 1st IEEE Symp. on Logic in Computer Science*, pp. 332–344, Jun 1986.
35. P. Wolper. Temporal logic can be more expressive. *Information and Computation* 56, pp. 72–99, 1983.
36. P. Wolper, M. Y. Vardi, A. P. Sistla. Reasoning about infinite computation paths. In *Proc. 24th IEEE Symp. on the Foundations of Computer Science*, pp. 185–194, IEEE Computer Society Press, Nov 1983.

Don't Know in Probabilistic Systems

Harald Fecher[1], Martin Leucker[2], and Verena Wolf[3]

[1] Institute of Informatics, University of Kiel, Germany
[2] Institute of Informatics, TU Munich, Germany
[3] Institute of Informatics, University of Mannheim, Germany

Abstract. In this paper the abstraction-refinement paradigm based on 3-valued logics is extended to the setting of probabilistic systems. We define a notion of abstraction for Markov chains. To be able to relate the behavior of abstract and concrete systems, we equip the notion of abstraction with the concept of simulation. Furthermore, we present model checking for abstract probabilistic systems (abstract Markov chains) with respect to specifications in probabilistic temporal logics, interpreted over a 3-valued domain. More specifically, we introduce a 3-valued version of probabilistic computation-tree logic (PCTL) and give a model checking algorithm w.r.t. abstract Markov chains.

1 Introduction

Abstraction is one of the most successful techniques for fighting the state space explosion problem in model checking [4]. Abstractions hide some of the details of the verified system, thus resulting in a smaller model. In the seminal papers on abstraction-based model checking, *conservative* abstractions for *true* have been studied. In this setting, if a formula is true in the abstract model then it is also true in the concrete (precise) model of the system. However, if it is false in the abstract model then nothing can be deduced for the concrete one [3].

In the 3-valued setting, the goal is to define abstractions that are conservative for both true and false. Therefore, a third value *indefinite* (also called *don't know*), denoted by ?, is introduced that identifies when too much information is hidden to decide whether the formula evaluates to true or false in the concrete system. Thus, *indefinite* indicates that the abstract system has to be *refined*, meaning that less information should be concealed.

Kripke Modal Transition Systems (KMTS, [13]) have become a popular device to model abstractions of transition systems. In the abstraction process, states of the concrete system are grouped together in the abstract system. Transitions between sets of concrete states are then classified as *must* or *may* edges. Very roughly, may edges are a kind of over approximation while must edges are a kind of under approximation.

In this paper, we study abstractions for (labeled discrete-time) Markov chains (MCs). MCs are a typical underlying model for sequential probabilistic programs or probabilistic process algebras [19]. In simple words, MCs are transition systems where the transitions are enriched with transition probabilities. To get an

A. Valmari (Ed.): SPIN 2006, LNCS 3925, pp. 71–88, 2006.

abstraction in the same spirit as the one for KMTS, one could again group states of the concrete system together to obtain an abstract system. Then we have to come up with a suitable notion of over and under approximation of transitions. We suggest to label transitions by intervals of probabilities, similar as in [15, 20]. The lower bound of an interval represents an under approximation while the upper bound is used for the over approximation.

This motivates to define the notion of *Abstract Markov Chains* (AMCs) as a kind of transition system where transitions are labeled with intervals of probabilities. To compare the behavior of a given AMC and a given MC, we introduce a simulation relation, called probabilistic simulation. We call an AMC M' coarser or an abstraction of AMC M if M' simulates M and vice versa M is called finer or a refinement of M'. We show that the abstractions obtained by the process mentioned above are in the simulation relation.

When AMCs are used in the context of abstraction, we motivate that only certain combinations of intervals are meaningful and call such AMCs *delimited*. *Cutting* arbitrary AMCs to delimited ones, also during the model checking process, will give more precise results at (nearly) no cost, as we will describe.

Our main motivation for abstraction is model checking. For probabilistic systems, Jonsson and Hansson introduced Probabilistic Computation Tree Logic (PCTL) [10] that allows formulation of statements involving the measure of certain paths. We give PCTL a 3-valued semantics over AMCs. The semantics is defined, as we show, in the right manner w.r.t. abstractions: If a formula evaluates to true or false in the abstract system, it does so in the concrete system. If the result is *indefinite*, nothing can be said about the concrete system.

We then present (two versions of) a model checking algorithm for AMCs and 3-valued PCTL. The gist of our algorithms is to use 3-valued combinations instead of boolean (as in the 2-valued case) for state formulas and to compute measures for each path property similar as in the setting of Markov decision processes [1, 7].

Recently, 3-valued-based model checking and refinement has gained a lot of interest. A framework for 3-valued abstraction is introduced in [13, 8]. In [17, 16, 2], model checking of 3-valued (or multi-valued) versions of CTL or CTL* have been studied. Game-based approaches allow an elegant treatment of refinement and have been presented in [18, 9] in the setting of CTL and respectively the μ-calculus.

General issues for abstractions of probabilistic systems are discussed in [12, 14] while we concentrate on a specific abstraction together with dedicated model checking algorithms. The closest works to ours are [6] and [11]. In [6], Markov decision processes are proposed for abstracting of MCs. However, they only consider reachability properties while we study PCTL model checking. More importantly, our notion of simulation is coarser—thus allowing for coarser and therefore smaller abstractions—while maintaining soundness w.r.t. 3-valued PCTL. In [11][1], criterias have been engineered that guarantee an abstraction to be optimal (in some sense). While, of course, such an optimal abstraction sounds

---

[1] We thank the author for providing us the as yet unpublished manuscript.

preferable, the approach loses some of its elegance since—in simple words—it requires storage of much information. Furthermore, it is not clear (to us) how to obtain this information without constructing the underlying MC.

We conclude our paper by discussing the pros and cons of the different approaches in detail and order them w.r.t. their precision (in a sense made precise below).

Outline AMCs are derived in the next section. Before, introducing 3-valued PCTL in Section 4, we discuss the relation of measures of paths in finer and coarser systems first for reachability properties, in Section 3. The model checking algorithms for PCTL is given in Section 5. We compare our framework with existing ones in Section 6.

2   Abstract Markov Chains

To introduce our notion of abstraction, let us consider the Markov chain shown in Figure 1(a). A Markov chain consists of states labeled with propositions. The states are connected by transitions that are labeled with probabilities for taking the corresponding transitions. Following the idea of Kripke Modal Transition Systems, states of the concrete system are grouped together in the abstract system. For example, s_5 and s_6 form the abstract state A_2 (Figure 1(b)). While in the case of transition systems, we obtain so-called *may-* and *must*-transitions denoting that there may be a transition from one state to the other, or, there is a transition for sure, we deal with lower and upper bounds on the transition probabilities here. For example, we say that we move from A_2 to A_1 with some probability in $[0, \frac{1}{4}]$ since we either cannot move to A_1 (when in s_6) or move to A_1 with probability $\frac{1}{4}$ (when in s_5). This motivates the definition of an *abstract* Markov chain. Let us first fix some notation:

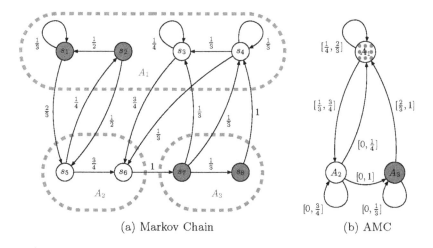

(a) Markov Chain   (b) AMC

Fig. 1. A Markov chain and its abstraction

Let AP be a nonempty finite set of *propositions* and $\mathbb{B}_3 = \{\perp, ?, \top\}$ the three valued truth domain. Let X be a finite set. For $Y, Y' \subseteq X$ and a function $Q : X \times X \to \mathbb{R}$ let $Q(Y, Y') = \sum_{y \in Y} \sum_{y' \in Y'} Q(y, y')$. We omit brackets if Y or Y' is a singleton. The function $Q(x, \cdot)$ is given by $x' \mapsto Q(x, x')$ for all $x' \in X$. Furthermore let $psdistr(X) = \{f : X \to [0, 1]\}$ be the set of all *pseudo distribution functions* on X and $distr(X) = \{f \in psdistr(X) \mid \sum_{x \in X} f(x) = 1\}$ the set of *distributions* on X.

Definition 1. *An* abstract Markov chain *(AMC) is a tuple* (S, P^l, P^u, L) *where:*

- S *is a finite set of states,*
- $P^l, P^u : S \times S \to [0, 1]$ *are matrices describing the lower and upper bounds for the transition probabilities between states such that for all $s, s' \in S$, $P^l(s, \cdot)$ and $P^u(s, \cdot)$ are pseudo distribution functions and*

$$P^l(s, s') \leq P^u(s, s') \text{ and } P^l(s, S) \leq 1 \leq P^u(s, S), \qquad (1)$$

- $L : S \times AP \to \mathbb{B}_3$ *is a labeling function that assigns a truth value to each pair of state and proposition.*

Note that with condition (1) we do not consider states without any outgoing transition. We call an AMC $M = (S, P^l, P^u, L)$ a *Markov chain* (MC) if $P^l = P^u =: P$. Note that in this case $P(s, \cdot) \in distr(S)$, for all $s \in S$. Let X be a finite set. Let g^l, g^u be a pair of functions in $psdistr(X)$ with $g^l(x) \leq g^u(x)$ for all $x \in X$. We write $g(x)$ for the interval $[g^l(x), g^u(x)] \subseteq [0, 1]$ and $distr(g)$ for the set $\{f \in distr(X) \mid \forall x \in X : f(x) \in g(x)\}$. If $g^l = Q^l(x, \cdot)$ and $g^u = Q^u(x, \cdot)$ for some $Q^l, Q^u \in psdistr(X \times X)$ we put $distr(Q(x, \cdot)) = distr(g)$.

Let us now formalize the notion of abstraction:

Definition 2. *Let* $M = (S, P^l, P^u, L)$ *be an AMC and* $\mathcal{A} = \{A_1, A_2, \ldots, A_n\} \subseteq 2^S$ *a partition of S, i.e.* $A_i \neq \emptyset$, $A_i \cap A_j = \emptyset$ *for* $i \neq j$, $1 \leq i, j \leq n$ *and* $\bigcup_{i=1}^n A_i = S$. *Then the* abstraction *of M induced by $\mathcal{A}$ is the AMC* $abstract(M, \mathcal{A}) = (\tilde{S}, \tilde{P}^l, \tilde{P}^u, \tilde{L})$ *given by*

- $\tilde{S} = \mathcal{A}$,
- $\tilde{P}^l(A_i, A_j) = \min_{s \in A_i} P^l(s, A_j)$ *and* $\tilde{P}^u(A_i, A_j) = \max_{s \in A_i} P^u(s, A_j)$.
- *For* $a \in AP$ *the labeling of an abstract state (also called* macro state*)* $A \in \mathcal{A}$ *is given by*

$$\tilde{L}(A, a) = \begin{cases} \top, & \text{if } L(s, a) = \top \text{ for all } s \in A, \\ \perp, & \text{if } L(s, a) = \perp \text{ for all } s \in A, \\ ?, & \text{otherwise.} \end{cases}$$

Example 1. Figure 1 (a) illustrates a MC with 8 states. These states are grouped together, denoted by the dashed grey circles, to form the abstract system with three states.[2] The intervals of probabilities are obtained as described before. For simplicity we consider a single proposition $a \in AP$ that holds exactly in all grey shaded states. Thus, in the abstract system, we get $\tilde{L}(A_1, a) =?$, $\tilde{L}(A_2, a) = \perp$ and $\tilde{L}(A_3, a) = \top$.

---

[2] Note that the question of how to partition the state space usually depends on where MCs are used and is beyond the scope of this paper.

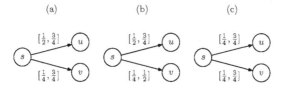

Fig. 2. Sharpening and widening the intervals

Scheduler. In the setting of AMCs, in every state s, there is a choice for the distribution yielding the probabilities to reach successor states. This non-determinism can be resolved by means of a scheduler: A (history-dependent) *scheduler* for a state s_0 is a function $\eta : s_0 S^* \rightarrow distr(S \times S)$ that maps each sequence of states $s_0 \ldots s$ to a distribution in $distr(P(s, \cdot))$. The set of all schedulers for an AMC M starting in state s_0 is denoted by $\mathcal{S}(M, s_0)$. We write $\mathcal{S}(s_0)$ if M is clear from the context.

Delimited AMCs. Since a scheduler is defined to select only distributions (rather than pseudo distributions), we can sharpen the definition of AMCs, motivated as follows (see also [20]):

Consider the AMC M in Figure 2, (a)[3]. Assume that one chooses the value $\frac{3}{4}$, i.e. $P^u(s, v) = P^l(s, v) = \frac{3}{4}$, from the interval $[\frac{1}{4}, \frac{3}{4}]$ labeling the transition from state s to v. But then, the transition probability from state s to u is $P(s, u) = 1 - P(s, v) = \frac{1}{4} \notin [\frac{1}{2}, \frac{3}{4}]$. This problem does not occur in case (b) and (c) of Figure 2. The AMC in case (b) is "finer" than (a) since $[\frac{1}{4}, \frac{1}{2}] \subset [\frac{1}{4}, \frac{3}{4}]$, whereas case (c) is more abstract than (a). In the following we will "cut" AMCs so that cases with "non-constructive" information do not occur and give a transformation that refines an AMC such that the conditions are fulfilled. Thus, for the example, we change from case (a) to the finer model of (b) rather than to (c).

Definition 3. *For a finite set X let $g^l, g^u \in psdistr(X)$ with $g^l(x) \leq g^u(x)$ for all $x \in X$. The* cut *of g^l and g^u is the pair $cut(g^l, g^u) = (f^l, f^u)$ given by*

$$f^l(x) = \min\{h(x) \mid h \in distr(g)\} \qquad f^u(x) = \max\{h(x) \mid h \in distr(g)\}$$

We call an AMC $M = (S, P^l, P^u, L)$ delimited *iff for all $s \in S$ it holds that*

$$cut(P^l(s, \cdot), P^u(s, \cdot)) = (P^l(s, \cdot), P^u(s, \cdot)).$$

Summing up, *cut* deletes values that cannot be completed to a distribution, so no scheduler of an AMC gets lost:

Lemma 1. *Let $M = (S, P^l, P^u, L)$ be an AMC and $M' = (S, cut(P^l, P^u), L)$ the delimited version of M. Then for all $s \in S$,*

$$\mathcal{S}(M, s) = \mathcal{S}(M', s)$$

---

[3] We sometimes omit outgoing transitions in examples from now on.

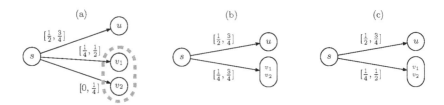

Fig. 3. Cutting abstraction: (a) abstracted to (b) delimited to (c)

Note that the *cut* operator is easy to calculate, e.g., the lower bound of the transition probability for s to s' will be $\max\{P^l(s, s'), 1 - \sum_{s'' \neq s'} P^u(s, s'')\}$ in the delimited version. If a lower bound is adapted no upper bound has to be adapted and vice versa.

If we construct $abstract(M, \mathcal{A})$ we always receive a delimited AMC if M is a MC. This is not necessarily the case if M is an AMC, even if M is delimited, as Figure 3 shows.

Remark 1. In the following we assume that w.l.o.g. all considered AMCs are delimited unless otherwise stated.

Extreme Distributions. As will become apparent in the following, distributions taking up values on the borders of intervals, called extreme distributions, are of special interest. Let $g^l, g^u \in psdistr(X)$ with $g^l(x) \leq g^u(x)$ for all $x \in X$ and $cut(g^l, g^u) = (g^l, g^u)$. For $X' \subseteq X$ let $ex_{min}(g^l, g^u, X')$ be the set of distributions $h \in distr(g)$ such that $X' = \emptyset$ implies $h = g^l = g^u$ and $X' \neq \emptyset$ implies

$$\exists x \in X'.h(x) = g^l(x) \wedge h \in ex_{min}(cut(g^l, g^u[x \mapsto g^l(x)]), X' \setminus \{x\}),$$

where $f[s \mapsto n]$ denotes the function that agrees everywhere with f except at s where it is equal to n. Dually, let $ex_{max}(g^l, g^u, X')$ be the set of distributions $h \in distr(g)$ such that $X' = \emptyset$ implies $h = g^l = g^u$ and $X' \neq \emptyset$ implies

$$\exists x \in X'.h(x) = g^u(x) \wedge h \in ex_{max}(cut(g^l[x \mapsto g^u(x)], g^u), X' \setminus \{x\}).$$

Definition 4. *We say that a distribution* $h \in distr(g)$ *min-extreme if* $h \in ex_{min}(g^l, g^u, X)$ *and max-extreme if* $h \in ex_{max}(g^l, g^u, X)$. h *is called extreme if it is min-extreme or max-extreme.*

Simulation. To compare the behavior described by two AMCs, we introduce the notion of probabilistic simulation that is an extension of probabilistic simulation for MCs [15].

Definition 5. *Let* $M = (S, P^l, P^u, L)$ *be an AMC. We call* $\mathcal{R} \subseteq S \times S$ *a probabilistic simulation iff* $s\mathcal{R}s'$ *implies:*

1. $\forall a \in AP : (L(s', a) \neq ?) \Longrightarrow L(s', a) = L(s, a)$,
2. *for each* $h \in distr(P(s, \cdot))$ *there exists* $h' \in distr(P(s', \cdot))$ *and* $\delta \in distr(S \times S)$ *such that for all* $u, v \in S$

   (i) $\delta(u, v) > 0 \Longrightarrow u\mathcal{R}v$,   (ii) $\delta(u, S) = h(u)$,   (iii) $\delta(S, v) = h'(v)$.

We write $s \preceq s'$ iff there exists a probabilistic simulation $\mathcal{R}$ with $s\mathcal{R}s'$. For AMC $M_i = (S_i, P^l{}_i, P^u{}_i, L_i)$, $s_i \in S_i$, $i = 1, 2$ we write $s_1 \preceq s_2$ iff there exists a probabilistic simulation $\mathcal{R}$ on $S_1 \cup S_2$ with $s_1\mathcal{R}s_2$ in the composed AMC of M_1 and M_2 (which is constructed in the obvious way, assuming $S_1 \cap S_2 = \emptyset$).

Note that if $s \preceq s'$ then all possible distributions h of s are matched by a distribution h' of s'. The opposite does not hold, i.e., the set $distr(P(s', \cdot))$ may contain distributions that can not be simulated by a distribution of s.

The previously defined abstraction operator induces a simulation:

Theorem 1. *Let* $M = (S, P^l, P^u, L)$ *be an AMC and* $abstract(M, \mathcal{A})$ *an abstraction of* M *induced by a partition* $\mathcal{A}$ *of* S. *Then* s *is simulated by its macro state, i.e. for all* $s \in S, A \in \mathcal{A}$

$$s \in A \implies s \preceq A.$$

Example 2. Consider the MC M of Example 1, Figure 1. We have $s_4 \preceq A_1$, for instance: Let $\mathcal{R} = \{(s_i, A_1) \mid 1 \leq i \leq 4\} \cup \{(s_5, A_2), (s_6, A_2)\} \cup \{(s_7, A_3), (s_8, A_3)\}$. Since $\tilde{L}(a, A_1) = ?$ condition (1) of Definition 5 is trivially fulfilled. Checking condition (2) for (s_4, A_1) yields: $\delta(s_3, A_1) = \delta(s_4, A_1) = \delta(s_6, A_2) = \frac{1}{3}$ and 0 for all remaining pairs. Then $h' \in distr(\mathcal{A})$ with $h'(A_1) = \delta(s_3, A_1) + \delta(s_4, A_1) = \frac{2}{3}$, $h'(A_2) = \frac{1}{3}$, and $h'(A_3) = 0$ is an element of $distr(\tilde{P}(A_1, \cdot))$ such that condition (2) is fulfilled.

3   Measures and Simulation

Let us define a notion of measure for AMCs and discuss how measures are related w.r.t. simulation. Here, we study reachability properties. In the next section, we extend our study to a three-valued version of Probabilistic Computation Tree Logic (PCTL).

A nonempty set Ω of possible outcomes of an experiment of chance is called *sample space*. A set $\mathfrak{B} \subseteq 2^\Omega$ is called *Borel field* (or σ-algebra) over Ω if it contains Ω, $\Omega \setminus E$ for each $E \in \mathfrak{B}$, and the union of any countable sequence of sets from $\mathfrak{B}$. The subsets of Ω that are elements of $\mathfrak{B}$ are called *measurable* (w.r.t. $\mathfrak{B}$). A Borel field $\mathfrak{B}$ is *generated* by an at most countable set $\mathcal{E}$, denoted by $\mathfrak{B} = \langle \mathcal{E} \rangle$, if $\mathfrak{B}$ is the closure of $\mathcal{E}$'s elements under complement and countable union.

A *probability space* is a triple $\mathcal{PS} = (\Omega, \mathfrak{B}, \text{Prob})$ where Ω is a sample space, $\mathfrak{B}$ is a Borel field over Ω, and Prob is a mapping $\mathfrak{B} \to [0, 1]$ such that $\text{Prob}(\Omega) = 1$ and $\text{Prob}(\bigcup_{i=1}^\infty E_i) = \sum_{i=1}^\infty \text{Prob}(E_i)$ for any sequence $E_1, E_2, \ldots$ of pairwise disjoint sets from $\mathfrak{B}$. We call Prob a *probability measure*.

For an AMC $M = (S, P^l, P^u, L)$, let $\Omega = S^\omega$ be the set of *trajectories* (also called *paths*) of M. Let $\mathfrak{B}$ be the Borel field generated by $\{\mathcal{C}(\pi) \mid \pi \in S^*\}$, where $\mathcal{C}(\pi) = \{\pi' \in \Omega \mid \pi \text{ is a prefix of } \pi'\}$ is the *basic cylinder set* of π. A scheduler $\eta \in \mathcal{S}(M, s_0)$ induces a probability space $\mathcal{PS}^\eta = (\Omega, \mathfrak{B}, \text{Prob}^\eta)$ as follows: Prob^η is uniquely given by $\text{Prob}^\eta(\Omega) = 1$ and, for $n \geq 1$, $\text{Prob}^\eta(\mathcal{C}(s_0 s_1 \ldots s_n)) =$

$h_1(s_1) \ldots h_n(s_n)$, where $h_i = \eta(s_0 \ldots s_{i-1})$, for $i \in \{1, \ldots, n\}$, is the probability distribution selected by η. We set $\mathrm{Prob}^\eta(\mathcal{C}(s_0' s_1' \ldots s_n')) = 0$ if $s_0' \neq s_0$. Furthermore, we put $\pi(s) = \mathcal{C}(s)$ and for $n = 0, 1, 2, \ldots$ let $\pi[n]$ denote the n-th state of π.

When interested in the infimum of probabilities of measurable sets w.r.t. all schedulers, it suffices to consider only extreme distributions, which take values only at boundaries of intervals. A scheduler is called *extreme* iff it only chooses extreme distributions. The set of all extreme schedulers for state s is denoted by $\mathcal{ES}(M, s)$ and $\mathcal{ES}(s)$ if M is known.

Theorem 2. *For state s in an AMC, we have for every measurable set Q of the induced probability space that*

$$\inf_{\eta \in \mathcal{ES}(s)} \mathrm{Prob}^\eta(Q) = \inf_{\eta \in \mathcal{S}(s)} \mathrm{Prob}^\eta(Q)$$

The previous theorem can easily be shown as follows: Take a scheduler η and show that the measure is reduced (or stays the same) when changing η to an extreme distribution.

Note that while there are typically infinitely many distributions leading from one state to the other in an AMC, there are only finitely many extreme distributions.

Let us compare the notion of AMCs with the one of Markov decision processes (MDPs) in the three-valued setting: A *Markov decision process* (MDP) is a tuple $M = (S, \Sigma, Prob, L)$, where S is a finite set of states, Σ is a non-empty finite set of letters, $Prob : S \times \Sigma \rightharpoonup distr(S)$ is a partial function that yields for a state s and a given letter σ a distribution function for successor states. $L : S \times AP \to \mathbb{B}_3$ is a labeling function that assigns a truth value to each pair of state and proposition.

The MDP $M' = MDP(M)$ induced by an AMC $M = (S, P^l, P^u, L)$ is given as $M' = (S, \Sigma, Prob, L)$ where $\Sigma = \{\sigma_h \mid h \in distr(P(s, \cdot))$ for some $s \in S$ and h is extreme$\}$, $Prob$ is such that $Prob(s, \sigma_h) = h$ if $h \in distr(P(s, \cdot))$ and h is extreme and $Prob(s, \sigma_h)$ is undefined otherwise.

Thus, $MDP(M)$ defines a Markov decision process with the same state space as M but with (finitely-many) extreme distributions. The notion of schedulers carries over in the expected manner, i.e. $\mathcal{ES}(M, s) = \mathcal{ES}(MDP(M), s)$ for all states s. More importantly, the infimum of the measure of some measurable set with respect to some scheduler class obviously coincides, due to Theorem 2.

For the remainder of this section, let us now concentrate on reachability properties. More specifically, for an AMC M and s one of its state, a proposition $a \in AP$, $\alpha \in \mathbb{B}_3$ and $n = 0, 1, 2, \ldots$, let, $Reach(s, a, \alpha, n) := \{\pi \in \pi(s) \mid L(\pi[n], a) = \alpha$ and for all $k < n, L(\pi[k], a) \neq \alpha\}$ and

$$Reach(s, a, \alpha) = \bigcup_{n \geq 0} Reach(s, a, \alpha, n)$$

For reachability properties, it was shown in the setting of Markov decision processes (MDPs), that the infimum with respect to all schedulers agrees with the one when only so-called simple schedulers are considered [7]. A scheduler $\eta \in \mathcal{S}(M, s)$ is called *simple* iff for all $\pi, \pi' \in S^*$, $s' \in S$, we have $\eta(s\pi s') = \eta(s\pi's')$, meaning that the choice does not depend on the history π. Thus, a similar result holds for AMCs as well. The set of simple schedulers that choose only extreme distributions is denoted by $\mathcal{SES}(M, s)$ for AMC or MDP M. Since there are only finitely many simple extreme schedulers, the infimum is indeed a minimum. Thus, we get

Lemma 2. *For state s, $a \in AP$, and $\alpha \in \mathbb{B}_3$ it holds that*

$$\inf_{\eta \in \mathcal{S}(s)} Prob^\eta(Reach(s, a, \alpha))$$
$$= \inf_{\eta \in \mathcal{SES}(s)} Prob^\eta(Reach(s, a, \alpha))$$
$$= \min_{\eta \in \mathcal{SES}(s)} Prob^\eta(Reach(s, a, \alpha))$$

Let us now compare the behavior of two AMCs w.r.t. abstraction, i.e., simulation. We give the intuition of the following Lemma first. Let $s_0 \preceq s_0'$. When scheduler $\eta \in \mathcal{S}(s_0)$ chooses some distribution h_0, there is, according to the definition of simulation, a corresponding $h_0' \in distr(P(s_0', \cdot))$. This implies that for every state s_1 reachable by h_0 with positive probability, there is a set of states $s_{1_1}', \ldots, s_{1_{k_1}}'$ reachable by h_0' with positive probability, each simulating s_1. Now, for $s_0 s_1$, we can argue in the same fashion: For $\eta(s_0 s_1) = h_1$ there is a corresponding h_{1_i}' for each $s_0' s_{1_i}'$, and so on...

Let us be more precise: For a scheduler $\eta \in \mathcal{S}(s_0)$ we define a scheduler $\eta' \in \mathcal{S}(s_0')$ inductively as follows: For $h = \eta(s_0)$ define $\eta'(s_0') = h'$, where h' is as in the definition of the simulation relation. Similarly, let $s_0 \ldots s_n$ be a sequence of states such that $Prob^\eta(\mathcal{C}(s_0 \ldots s_n)) > 0$ and $h = \eta(s_0 \ldots s_n)$. By induction, there is a set of states $s_{n_1}', \ldots s_{n_k}'$ each simulating s_n. For each $s_{n'}' \in \{s_{n_1}', \ldots s_{n_k}'\}$, define $\eta'(s_0' \ldots s_{n'}') = h'$, where h' is as in the definition of the simulation relation.

Lemma 3. *For $\alpha \in \{\top, \bot\}$, $a \in AP$ it holds that $s \preceq s'$ implies*

$$\inf_{\eta \in \mathcal{S}(s)} Prob^\eta(Reach(s, a, \alpha)) \geq \inf_{\eta' \in \mathcal{S}(s')} Prob^{\eta'}(Reach(s', a, \alpha))$$

The previous lemma can be shown by induction on n, where n is the position where the proposition a has value α for the first time. Induction hypothesis is that

$$Prob^\eta(Reach(s, a, \alpha, n)) = Prob^{\eta'}(Reach(s', a, \alpha, n))$$
$$\geq \inf_{\eta'' \in \mathcal{S}(s)} Prob^{\eta''}(Reach(s', a, \alpha, n))$$

where η' is the scheduler constructed for η as described above and η may be the one for which the infimum is taken.

Note that for the supremum, the corresponding result only holds when adding the paths that reach a state for which a evaluates to ?:

Lemma 4. *For $\alpha \in \{\top, \bot\}$, $a \in AP$ we have that $s \preceq s'$ implies*

$$\sup_{\eta \in \mathcal{S}(s)} Prob^\eta(Reach(s, a, \alpha)) \leq \sup_{\eta' \in \mathcal{S}(s')} Prob^{\eta'}(Reach(s', a, \alpha) \cup Reach(s', \eta', a, ?))$$

Thus, Lemma 2 and Lemma 3 yield that the lower bound for some reachability property in the coarser system is less or equal than in the finer system.

Theorem 3. *Let s, s' be states in an AMC with $s \preceq s'$ and $a \in AP$, and $\alpha \in \{\top, \bot\}$. Then*

$$\min_{\eta \in \mathcal{S}(s)} Prob^{\eta}(Reach(s, a, \alpha)) \geq \min_{\eta' \in \mathcal{SES}(s')} Prob^{\eta'}(Reach(s', a, \alpha))$$

In simple words, the previous theorem says that when the minimum of a reachability property is at least p in the coarser system, it is so in the finer system as well.

4   3-Valued PCTL

Recall that AP denotes a nonempty finite set of *propositions*. The set of *Probabilistic Computation-Tree Logic (PCTL)* [10,5] formulas over AP, denoted by PCTL, is the set of *state-formulas* φ inductively defined as follows:

$$\varphi ::= \text{true} \mid a \mid \varphi \wedge \varphi \mid \neg\varphi \mid [\Phi]_{\bowtie p} \qquad \Phi ::= X\varphi \mid \varphi \, \mathcal{U} \, \varphi$$

where $\bowtie \in \{\leq, <, \geq, >\}$, $p \in [0, 1]$ and $a \in AP$. The formulas defined by Φ are called *path-formulas*[4].

In the setting of AMCs, a state might no longer just satisfy or refuse a formula, but a third value ? (don't know) is appropriate. Consequently, we define the satisfaction of a formula w.r.t. a state as a function into $\mathbb{B}_3$, which forms a complete lattice ordering the elements as $\bot < ? < \top$. Joins and meets in this lattice are denoted by $\sqcup$ and $\sqcap$, respectively. Complementation is denoted by $\overline{}$, where $\top$ and $\bot$ are complementary to each other while $\overline{?} = ?$.

When a formula evaluates in a state to $\top$ or $\bot$, we sometimes say that the result is *definite*. Otherwise, we say that it is *indefinite*. Similarly, we say the result holds for sure or is violated for sure if it evaluates to $\top$ respectively $\bot$. We say it may be true or may be false if it evaluates to ?.

Given an AMC $M = (S, P^l, P^u, L)$ and a PCTL formula φ we define the satisfaction function $[s, \varphi]$ for state $s \in S$ and $[\pi, \Phi]$ for trajectory $\pi \in S^{\omega}$ inductively as shown in Figure 4, where $Pr^l(s, \Phi, \alpha) = \inf_{\eta \in \mathcal{SES}(s)} Prob^{\eta}(\{\pi \in \pi(s) \mid [\pi, \Phi] = \alpha\})$ for $\alpha \in \mathbb{B}_3$. For the cases $\bowtie \, = \, <$ and $\bowtie \, = \, >$ the value of $[s, [\Phi]_{\bowtie p}]$ is similar to the cases $\leq$ and $\geq$, respectively, but we exchange $\leq$ by $<$ and vice versa.

To understand why the above semantics is sound with respect to the notion of simulation in Definition 5 we discuss each operator in the following and state the soundness result later in Theorem 4.

Case true, false, a, $\wedge$, $\neg$: The semantics is defined as expected for the base and boolean cases.

---

[4] To simplify the presentation, we omit the bounded until operator given in [10], which could easily be added.

$[s, \text{true}]$	$= \top$	$[s, \text{false}]$	$= \bot$
$[s, a]$	$= L(s, a)$		
$[s, \varphi_1 \wedge \varphi_2]$	$= [s, \varphi_1] \sqcap [s, \varphi_2]$	$[s, \neg \varphi_1]$	$= \overline{[s, \varphi_1]}$

$$[s, [\Phi]_{\geq p}] = \begin{cases} \top & \text{if } Pr^l(s, \Phi, \top) \geq p \\ \bot & \text{if } Pr^l(s, \Phi, \bot) > 1 - p \\ ? & \text{otherwise} \end{cases} \quad [s, [\Phi]_{\leq p}] = \begin{cases} \top & \text{if } Pr^l(s, \Phi, \bot) \geq 1 - p \\ \bot & \text{if } Pr^l(s, \Phi, \top) > p \\ ? & \text{otherwise} \end{cases}$$

$$[\pi, X \varphi_1] = [\pi[1], \varphi_1]$$

$$[\pi, \varphi_1 \, \mathcal{U} \, \varphi_2] = \begin{cases} \top & \text{if } \exists i.([\pi[i], \varphi_2] = \top \text{ and } \forall 0 \leq j < i.[\pi[j], \varphi_1] = \top) \\ \bot & \text{if } \forall i.([\pi[i], \varphi_2] \neq \bot \implies \exists 0 \leq j < i.[\pi[j], \varphi_1] = \bot) \\ ? & \text{otherwise,} \end{cases}$$

Fig. 4. Semantics of PCTL formulas

Case X and $\mathcal{U}$: The truth value of $[\pi, X \varphi_1]$ equals the result of φ_1 in state $\pi[1]$. A trajectory π satisfies the formula $\varphi_1 \, \mathcal{U} \, \varphi_2$ for sure, if φ_1 holds for sure until φ_2 holds for sure. It is violated, if either φ_2 is always wrong for sure, or otherwise φ_1 is violated before.

Case $[\Phi]_{\geq p}$: For $[\Phi]_{\geq p}$, the situation is slightly more involved. First, we remark that Lemma 2 holds also for PCTL path properties, i.e. that is suffices to consider simple extreme schedulers instead of arbitrary ones.

Lemma 5. *Let M be an AMC, s one of its states, Φ a path property of PCTL, $\alpha \in \mathbb{B}_3$, and $Q = \{\pi \in \pi(s) \mid [\pi, \Phi] = \alpha\}$. Then*

$$\inf_{\eta \in \mathcal{S}(s)} Prob^\eta(Q) = \inf_{\eta \in \mathcal{SES}(s)} Prob^\eta(Q) = \min_{\eta \in \mathcal{SES}(s)} Prob^\eta(Q)$$

In view of the simulation relation we can show that coarser systems yield even lower bounds than finer systems.

Lemma 6. *For states s, s' in an AMC with $s \preceq s'$ and Φ a path property of PCTL, $\alpha \in \{\top, \bot\}$, $Q = \{\pi \in \pi(s) \mid [\pi, \Phi] = \alpha\}$, $Q' = \{\pi \in \pi(s') \mid [\pi, \Phi] = \alpha\}$ we have*

$$\min_{\eta \in \mathcal{SES}(s)} Prob^\eta(Q) \geq \min_{\eta' \in \mathcal{SES}(s')} Prob^{\eta'}(Q')$$

The previous lemmas can easily be shown as their counterparts for reachability properties listed in the previous section.

For $[\Phi]_{\geq p}$, we measure the paths starting in s for which Φ evaluates to $\top$ and check whether the lower bound of this measure is greater or equal to p. If so, the result is $\top$ and for a finer state s' with $s' \preceq s$ this measure is also greater than p.

For scheduler $\eta \in \mathcal{SES}(M, s')$ we set $p_\alpha^\eta = Prob^\eta(\{\pi \in \pi(s') \mid [\pi, \Phi] = \alpha\})$ and observe that $\sum_{\alpha \in \mathbb{B}_3} p_\alpha^\eta = 1$. If the measure of the paths starting in s for which Φ evaluates to $\bot$ is greater than $1 - p$, then this is also the case for s', i.e. $p_\bot^\eta > 1 - p$. Therefore, this leaves less than $1 - (1 - p) = p$ for $p_\top^\eta + p_?^\eta$. In other words, even if $p_?^\eta$ is added to $p_\top^\eta$, the constraint $\geq p$ cannot be met. Therefore, we decide for $\bot$.

Case $[\Phi]_{\leq p}$*:* For $[\Phi]_{\leq p}$, we consider the measure of paths starting in s for which Φ evaluates to $\top$. If the lower bound is already bigger than p, it is so especially so for s' and we decide for $[\Phi]_{\leq p}$ as $\bot$. Similarly, if for enough paths Φ evaluates to $\bot$, we can be sure that the measure of paths satisfying Φ is small. If $Pr^l(s, \Phi, \bot) \geq 1 - p$ then in the finer system for all $\eta \in \mathcal{SES}(M, s')$ we get $p_\bot^\eta \geq 1 - p$. But then $p_?^\eta + p_\top^\eta \leq 1 - (1 - p) = p$. In other words, even if $p_?^\eta$ is added to $p_\top^\eta$, the constraint $\leq p$ is fulfilled and we go for $\top$.

The following theorem states that our framework developed so far can indeed be used for abstraction based model checking and follows easily from Lemma 6 and the discussion above. In simple words, it says that the result of checking a formula in the abstract system agrees with the one for the finer system, unless it was indefinite.

Theorem 4. *Let s and s' be two states of an AMC M with $s \preceq s'$. Then for all $\varphi \in PCTL$:*

$$[s', \varphi] \neq ? \ implies \ [s, \varphi] = [s', \varphi].$$

Observe that the 3-valued PCTL semantics of an MC understood as an AMC coincides with the usual 2-valued PCTL semantics for Markov chains.

5   Model Checking 3-Valued PCTL

In this section, we discuss two model checking algorithms for 3-valued PCTL. As for CTL, both model checking algorithms work bottom-up the parse tree of φ. Hence, it suffices to describe their steps inductively on the structure of φ. Each state s is labeled with a function t_s assigning to each subformula its truth value. t_s is defined directly for true, false, a, $\varphi_1 \wedge \varphi_2$, and $\neg \varphi_1$ according to the definition of their semantics. For $[\Phi]_{\bowtie p}$, t_s can easily be determined, provided the lower bound of a measure of paths for some path property (denoted by Pr^l in Figure 4) can be computed. Therefore, it remains to show how to compute the lower bound of the measure of paths for which an until or next-step formula evaluates to $\top$, $\bot$, and $?$. Let us discuss $\Phi := \varphi_1 \, \mathcal{U} \, \varphi_2$. The treatment of the next-step operator is similar but easier and is omitted here. Thanks to Theorem 2, computing the measure for an until property becomes (technically) easy, since only extreme distributions have to be considered.

Reduction to MDP Model Checking. The first idea is to convert an AMC M to an MDP $MDP(M)$ and reuse existing methods for computing path properties on MDPs. Before translating M, we can assume that for every state, we know the truth values of φ_1 and φ_2. We annotate $MDP(M)$ with (two-valued) propositions corresponding to the values of φ_1 and φ_2 in M. More specifically, label a state s of $MDP(M)$ by the (new) propositions a_{φ_1} and a_{φ_2}, if φ_1 respectively φ_2 evaluates to $\top$ in s. Label s by propositions $\bar{a}_{\varphi_1}$ and $\bar{a}_{\varphi_2}$, if φ_1 respectively φ_2 are $\bot$. Now, considering the semantics of the until operation as shown in Figure 4, it is easy to see that $\varphi_1 \, \mathcal{U} \, \varphi_2$ on a path of M evaluates to $\top$ iff $a_{\varphi_1} \, \mathcal{U} \, a_{\varphi_2}$ on the same path (of $MDP(M)$) evaluates to true. Similarly, it is easy to see that $\varphi_1 \, \mathcal{U} \, \varphi_2$ on a path of M evaluates to $\bot$ iff $\neg(\neg\bar{a}_{\varphi_1} \, \mathcal{U} \, \neg\bar{a}_{\varphi_2})$ evaluates to true.

Using the reduction to an MDP model checking problem for until properties, we have completed the first algorithm that is mainly used to give an upper bound on the complexity of the model checking problem.

Complexity. Computing the semantics for an AMC M and a formula $\varphi \in$ PCTL bottom-up for every state can be done in linear time, provided the measures for path properties are given. For every state s with k outgoing transitions, one can obtain, in the worst case, $k!$ extreme distributions. Thus, the size of $MDP(M)$ is at most exponential in the size of M, where, as expected, the size of M, denoted by $|M|$ is the number of states plus the number of transitions, i.e., pairs (s, s') for which $P^l(s, s') > 0$. Computing the measure for a path property in an MDP M' is polynomial with respect to the size of M' (states plus non-zero transitions) [7]. Thus, overall, we get:

Theorem 5. *Given an AMC $M = (S, P^l, P^u, L)$ and a PCTL formula φ, then the algorithm outlined in this section labels every state $s \in S$ with $t_s(\psi) = [s, \psi]$ for each subformula ψ of φ in time polynomial w.r.t. $O(2^{|M| \log |M|})$ and linear w.r.t. the size of φ, where $|M|$ denotes the size of M.*

Fixpoint Computation. The reduction to an MDP for computing path properties suffers from the effort spent for computing all extreme distributions. Therefore, we have implemented a version of the algorithm that is based on fixpoint iteration. This algorithm, while (only) approximating the minimal result in question, chooses (and computes) extreme distributions in an on-the-fly fashion, leading to huge space gains.

Our approach is inspired by the treatment in [1, 5] done for MDPs. Let us define the sets:

$$
\begin{aligned}
W_\top^+ &= \{s \mid t_s(\varphi_2) = \top\} \\
W_\top^- &= \{s \mid t_s(\varphi_2) \neq \top \text{ and } t_s(\varphi_1) \neq \top\} \\
W_\bot^+ &= \{s \mid t_s(\varphi_2) = \bot \text{ and } t_s(\varphi_1) = \bot\} \\
W_\bot^- &= \{s \mid t_s(\varphi_2) \neq \bot\}
\end{aligned}
$$

To simplify our presentation, we say that Φ evaluates in a state to some value in $\mathbb{B}_3$ if it evaluates to that value on all paths starting in this state.

Φ holds in $W_\top^+$ for sure and is violated for sure in $W_\top^-$. However, the result is $\bot$ in $W_\bot^+$ since φ_1 as well as φ_2 is $\bot$. In $W_\bot^-$ the formula is not necessarily violated.

Let p_α^{min} abbreviate $(Pr^l(s, \Phi, \alpha))_{s \in S}$. We obtain p_α^{min} as least fixpoint of the iteration described in the following:

First, let Del be the set of all pairs of delimited pseudo distribution functions on S and $b \in \{l, u\}$. Consider the minimization/maximization function $\xi^b :$ $2^S \times \text{Del} \times (S \to [0, 1]) \to [0, 1]$ that is given by $\xi^b(\emptyset, (g^l, g^u), x) = 0$ and for $S' \neq \emptyset$

$$\xi^l(S',(g^l,g^u),x) = g^l(s^l) \cdot x(s^l) + \xi^l(S' \setminus \{s^l\}, cut(g^l,g^u[s^l \mapsto g^l(s^l)]),x)$$
$$\text{if } x(s^l) = \min_{s' \in S'} x(s'),$$

$$\xi^u(S',(g^l,g^u),x) = g^u(s^u) \cdot x(s^u) + \xi^u(S' \setminus \{s^u\}, cut(g^l[s^u \mapsto g^u(s^u)],g^u),x)$$
$$\text{if } x(s^u) = \max_{s' \in S'} x(s').$$

Note that $\xi^b(S,(g^l,g^u),x)$ sorts the states $s \in S'$ according to their values in x and chooses $h \in distr(g)$ that minimizes/ maximizes the value $\sum_{s \in S} h(s) \cdot x(s)$.[5]

Let $S^+, S^- \subseteq S$. We use ξ^b to define the function $\mathrm{F}^b_{(S^-,S^+)} : (S \to [0,1]) \to (S \to [0,1])$ that determines the next iteration step by

$$\mathrm{F}^b_{(S^-,S^+)}(x)_{(s)} = \begin{cases} 1 & \text{if } s \in S^+, \\ 0 & \text{if } s \in S^-, \\ \xi^b(S,(P^l(s,\cdot),P^u(s,\cdot)),x) & \text{otherwise.} \end{cases}$$

Furthermore, let x_0 denote the function that maps everything to 0.

Theorem 6. *The least fixpoint (w.r.t. point wise extension of the order of the real numbers) of the function $\mathrm{F}^b_{(S^-,S^+)}$ can be used to calculate the values p^{min}_α:*

$$p^{min}_\top(s) = (\sqcup_{n \in \mathbb{N}} \mathrm{F}^l_{(W^-_\top,W^+_\top)}{}^{(n)}(x_0))_{(s)}$$
$$p^{min}_\bot(s) = 1 - (\sqcup_{n \in \mathbb{N}} \mathrm{F}^u_{(W^+_\bot,W^-_\bot)}{}^{(n)}(x_0))_{(s)}.$$

The proof goes along the lines of the proof for MDPs (see [1, Chapter 3] for details).

Let us give an example showing that the *cut* in the definition of the fixpoint operator in Theorem 6 to calculate the probabilities for $[\Phi]_{\bowtie p}$ is indeed important:

Example 3. Let us consider the AMC shown in Figure 3 (a) (page 76) and $\Phi = \varphi_1 \, \mathcal{U} \, \varphi_2$. Assume that $t_s(\varphi_1) = t_{v_2}(\varphi_1) = t_u(\varphi_2) = \top$ and all remaining truth values for φ_1 and φ_2 are $\bot$. Furthermore, assume that there is a $[1,1]$-transition from v_2 back to itself. Then we get: $W^+_\top = \{u\}$ and $W^-_\top = \{v_1\}$. For example, the maximization function ξ^u chooses $P^l(s,u) = P^u(s,u) = \frac{3}{4}$ since $1 = \max\{1,0,0\} = \max\{x(u),x(v_1),x(v_2)\}$ after the first iteration step and due to the *cut* operation $P(s,v_1) = [\frac{1}{4},\frac{1}{4}]$ and $P(s,v_2) = [0,0]$. Hence, $Pr^u(s,\Phi,\top) = \frac{3}{4} \cdot 1 + \frac{1}{4} \cdot 0 + 0 \cdot 0 = \frac{3}{4}$. $W^+_\bot = \{v_1,v_2\}$ and $W^-_\bot = \{u\}$. Altogether we get $Pr(s,\Phi,\top) = [\frac{1}{2},\frac{3}{4}]$, $Pr(s,\Phi,\bot) = [\frac{1}{4},\frac{1}{2}]$, $Pr(s,\Phi,?) = [0,0]$. Note that we get the intervals shown in Figure 3 (c). Thus, the subsequent cut in the definition of the fixpoint operator is necessary since the values in Figure 3 (b) yield less precise results.

---

[5] The function ξ^b is well defined, i.e., the same value is obtained if another maximal/minimal state s' is considered. This follows from the fact that $\min\{\sum_{s \in S'} h(s) \mid h \in distr(g)\} = \min\{\sum_{s \in S'} h(s) \mid h \in distr(cut(g^l,g^u[s' \mapsto g^l(s')]))\}$ for all $S' \subseteq S$ with $s' \in S'$.

6 Alternatives to AMCs

Let us discuss alternative approaches for abstraction of Markov chains. For reasons of space limitation, we keep the discussion informal.

Generally, *Markov Decision Processes* (MDPs) are considered to be abstractions for Markov chains. MDPs extend the model of MCs by allowing several distribution functions in each state (see Figure 5 (c)).

Thus, when merging states to obtain an abstraction, one could define the corresponding distribution functions, as indicated in Figure 5 (a)–(c). Hence, the result would be an MDP. Now, one might be tempted to use existing model checking theory for PCTL and MDPs to reason about the underlying Markov chain. However, this is not possible since, as far as we know, there is no 3-valued notion of PCTL for MDPs (not to mention, we need one that suits the role in the abstraction defined here).

When interested in reachability properties, the approach is possible and was pursued in [6]. Let us call the approach *AMDP*. Actually, the model checking algorithms presented in the previous section considers the AMC as an MDP with extreme distributions, but only when computing the minimal probabilities of path properties.

Of course, one could have developed such a 3-valued version of PCTL for MDPs as opposed for AMCs, as done here. But actually, the 3-valued PCTL semantics given in Section 4 can easily be taken over for such a 3-valued PCTL semantics for MDPs.

However, there is an intrinsic difference in the approach using AMCs and the one based on MDPs. An MDP can easily be abstracted to an AMC. For example, for the MDP shown in Figure 5 (c), we would get the AMC shown in Figure 5 (d). But using intervals, one *reduces more* information.

This has two implications, one theoretical and one practical. Our semantics for PCTL path properties compares only extreme distributions. Probabilities that are not the bound of some transition probability interval are not considered. However, we might consider *all* extreme distributions. For example, one extreme distribution for the AMC in Figure 5 (d) is $(u \mapsto \frac{4}{10}, v_1 \mapsto \frac{2}{10}, w \mapsto \frac{3}{10}, v_2 \mapsto \frac{1}{10})$, which is not present in Figure 5 (c). Now, consider $\varphi = [X(a_u \vee a_w)]_{\leq \frac{6}{10}}$, where

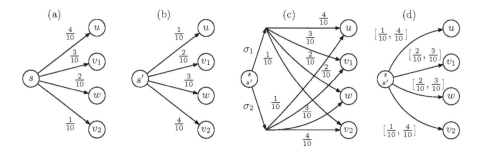

Fig. 5. Abstraction by MDPs vs. AMCs

proposition a_u (a_w) is $\top$ in state u (respectively w) and $\bot$ in all other states. Then the macro state in Figure 5 (c) provides $\top$ for φ but for the AMC in Figure 5 (d) the result is ?. Thus, our results might sometimes be less precise. From the practical side, using MDPs, one reduces the number of states but basically all distributions are kept. But storing all distributions causes no memory savings and it is questionable whether such an abstraction does indeed satisfy practical needs. In our approach, on the other hand, if, for example, a third distribution denoted by σ_3 with $(u \mapsto \frac{2}{10}, v_1 \mapsto \frac{2}{10}, w \mapsto \frac{3}{10}, v_2 \mapsto \frac{3}{10})$ would be present in Figure 5 (c), we obtain the same AMC, thus, reducing the memory requirments.

A different approach was taken in [11]. There, criterias have been engineered that guarantee an abstraction to be optimal (in some sense). Let us call this approach O. While, of course, such an optimal abstraction sounds preferable, it turns out that neither AMCs nor MDPs carry enough information to be optimal. In simple words, the approach loses some of its elegance since it requires to store much information. Furthermore, it is not clear (to us) how to obtain this information without constructing the underlying Markov chain. The author of [11] therefore suggests as well a more simple approximation of the optimal abstraction, which we call S. In simple words, S is similar to AMCs but does not use the cut operator to optimize the information present in AMCs.

Let us discuss Example 15 of [11]: Consider Figure 6 and $\Phi = [X\neg a_{u_1}]_{>0}$ where a_{u_1} is true in u_1 and false in all other states. For the approach S the result in u_0 is ? because the sum of the two zero values of the lower bounds to the direct successors u_d and u_0 are added which yields $0 + 0 = 0$ (see [11, Example 15]). In our setting after the first chosen zero value, say $P^l(u_0, u_d) = P^u(u_0, u_d) = 0$ through the *cut* the next choice is $P^l(u_0, u_0) = 1 - 0.01 = 0.99$. The resulting extrem distribution is $(u_d \mapsto 0, u_0 \mapsto 0.99, u_1 \mapsto 0.01)$ which leads to $[u_0, \Phi] = \top$. Thus, results based on S are less precise than the results obtained with our method. In terms of memory, S and AMC are comparable, provided the fixpoint computation method is used. Note that [11] does not address the question of model checking.

Summarizing, with abstraction one loses information usually by reducing space requirements. All approaches have in common, that states are grouped together to form an abstract system. They differ in the information that is kept for transitions. By means of precision, we can order the approaches $S < AMC < AMDP < O$, where $a < b$ means that a is less precise than b, when for some concrete system, the same states are grouped together. In terms of memory

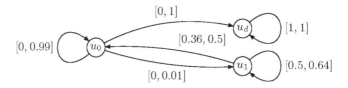

Fig. 6.

usage, we can order the approaches as $S = AMC < AMDP < O$, where $a < b$ means that a consumes less memory than b, when for some concrete system, the same states are grouped together.

7   Conclusion

In this paper, we have extended the abstraction-refinement paradigm based on three-valued logics to the setting of probabilistic systems. We have given a notion of abstraction for Markov chains. In simple words, abstract Markov chains are transition systems where the edges are labeled with intervals of probabilities. We equipped the notion with the concept of simulation to be able to relate the behavior of abstract and concrete systems.

We have presented model checking for abstract probabilistic systems (i.e. abstract Markov chains) with respect to specifications in a probabilistic temporal logic, interpreted over a 3-valued domain. More specifically, we studied a 3-valued version of PCTL. The model checking algorithm turns out to be quite similar to the ones developed in the setting of checking PCTL specifications of Markov decision processes. Thus, using the intuitive concept of intervals allows to refrain from saving all probability distributions present in concrete systems but storing only boundaries, while allowing to adapt existing theory of model checking probabilistic systems.

Our work can be extended into several directions. First, further insight in which and how to split states is desirable, when the model checking result is indefinite. It would also be interesting to extend our setting towards the more expressive logic PCTL* or to the setting of continuous-time Markov chains.

References

1. Christel Baier. *On the algorithmic verification of probabilistic systems*. Universität Mannheim, 1998. Habilitation Thesis.
2. M. Chechik, B. Devereux, S. Easterbrook, and A. Gurfinkel. Multi-valued symbolic model-checking. *ACM Transactions on Software Engineering and Methodology (TOSEM)*, 12:371–408, 2003.
3. E. Clarke, O. Grumberg, and D. Long. Model Checking and Abstraction. In *Proc. of POPL*, pages 342–354, New York, January 1992. ACM.
4. E.M. Clarke, O. Grumberg, and D.A. Peled. *Model Checking*. MIT press, December 1999.
5. C. Courcoubetis and M. Yannakakis. The complexity of probabilistic verification. *Journal of the ACM*, 42(4):857–907, July 1995.
6. P. D'Argenio, B. Jeannet, H. Jensen, and K. Larsen. Reduction and refinement strategies for probabilistic analysis. In *PAPM-PROBMIV*, pages 57–76, 2002.
7. Luca de Alfaro. *Formal Verification of Probabilistic Systems*. PhD thesis, Stanford University, 1997. Technical report STAN-CS-TR-98-1601.
8. P. Godefroid and R. Jagadeesan. On the expressiveness of 3-valued models. In *Verification, Model Checking and Abstract Interpretation (VMCAI)*, volume 2575 of *LNCS*, pages 206–222, 2003.

9. O. Grumberg, M. Lange, M. Leucker, and S. Shoham. *Don't know* in the μ-calculus. In *Proc. VMCAI'05*, volume 3385 of *LNCS*. Springer, 2005.

10. H. Hansson and B. Jonsson. A logic for reasoning about time and reliability. *Formal Aspects of Computing*, 6:512–535, 1994.

11. M. Huth. On finite-state approximants for probabilistic computation tree logic. *Theoretical Computer Science*. to appear.

12. M. Huth. An abstraction framework for mixed non-deterministic and probabilistic systems. In *Validation of Stochastic Systems*, pages 419–444, 2004.

13. M. Huth, R. Jagadeesan, and D. Schmidt. Modal transition systems: A foundation for three-valued program analysis. In *European Symposium on Programming (ESOP)*, volume 2028, pages 155–169, 2001.

14. Michael Huth. Abstraction and probabilities for hybrid logics. In *Qualitative Aspects of Programming Languages*, 2004.

15. B. Jonsson and K. Larsen. Specification and refinement of probabilistic processes. In *Proc. 6th IEEE Int. Symp. on Logic in Computer Science*, 1991.

16. B. Konikowska and W. Penczek. Model checking for multi-valued computation tree logics. In *Beyond two: theory and applications of multiple-valued logic*, pages 193–210. Physica-Verlag GmbH, 2003.

17. B. Konikowska and W. Penczek. On designated values in multi-valued CTL* model checking. *Fundamenta Informaticae*, 60(1–4):221–224, 2004.

18. S. Shoham and O. Grumberg. A game-based framework for CTL counterexamplesand 3-valued abstraction-refinemnet. In *Computer Aided Verification (CAV)*, volume 2725 of *LNCS*, pages 275–287, 2003.

19. R. van Glabbeek, S. Smolka, B. Steffen, and C. Tofts. Reactive, generative, and stratified models of probabilistic processes. In *Logic in Computer Science*, pages 130–141, 1990.

20. W. Yi. Reasoning about uncertain information compositionally. In *Proc. of the 3rd International School and Symposium on Real-Time and Fault-Tolerant Systems*, volume 863 of *LNCS*. Springer, 1994.

Symbolic Model Checking of Stochastic Systems: Theory and Implementation

Matthias Kuntz and Markus Siegle

Department of Computer Engineering,
University of the Federal Armed Forces Munich, Germany

Abstract. This paper presents IM-SPDL, a stochastic extension of the modal logic PDL, which supports the specification of complex performance and dependability requirements. The logic is interpreted over extended stochastic labelled transition systems (ESLTS), i.e. transition systems containing both immediate and Markovian transitions. We define the syntax and semantics of the new logic and show that IM-SPDL provides powerful means to specify path-based properties with timing restrictions. In general, paths can be characterised by regular expressions, also called programs, where the executability of a program may depend on the validity of test formulae. For the model checking of IM-SPDL time-bounded path formulae, a deterministic program automaton is constructed from the requirement. Afterwards the product transition system between this automaton and the ESLTS is built and subsequently transformed into a continuous time Markov Chain (CTMC) on which numerical analysis is performed. Empirical results given in the paper show that model checking IM-SPDL can be realised efficiently in practice.

Keywords: Stochastic systems, performance and dependability analysis, symbolic model checking, model checking software.

1 Introduction

It is extremely important to develop techniques for constructing and analysing distributed, concurrent hard- and software systems, which have become part of our daily life. Such systems must work correctly and meet high performance and dependability requirements. Our approach to the combined analysis of functional, performance and dependability aspects (the latter two commonly known as performability) is based on the formal verification of a stochastic model which describes both functional and temporal aspects of behaviour.

Such models can be constructed with the help of high-level formalisms, where stochastic Petri nets and stochastic process algebras are among the most popular ones. Generalised stochastic Petri nets (GSPNs) [1] offer two types of transitions: Timed transitions, associated with an exponentially distributed delay, and immediate transitions which, once enabled, fire without delay. Immediate transitions have been shown to be very useful for the modelling of complex synchronisation or cooperation schemes, for representing probabilistic decisions or simply for

A. Valmari (Ed.): SPIN 2006, LNCS 3925, pp. 89–107, 2006.

modelling bookkeeping activities which consume only negligible time. For this reason, immediate activities are also an integral part of the Stochastic Activity Network (SAN) modelling formalism [25] as implemented in the Möbius modelling framework [10] for the modelling and analysis of performability properties of distributed systems. For similar reasons, immediate transitions have also been included, in the form of immediate actions, into several stochastic process algebras, such as TIPP [13], EMPA [8] and IMC [12]. Overall, one may say that immediate transitions are a very valuable and often used modelling feature.

While there has been substantial work on the model checking of stochastic systems, the aspect of immediate transitions has not been considered in this context. In this paper, we present an extension of the modal logic PDL [11], called IM-SPDL (immediate and Markovian stochastic PDL), which can be used for specifying requirements for models that contain both immediate and Markovian transitions. Such a model we call extended stochastic labelled transition system (ESLTS), since it has two types of transitions and carries action labels as well as state labels. As the paper shall explain, IM-SPDL is a very powerful logic in that it allows its user to specify requirements which are based on the probability measure of sets of execution paths, where regular expressions of actions and so-called tests are used to characterise the set of satisfying paths. The model checking of IM-SPDL time-bounded path formulae follows an automaton-based approach: From the requirement, a deterministic program automaton is constructed, and subsequently the product transition system between this automaton and the ESLTS is built and thereafter transformed into a continuous time Markov Chain (CTMC) on which numerical analysis is performed.

Related Work. In recent years, many efforts have been made to devise temporal logics for the specification of system properties in the area of performance analysis, where the underlying model is a labelled Markov chain. One result of these efforts is the logic CSL (continuous stochastic logic) [6], introduced by [3] and extended in [7] with an operator to reason about steady-state behaviour. CSL allows the specification of certain types of performability measures (cf. [5]), but the specification of these measures is completely state-oriented, i.e. based on atomic propositions. In [15] an action-based variant of CSL, called aCSL, was proposed, which is not based on atomic propositions but on sequences of named actions and therefore more suitable for action-oriented formalisms such as process algebras. In [14] it was shown how to employ the logic aCSL for performability modelling. A first combination of the state-oriented and action-oriented approach was the logic aCSL+ [22], where regular expressions of actions are used to characterise satisfying paths. In [18] we presented the first ideas of a stochastic extension of the logic PDL (SPDL) which also combines state-oriented and action-oriented features, and where paths can be specified via regular expressions of actions and so-called tests. The logic asCSL [4], inspired by the path-based reward variables of [23], follows a similar motivation. However, we emphasise the fact that the model to be checked by all logics mentioned in this paragraph is a labelled CTMC which is not allowed to contain immediate transitions.

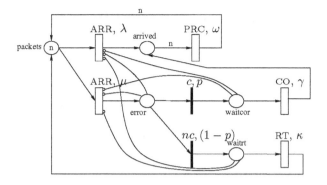

Fig. 1. GSPN-style model of a fault-tolerant packet collector

Organisation of the Paper. This paper is organised as follows: In Sec. 2, we introduce ESLTS, the class of models which we consider. Sec. 3 defines the syntax and semantics of the new logics IM-SPDL. In Sec. 4, we show how model checking of IM-SPDL path formulae can be carried out, by constructing a product transition system on which numerical analysis is performed. Sec. 5 presents some empirical results obtained from a prototype implementation. Finally, in Sec. 6 we summarise the results and give pointers to future research.

Example 1 (Running example: Fault-tolerant packet collector). Throughout this paper, we use the example of a fault-tolerant packet collector. Fig. 1 shows the GSPN-style specification of this simple system which has the following repeating behaviour: n data packets arrive independently, are stored, and then all n data packets are jointly processed. Arrivals can either be error-free (upper transition *ARR*, rate λ) or erroneous (lower transition *ARR*, rate μ). Rather unusual for GSPNs, there are two timed transitions bearing the same name, *ARR*, which expresses the fact that these transitions are not distinguishable by an observer. If a data packet contains an error, this error can be correctable (immediate transition c) with a certain probability p, or non-correctable (immediate transition nc) with the complementary probability. In the case of a correctable error, the error is corrected (transition *CO*) and more data packets can be received. If the error is non-correctable, the data packet has to be retransmitted (transition *RT*). During the processing of an erroneous packet, no new packet can arrive, which is modelled by the inhibitor arcs from places *error*, *waitcor*, and *waitrt* to the *ARR* transitions of the model. □

2 Model: Extended Stochastic Labelled Transition Systems

The model of the logic IM-SPDL is an extended stochastic labelled transition system (ESLTS). An ESLTS has two types of transitions, immediate and Markovian transitions. Immediate transitions are untimed transitions, whereas Markovian transitions are associated with an exponentially distributed delay.

Definition 1 (Extended Stochastic Labelled Transition System). An extended stochastic labelled transition system (ESLTS) is a quintuple $\mathcal{M} := (S, L, R_I, R_M, s)$, where:

- S is a finite set of states.
- $L : S \mapsto 2^{\mathsf{AP}}$ is the state labelling function that associates with every state $s \in S$ the set of atomic propositions which hold in that state. AP is the set of atomic propositions.
- $R_I : S \times \mathsf{Act}_I \times I\!P \times S$ is the immediate transition relation, where $I\!P = (0, 1]$. If $(s, a, p, s') \in R_I$, we write $s \overset{a,p}{\dashrightarrow} s'$. Act_I is a finite set of immediate action labels, i.e. actions, that are associated with immediate transitions, and $p \in I\!P$ is a probability. The probabilities associated with the immediate transitions leaving a particular state must sum up to 1 (provided that the state has at least one emanating immediate transition).
- $R_M : S \times \mathsf{Act}_M \times I\!R \times S$ is the Markovian transition relation. Act_M is a finite set of Markovian action labels, i.e. actions, that are associated with Markovian transitions. We require that $\mathsf{Act}_I \cap \mathsf{Act}_M = \emptyset$. If $(s, a, \lambda, s') \in R_M$, we write $s \overset{a,\lambda}{\longrightarrow} s'$.
- $s \in S$ is the unique initial state of $\mathcal{M}$.

Example 2 (ESLTS of packet collector). In Fig. 2, the ESLTS $\mathcal{M}$ for the packet collector GSPN from Fig. 1 is shown, where we assume that the number n of data packets that are to be processed is equal to four.

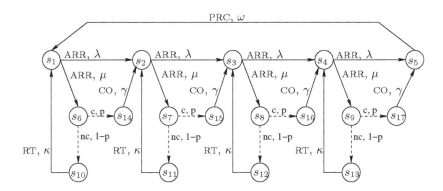

Fig. 2. ESLTS of the GSPN model for $n = 4$

The system has the following state labels:

$$L(s_5) = \{\mathsf{full}\}, \quad L(s_6) = ... = L(s_9) = \{\mathsf{error}\},$$
$$L(s_{10}) = ... = L(s_{13}) = \{\mathsf{waitrt}\}, \quad L(s_{14}) = ... = L(s_{17}) = \{\mathsf{waitcor}\}$$

The sets of immediate and Markovian actions are given as follows:

$$\mathsf{Act}_I := \{nc, c\}, \quad \mathsf{Act}_M := \{ARR, RT, CO, PRC\}$$

For example, transitions $s_6 \xdashrightarrow{nc,1-p} s_{10}$ and $s_6 \xdashrightarrow{c,p} s_{14}$ are immediate, whereas $s_1 \xrightarrow{ARR,\lambda} s_2$ and $s_{14} \xrightarrow{CO,\gamma} s_2$ are Markovian transitions. $\qquad\square$

Since an ESLTS may have two types of transitions, there are two types of states, vanishing and tangible states.

Definition 2 (Vanishing and tangible states). A state of an ESLTS is called *vanishing* if it possesses at least one outgoing immediate transition. Otherwise the state is called *tangible*.

A vanishing state is left as soon as it is entered, i.e. its sojourn time is zero. A tangible state has at least one outgoing Markovian, but no immediate transition (unless it is absorbing), therefore its sojourn time is governed by an exponential distribution whose rate parameter λ equals the sum of all the rates of the Markovian transitions emanating from that state. In the context of compositional modelling formalisms, such as stochastic process algebras, a further refinement of the notions of tangible/vanishing states is possible [26]. However, as our model checking approach is independent of any high-level modelling formalism, as long as the model to be checked is a single ESLTS which is considered in isolation, it suffices to distinguish between vanishing and tangible states.

Example 3. In Fig. 2 states s_6, s_7, s_8, and s_9 are vanishing, the remaining states are tangible. $\qquad\square$

For the semantics of the logic IM-SPDL, the following notion of a path is of great importance:

Definition 3 (Paths in $\mathcal{M}$). An infinite path σ of an ESLTS $\mathcal{M}$ is a sequence of transitions of the form $s_0 \xrightarrow{a_0,t_0} s_1 \xrightarrow{a_1,t_1} s_2 \ldots$ where:

- $t_i = \tau(\sigma,i) \in \mathbb{R}_{\geq 0}$ is the real-valued sojourn time in s_i before passing to s_{i+1}.
- if $a_i \in \mathsf{Act}_M$, then $\exists \lambda : (s_i, a_i, \lambda, s_{i+1}) \in R_M$ and $t_i > 0$ is the sojourn time in state s_i (i.e. t_i is the value drawn from an exponential distribution).
- if $a_i \in \mathsf{Act}_I$, then $\exists p : (s_i, a_i, p, s_{i+1}) \in R_I$ and $t_i = 0$ is the sojourn time in state s_i.
- $\sigma[i]$ is the $(i+1)$st state on path σ.
- $\sigma@t$ is the state at time point t.
- $a[i]$ is the $(i+1)$st action on path σ.

A finite path σ is a finite sequence of transitions of the form: $s_0 \xrightarrow{a_0,t_0} s_1 \xrightarrow{a_1,t_1} s_2 \ldots s_{n-1} \xrightarrow{a_{n-1},t_{n-1}} s_n$, where s_n is an absorbing state. For a finite path, $\tau(\sigma,i)$ is defined for $i < n$ as for infinite paths, and for $i = n$ we define $\tau(\sigma,i) = \infty$. The set $\mathsf{PATH}^{\mathcal{M}}(s) := \{\sigma \mid \sigma[0] = s\}$ is the set of all finite or infinite paths with initial state s.

3   Syntax and Semantics of IM-SPDL

The logic IM-SPDL is a stochastic extension of PDL [11], a multi-modal program logic. Beside the standard ingredients such as propositional logic and the modal ◇-operator ("possibly"), PDL enriches the ◇-operator with so-called regular programs which are basically regular expressions of actions and tests (cf. Def. 5 below). If Φ and Ψ are PDL formulae and ρ is a program, then $\Phi \vee \Psi$, $\neg\Phi$ and $\langle\rho\rangle\Psi$ are formulae. $\langle\rho\rangle\Psi$ means that it is possible to execute program ρ, thereby ending up in a state that satisfies Ψ.

With respect to PDL we have added the following operators to obtain IM-SPDL: A path operator that extends the original PDL $\langle.\rangle$-operator by specifying time bounds within which the Ψ state has to be reached, a probabilistic path quantifier $\mathcal{P}_{\bowtie p}$ to reason about the transient probabilistic behaviour of a system, and a steady-state operator $\mathcal{S}_{\bowtie p}$ to reason about the behaviour of the system once stationarity of the underlying Markov chain is reached.

3.1   Syntax of IM-SPDL

The formulae of IM-SPDL are formally defined as follows:

Definition 4 (Syntax of IM-SPDL). Let $p \in [0,1]$ be a probability and $q \in \mathsf{AP}$ an atomic proposition and $\bowtie \in \{\leq, <, \geq, >\}$ a comparison operator. The state formulae Φ of SPDL are defined as follows:

$$\Phi := q \big| \Phi \vee \Phi \big| \neg\Phi \big| \mathcal{S}_{\bowtie p}(\Phi) \big| \mathcal{P}_{\bowtie p}(\phi) \big| (\Phi)$$

Path formulae ϕ are defined by:

$$\phi := \Phi[\rho]^I \Phi$$

where Φ is a state formula as defined above, and I is the closed time interval $[t, t']$ of the real axis. The symbol ρ represents a program as defined by Def. 5.

Definition 5 (Programs). Let $\mathsf{Act} = \mathsf{Act}_I \cup \mathsf{Act}_M$ be a set of actions, which are also called atomic programs, and TEST be a set of IM-SPDL state formulae. A program ρ is defined by the following grammar:

$$\rho := \epsilon \big| \Phi?; a \big| \rho; \rho \big| \rho \cup \rho \big| \rho^* \big| \Phi?; \rho \big| (\rho)$$

where $\epsilon \notin \mathsf{Act}$ is the empty program, $a \in \mathsf{Act}$ and $\Phi \in \mathsf{TEST}$.

The operators ; (sequential composition), $\cup$ (choice), and $*$ (Kleene star) have their usual meaning. The operator $\Phi?; \rho$ (resp. $\Phi?; a$) is the so-called test operator (also called guard operator). Its informal semantics is as follows: Test whether Φ holds in the current state of the model. If this is the case, then execute program ρ, otherwise ρ is not executable. Def. 5 requires that every atomic program is preceded by a test formula Φ, but this can be the trivial test (i.e. $\Phi = \mathsf{true}$). From standard automata theory it is known that regular expressions coincide with regular languages, i.e. sets of words that are generated according to the rules of regular expressions. Programs as defined in Def. 5 can be seen as regular expressions over the alphabet $\Sigma = \mathsf{TEST} \times (\mathsf{Act} \cup \epsilon)$. Words that are generated from programs in IM-SPDL will be referred to as *program instances*. The set of these program instances is called, as before, a language.

The length of a program instance r, denoted by $|r|$, is the number of elements from Σ occuring in it. For $0 \leq i < |r|$, $r[i]$ is the $(i+1)$st element of r. $TF(r[i])$ denotes the test formula part of $r[i]$, and $Act(r[i])$ denotes the action part of $r[i]$.

Example 4 (Programs and program instances). Let $\mathsf{Act} = \mathsf{Act}_I \cup \mathsf{Act}_M$ as in Ex. 2 be the set of atomic programs, and $\mathsf{TEST} = \{\mathsf{error}, \mathsf{full}, ..., \neg\mathsf{error}, \neg\mathsf{full}, ...\}$ the set of test formulae. Using the grammar from Def. 5, possible programs are[1]

$$\rho_1 = ARR; (\neg\mathsf{error}?; ARR)^*; c; CO; ARR^* \text{ and}$$
$$\rho_2 = (\neg\mathsf{full}?; ARR); c; CO; (\mathsf{full}?; \epsilon).$$

Some program instances of ρ_1 are:

$$q = ARR; c; CO; ARR; ARR,$$
$$r = ARR; (\neg\mathsf{error}?; ARR); c; CO \text{ and}$$
$$s = ARR; (\neg\mathsf{error}?; ARR); (\neg\mathsf{error}?; ARR); c; CO; ARR.$$

For r it holds that $|r| = 4$, $Act(r[1]) = ARR$ and $TF(r[1]) = \neg\mathsf{error}$.   □

3.2 Semantics of IM-SPDL

Before we give the formal semantics of IM-SPDL, we provide an informal explanation. The meaning of negation $(\neg\Phi)$ and disjunction $(\Phi \vee \Psi)$ is as usual. $\mathcal{S}_{\bowtie p}(\Phi)$ asserts that the steady-state probability of the set of Φ-states, i.e. the probability to reside in a Φ-state once the system has reached stationarity, satisfies the boundary as given by $\bowtie p$. $\mathcal{P}_{\bowtie p}(\phi)$ asserts that the probability measure of the paths that satisfy ϕ is within the bounds as given by $\bowtie p$. Path formula $\Phi[\rho]^{[t,t']}\Psi$ means that a state that satisfies Ψ is reached within at least t but at most t' time units, and that all preceding states must satisfy Φ. Additionally, the action sequence of the path to the Ψ state must correspond to the action sequence of a word from the language $\mathcal{L}_\rho$ (the language induced by program ρ) and all test formulae that are part of program ρ must be satisfied by the corresponding states on the path.

Definition 6 (State probabilities). The probability to be in state s' at time point t, provided that the system is in state s at time 0, is given by

$$\pi^{\mathcal{M}}(s, s', t) = Pr\{\sigma \in \mathsf{PATH}^{\mathcal{M}}(s) | \sigma@t = s'\}$$

The set of paths $\{\sigma \in \mathsf{PATH}^{\mathcal{M}}(s) | \sigma@t = s'\}$ is measurable (see [6]), and Pr denotes this probability measure.

---

[1] For better readability we often omit the trivial test formula, i.e. we write a instead of $(true?; a)$.

The definition for steady-state probabilities is similar, taking into account that steady-state means 'on the long run':

$$\pi^{\mathcal{M}}(s, s') = lim_{t \to \infty} \pi^{\mathcal{M}}(s, s', t)$$

These definitions can be extended to sets of states: For $S' \subseteq S$:

$$\pi^{\mathcal{M}}(s, S', t) := \sum_{s' \in S'} \pi^{\mathcal{M}}(s, s', t) \quad \text{and} \quad \pi^{\mathcal{M}}(s, S') := \sum_{s' \in S'} \pi^{\mathcal{M}}(s, s').$$

We are now ready to give the formal semantics of IM-SPDL.

Definition 7 (Semantics of IM-SPDL). The semantics of state formulae is defined as follows:

$$\mathcal{M}, s \models q \Longleftrightarrow q \in L(s)$$
$$\mathcal{M}, s \models \neg\Phi \Longleftrightarrow \mathcal{M}, s \not\models \Phi$$
$$\mathcal{M}, s \models (\Phi \vee \Psi) \Longleftrightarrow \mathcal{M}, s \models \Phi \text{ or } \mathcal{M}, s \models \Psi$$
$$\mathcal{M}, s \models \mathcal{S}_{\bowtie p}(\Phi) \Longleftrightarrow \pi^{\mathcal{M}}(s, Sat(\Phi)) \bowtie p$$
$$\mathcal{M}, s \models \mathcal{P}_{\bowtie p}(\phi) \Longleftrightarrow Prob^{\mathcal{M}}(s, \phi) \bowtie p$$

$Sat(\Phi)$ is the set of states that satisfy Φ, and $Prob^{\mathcal{M}}(s, \phi)$ is the probability measure of all paths $\sigma \in \mathsf{PATH}(s)$ that satisfy ϕ:

$$Prob^{\mathcal{M}}(s, \phi) := Pr\{\sigma \in \mathsf{PATH}^{\mathcal{M}}(s) | \mathcal{M}, \sigma \models \phi\}$$

For the semantics of path formulae we have to relate the instances of the program ρ to words on paths in the ESLTS $\mathcal{M}$.

Definition 8 (Words on paths). The word $\mathcal{W}^k$ of length $k \geq 0$ on a path $\sigma \in \mathsf{PATH}^{\mathcal{M}}$ is defined as follows:

$$\mathcal{W}^0(\sigma) := \epsilon$$
$$\mathcal{W}^k(\sigma) := \mathcal{W}^{k-1}(\sigma) \circ a[k-1]$$

$$\text{where} \quad a[k-1] \in \mathsf{Act}_M \wedge \sigma[k-1] \xrightarrow{a[k-1], t_{k-1}} \sigma[k] \quad \text{or}$$

$$a[k-1] \in \mathsf{Act}_I \wedge \sigma[k-1] \xrightarrow{a[k-1], 0} \sigma[k].$$

For $i = 0, 1, \ldots, k-1$, $\mathcal{W}^k(\sigma)[i]$ denotes the $i + 1$st action on path σ.

Example 5. Consider a path $\sigma := s_1 \xrightarrow{ARR, t_1} s_6 \xrightarrow{c, 0} s_{14} \xrightarrow{CO, t_2} s_2 \xrightarrow{ARR, t_3} \ldots$ of the ESLTS from Fig. 2. The word of length 2 induced by σ is (ARR, c), the word of length 4 is (ARR, c, CO, ARR) and $\mathcal{W}^4(\sigma)[2] = CO$. $\square$

Definition 9 (Semantics of path formulae). The semantics of path formulae is defined as follows:

$$\mathcal{M}, \sigma \models \Phi[\rho]^{[t, t']}\Psi \iff \exists k \big(\mathcal{M}, \sigma[k] \models \Psi \wedge \forall 0 \leq i < k(\mathcal{M}, \sigma[i] \models \Phi)$$
$$\wedge \quad time\_restriction$$
$$\wedge \quad program\_matching\big)$$

The first line states that there must be a state $\sigma[k]$ that satisfies Ψ and that all preceding states must satisfy Φ. The formula *time_restriction* is defined as follows:

$$time\_restriction :=$$

(1) $\left((t = 0 \wedge \sum_{i=0}^{k-1} t_i \leq t') \vee\right.$

(2) $\left(t \neq 0 \wedge ((t \leq \sum_{i=0}^{k-1} t_i \leq t') \vee (\sum_{i=0}^{k-1} t_i < t \wedge \sum_{i=0}^{k} t_i > t \wedge \sigma[k] \models \Phi)))\right)$

It expresses the restrictions stemming from the time bounds that are imposed on paths. In line (1), if the lower time bound is zero, then the only requirement is to reach a Ψ-state before more than t' time units have passed. Line (2) covers the case where the lower time bound is greater than zero. In this case, either the entry time into state $\sigma[k]$ must lie within the interval $[t, t']$, or if the entry time is less than t, then the sojourn time in $\sigma[k]$ plus the sojourn times in the previous states must be greater than t. The formula *program_matching* is defined as follows:

$$program\_matching :=$$

(1) $(\exists r \in \mathcal{L}(\rho) \wedge |r| = k \wedge Act(r[k-1]) \neq \epsilon \wedge$

    $\forall 0 \leq i \leq k-1(Act(r[i]) = \mathcal{W}^{(k)}(\sigma)[i] \wedge \mathcal{M}, \sigma[i] \models TF(r[i]))) \vee$

(2) $(\exists r \in \mathcal{L}(\rho) \wedge |r| = k+1 \wedge Act(r[k]) = \epsilon \wedge \sigma[k] \models TF(r[k]) \wedge$

    $\forall 0 \leq i \leq k-1(Act(r[i]) = \mathcal{W}^{(k)}(\sigma)[i] \wedge \mathcal{M}, \sigma[i] \models TF(r[i])))$

This formula expresses that the word induced on path σ must be matched by the corresponding action parts of a program instance r and that the tests appearing in the program must be satisfied by the appropriate states on the path. There are two possibilities, as indicated in the formula: (1) If the last element of r is of the form $\Phi?; a$, where $a \neq \epsilon$, the corresponding state must satisfy the test formula and the last transition on the path must have a label identical to the action part of $r[k-1]$. (2) If the last element of r is of the form $\Phi?; \epsilon$, i.e. has an empty action part, then it only has to be checked whether the corresponding state on the path satisfies the test formula.

Example 6 (IM-SPDL formulae). With respect to the ESLTS $\mathcal{M}$ of Fig. 2 we specify four example requirements:

- Is the probability to receive four data packets with at most one packet containing a non-correctable error within 5 time units greater than 0.9?

$$\Phi_1 := \mathcal{P}_{>0.9}(\neg full \, [ARR^*; nc; RT; ARR^* \cup ARR^*]^{[0,5]} \, full)$$

- Is the probability to reach a state in which the buffer is full with a single arrival greater than zero?

$$\Phi_2 := \mathcal{P}_{>0}(\neg full \, [ARR]^{[0,\infty]} \, full)$$

Requirement Φ_2 characterises state s_4.

– Is the probability that the buffer is full after at most 7.3 time units greater than 75 percent, if the following side conditions must be met: The only packet that contains an error is the fourth packet. This error must be correctable.

$$\Phi_3 := \mathcal{P}_{>0.75}(\text{true } [ARR^*; (\Phi_2?; ARR); c; CO]^{[0,7.3]} \text{ true})$$

– In steady-state, is the probability that the system is currently processing either a correctable or a non-correctable error, less than 3%?

$$\Phi_4 := \mathcal{S}_{<0.03}(\text{waitcor} \vee \text{waitrt}) \qquad \qquad \square$$

4   Model Checking IM-SPDL

In this section, we describe the model checking algorithm for the logic IM-SPDL. Central for this are the notions of program automata and product transition systems which we introduce in the sequel. Due to restricted space we will only describe the general idea of how to model check IM-SPDL path formulae, full details can be found in [19].

4.1   General Idea

The overall model checking algorithm for IM-SPDL is similar to that of CTL in the sense that we start by checking elementary subformulae and then proceed to the checking of more and more complex subformulae until the overall formula has been checked. Model checking propositional logic subformulae works as for CTL. Steady-state subformulae are checked in three steps as follows:

1. The ESLTS $\mathcal{M}$ is transformed into a state-labelled CTMC $\mathcal{M}'$, by eliminating the vanishing states, as described, for instance, in [2].
2. On $\mathcal{M}'$, model checking the steady-state operator works as for CSL [6]. Step 2 yields the verification results for the tangible states only.
3. During step 1, for each vanishing state the probability to reach a certain tangible state as the next tangible state is recorded. These probabilities are now combined with the results of step 2 in order to obtain the verification results for the vanishing states.

The basic model checking procedure for IM-SPDL path formulae with leading $\mathcal{P}_{\bowtie p}$ operator is more involved: We assume that we want to check whether state s of a given ESLTS $\mathcal{M}$ satisfies the formula $\mathcal{P}_{\bowtie p}(\phi)$, where $\phi = \Phi[\rho]^{[t,t']}\Psi$. The basic idea is to reduce the IM-SPDL model checking problem $\mathcal{M}, s \models \mathcal{P}_{\bowtie p}(\phi)$ to the CSL model checking problem of deciding whether $\mathcal{M}^*, s^* \models \mathcal{P}_{\bowtie p}(\mathsf{F}^{[t,t']}\mathsf{succ})$ for a CTMC $\mathcal{M}^*$ (to be constructed) and a state s^* of $\mathcal{M}^*$. A path satisfies the CSL path formula $\mathsf{F}^{[t,t']}\mathsf{succ}$, if within the time interval $[t,t']$ a state is reached that satisfies the new atomic proposition succ. We take the following steps:

1. From the program ρ we derive a deterministic program automaton $\mathcal{A}_\rho$, which is a variant of deterministic finite automata.
2. Using the given ESLTS $\mathcal{M}$ and the program automaton $\mathcal{A}_\rho$, we construct a product ESLTS (PESLTS) $\mathcal{M}^\times$. The state space of $\mathcal{M}^\times$ is the product between $\mathcal{M}$ and $\mathcal{A}_\rho$, i.e. states are of the form (s_i, z_i), where s_i is a state of $\mathcal{M}$ and z_i a state of $\mathcal{A}_\rho$. In addition, $\mathcal{M}^\times$ contains an absorbing error state with the new state label fail. The transitions in $\mathcal{M}^\times$ are labelled with rates in the case of Markovian transitions and with probabilities in the case of immediate transitions. The purpose of building this PESLTS is to check whether $\phi = \Phi[\rho]^{[t,t']}\Psi$ is functionally satisfiable in $\mathcal{M}$ or not.
3. In order to compute the probability measure of the paths satisfying ϕ we proceed as follows:
   (a) All states (s_i, z_i) of $\mathcal{M}^\times$ for which s_i is a Ψ-state and z_i is an accepting state are replaced by a single absorbing goal state, with the special state label succ (for "success"). All transitions leading to a state (s_j, z_j) of the kind just described are redirected to this succ-state.
   (b) The PESLTS $\mathcal{M}^\times$ is transformed into a CTMC $\mathcal{M}^*$ by eliminating vanishing states as in [2].
4. On $\mathcal{M}^*$ we can compute the probability measure of all paths satisfying the CSL formula $\mathcal{P}_{\bowtie p}(\mathsf{F}^{[t,t']}\mathsf{succ})$, which is equivalent to the probability measure of the paths satisfying the original formula $\mathcal{P}_{\bowtie p}(\phi)$ in the original model $\mathcal{M}$.

4.2 Program Automata

According to Sec. 4.1 we have to derive an automaton from a given program ρ. This is done by the following steps:

- At first, we construct from ρ a non-deterministic program automaton (NPA) $\mathcal{N}_\rho$. The definition of NPA is identical to that of non-deterministic finite automata as known from standard automata theory, albeit with special input alphabet Σ as introduced above in Sec. 3.1.
- Secondly, we turn $\mathcal{N}_\rho$ into a deterministic program automaton (DPA) $\mathcal{A}_\rho$. DPAs are formally defined in Def. 10. From this definition, it follows that the determinisation of an NPA is quite different from making a non-deterministic finite automaton deterministic. We will exemplify and justify our approach in example 7.

Definition 10 (Deterministic program automaton DPA). A DPA $\mathcal{A}$ is a quintuple $(Z_\mathcal{A}, \Sigma_\mathcal{A}, z^{Start}, E_\mathcal{A}, \delta_\mathcal{A})$ where

- $Z_\mathcal{A}$ is a finite set of states,
- $\Sigma_\mathcal{A} = \mathsf{TEST} \times (\mathsf{Act} \cup \epsilon)$ is the input alphabet,
- $z_\mathcal{A}^{Start} \in Z_\mathcal{A}$ is the initial state,
- $E_\mathcal{A} \subseteq Z_\mathcal{A}$ is the set of accepting states and
- $\delta_\mathcal{A} : Z_\mathcal{A} \times \Sigma_\mathcal{A} \to Z_\mathcal{A}$ is the state transition function which has to satisfy the following condition: If a state z possesses more than one outgoing transition then, either the action parts of the labellings of all outgoing transitions must

be pairwise different, or if there are two or more transitions whose action parts are identical, then the test formula parts of them must not be true at the same time.

Our model checking approach relies on the following theorem:

Theorem 1. *For every NPA, an equivalent DPA can be constructed.*

Although Theorem 1 seems quite obvious, it should be noted that its proof [16] is not the same as the equivalence proof of deterministic and non-deterministic finite automata from standard automata theory, since the input symbols have both a test part and an action part, and during determinisation the semantics of the test part must be taken into account. Instead of a formal proof of Theorem 1, we consider the following illustrative example:

Example 7 (NPA and DPA). Fig. 3 shows a non-deterministic program automaton $\mathcal{N}_\rho$ for the program $\rho = ARR^*; (\Phi_2?; ARR); c; CO$ (taken from Ex. 6, requirement Φ_3). The automaton is non-deterministic since the arcs emanating from state A, labelled with ARR (which is equivalent to $(true?; ARR)$) and $(\Phi_2?; ARR)$, have identical action label and the test parts are not disjoint. We cannot directly use such a non-deterministic automaton for our model checking algorithm, as the product construction explained in Sec. 4.3 could modify the stochastic behaviour of $\mathcal{M}$ and thus lead to wrong numerical results. Therefore we first construct a deterministic program automaton $\mathcal{A}_\rho$, which is shown in Fig 4. In $\mathcal{A}_\rho$, no two transitions are activated at the same time. This determinisation guarantees that the product automaton will preserve the branching structure and therefore the stochastic behaviour of $\mathcal{M}$.   □

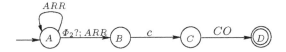

Fig. 3. Non-deterministic program automaton $\mathcal{N}_\rho$ for the program of Φ_3

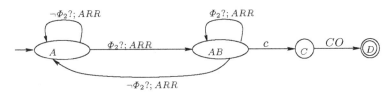

Fig. 4. Deterministic program automaton $\mathcal{A}_\rho$ for the program of Φ_3

4.3   Product ESLTS Construction and Analysis

The central part of model checking probabilistic path formulae is the construction of the PESLTS of the model $\mathcal{M}$ and the DPA $\mathcal{A}_\rho$ for the program ρ of the path formula that is to be checked. In this section, we describe by means of an example how this PESLTS is generated.

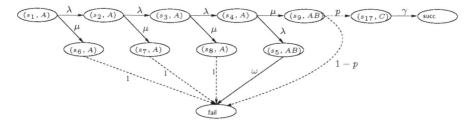

Fig. 5. Product ESLTS $\mathcal{M}^\times$

Example 8 (Constructing the PESLTS). Let the ESLTS $\mathcal{M}$ from Fig. 2 and the DPA $\mathcal{A}_\rho$, shown in Fig. 4, be given. We now explain by example, how their PESLTS $\mathcal{M}^\times$, shown in Fig. 5, is constructed:

- The combinations of the transitions $s_1 \xrightarrow{ARR,\lambda} s_2$ in $\mathcal{M}$ and $A \xrightarrow{\neg\Phi_2?;ARR} A$ in $\mathcal{A}_\rho$ leads to the transition $(s_1, A) \xrightarrow{\lambda} (s_2, A)$ in $\mathcal{M}^\times$.

- In $\mathcal{M}$, transition $s_1 \xrightarrow{ARR,\mu} s_6$ is also possible, therefore $\mathcal{M}^\times$ also has the transition $(s_1, A) \xrightarrow{\mu} (s_6, A)$.

- Transition $(s_9, AB) \overset{p}{\dashrightarrow} (s_{17}, C)$ in $\mathcal{M}^\times$ stems from the transition $s_9 \overset{c,p}{\dashrightarrow} s_{17}$ in $\mathcal{M}$ and $AB \xrightarrow{c} C$ in $\mathcal{A}_\rho$.

- Transition $(s_6, A) \overset{1}{\dashrightarrow}$ fail is composed of the transitions $s_6 \overset{c,p}{\dashrightarrow} s_{14}$ and $s_6 \overset{nc,1-p}{\dashrightarrow} s_{10}$ in $\mathcal{M}$, since in state A neither a c nor an nc transition is possible. Therefore in $\mathcal{M}^\times$ we obtain the transitions $(s_6, A) \overset{p}{\dashrightarrow}$ fail and $(s_6, A) \overset{1-p}{\dashrightarrow}$ fail which can be replaced by a single immediate transition that has probability one.

- In state C there is a transition $C \xrightarrow{CO} D$, where D is an accepting state, and in $\mathcal{M}$ there is a transition $s_{17} \xrightarrow{CO,\gamma} s_5$. In $\mathcal{M}^\times$ this leads to transition $(s_{17}, C) \xrightarrow{\gamma}$ succ, which stems from the fact that the automaton goal state D is accepting and that the goal state s_5 of the ESLTS satisfies $\Psi = \text{true}$, i.e. state (s_5, D) satisfies the conditions of Sec. 4.1, item 3(a). □

After the product ESLTS $\mathcal{M}^\times$ has been constructed, its vanishing states are eliminated. We explain this elimination by means of the example:

Example 9 (Elimination of vanishing states). Let the PESLTS $\mathcal{M}^\times$ from Fig. 5 be given. The vanishing states (s_6, A), (s_7, A), (s_8, A) and (s_9, AB) are eliminated, thereby redirecting their incoming arcs to the respective successor states[2] and weighing them with the corresponding probabilities. This leads to the labelled CTMC $\mathcal{M}^*$ shown in Fig. 6. □

---

[2] In general, sequences and even cycles of immediate transitions are possible, which situation can be handled by several published elimination algorithms.

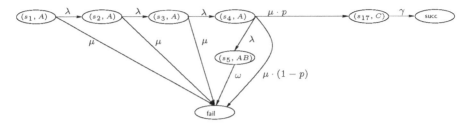

Fig. 6. $\mathcal{M}^*$: Result of the elimination of vanishing states

4.4 Complexity

It is known that the time complexity of model checking CSL is linear in the number of transitions of the model, the uniformisation rate (determined by the largest exit rate of any state of the model), and the involved time bound [6]. For model checking IM-SPDL probabilistic path formulae, a product transition system must be constructed first whose size, in the worst case, is the product of the original model and the program automaton at hand. However, in spite of this potential blow-up of the state space, in most practical cases (like the ones in Sec. 5) the product transition system remains small (even smaller than the original model), since the program automaton typically restricts the possible behaviour of the original model and only the reachable portion of the product transition system needs to be constructed.

5 Empirical Results

This section presents empirical results of model checking IM-SPDL requirements, obtained with the help of the tool CASPA [20] which we have recently extended by model checking features.

5.1 The Tool CASPA

In CASPA the system to be checked is specified with the help of a stochastic process algebra (SPA) language, which is augmented by constructs for describing performability requirements as well as classical performance and dependability measures. Fig. 7 shows the building blocks of CASPA and their interaction. CASPA is a fully symbolic model checker, i.e. it relies completely on multi-terminal binary decision diagrams (MTBDDs), both for representing the transition system and for implementing the verification algorithms. In our experience, MTBDDs are superior to explicit representations in that they enable the compact storage of very large state spaces, where the symbolic representation of the ESLTS from the SPA specification can be generated very efficiently [17]. The use of MTBDDs thus enables the generation and storage of state spaces whose sizes are prohibitive in the case of explicit storage schemes. Using extensions of MTBDDs and efficient algorithms for numerical analysis, as implemented in the tool PRISM [21], it is possible to analyse very large systems.

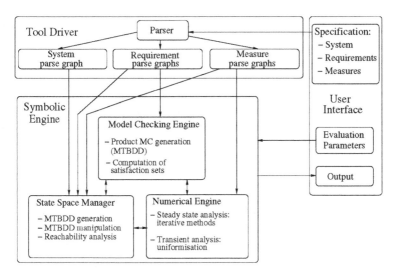

Fig. 7. Architecture of CASPA

5.2   Case Studies

Fault-Tolerant Packet Collector. We check the path-based requirements Φ_1 and Φ_3 from Ex. 6. Table 1 shows the model checking times[3] for different values of the model parameter n. Columns "States $\mathcal{M}^*$" denote the number of states of the final transition system $\mathcal{M}^*$, obtained by eliminating the vanishing states from the respective product transition system $\mathcal{M}^\times$. For the model checking of Φ_1 and Φ_3, most of the time is needed for generating the product ESLTS, since the times for constructing the DPA and for eliminating the vanishing states were found to be negligible.

For Φ_1 the number of states for the PESLTS is about half the number of states of the original model because the requirement states that either all packets should be error-free or at most one packet may contain an incorrectable error. Likewise, we observe that for Φ_3 the number of states of the PESLTS is also smaller than for the original model. This is due to the fact that we are only interested in the paths that result from a single correctable error that occurs in the last packet to be received. This restricts the number of states, as all other transitions not being labelled with the appropriate actions in the respective states can be redirected to a single absorbing error state.

According to Table 1, the numerical analysis (N.A.) times are small compared to the generation times. However, model checking of Φ_1 consumes more time than that of Φ_3 because the number of states of the PESLTS is larger for Φ_1 (but the construction times for both PESLTSs are roughly the same).

Kanban System. The Kanban manufacturing system was first described as a generalised stochastic Petri net in [9]. We consider a Kanban system with four

---

[3] All execution times are given in seconds, measured on a 3.0 GHz Pentium IV with 1GB of memory, running SuSe Linux 9.0.

Table 1. Model checking statistics for fault-tolerant packet collector for Φ_1 and Φ_3

n:	States:	Φ_1			Φ_3		
		States $\mathcal{M}^*$:	Gen. Time:	N.A. Time:	States $\mathcal{M}^*$:	Gen. Time:	N.A. Time:
5,000	20,001	10,002	1.69	0.32	5,003	1.80	0.11
15,000	60,001	30,002	6.09	1.08	15,003	6.70	0.32
30,000	120,001	60,002	13.72	2.20	30,003	14.59	0.68
50,000	200,001	100,002	25.88	3.57	50,003	28.12	1.16

cells, a single type of Kanban cards and the possibility that some workpieces may need to be reworked (i.e. moved back to the same cell).

The Kanban system demonstrates the usefulness of symbolic data structures for representing large state spaces. Table 2 gives the model statistics, where the scaling parameter n denotes the number of Kanban cards. For $n = 12$ and a reachable state space of more than 5.5 billion states only $32,324$ MTBDD nodes are required. Generating the state space from the given SPA specification and restricting it to its reachable portion takes only about 17 seconds in the case of $n = 12$. Consider the following requirements (only textual definitions are given):

- Φ_1: The probability, that within t time units a single workpiece needs exactly three reworks, should be below p.
- Φ_2: The requirement, that a job needs three reworks in the first cell and zero reworks in the second cell within a given time bound, should be satisfied with a probability of p?
- Φ_3 : The steady-state probability that cell 3 or 4 is blocked, i.e. the maximum number of Kanban cards is reached, should be below p.

From the results given in Table 3 we observe that for requirements Φ_1 and Φ_2 the state space of the PESLTS is dramatically smaller than that of the original system, which stems from the fact that in both cases only very specific paths in the system are of interest. The table also gives the generation time for the PESLTS for Φ_1 and Φ_2 with varying n. For Φ_3 the state space size is the same as for the original model, since in the case of a steady-state requirement no PESLTS has to be generated. For Φ_1 and Φ_2 the numerical analysis time is small compared to the generation time (because the size of the PESLTS is very small). For Φ_3

Table 2. Model statistics for the Kanban system

n:	States:	Transitions:	Model Gen. Time:	MTBDD Nodes:
5	2,546,432	2.446e+07	0.42	5,392
6	11,261,376	1.15709e+08	0.94	8,086
7	41,644,800	4.45046e+09	1.59	10,389
10	1,005,927,208	1.20322e+10	8.37	23,245
11	2,435,541,472	2.98062e+10	12.90	27,425
12	5,519,907,575	6.88839e+10	17.22	32,324

Table 3. Model checking statistics for Kanban for Φ_1 to Φ_3

n:	Φ_1			Φ_2			Φ_3	
	States $\mathcal{M}^*$:	Gen. Time :	N.A. Time:	States $\mathcal{M}^*$:	Gen. Time:	N.A. Time:	Gen. Time:	N.A. Time:
5	44	0.39	$< 10^{-6}$	42	0.19	$< 10^{-6}$	0.42	164
6	53	0.91	$< 10^{-6}$	53	0.93	$< 10^{-6}$	0.94	1093
7	62	1.71	$< 10^{-6}$	54	1.91	$< 10^{-6}$	1.59	75,600
10	89	7.76	0.01	108	7.71	0.03	8.37	–
11	98	12.88	0.03	119	11.46	0.04	12.90	–
12	107	16.03	0.05	130	17.89	0.09	17.22	–

Table 4. Model checking statistics for FTMCS for Φ

Config.:	States:	Φ		
		States $\mathcal{M}^*$:	Gen. Time:	N.A. Time:
C1	753,664	4,098	0.06	0.02
C2	2,152	33	0.02	$< 10^{-6}$
C3	889	11	0.01	$< 10^{-6}$
C4	123,760	134	0.03	0.01

numerical analysis for the cases $n \geq 10$ was not feasible (indicated by "–" in the table), since the allocation of a solution vector in main memory for more than one billion states is not possible on a common workstation, not to speak of the solution time.

Fault-Tolerant Multi Computer System (FTMCS). This computer system, originally described in [24], comes in different configurations, thereby achieving different degrees of fault-tolerance (due to the replication of certain components). For example, configuration $C1$ has three computers and three memory modules of which at least one must be operational for the entire system to be operational. Requirement Φ which we check here, a time-bounded probabilistic path formula, describes a system failure which is only due to memory failures, no failures of other components shall contribute to this situation. Table 4 shows that, for all considered configurations, the state space size of $\mathcal{M}^*$ is very small compared to the size of the system, since only a very restricted number of paths is of interest, such that many transitions are redirected to the absorbing failure state.

6   Conclusions and Future Work

In this paper, we have introduced the logic IM-SPDL, a state- and action-oriented logic whose semantic model contains both Markovian and immediate transitions. We have shown how the model checking of IM-SPDL path formulae can be carried out with the help of a product transition system construction. The papers also presented some empirical results, obtained with our tool CASPA, which showed the feasibility and efficiency of the proposed method in spite of the theoretical worst-case complexity of the model checking algorithm.

As future work, it would be interesting to check whether the validity of IM-SPDL is invariant with respect to some notion of bisimulation, as is the case for other stochastic temporal logics. Such a result would enable reductions of the state space prior to model checking, which could be of great value, in particular in connection with compositional model checking approaches. We also plan to extend IM-SPDL with random time bounds, i.e. we intend to replace the fixed time bounds by time bounds whose value is drawn from a random variable.

References

1. M. Ajmone Marsan, G. Balbo, and G. Conte. A Class of Generalized Stochastic Petri Nets for the Performance Evaluation of Multiprocessor Systems. *ACM Transactions on Computer Systems*, 2(2):93–122, May 1984.
2. M. Ajmone Marsan, G. Balbo, G. Conte, S. Donatelli, and G. Franceschinis. *Modelling with Generalized Stochastic Petri Nets*. Wiley, 1995.
3. A. Aziz, K. Sanwal, V. Singhal, and R. Brayton. Verifying continuous time Markov chains. In R. Alur and T.A. Henzinger, editors, *Computer-Aided Verification*, volume LNCS 1102, pages 146–162. Springer, 1996.
4. C. Baier, L. Cloth, B. Haverkort, M. Kuntz, and M. Siegle. Model Checking Action- and State-labelled Markov Chains. In *Int. Conf. on Dependable Systems and Networks: Performance and Dependability Symposium*, pages 701–710. IEEE Computer Society Press, 2004.
5. C. Baier, B. Haverkort, H. Hermanns, and J.-P. Katoen. On the logical characterisation of performability properties. In *ICALP*, pages 780–792. Springer, LNCS 1853, 2000.
6. C. Baier, B. Haverkort, H. Hermanns, and J.P. Katoen. Model-Checking Algorithms for Continuous-Time Markov Chains. *IEEE Trans. Software Eng.*, 29(7):1–18, July 2003.
7. C. Baier, J.-P. Katoen, and H. Hermanns. Approximate Symbolic Model Checking of Continuous-Time Markov Chains. In J.C.M. Baeten and S. Mauw, editors, *Conurrency Theory*, volume LNCS 1664, pages 146–162. Springer, 1999.
8. M. Bernardo and R. Gorrieri. A Tutorial on EMPA: A Theory of Concurrent Processes with Nondeterminism, Priorities, Probabilities and Time. *Theoretical Computer Science*, 202:1–54, 1998.
9. G. Ciardo and M. Tilgner. On the use of Kronecker operators for the solution of generalized stochastic Petri nets. Technical Report 96-35, ICASE, 1996.
10. D. Deavours, G. Clark, T. Courtney, D. Daly, S. Derisavi, J. Doyle, W.H. Sanders, and P. Webster. The Moebius Framework and its Implementation. *IEEE Transactions on Software Engineering*, 28(10):956–969, 2002.
11. M. Fischer and R. Ladner. Propositional dynamic logic of regular programs. *J. Comput. System Sci.*, 18:194–211, 1979.
12. H. Hermanns. *Interactive Markov Chains and the Quest for Quantified Quality*. Springer, LNCS 2428, 2002.
13. H. Hermanns, U. Herzog, U. Klehmet, V. Mertsiotakis, and M. Siegle. Compositional performance modelling with the TIPPtool. *Performance Evaluation*, 39(1-4):5–35, January 2000.

14. H. Hermanns, J.-P. Katoen, J. Meyer-Kayser, and M. Siegle. Implementing a Model Checker for Performability Behaviour. In *Proc. Fifth Int. Workshop on Performability Modeling of Computer and Communication Systems (PMCCS-5)*, pages 110–115, Erlangen, Germany, 2001.

15. H. Hermanns, J.P. Katoen, J. Meyer-Kayser, and M. Siegle. Towards model checking stochastic process algebra. In *Integrated Formal Methods*, volume LNCS 1945, pages 420–439. Springer, 2000.

16. M. Kuntz. *Symbolic Semantics and Verification of Stochastic Process Algebras*. PhD thesis, Universität Erlangen-Nürnberg, Institut für Informatik 7, 2006 (to appear).

17. M. Kuntz and M. Siegle. Deriving symbolic representations from stochastic process algebras. In *Process Algebra and Probabilistic Methods, Proc. PAPM-PROBMIV'02*, pages 188–206. Springer, LNCS 2399, 2002.

18. M. Kuntz and M. Siegle. A Stochastic Extension of the Logic PDL. In *Sixth Int. Workshop on Performability Modeling of Computer and Communication Systems (PMCCS-6)*, pages 58–61, 2003.

19. M. Kuntz and M. Siegle. A Stochastic Extension of the Logic PDL. Technical Report 2004-5, Universität der Bundeswehr München, Dept. of Computer Science, 2004. (http://fakinf.informatik.unibw-muenchen.de/~msiegle/PAPERS/TR_2004_5.ps.gz).

20. M. Kuntz, M. Siegle, and E. Werner. CASPA - A Tool for Symbolic Performance and Dependability Evaluation. In *Proceedings of EPEW'04 (FORTE satellite workshop)*, pages 293 – 307. Springer, LNCS 3236, 2004.

21. M. Kwiatkowska, G. Norman, and D. Parker. Probabilistic symbolic model checking with PRISM: A hybrid approach. *International Journal on Software Tools for Technology Transfer (STTT)*, 6(2):128–142, 2004.

22. J. Meyer-Kayser. Verifikation stochastischer prozessalgebraischer Modelle mit aCSL+. Technical Report IB 01/03, Universität Erlangen-Nürnberg, Institut für Informatik 7, 2003 (in German).

23. W.D. Obal and W.H. Sanders. State-space support for path-based reward variables. *Performance Evaluation*, 35(3-4):233–251, 1999.

24. W. H. Sanders and L. M. Malhis. Dependability evaluation using composed SAN-based reward models. *Journal of Parallel and Distributed Computing*, 15(3):238–254, 1992.

25. W. H. Sanders and J. F. Meyer. Stochastic Activity Networks: Formal Definitions and Concepts. In *Lectures on Formal Methods and Performance Analysis*, pages 315–343. Springer, LNCS 2090, 2001.

26. M. Siegle. *Behaviour analysis of communication systems: Compositional modelling, compact representation and analysis of performability properties*. Shaker Verlag, Aachen, 2002.

Parallel and Distributed Model Checking in Eddy*

Igor Melatti, Robert Palmer, Geoffrey Sawaya, Yu Yang, Robert Mike Kirby, and Ganesh Gopalakrishnan

School of Computing, University of Utah
{melatti, rpalmer, sawaya, yuyang, kirby, ganesh}@cs.utah.edu

Abstract. Model checking of safety properties can be scaled up by pooling the CPU and memory resources of multiple computers. As compute clusters containing 100s of nodes, with each node realized using multicore (e.g., 2) CPUs will be widespread, a model checker based on the *parallel* (shared memory) and *distributed* (message passing) paradigms will more efficiently use the hardware resources. Such a model checker can be designed by having each node employ *two* shared memory threads that run on the (typically) two CPUs of a node, with one thread responsible for state generation, and the other for efficient communication, including (i) performing overlapped asynchronous message passing, and (ii) aggregating the states to be sent into larger chunks in order to improve communication network utilization. We present the design details of such a novel model checking architecture called *Eddy*. We describe the design rationale, details of how the threads interact and yield control, exchange messages, as well as detect termination. We have realized an instance of this architecture for the Murphi modeling language. Called Eddy_Murphi, we report its performance over the number of nodes as well as communication parameters such as those controlling state aggregation. Nearly linear reduction of compute time with increasing number of nodes is observed. Our thread task partition is done in such a way that it is modular, easy to port across different modeling languages, and easy to tune across a variety of platforms.

1 Introduction

This paper studies the following question:

> Given that shared memory programming will be supported by multicore chips (multi-CPU shared memory processors) programmed using lightweight threads, and given that such shared memory processors will be interconnected by high bandwidth message passing networks, how best to design a safety model checker that is (i) efficient for such hardware platforms, and (ii) is modular to permit multiple implementations for different modeling languages?

---

* Supported in part by NSF award CNS-0509379 and SRC Contract 2005-TJ-1318.

A. Valmari (Ed.): SPIN 2006, LNCS 3925, pp. 108–125, 2006.

The importance of this question stems from many facts. First of all, basic finite-state model checking must continue to scale for large-scale debugging. Multiple CPUs per node are best exploited by multi-threaded code running on the nodes; the question, however, is how to organize the threads for high efficiency and modularity, especially given that thread programming is error-prone. Moreover, most parallel versions of safety model checkers employ hash tables distributed across the nodes, with new states possibly sent across the interconnect to be looked up in these tables (as was done since the very first model checkers of this kind, namely Stern and Dill [1] and Lerda and Sisto [2]); we do not deviate from this decision. What we explore in this paper is whether, by specializing the threads running within each node to specific tasks, (i) the state generation efficiency can be kept high, (ii) communication of states across the interconnect can be performed efficiently, and (iii) the overall code remains simple and modular to be trustworthy.

We have developed a parallel *and* distributed model checking architecture called Eddy that meets the above objectives. A specific model checker following this architecture, called Eddy_Murphi (for the Murphi [3] modeling language) has been developed and released. To the best of our knowledge, such a model checker has previously not been discussed in the literature. There are a wide array of choices available in deciding how to go about designing such a model checker. The decisions involved are how to allocate the CPUs of each compute node to support state generation, hash-table lookup, coalescing states into bigger *lines* before shipment, overlapped computation and communication, and handling distributed termination. Many of these choices may not achieve high performance, and may lead to tricky code. We are placing a great deal of importance on achieving simple and maintainable code, allowing the model checker to be easily re-targeted for a different modeling language, and even make the model checker self calibrating over a wide range of hardware platforms. While much remains to be explored as well as implemented, Eddy_Murphi has realized many of the essential aspects of the Eddy architecture. In particular, Eddy_Murphi employs shared memory CPU threads in each node running POSIX PThreads [4, 5] code, with the nodes communicating using the Message Passing Interface (MPI, [6]). It dramatically reduces the time taken to model check several non-trivial Murphi models, including cache coherence protocols.

We have also: (i) ported Eddy_Murphi to work using a Win32 porting of PThreads [7] as well as Microsoft Compute Cluster Server 2003 [8]; (ii) created Eddy_SPIN, a *preliminary* distributed model checker for Promela[1]. Both Eddy_SPIN and Eddy_Murphi are based on the same architecture: while the state generation ("worker") thread more or less executes the reachability computation aspects of the standard sequential SPIN or Murphi, the communication threads are *organized in an identical manner*. In the rest of the paper, we will focus on the internal organization of Eddy_Murphi, the impact of its performance over the

---

[1] Eddy_SPIN was based on a refactored implementation of SPIN [9] which did not exhibit the scalability advantages reported here for Eddy_Murphi owing to its very high overheads; this will be corrected in our next implementation.

number of nodes as well as communication parameters such as those controlling state aggregation, as well as scalability results from a catalog of benchmarks. Since we do not have the ability to compare "apples to apples" with other existing model checkers, our contributions fall in the following categories. (i) We provide a detailed description of the algorithms used in Eddy_Murphi. (ii) We report the performance of Eddy_Murphi across a wide spectrum of examples. In one case, Eddy_Murphi model-checked a very huge protocol in 9 hours using 60 nodes when sequential Murphi had not enough memory resources to verify it and a disk-based sequential Murphi [10][2] did not finish even after a week. (iii) In [11], we provide extensive experimental results, the full sources of Eddy_Murphi, as well as a Promela verification model that explicates the detailed organization of its thread and message passing code.

The rest of this paper is organized as follows. Section 1.1 presents specific design considerations that lead to the selection of a natural architecture and implementation for Eddy. Section 2 presents the algorithm used by Eddy. Section 3 has our experimental results. Section 4 concludes.

Related Work: Parallel and distributed model checking has been a topic of growing interest, with a special conference series (PDMC) devoted to the topic. An exhaustive literature survey is beyond the scope of this paper. Many distributed model-checkers based on message passing have been developed for Murphi and SPIN. Distributed BDD-based verification tools have been widely studied (e.g., [12]). In [13], a multithreaded SAT solver is described. The idea of coalescing states into larger messages for better network utilization in the context of model checking was pointed out in [14]. Previous parallel Murphi versions has been devised by Stern and Dill [15], Sivaraj and Gopalakrishnan [16], and Kumar and Mercer [17]. As said earlier, a parallel and distributed framework for safety model checking similar to Eddy is believed to be new.

1.1 Design Considerations for Eddy

Our main goal is to have the two threads used in Eddy run without too many synchronizations. This increases the intra node parallelism. Furthermore, if thread-binding to CPUs is available (depending on the underlying OS), then context-switching overhead can also be reduced. Hence, we design our two threads to have complementary tasks, thus maximizing the parallelism between them. One thread will be responsible for state generation, hash table lookup and error analysis, while the other one will handle the communication part, i.e. receiving and sending messages. We also give to this latter thread the task to group up states to be communicated in a big coalesced chunk of memory called a *line*. We experimentally show that this is far more efficient than suffering the overhead of sending individual states across.

Terminology: A *Nondeterministic Finite State System* (shortened *NFSS* in the following) S is a 4-tuple $(S, I, \mathcal{A}, \texttt{next})$, where S is a finite set of states, $I \subseteq S$

---

[2] This version of Murphi is able to limit the performance slowdown due to disk usage to an average factor of 3.

```
FIFO_Queue Q = ∅;  /* BF consumption queue */
HashTable T = ∅;  /* for visited states */

/* Returns true iff φ holds in all the reachable states */
bool BFS(NFSS S, SafetyProperty φ)
{
  let S = (S, I, A, next);
  /* is there an initial state which is an error state? */
  foreach s in I {
    if (!IfNotVisitedCheckEnqueue(s))
      /* IfNotVisitedCheckEnqueue returned false, thus s is
         an error state and S does not satisfy φ */
      return false;
  }
  /* visit */
  while (Q ≠ ∅) {
    s = Dequeue(Q);
    /* s expansion */
    foreach (s_next, a) in next(s) {
      if (!IfNotVisitedCheckEnqueue(s_next))
        return false;
    } /* foreach */
  } /* while */
  /* error not found, S satisfies φ */
  return true;
} /* BFS() */

/* returns false if s is an error state (i.e. does not
   satisfy φ), true otherwise */
bool IfNotVisitedCheckEnqueue(s, AP φ)
{
  if (s is not in T) {
    if (!φ(s))
      return false;
    HashInsert(T, s);
    Enqueue(Q, s);
  }
  return true;
} /* IfNotVisitedCheckEnqueue() */
```

Fig. 1. Explicit Breadth–First Search

is the set of the initial states, A is a finite set of labels and **next** : $S \rightarrow 2^{S \times A}$ is a function taking a state s as argument and returning a set **next**(s) of pairs $(t, a) \in S \times A$. Given an NFSS $S = (S, I, A, \textbf{next})$ and a property ϕ defined on states (i.e., $\phi : S \rightarrow \{true, false\}$), we want to verify if ϕ holds on all the states of S (i.e., for all $s \in S$, $\phi(s)$ holds). The algorithm in Figure 1 is what Murphi essentially implements[3]. We seek to parallelize this algorithm based on a number of established as well as new ideas. Our objective is to support distributed hash tables as in contemporary works. This assigns each state s to a home node $p(s)$ determined by a surjective partitioning function p that maps state vectors to node numbers lying in the range $\{1 \ldots N\}$. Kumar and Mercer [17] study the effect of partitioning on load balancing—an important consideration in parallel model checking. We consider the selection of partition functions to be orthogonal to our work.

Given all this, the state generation rate and the communication demands of a parallel safety model checker very much depends on many factors. The amount of work performed to generate the successor states of a given state is a critical consideration. In Murphi, for instance, each "rule" is a ⟨*guard, action*⟩ pair, with guards and actions being typically coarse-grained. Often, the guards and actions span several pages of code, often involving procedures and functions. In other modeling languages such as Promela and Zing [18], the amount of work to generate the successors of a given state can vary greatly. After gaining sufficient understanding, we hope to have a user-assisted calibration feature for all model checkers constructed following the Eddy architecture. In the rest of this paper, we assess results from our preliminary implementation.

2   A New Algorithm for Parallel Model Checking

We present the Eddy_Murphi algorithms in Section 2.1, after a brief overview of the MPI and PThread functions used.

MPI Functions Employed in Eddy_Murphi. MPI (Message Passage Interface, [19, 20, 6]) is a message-passing library specification, designed to ease the use of message passing by end users, library writers, and tool developers. It is in use in over 60% of the world's supercomputers and clusters. We now present a simplified description of the semantics of certain MPI functions used in our algorithm descriptions (we also take the liberty to simplify the names of these functions somewhat).

- MPI_Isend(obj, dest_node, msg_label) sends obj to dest_node, and the message is labeled msg_label. Note that this operation is non-blocking (the 'I' stands for *immediate*), i.e. it does not wait for the corresponding receive. Here, obj is an object of any type, dest_node is a node of the computing network, msg_label is the label message (chosen between *state, termination, termination probe*). The following always holds:
  - if msg_label is *state*, then obj is a set of states;
  - if msg_label is *termination probing*, then obj is a token structure (see Fig. 4);

---

[3] This rather straightforward algorithm is included in this paper to help contrast our distributed model checker.

- if **msg_label** is *termination*, then **obj** is a boolean value (to be assigned to the global variable **result**).
- **MPI_Iprobe(src_node, msg_label)** returns **true** if there is a message sent by the **src_node** node with the label **msg_label** for the current node. Otherwise, **false** is returned. As the 'I' suggests, also this call is non-blocking. If **src_node** is **ANY_SOURCE** instead of a specific node, then only the message label is checked.
- **MPI_Recv(src_node, msg_label)** returns the message sent by the **src_node** node to the current one with the label **msg_label**. We will call this function only after a successful call to **MPI_Iprobe**, thus we are always sure that a **MPI_Isend** had previously sent something to the current node with the given **msg_label**. Again, if **src_node** is **ANY_SOURCE**, then the current node is retrieving the message without checking which node is the sender (only the message label is checked).
- **MPI_Test(obj)** returns true iff **obj** has been successfully sent, i.e. if the sending has been completed. Note that this is necessary because we are using **MPI_Isend**, that performs an asynchronous sending operation. We will call this function only for test sending completion for states.
- **MPI_MyRank()** returns the rank or identifier of the node.

Finally, with **#MPI_Isend(msg_label)** (resp., **#MPI_Recv(msg_label)**), we denote the number of **MPI_Isend** (resp. **MPI_Recv**) performed with the message label **msg_label**. Note that here **msg_label** is always *state*, i.e. we count only the sending operations regarding sets of states.

PThread Functions Employed in Eddy_Murphi. POSIX PThread [4, 5] is a standardized programming interface for threads usage. In our model checker we use the following functions. Note that, w.r.t. the PThread standard, we again change the function interface to make their usage clearer:

- **pthread_create(f)** creates a new thread. Namely, the thread that calls this function continues its execution, whilst a new thread is started which executes the function **f**.
- **pthread_exit()** terminates the thread which calls it.
- **pthread_join()** called by the "main" thread (i.e. the one having called **pthread_create**), suspends the execution of this thread until the other one terminates (because of a **pthread_exit()**), unless it is already terminated.
- **pthread_yield()** Forces the calling thread to relinquish use of its processor.

2.1 Eddy_Murphi Algorithms

In Figures 2, 3 and 4, we show how the breadth-first (BF) visit of Figure 1 is modified in our parallel approach. Since we use a SPMD (Single Program Multiple Data) paradigm, *the code listed is executed on all the nodes of the computational network*. The *worker thread* is described in Figure 2, and the *communication thread* in Figures 3 and 4.

```
/* local data (each node has its own copy of this) */
FIFO_Queue Q = ∅; HashTable T = ∅;
bool Terminate = false; bool result = true;
FIFO_Queue_lines CommQueue[NumNodes] = ∅;
SafetyProperty φ;

bool ParBFS(NFSS S) {
 pthread_create(CommThread);
 if IAmRoot() { /* i.e., MPI_MyRank() == 0 */
  foreach s in I {
   if (!CheckState(s)) {Terminate = true; break;}
 } }
 while (!ParTerminate()) {
  (s, checked) = Dequeue(Q);
  if (!checked) { /* sent by some other node */
   if (s in T) continue;
   else HashInsert(T, s);
  }
  foreach (s_next, a) in next(s) {
   if (!CheckState(s_next)) {Terminate = true; break;}
 } }
 Terminate = true; pthread_join();
 return result;
} /* ParBFS() */

bool CheckState(state s) {/* false if error state found */
 owner_rank = owner(s);
 if (owner_rank == MPI_MyRank()) { /* this node owns s */
  if (s is not in T) {
   if (!φ(s)) {result = false; return false;}
   HashInsert(T, s); Enqueue(Q, (s, true));
  } /* otherwise, s is already visited */
 } else { /* this node does not own s */
  if (!φ(s)) {result = false; return false;}
  Enqueue_line(CommQueue[owner_rank], s);
 return true;
} /* CheckState() */

bool ParTerminate() { /* true if computation is over */
 if (Terminate) return true;
 if (Q ≠ ∅) return false;
 if (!Terminate) sleep;
 if (Terminate) return true;
 return false; /* here, new states are in Q */
} /* ParTerminate() */
```

Fig. 2. Worker thread

```
CommThread() { /* Communication thread */
 while (true) {
  ProcMess(); /* if termination was received, exits */
  if (Terminate) End(true); /* φ does not hold */
  DoSends();
  Free_lines(CommQueue); /* tests sending completion */
  StableCondTokenProc(); /* termination probing */
} } /* CommThread() */

ProcMess() { /* Processes incoming messages */
 if (MPI_Iprobe(ANY_SOURCE, state)) ReceiveStates();
 if (MPI_Iprobe(ANY_SOURCE, termination)) {
  /* some other nonroot node found an error, or the root
     decided the search is finished */
  result = MPI_Recv(ANY_SOURCE, termination);
  End(false);
 }
 if (MPI_Iprobe(prev_ring_node, termination probing))
  ReceiveTermProb();
} /* ProcessMessages() */

ReceiveStates() { /* Processes incoming state messages */
 S = MPI_Recv(ANY_SOURCE, state);
 foreach state s in S {Enqueue(Q, (s, false));}
 /* here Q might be empty because of thread scheduling */
 if (worker sleeping && Q ≠ ∅)
  wake the worker thread up; /* wake up and work */
} /* ReceiveStates() */

DoSends() { /* Try to send what it is now in CommQueue */
 foreach computing node n different from MPI_MyRank() {
  while (lines_ready(CommQueue[n])) {
   S = Dequeue_line(CommQueue[n]);
   MPI_Isend(S, n, state);
} } } /* DoSends() */

End(bool broadcast){ /* Shuts down CommThread() */
 if (broadcast) { /* terminate all the other nodes */
  foreach computing node n
   MPI_Isend(result, n, termination);
 }
 Terminate = true; /* also the worker thread terminates */
 if (worker sleeping)
  wake the worker thread up; /* wake up and die */
 pthread_exit();
} /* End() */
```

Fig. 3. Communication thread (continues in Fig. 4)

```
/* Local data (each node has its own copy of this) */
bool TokenValid = IAmRoot();
struct { int snt; int rcvd; } token;

/* Possibly starts or continues the token passing */
StableCondTokenProc() {
 if (TknVldAndNthngToDo()) {
  /* initially, only the root might enter */
  if (IAmRoot()) {
   /* token processing to see if we can terminate */
   token.snt = token.rcvd = 0;
  } else {
   token.snt += #MPI_Isend(state);
   token.rcvd += #MPI_Recv(state);
  }
  MPI_Isend(token, next ring node, termination probing);
  TokenValid = false; /* token sent away... */
} } } /* StableCondTokenProc() */

/* True iff token valid and nothing can be done locally */
bool TknVldAndNthngToDo() {
 if (TokenValid && worker sleeping) {
  Try DoSends(), then ProcessMessages();
  return (no operation performed);
 }
 return false;
} } /* TknVldAndNthngToDo() */

/* Processes incoming termination probing messages */
ReceiveTermProb() {
 token = MPI_Recv(ANY_SOURCE, termination probing);
 TokenValid = true;
 if (TknVldAndNthngToDo()) {
  /* basing on local information, the computation can be
     terminated */
  if (!IAmRoot()) {
   /* rehop the token, after having modified it */
   token.snt += #MPI_Isend(state);
   token.rcvd += #MPI_Recv(state);
   MPI_Isend(token, next_ring_node, termination probing);
   TokenValid = false; /* token sent away... */
  } else { /* the token has finished its tour */
   if (token.snt + #MPI_Isend(state) ==
       token.rcvd + #MPI_Recv(state))
    End(true);
   /* otherwise, the computation will continue */
} } } /* ReceiveTermProb() */
```

Fig. 4. Communication thread (functions for termination)

The worker thread is somewhat similar to the standard BF visit of Figure 1, but with important changes. One is that only the computation root node generates the start states. However, the most important change is in the handling of the local consumption queue Q.

In fact, whenever a new state s is generated, and s turns out not to be an error state, then a states distribution function (called owner() in Figure 2) determines if s belongs to the current node or not. In the first case, the current node inserts s in Q as well as in the local hash table, unless it was already visited, as it happens in a standalone BF. In the second case, s will be sent to the node $p(s)$ owing it; $p(s)$ will eventually then explore s upon receiving it.

However, in order to avoid too many messages between nodes, we use a queuing mechanism that allows to group as many states as possible in a unique message. To this aim, the worker thread enqueues s in a *communication queue* (CommQueue in Fig. 2). Then, the communication thread will eventually dequeue s from CommQueue and send it $p(s)$. The details of this queuing mechanism will be explained in Section 2.2.

Note that only the worker thread can dequeue states from the local BF consumption queue Q. On the other hand, the enqueuing of states in Q is performed both by the worker thread (see function CheckState() in Fig. 2) and the communication thread. This latter case happens as a result of receiving states from some other node (see function ReceiveStates() in Fig. 3). Since the states received from other nodes could be both new or already visited, the worker thread performs a check after having dequeued a state received from another node. To distinguish between local generated states (already checked for being new or not) and received states (on which the check has to be performed), Q stores pairs (state, boolean) instead of states.

As for the communication thread, it consists of an endless loop essentially trying to receive and send messages. As stated earlier, there are three type of messages, each carrying:

- states; this kind of messages can be exchanged by every couple of nodes, where the sender is the node generating the states and the receiver is the node owning the states. More details on the sending of this kind of messages are in Section 2.2.
- termination probings; here, MPI node ranks are used to imagine the computation network to form a ring on which the termination probing message is exchanged only between neighbors. This allows us to call the termination probing message a *token*. Thus, each node receiving a token from its left neighbor, will forward it to its right neighbor. However, the forwarding is performed only when the current node is unable to do anything locally (i.e., the worker thread is sleeping due to empty BF consumption queue and there are no messages to be sent or received).

  The token message chain can be started only by the root node and ends when the root node receives the token back by the last node. Since every node updates the global sent and received message counting on the token before forwarding it, if the root finds the two counter to match then the parallel computation is over. In fact, this implies that all the nodes are inactive (i.e. with the worker thread sleeping) and all messages that have been sent have also been received.

– termination; message of this kind are always broadcasted by one node to all the others. Namely, the source can be either the root node (when the termination probing is successfully terminated) or any node. In the first case, all the reachable states have been globally visited, and the system is correct w.r.t. the invariant property ϕ we want to verify. In the second case, there is an error state somewhere (i.e. a state s such that $\phi(s) = 0$), and the termination message will be sent by the node which has discovered it (note that it could be also the root node, and that more than one error state could be discovered at the same time by different nodes).

2.2   The Communication Queue Mechanism

A more detailed description is needed for the communication queue handling (i.e. CommQueue in Figures 2 and 3). The purpose of this data structure is to avoid sending each state separately: on the contrary, it allows to group up as many states as reasonable, thus reducing the communication overhead. Of course, grouping is possible only if the destination is the same, thus there is a communication queue for every possible destination node[4].

Differently from Q, which is a traditional FIFO queue (storing pairs (state, boolean)), each communication queue is organized as an array of arrays of states. We will refer to each array of states as a *line*, thus our parallel algorithm depends on two parameters:

NumLines the number of lines used;
LineSize the number of states for each line.

In Figures 2 and 3, there are four functions accessing CommQueue. In order to explain how they work, we have to say that at every execution time there is only one *active* line (i.e. the line on which the states are currently added), while the other lines status can be:

waiting to be sent these lines already contain all the LineSize states they are allowed to, and they are waiting to be sent;
currently being sent also these lines are filled up, but they have already been passed to MPI_Isend; however, the sending operation is still not terminated. Following the MPI standard specification, the contents of these lines cannot by accessed until the sending operation has been successfully completed;
waiting to be active these lines contain no states, or have already been successfully sent, so their content can be overwritten with new states.

Thus, three line index lists are maintained, one for each of these line types; we will call the former list WTBS, the second one CBS and the latter WTBA. Initially,

---

[4] Indeed, our implementation uses NumNodes − 1 communication queues per node, while in Figure 2 NumNodes queues are declared. This allows to simplify our pseudocode.

the first line is the active one, WTBA contains all the other NumLines − 1 lines and WTBS and CBS are empty.

We are now ready to give the semantics of the four functions manipulating commQueue:

Enqueue_line(CommQueue, state) called by the worker thread, adds **state** at the end of the active line of CommQueue. It also handles the active line filling, by properly modifying WTBS and WTBA.

Dequeue_line(CommQueue) called by the communication thread, returns the first line ready to be sent in CommQueue, and properly modifies WTBS and CBS. If there are no ready lines, and the worker thread is sleeping, then the active line is returned.

lines_ready(CommQueue) returns true if Dequeue_line returns (a line with) at least one state.

Free_lines(CommQueues) calls MPI_Test on all the lines currently being sent (no matter which queue they belong). Those lines passing the test are moved to the WTBA list.

A more detailed pseudocode describing these function can be found in Fig. 5.

Summing up, the evolution of a line status is shown in Fig. 6, where we use the list acronyms to denote the status of the lines that are stored in them. As for the events causing the status transitions, if l is the line under analysis then the following holds:

1. is triggered when a call to Enqueue_line fills up the active line and l is the first of the WTBA list;
2. is triggered when a call to Enqueue_line fills up the active line (which coincides with l)
3. is triggered when a call to Dequeue_line returns l;
4. is triggered when a call to Free_line finds l to be entirely sent.

Finally, note that the initial state of the automaton in Fig. 6 is Active for the first line in the lines array, and WTBA for all the others.

2.3 Algorithm Rationale

In parallel algorithms for model checking proposed to date, nodes alternate between state generation, state sending, and state receiving. With only one thread available, providing maximal overlap between these activities requires the use of non-blocking MPI communications amidst the rather intricate state generation steps of a model checker. This can render the code brittle, non-portable, and ultimately inadequately concurrent. In contrast, in our design, state generation and communication are in two threads which, on an increasing number of hardware platforms, map onto multi-core CPUs. Through the use of threading and the lines queues, we minimize the time that a worker spends in a waiting state. The threading itself allows the worker not to be kept waiting for communication handling. In fact, there are only two other events that cause the worker thread to wait:

```
/* Puts s in the active line, and handles filling */
void Enqueue_line(FIFO_Queue_line Q, state s) {
 while (1) { /* breaked once there is an active line */
  if (Q.active_line is defined) {
   Q.active_line = Q.active_line ∪ s;
   if (length(Q.active_line) == LineSize) {
    Q.WTBS = Q.WTBS ∪ Q.active_line;
    if (Q.WTBA == ∅) undefine Q.active_line;
    else {
     Q.active_line = head(Q.WTBA);
     Q.WTBA = tail(Q.WTBA);
     Clear(Q.active_line);/* length(Q.active_line) == 0 */
    } }
   break; /* exits while(1) */
  }
  if (Terminate) break; /* exits while(1) */
  if (too much iterations without an active line found)
   pthread_yield(); /*yields to the communication thread*/
} } } /* Enqueue_line() */

/* Returns a line that can be sent away */
state_array Dequeue_line(FIFO_Queue_line Q) {
 if (Q.WTBS ≠ ∅) {
  ret = head(Q.WTBS);
  Q.WTBS = tail(Q.WTBS);
  Q.CBS = Q.CBS ∪ ret;
  return ret;
 }
 else if (worker sleeping) return Q.active_line;
 else return NULL;
} /* Dequeue_line() */

bool lines_ready() { /* Can something  be sent? */
 if (Dequeue_line can return at least one state)
  return true;
 else return false;
} /* lines_ready() */

/* Checks for sending completion */
void Free_lines(FIFO_Queue_lines Qs) {
 foreach computing node n different from MPI_MyRank() {
  foreach line l in Qs[n].CBS {
   if (MPI_Test(l)) {
    Q.WTBA = Q.WTBA ∪ l; /* with length(l) == 0 */
    remove l from Q.CBS;
} } } } /* Free_lines() */
```

Fig. 5. Communication queue handling

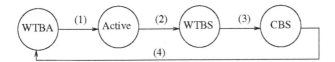

Fig. 6. Evolution of a line status

- When the consumption queue is empty (function **ParTerminate** in Figure 2); in this case, the worker thread enters a sleeping status, waiting for some other node to send some new states, or for termination. However, the wait for new states to be processed could be extended if the communication threads keep sending small lines (i.e., containing too few states) to the other nodes. It should be clear that it is more convenient to send as many states as possible in one shot. To achieve this, it is sufficient to set **LineSize** to an adequately high number. Note however that setting this parameter to a too high number may cause a delay in the sending of the states, thus causing other nodes to be idle.
- When there are no available lines in **WTBA** of the communication queue for some node; thus, all the lines are in **WTBS** or **CBS** (in this case, the worker loops in the **while(1)** statement of function **Enqueue_lines** in Figure 5). In this case, after a given number of attempts, the worker thread yields to the communication thread, so that some line becomes available earlier. Note that at each iteration the worker also checks if **Terminate** has been set as a result of receiving a termination message (without this check, deadlocks are possible if a termination message is received when the worker is inside **Enqueue_lines**). This problem can be mitigated by properly choosing the number of lines and their length. If there are too few lines, then the worker thread will often be stopped in a waiting status when trying to submit states to the communication queues. Thus, the parameter **NumLines** should be as high as possible.

However, **NumLines** and **LineSize** cannot be set indefinitely high, since they are memory consuming: e.g., if 10 bytes are needed to represent a state in a given model to be verified, then having 1024 lines each with 1024 states on a 50-nodes computation will result in about 500MB RAM memory requirement for each node. This will reduce the space for hash table and consumption queue, so affecting the worker thread performances.

Fortunately, we will show that 1024 or 512 states are a good value for **LineSize**, whilst **NumLines** can be much smaller, e.g. 8 or 16. *In fact, the number of lines merely needs to be large enough to allow overlap of the two threads.*

3 Experimental Results

To assess the feasibility of our approach, we implemented our parallel algorithm within the model checker Murphi [21]. We will call the resulting verifier Eddy_Murphi [11].

We use Eddy_Murphi to run different kinds of experiments. All the experiments we run are computed as an average over at least two runs, and were repeated until an acceptable standard deviation was reached (all details provided at [11]).

Initially, we tune the communication parameters, i.e. the number of lines (NumLines), and the size of each line (LineSize). To do this, we use the protocol sci [15], available within the standard Murphi distribution, modifying its parameters in a way such that it has now a fairly high number of states (approx. 2.7×10^6). We then run different verifications on sci, changing the values for NumLines and LineSize; these values, as already said in Sect. 2.3, are chosen to be low for NumLines and high for LineSize; we also change the number of nodes. The results are in Table 1, where **NL** stand for NumLines, **LS** for LineSize and **Time %** is the ratio between the execution time for Eddy_Murphi and the execution time for standard Murphi. In Table 1, we report only the four best configurations for our parameters, ordered by decreasing time. It is clear that the best results are obtained with 1024 states for each line, and with a number of lines between 8 and 32. To keep memory occupation small enough, we choose 8 lines with 1024 states each.

Table 1. Experimental results for the parameter tuning, carried out on a multi-core 120-nodes cluster; each node has 2 Intel XEON processors at 2.4 GHz, with 2GB of RAM

40 Nodes			20 Nodes			10 Nodes		
NL	**LS**	**Time %**	**NL**	**LS**	**Time %**	**NL**	**LS**	**Time %**
32	1024	0.023984	32	1024	0.046594	16	1024	0.106446
16	1024	0.023989	2	1024	0.046677	32	1024	0.106805
8	1024	0.024058	16	1024	0.046717	8	1024	0.106833
2	1024	0.024136	8	1024	0.046884	1	512	0.107657

Next, we use these parameters values to compare the performances of Eddy_Murphi with (standard) Murphi. In these experiments we use five protocols from the Murphi distribution, in order to be able to compare the performances of Eddy_Murphi vs Murphi. These protocols have been chosen in such a way that their number of states is high enough to make the use of parallel model checker meaningful; indeed, they all have between 10^6 and 10^8 states.

The results are in Fig. 7, where we graph the speedup obtained by Eddy_Murphi w.r.t. Murphi (the inverse of Table 1, i.e. $\frac{\text{Murphi time}}{\text{Eddy\_Murphi time}}$) as a function of the number of compute nodes. Fig. 7 shows that we obtain a nearly linear speedup on almost all the examples, and that on all examples we are considerably faster than standalone Murphi. Moreover, note that the protocol peterson is the only one not showing a linear speedup: running the verification on 40 nodes is worse than on 30. However, this is due to the particular state partition function we use (i.e. the implementation we chose for function

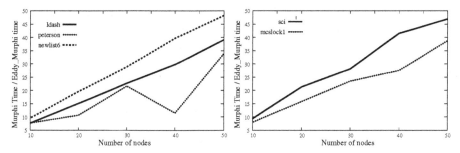

Fig. 7. Experimental results for performances comparison with standard Murphi, carried out on the same cluster of Table 1

owner in Fig. 2): on this protocol, for 30 nodes we have that each node owns about $\frac{n}{30}$ states, but this does not hold for 40 nodes. Here, we do not address state partition functions performances, since this is an orthogonal problem to our work.

Note that a previous parallel version of Murphi was already developed [22]. We could not re-run the parallel Murphi implementation of [22] because it was developed for the Berkeley NOW hardware which is unavailable. However, when using an MPI porting (reported by [16]), we do not observe the speedup mentioned in [22], and it is always much slower than standard Murphi. This is probably due to the fact that now CPUs are faster, and that the clusters network used in [22] are optimized for message passing, which is not the case with MPI, that privileges the portability. Parallel Murphi implementations were also reported by [17], but we were not able to obtain a reliable version of this code.

Finally, we present a very large protocol whose verification is not feasible on a standalone machine. This is the case of the FLASH protocol [23] with 5 processors and 2 data values as parameters. This protocol has more than 3×10^9 states, and its verification with standard Murphi would require a huge amount of RAM memory (assuming 40 bits for each state in hash compaction, we would need 15 GB of RAM for the hash table only), as well as an unacceptable computational time. On the other hand, by using a disk version of Murphi [10], the computation lasts more than 1 week (we do not know the exact amount of time, but a projection based on the first part of the verification leads to a probable execution time of 3 weeks). However, we successfully completed the verification of this protocol with Eddy_Murphi on 60 nodes in approximately 9 hours.

4   Conclusions

We have developed a novel algorithm and an associated framework for shared memory *and* distributed memory model checking of safety properties, called "Eddy." This is the first such model checker that we are aware of. Eddy meets many goals that we had originally set forth. One important goal was to ensure a clean separation of concerns between *next-state generation* and *communication* during distributed model checking. This, in turn, has several advantages. One advantage is that it makes the code easier to understand, validate, and modify. It also helps make the model checking framework more generic by allowing us to replace the next-state generation logic (e.g., switch over from, say, Murphi to SPIN or Zing) without changing the communication management part very much. Another advantage is the increased concurrency possible when the next-state generation and communication management activities are run as two separate threads. Last but not least, the two threads running per node of Eddy can exploit the two separate CPUs of dual-core CPUs that will become widely available soon. These threads will then have lower or no context-switch overheads, and also utilize the cache memories of the CPUs much more effectively. Eddy optimizes communication in several ways: (i) by not sending individual states, but rather much more bulky units that collect several states before shipment, the interconnection utilization vastly improves. (ii) by performing multiple asynchronous *sends* in an overlapped manner, the overall throughput improves.

Our experiments confirm that the Eddy algorithm is quite robust and scales extremely well on a wide variety of nodes as well as communication parameters such as those controlling state aggregation. In particular, large instances of the Stanford FLASH protocol that cannot be verified through sequential model checking on powerful uniprocessors can now be verified quite fast using multiple nodes. The measurements reported in this paper indicate the actual speedups obtained as well as the impact of line sizes and the number of lines on performance.

As part of future work, we hope to combine other optimizations with Eddy. Some of the ideas under consideration are: (i) the use of other ways to record visited states per node, including disk-based algorithms [10], and the use of minimal automata [24], (ii) the use of thread-pools if multiple CPUs are available per node (e.g. hyper-threaded multi-cores), and (iii) self-calibrating versions of Eddy that set its communication thread parameters based on the measured network characteristics.

References

1. U. Stern and D. Dill. Parallelizing the Murφ verifier. *Formal Methods in System Design*, 18(2):117–129, 2001. (Journal version of their CAV 1997 paper).
2. F. Lerda and R. Sisto. Distributed-memory model checking with SPIN. In *Proc. of SPIN 1999*, volume 1680 of *LNCS*. Springer, 1999.
3. D. L. Dill. The mur*phi* verification system. In *Proc. of CAV 1996*, volume 1102 of *Lecture Notes in Computer Science*, pages 390–393. Springer, 1996.
4. D. R. Butenhof. *Programming with POSIX Threads*. Addison-Wesley, 1997.
5. POSIX PThreads http://www.llnl.gov/computing/tutorials/pthreads/.
6. MPI tutorial http://www-unix.mcs.anl.gov/mpi/tutorial/gropp/talk.html.
7. PThreads Win32 home page http://sourceware.org/pthreads-win32/.
8. MCCS 2003 http://www.microsoft.com/windowsserver2003/ccs/overview.mspx.
9. R. Palmer and G. Gopalakrishnan. Refactoring spin for safety. Technical report, University of Utah, July 2005.

10. G. Della Penna, B. Intrigila, I. Melatti, E. Tronci, and M. Venturini Zilli. Exploiting transition locality in automatic verification of finite state concurrent systems. *Software Tools for Technology Transfer*, 6(4):320–341, 2004.

11. Eddy_Murphi distribution
http://www.cs.utah.edu/formal_verification/software/murphi/eddy_murphi/.

12. O. Grumberg, T. Heyman, N. Ifergan, and A. Schuster. Achieving speedups in distributed symbolic reachability analysis through asynchronous computation. In *Proc. of CHARME 2005*, volume 3725 of *Lecture Notes in Computer Science*, pages 129–145. Springer, 2005.

13. Y. Feldman, N. Dershowitz, and Z. Hanna. Parallel multithreaded satisfiability solver: Design and implementation. In *Proc. of PDMC 2004*, volume 128 issue 3 of *Electronic Notes in Theoretical Computer Science*, pages 75–90. Elsevier, 2005.

14. R. Kumar and E. Mercer. Scalable distributed model checking: Experiences, lessons, and expectations. In *Proc. of PDMC 2003*, volume 89 issue 1 of *Electronic Notes in Theoretical Computer Science*, page 3. Elsevier, 2003.

15. U. Stern and D. L. Dill. Automatic verification of the sci cache coherence protocol. In *Proc. of CHARME 1995*, volume 987 of *Lecture Notes in Computer Science*, pages 21–34. Springer, 1995.

16. H. Sivaraj and G. Gopalakrishnan. Random walk based heuristic algorithms for distributed memory model checking. In *Proc. of PDMC 2003*, volume 89 issue 1 of *Electronic Notes in Theoretical Computer Science*, pages 51–67. Elsevier, 2003.

17. R. Kumar and E. Mercer. Load balancing parallel explicit state model checking. In *Proc. of PDMC 2004*, volume 128 issue 3 of *Electronic Notes in Theoretical Computer Science*, pages 19–34. Elsevier, 2004.

18. T. Andrews, S. Qadeer, S. K. Rajamani, J. Rehof, and Y. Xie. Zing: A model checker for concurrent software. Technical report, Microsoft Research, 2004.

19. W. Gropp, E. Lusk, and A. Skjellum. *Using MPI: Portable Parallel Programming with the Message-Passing Interface*. MIT Press, 1999.

20. MPI official specification http://www.mpi-forum.org/docs/docs.html.

21. Murphi distribution http://sprout.stanford.edu/dill/murphi.html.

22. U. Stern and D. Dill. Parallelizing the murφ verifier. In Orna Grumberg, editor, *Proc. of CAV 1997*, volume 1254 of *Lecture Notes in Computer Science*, pages 256–278. Springer, 1997.

23. J. Kuskin and D. Ofelt et al. The Stanford FLASH multiprocessor. In *Proc. of SIGARCH 1994*, pages 302–313, May 1994.

24. G.J. Holzmann and A. Puri. A minimized automaton representation of reachable states. *Software Tools for Technology Transfer*, 3(1):270–278, 1998.

Distributed On-the-Fly Model Checking and Test Case Generation

Christophe Joubert[1] and Radu Mateescu[1,2]

[1] INRIA Rhône-Alpes / VASY
655, avenue de l'Europe, F-38330 Montbonnot St Martin, France
[2] ENS Lyon / LIP / PLUME
46, allée d'Italie, F-69364 Lyon, France
{Christophe.Joubert, Radu.Mateescu}@inria.fr

Abstract. The explicit-state analysis of concurrent systems must handle large state spaces, which correspond to realistic systems containing many parallel processes and complex data structures. In this paper, we combine the on-the-fly approach (incremental construction of the state space) and the distributed approach (state space exploration using several machines connected by a network) in order to increase the computing power of analysis tools. To achieve this, we propose MB-DSOLVE, a new algorithm for distributed on-the-fly resolution of multiple block, alternation-free boolean equation systems (BESs). First, we apply MB-DSOLVE to perform distributed on-the-fly model checking of alternation-free modal μ-calculus, using the standard encoding of the problem as a BES resolution. The speedup and memory consumption obtained on large state spaces improve over previously published approaches based on game graphs. Next, we propose an encoding of the conformance test case generation problem as a BES resolution from which a diagnostic representing the complete test graph (CTG) is built. By applying MB-DSOLVE, we obtain a distributed on-the-fly test case generator whose capabilities scale up smoothly w.r.t. well-established existing sequential tools.

1 Introduction

The explicit-state verification of concurrent finite-state systems is confronted in practice with the *state explosion* problem (prohibitive size of the underlying state spaces), which occurs for realistic systems containing many parallel processes and complex data structures. Various approaches have been proposed for combating state explosion: *on-the-fly* verification constructs the state space in a demand-driven way, thus allowing the detection of errors without a priori building the entire state space, and *distributed* verification uses the computing resources of several machines connected by a network, thus allowing to scale up the capabilities of verification tools by one or two orders of magnitude [5, 17]. Practical experience suggests that combining these two techniques leads potentially to better results than using them separately [3, 13, 21].

A. Valmari (Ed.): SPIN 2006, LNCS 3925, pp. 126–145, 2006.

Given that verification tools are complex pieces of software, their design should promote modular architectures and intermediate representations, in order to reuse existing achievements as much as possible. *Boolean Equation Systems* (BESs) [23] are a useful intermediate representation for various verification problems, such as model checking of modal μ-calculus [1, 23], equivalence checking [2, 26], and partial order reduction [31]. Numerous sequential algorithms for on-the-fly BES resolution were proposed [1, 23, 29], some of them being subject to generic implementations, such as the CÆSAR_SOLVE library [26, 28], which serves as computing engine for the model checker EVALUATOR [29, 26], the equivalence checker BISIMULATOR [26, 4], and the reductor TAU_CONFLUENCE [31, 28], developed within the CADP toolbox [11]. Due to their modular architecture, distributed versions of these tools can be obtained in a straightforward manner by developing distributed BES resolution algorithms, such as DSOLVE [18], which handles BESs with a single equation block and underlies the distributed version of BISIMULATOR [17].

In this paper, we propose MB-DSOLVE, a new distributed on-the-fly resolution algorithm for multiple block, alternation-free BESs. The algorithm is based upon a distributed breadth-first exploration of the *boolean graph* [1] representing the dependencies between boolean variables of a BES. Our first application of MB-DSOLVE was the distributed on-the-fly model checking of alternation-free μ-calculus formulas (as computing engine for EVALUATOR), using the standard translation of the problem into a BES resolution [20, 1]. The only existing distributed on-the-fly algorithm for solving this problem was proposed in [5] and is based on *game graphs*, stemming from a game-based formulation of the problem [32]. The latest version of this algorithm, called PTCL1 and implemented in the model checker UPPDMC [13], has an extension, called PTCL2, which is also able to handle μ-calculus formulas of alternation depth 2 [22] and exhibits good performance on large state spaces, such as those of the VLTS benchmark suite[1]. Although the two algorithms MB-DSOLVE and PTCL1 are graph-based and therefore similar in spirit, MB-DSOLVE allows all machines involved in the distributed computation to handle simultaneously all equation blocks of a BES, thus potentially reaching a higher degree of concurrency than PTCL1, which at a given moment synchronizes and employs all machines to solve a precise part, called *component*, of the game graph. This intuition is confirmed experimentally on large states spaces from the VLTS benchmark.

Our second application of MB-DSOLVE was the distributed on-the-fly generation of conformance test cases from specifications and test purposes (both given as state spaces), following the approach advocated in the TGV tool [16]. To achieve this, we proposed an encoding of the test generation problem as a BES resolution from which a diagnostic representing the *Complete Test Graph* (CTG) is built, and we implemented it within CADP in a tool named EXTRACTOR. This led to sequential and distributed test case generation functionalities, obtained by applying the algorithms of CÆSAR_SOLVE optimized for disjunctive/conjunctive BESs [28] and MB-DSOLVE, respectively. The BES technology proved again its

---

[1] http://www.inrialpes.fr/vasy/cadp/resources/benchmark_bcg.html

usefulness: the performance of the sequential version of EXTRACTOR exhibits comparable performances with the optimized algorithms of TGV, and the distributed version scales smoothly to larger systems. As far as we know, this is the first attempt of building a distributed on-the-fly conformance test generator.

Related Work. Distributed model checking has also been investigated in the framework of Linear Temporal Logic (LTL) [24]. The first distributed model checking algorithm proposed for LTL [21] was based upon a non-nested DFS traversal of the state space, which allowed to check only safety properties. Although its complexity was not estimated precisely, an implementation of this algorithm on networks of workstations (NOWs) improved the capabilities of SPIN [14] for the analysis of systems exceeding the memory of a single machine.

This work was continued in [3], leading to an extended algorithm able to perform a distributed nested DFS and thus to check full LTL properties. The new algorithm, which has a cubic time complexity and a linear space complexity in the size of the state space, allowed to verify systems that could not be handled by the sequential version of SPIN. This algorithm could still be improved by allowing several DFS traversals to be performed concurrently.

Paper Outline. Section 2 recalls basic definitions of BESs and describes in detail the MB-DSOLVE resolution algorithm. Section 3 translates the problems of model checking alternation-free μ-calculus formulas and of conformance test case generation into BES resolutions. Section 4 shows experimental data comparing the performance of the distributed tools with their sequential versions and with other similar distributed tools. Finally, Section 5 gives some concluding remarks and directions for future work.

2   Distributed Local Resolution of Alternation-Free BESs

We first define the framework underlying the manipulation of alternation-free BESs, and then we present the MB-DSOLVE algorithm for distributed on-the-fly resolution.

2.1   Alternation-Free BESs

A Boolean Equation System (BES) [1,23], defined over $\mathcal{X}$, a set of boolean variables, is a tuple $B = (x, M_1, ..., M_n)$, where $x \in \mathcal{X}$ is a boolean variable and M_i are equation blocks ($i \in [1, n]$). Each block $M_i = \{x_{ij} \overset{\sigma_i}{=} op_{ij} \boldsymbol{X}_{ij}\}_{j \in [1, m_i]}$ is a set of minimal (*resp.* maximal) fixed point equations of sign $\sigma_i = \mu$ (*resp.* $\sigma_i = \nu$). The right-hand side of each equation ij of block M_i is a pure disjunctive or conjunctive formula obtained by applying a boolean operator $op_{ij} \in \{\vee, \wedge\}$ to a set of variables $\boldsymbol{X}_{ij} \subseteq \mathcal{X}$. The boolean constants false and true abbreviate the empty disjunction $\vee \emptyset$ and the empty conjunction $\wedge \emptyset$. A variable x_{ij} depends upon a variable x_{kl} if $x_{kl} \in \boldsymbol{X}_{ij}$. A block M_i depends upon a block M_k if some variable of M_i depends upon a variable defined in M_k. A block is *closed* if it does not depend upon any other blocks. A BES is *alternation-free* if there are no cyclic dependencies between its blocks; in this case, the blocks are sorted topologically such that a block M_i only depends upon blocks M_k with $k > i$. The *main* variable x must be defined in block M_1.

The semantics $[\![op\{x_1, ..., x_k\}]\!]\delta$ of a formula $op\{x_1, ..., x_k\}$ w.r.t. $\mathbb{B} = \{\mathsf{false}, \mathsf{true}\}$ and a context $\delta : \mathcal{X} \to \mathbb{B}$, which must initialize all variables $x_1, ..., x_k$, is the boolean value $\delta(x_1)\ op\ ...\ op\ \delta(x_k)$. The semantics $[\![M_i]\!]\delta$ of a block M_i w.r.t. a context δ is the σ_i-fixed point of a vectorial functional $\Phi_{i\delta} : \mathbb{B}^{m_i} \to \mathbb{B}^{m_i}$ defined as $\Phi_{i\delta}(b_1, ..., b_{m_i}) = ([\![op_{ij}\boldsymbol{X}_{ij}]\!](\delta \oslash [b_1/x_{i1}, ..., b_{m_i}/x_{im_i}]))_{j\in[1,m_i]}$, where $\delta \oslash [b_1/x_{i1}, ..., b_{m_i}/x_{im_i}]$ denotes a context identical to δ except for variables $x_{i1}, ..., x_{im_i}$, which are assigned values $b_1, ..., b_{m_i}$, respectively. The semantics of an alternation-free BES is the value of its main variable x given by the solution of M_1, i.e., $\delta_1(x)$, where the contexts δ_i are calculated as follows: $\delta_n = [\![M_n]\!][]$ (the context is empty because M_n is closed), $\delta_i = ([\![M_i]\!]\delta_{i+1}) \oslash \delta_{i+1}$ for $i \in [1, n-1]$ (a block M_i is interpreted in the context of all blocks M_k with $k > i$).

The *local* (or *on-the-fly*) resolution of an alternation-free BES $B = (x, M_1, ..., M_n)$ consists in computing the value of x by exploring the right-hand sides of the equations in a demand-driven way, without explicitly constructing the blocks. Several sequential on-the-fly BES resolution algorithms are available [1, 23, 7]; here we adopt the approach proposed in [1], which formulates the resolution problem in terms of a *boolean graph* representing the dependencies between boolean variables. A boolean graph is a triple $G = (V, E, L)$, where $V = \{x_{ij} \mid i \in [1, n] \wedge j \in [1, m_i]\}$ is the set of *vertices* (boolean variables), $E : V \to 2^V$, $E = \{x_{ij} \to x_{kl} \mid x_{kl} \in \boldsymbol{X}_{ij}\}$ is the set of *edges* (dependencies between variables), and $L : V \to \{\vee, \wedge\}$, $L(x_{ij}) = op_{ij}$ is the *vertex labeling* (disjunctive or conjunctive). An example of BES with three blocks and its associated boolean graph is shown on Figure 2.

The resolution of variable x amounts to perform a forward exploration of the dependencies going out of x, intertwined with a backward propagation of stable variables (whose value is determined) along dependencies; the resolution terminates either when x becomes stable (after propagation of some stable successors) or when the portion of boolean graph reachable from x is completely explored.

2.2 Distributed Local Resolution Algorithm

The algorithm we propose for distributed on-the-fly resolution of multiple block, alternation-free BESs is called MB-DSOLVE (*Multiple Block Distributed SOLVEr*). We consider a computing architecture consisting of P machines (called *nodes*), numbered from 1 to P, interconnected via a network and communicating by message-passing. Examples of such architectures are NOWs and clusters of PCs. For simplicity, we assume that each node executes a single instance of MB-DSOLVE, called *worker*, although in practice there may be several worker instances running on the same node.

The resolution of an alternation-free BES $B = (x, M_1, ..., M_n)$ is done by means of two breadth-first traversals of the corresponding boolean graph, starting from x: a forward exploration of the dependencies of the variables being solved, and a backward propagation of stable variables. The traversals are done in a distributed manner, each worker node being responsible for solving a subset of the boolean variables defined in B, determined using a static hash function.

In addition to workers, a special process, called *supervisor*, usually executed on the end-user node (numbered 0), is responsible for initializing the distributed computation by copying files and launching workers on remote nodes, for collecting statistics about the BES resolution, and for detecting (normal and abnormal) termination. A description of the supervisor associated to the DSOLVE algorithm for solving single block BESs can be found in [18]. Its extension to multiple block BESs involves a multiplexing of the data structures for each equation block and of the distributed termination detection (DTD) algorithm in order to detect the partial termination of each block and the global termination of the resolution.

The function MB-DSOLVE, shown on Figure 1, describes the behavior of a worker node $i \in [1, P]$ participating to the distributed resolution on P nodes of the main variable $x \in V$ of an alternation-free BES $B = (x, M_1, ..., M_n)$ represented by its boolean graph $G = (V, E, L)$. The set of successors of a vertex x is noted $E(x)$. We assume that G is not entirely constructed, but is given implicitly by its successor function E, which allows to explore G on-the-fly. Boolean variables are distributed to worker nodes by means of a static hash function $h : V \rightarrow [1, P]$. The index of the block defining a variable is given by a function $b : V \rightarrow [1, n]$, $b(x_{ij}) = i$. Upon termination, the function MB-DSOLVE returns the boolean value computed for the main variable x.

Due to space limitations, only the main part of MB-DSOLVE is detailed on Figure 1. For instance, protocol and exchanged messages used of termination detection do not figure in the sketched algorithm. To each block k are associated, locally to node i, several information: a set $S_k^i \subseteq V$ containing the visited vertices; a BFS queue W_k^i storing the vertices visited but not explored yet; a set $B_k^i \subseteq V$ containing stable variables, whose values must be back-propagated; a set $R_k^i \subseteq V$ containing unstable variables with interblock predecessor dependencies (i.e., variables defined in block k and occurring in the rhs of some equation of another block l); and a set $Q_k^i \subseteq E$ storing the interblock transitions going from block k and pending to be explored. The counter $exp\_req_k^i$, initialized to 0, gives the number of interblock transitions starting from variables in block k locally to node i, which needs to be eventually traversed by propagating the values of stable target variables. To each vertex y_k^j are associated four fields: a counter $c(y_k^j)$, which keeps the number of y_k^j's successors that must be stabilized in order to make the value of y_k^j stable, its boolean value $v(y_k^j)$, a set $d(y_k^j)$ containing the vertices that currently depend upon y_k^j, and a boolean $stable(y_k^j)$ indicating if y_k^j has a stable value (i.e., if $c(y_k^j) = 0$ or if y_k^j belongs to a completely explored and stabilized portion of block k). These fields are set up by $initialize(y_k^j)$ as follows: the counter $c(y_k^j)$ is set to $|E(y_k^j)|$ if $\sigma_k = \mu$ and $L(y_k^j) = \wedge$ or $\sigma_k = \nu$ and $L(y_k^j) = \vee$, and to 1 otherwise; $v(y_k^j)$ is set to false if $\sigma_k = \mu$ and to true otherwise; $d(y_k^j)$ is initially empty; and $stable(y_k^j)$ is initially false.

At each iteration of the main while-loop (lines 6–17), received messages are processed first (lines 7–8). Then, the block with minimal index $l_i \in [1, n]$ that has

```
 1  MB-DSOLVE(x,(V,E,L),n,P,h,i) → B :
 2     if h(x) = i then
 3        S^i_{b(x)} := {x};  W^i_{b(x)} := put(x,nil);
 4        initialize(x)
 5     endif;  term^i_{b(x)} := false;
 6     while ¬term^i_{b(x)} do
 7        if IRECEIVE(msg_i, sender_i) then
 8           READ(msg_i, sender_i)
 9        elsif (l_i := HASSTABILITY) ≤ n then
10           STABILIZATION(l_i)
11        elsif (k_i := HASEXPANSION) ≥ 1 then
12           EXPANSION(k_i)
13        else
14           RECEIVE(msg_i, sender_i);
15           READ(msg_i, sender_i)
16        endif
17     endwhile;
18     return v(x)

19  READ(m_i, s_i):
20     case m_i is
21        Exp(x^{s_i}_k, y^i_l) → if k ≠ l then
22              Q^i_l ∪:= {(x^{s_i}_k, y^i_l)}
23              else EXPAND(x^{s_i}_k, y^i_l) endif
24        Evl(x^i_k, y^{s_i}_l) → if k ≠ l then
25              exp_req^i_k − := 1 endif;
26              if ¬stable(x^i_k) then
27                 STABILIZE(x^i_k, y^{s_i}_l) endif
28     endcase

29  STABILIZATION(l):
30     while B^i_l ≠ ∅ ∨ (term^i_l ∧ R^i_l ≠ ∅) do
31        if B^i_l ≠ ∅ then y^i_l := get(B^i_l);
32           B^i_l \ := {y^i_l} else y^i_l := get(R^i_l);
33           R^i_l \ := {y^i_l} endif;
34        forall w^j_k ∈ d(y^i_l) ∧ (B^i_l ≠ ∅ ∨ k ≠ l)
35              ∧¬term^i_{b(x)} ∧ ¬stable(w^j_k) do
36           if h(w^j_k) = i then
37              if k ≠ l then exp_req^i_k − := 1
38              endif; STABILIZE(w^j_k, y^i_l)
39           else SENDING(Evl(w^j_k, y^i_l), h(w^j_k))
40           endif
41        endfor; d(y^i_l) := ∅
42     endwhile

43  STABILIZE(w^i_k, y^j_l):
44     if ((L(w^i_k) = ∨) ∧ v(y^j_l)) ∨
45        ((L(w^i_k) = ∧) ∧ ¬v(y^j_l)) then
46        s(w^i_k) := y^j_l;  c(w^i_k) := 0;
```

```
47           stable(w^i_k) := true
48        else c(w^i_k) − := 1 endif;
49        if stable(w^i_k) then B^i_k ∪:= {w^i_k};
50           if w^i_k ∈ R^i_k then R^i_k \ := {w^i_k}
51        endif;  term^i_{b(x)} := stable(x)
52     endif

53  EXPANSION(k):
54     if W^i_k = nil then
55        forall (x^i_l, y^i_k) ∈ (Q^i_k)
56              ∧¬term^i_{b(x)} do
57           if j ≠ i ∨ ¬stable(x^j_l)
58              then EXPAND(x^j_l, y^i_k)
59           elsif l ≠ k then
60              exp_req^i_l − := 1 endif
61        endfor
62     else
63        x^i_k := head(W^i_k); W^i_k := tail(W^i_k);
64        forall y^j_l ∈ E(x^i_k) ∧ ¬term^i_{b(x)}
65              ∧¬stable(x^i_k) do
66           if k ≠ l then exp_req^i_k + := 1
67           endif;
68           if h(y^j_l) = i then
69              if k ≠ l then
70                 Q^i_l ∪:= {(x^i_k, y^j_l)}
71              else EXPAND(x^i_k, y^j_l) endif
72           else
73              SENDING(Exp(x^i_k, y^j_l), h(y^j_l))
74           endif
75        endfor
76     endif

77  EXPAND(x^j_k, y^i_l):
78     if y^i_l ∉ S^i_l then
79        S^i_l ∪:= {y^i_l};  initialize(y^i_l);
80        if c(y^i_l) ≠ 0 then
81           W^i_l := put(y^i_l, W^i_l)
82        else stable(y^i_l) := true endif;
83     endif;
84     if k ≠ l ∧ y^i_l ∉ R^i_l then
85        R^i_l ∪:= {y^i_l} endif;
86     if stable(y^i_l) then
87        if y^i_l ∈ R^i_l then R^i_l \ := {y^i_l}
88        endif;
89        if h(x^j_k) = i then
90           if k ≠ l then exp_req^i_l − := 1
91           endif; STABILIZE(x^j_k, y^i_l)
92        else B^i_l ∪:= {y^i_l};
93           d(y^i_l) ∪:= {x^j_k} endif
94     else d(y^i_l) ∪:= {x^j_k} endif
```

Fig. 1. Distributed local resolution of multiple block, alternation-free BES using its boolean graph

$$\text{block 1} \begin{cases} x_{1,1} \overset{\nu}{=} x_{2,1} \wedge x_{1,2} \\ x_{2,1} \overset{\nu}{=} x_{3,1} \wedge x_{1,3} \\ x_{3,1} \overset{\nu}{=} x_{3,1} \vee x_{1,3} \end{cases}$$

$$\text{block 2} \begin{cases} x_{1,2} \overset{\mu}{=} x_{2,1} \vee x_{1,3} \vee x_{2,2} \\ x_{2,2} \overset{\mu}{=} x_{1,2} \end{cases}$$

$$\text{block 3} \begin{cases} x_{1,3} \overset{\nu}{=} \text{false} \end{cases}$$

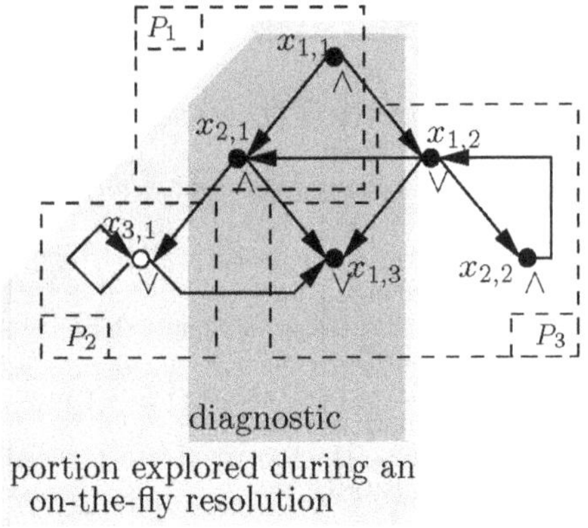

diagnostic

portion explored during an
on-the-fly resolution

Fig. 2. A multiple block, alternation-free BES, its partitioned boolean graph, and the result of a distributed on-the-fly resolution for $x_{1,1}$ on three nodes. Black and white vertices denote false and true variables, respectively.

stable variables not propagated yet (i.e., $B_l^i \neq \emptyset$) or that is completely explored but contains interblock predecessor dependencies not yet traversed by backward propagation of stable values (i.e., $term_l^i \wedge R_l^i$), is returned by HASSTABILITY and stabilized by STABILIZATION(l_i) (lines 9–10). If such block does not exist, the block k_i with maximal index that has a non-empty BFS queue (i.e., $W_k^i \neq nil$) or that is completely explored and contains pending resolution requests on unvisited variables (i.e., $exp\_req_k^i = 0 \wedge B_k^i = R_k^i = \emptyset \wedge term_k^i \wedge Q_k^i \neq \emptyset$), is returned by HASEXPANSION and explored with EXPANSION(k_i) (lines 11–12). Finally, if there is no more work on any block, the worker i remains blocked on reception, waiting, e.g., for termination detection messages sent by the supervisor (lines 14–15).

The boolean graph resolution begins with the successor generation (i.e., expansion) of main variable x (lines 63–75). Successors are then traversed in a breadth first (BFS) manner, and each of the new visited successor variables is either added to the set of interblock transitions going from block k and pending to be explored (line 70), either added to BFS heap (line 71) using primitive EXPAND (lines 77–94) locally to node i or sent to a remote node (lines 72–73) with a message Exp. The other novelty of MB-DSOLVE compared to DSOLVE is that primitive EXPANSION(k) explores interblock transitions whose destination block is k (lines 54–62) when the current visited portion of block k has completely been explored and detected stable by distributed partial termination detection. It does so by treating all such interblock transitions (lines 55–56) waiting to be explored, in order to minimize the number of partial termination detections of block k which involve costly internode synchronization.

Concerning the stabilization of variables, whose operation has a higher priority w.r.t. expansion, it is composed of two parts: one being focused on detection of block portion stability (i.e., passive stabilization) part of the distributed termination detection algorithm, and the other one being focused on the propagation of stable variables (i.e., active stabilization) (lines 30–42) either extracted from same block l (B_l^i) or from remote block l (R_l^i). Primitive STABILIZE (lines 43–52) is then invoked to update the value of variable w_k^i depending on the propagated value of y_l^j.

Distributed Generation of Diagnostics. The result of the distributed BES resolution must be accompanied by a diagnostic (example or counterexample) which provides the minimal amount of information needed for understanding the value computed for the main variable x. MB-DSOLVE computes diagnostic information in the form of a boolean subgraph rooted at x, following the approach proposed in [25]. The minimal information necessary for producing the diagnostic is stored as $s(w_k^i)$ (line 46), indicating the successor of variable w_k^i that stabilized it after a backward propagation (e.g., a true successor of an ∨-variable). This provides an implicit, distributed representation of the diagnostic, which can be explored on-the-fly once the resolution has finished.

Distributed Termination Detection for Equation Blocks. The variable $term_{b(x)}^i$ is set to true when distributed termination of the BES resolution is detected. Conditions of termination are: either the main variable x has been stabilized ($c(x) = 0$) during backward propagation (line 51), or the boolean graph has been completely explored, i.e., all local working sets of variables are empty ($\forall i \in [1, P], k \in [1, n] \cdot W_k^i = nil \wedge B_k^i = R_k^i = Q_k^i = \emptyset \wedge exp\_req_k^i = 0$) and no more messages are transiting through the network. MB-DSOLVE implements a mechanism for detecting the termination of the partial resolution of a block k on a node i ($term_k^i$). Contrary to the PTCL2 algorithm underlying the UPPDMC model checker, in which all nodes cooperate for solving a single block at a given time, our approach allows a fine-grain distribution of the BES resolution by allowing each node to work at the resolution of several blocks at the same time. The detection of the inactivity of nodes w.r.t. the resolution of a particular block improves the convergence of the distributed BES resolution by increasing the probability of finding a partially solved block from which stable values can be propagated backwards.

Our DTD is based on the four-counter method presented in [30] on a star-shaped topology with a central agent (the supervisor) whose role is asymmetric to worker nodes [15]. Activity status of workers is regularly sent to the supervisor, which therefore has a global view of the computation and is able to initiate the DTD for an equation block with higher probability of success than traditional ring-based DTD algorithms.

Example of Distributed Local Resolution. Figure 2 shows an alternation-free BES containing three equation blocks and its corresponding boolean graph, partitioned by the hash function onto three worker nodes P_1, P_2, P_3. Worker P_1 starts the exploration of the boolean graph by expanding the main variable $x_{1,1}$, whose successors $x_{2,1}$ and $x_{1,2}$ are solved locally by P_1 and sent to node P_3, respectively. Variables $x_{2,1}$ and $x_{1,2}$ can be expanded in parallel with the effect that $x_{3,1}$ is sent to node P_2, $x_{1,3}$ is sent to node P_3 (note that $x_{1,3}$ has an interblock predecessor dependency with $x_{2,1}$), and $x_{1,3}$, $x_{2,2}$ are solved locally by node P_3. Since $x_{1,3}$ is an $\vee$-vertex without successors (i.e., a constant false), its value is stable and can be propagated through backward dependencies to its predecessors; this stabilizes to false the $\wedge$-vertex $x_{2,1}$, but not the $\vee$-vertex $x_{1,2}$. The further propagation of $x_{2,1}$ stabilizes $x_{1,1}$ to false. To illustrate the fixed point operator, we can emphasize that the final value of $x_{3,1}$ is true since the variable is defined by a maximal fixed point boolean equation, and has an initial value true. Moreover, we should make clear that the block partitioning of the BES is specific to a problem resolution and totally independent from the hashing function used to distribute the BES onto remote computing nodes.

The light grey area delimits the portion of the boolean graph that was explored in order to complete the resolution of $x_{1,1}$. The dark grey area delimits the diagnostic (counterexample) associated to $x_{1,1}$, which is obtained by choosing, for each $\wedge$-variable x, the successor $s(x)$ which stabilized it to false, computed by MB-DSOLVE during propagation.

Complexity in Time, Memory, and Messages. MB-DSOLVE is based on the theory of boolean graphs underlying the sequential resolution algorithms for alternation-free BESs [1]. It consists roughly of two intertwined traversals (forward and backward) of the boolean graph, with a worst-case time complexity $O(|V| + |E|)$. The same bound applies for memory complexity, because of the backward dependencies stored during resolution for eventual propagations of stable variables. The communication cost of MB-DSOLVE can also be estimated, assuming that messages (excluding those for DTD) are sent for each *cross-dependency* (i.e., edge $(x, y) \in E \mid h(x) \neq h(y)$). Since the hash function h shares variables equally among nodes without *a priori* knowledge about locality, it also shares dependencies equally. Thus, the number of cross-dependencies can be evaluated to $((P - 1)/P) \cdot |E|$, since statistically only $|E|/P$ edges will be local to a node. Hence, the message complexity is $O(|E|)$, the worst-case being obtained with two messages (expansion and stabilization) exchanged per cross-dependency, i.e., at most $2 \cdot ((P - 1)/P) \cdot |E|$ messages. Our DTD algorithm has the same worst-case message complexity, but in practice it reveals to be very efficient, with only 0.01% of total exchanged messages used for DTD; this is due to the supervisor, which has an up-to-date global view of the computation.

3 Applications

We illustrate in this section the application of the MB-DSOLVE algorithm on two analysis problems defined on *Labeled Transition Systems* (LTSs): model checking of alternation-free μ-calculus formulas and generation of conformance test cases. An LTS is a tuple (S, A, T, s_0) containing a set of states S, a set of actions A, a transition relation $T \subseteq S \times A \times S$ and an initial state $s_0 \in S$. A transition $(s, a, s') \in T$, noted also $s \xrightarrow{a} s'$, states that the system can move from state s to state s' by executing action a (s' is an a-successor of s). Both problems can be formulated as the resolution of a multiple block, alternation-free BES, the second one essentially relying upon diagnostic generation for BESs. By applying MB-DSOLVE as BES resolution engine, we obtain distributed versions of the on-the-fly model checker EVALUATOR 3.5 [26] and the on-the-fly test generator TGV [16] of the CADP toolbox [11].

3.1   Model Checking for Alternation-Free Mu-Calculus

Modal μ-calculus [19] is a powerful fixed point based logic for specifying temporal properties on LTSs. Its formulas are defined by the following grammar (where X is a propositional variable):

$$\phi ::= \mathsf{false} \mid \mathsf{true} \mid \phi_1 \vee \phi_2 \mid \phi_1 \wedge \phi_2 \mid \langle a \rangle \, \phi \mid [a] \, \phi \mid X \mid \mu X.\phi \mid \nu X.\phi$$

Given an LTS (S, A, T, s_0), a formula ϕ denotes a set of states, defined as follows: boolean formulas have their usual set interpretation; modalities $\langle a \rangle \, \phi$ (*resp.* $[a] \, \phi$) denote the states having some (*resp.* all) a-successors satisfying ϕ; fixed point formulas $\mu X.\phi$ (*resp.* $\nu X.\phi$) denote the minimal (*resp.* maximal) solution of the equation $X = \phi$, interpreted over 2^S. The local model checking problem amounts to establish whether the initial state s_0 of an LTS satisfies a formula ϕ, i.e., belongs to the set of states denoted by ϕ.

The alternation-free fragment of the modal μ-calculus, noted L_μ^1 [8], is obtained by forbidding mutual recursion between minimal and maximal fixed point variables. L_μ^1 benefits from model checking algorithms whose complexity is linear in the size of the LTS (number of states and transitions) and the formula (number of operators), while still allowing to express useful properties, since it subsumes CTL [6] and PDL [9]. The model checking of L_μ^1 formulas on LTSs can be encoded as the resolution of an alternation-free BES [1]. We illustrate the encoding by considering the following formula, which states that the emission *snd* of a message is eventually followed by its reception *rcv* ('$-$' stands for 'any action' and '$\overline{a}$' stands for 'any action different from a'):

$$\nu X.([snd] \, \mu Y.(\langle - \rangle \, \mathsf{true} \wedge [\overline{rcv}] \, Y) \wedge [-] \, X)$$

The formula is translated first into a specification in HML with recursion [20], which contains two blocks of modal equations:

$$\{X \overset{\nu}{=} [snd] \, Y \wedge [-] \, X\}, \{Y \overset{\mu}{=} \langle - \rangle \, \mathsf{true} \wedge [\overline{rcv}] \, Y\}$$

Then, each modal equation block is converted into a boolean equation block by 'projecting' it on each state of the LTS:

$$\{X_s \overset{\nu}{=} \bigwedge\nolimits_{s \overset{snd}{\rightarrow} s'} Y_{s'} \wedge \bigwedge\nolimits_{s \rightarrow s'} X_{s'}\}_{s \in S}, \{Y_s \overset{\mu}{=} \bigvee\nolimits_{s \rightarrow s'} \mathsf{true} \wedge \bigwedge\nolimits_{s \overset{rcv}{\neq} s'} Y_{s'}\}_{s \in S}$$

A boolean variable X_s (*resp.* Y_s) is true iff state s satisfies the propositional variable X (*resp.* Y). Thus, the local model checking of the initial formula amounts to compute the value of variable X_{s_0} by applying a local BES resolution algorithm. This method underlies the on-the-fly model checker EVALUATOR 3.5 [29, 26] of CADP [11], which handles formulas of L_μ^1 extended with PDL-like modalities containing regular expressions over transition sequences.

3.2   Conformance Test Case Generation

Conformance testing aims at establishing that the implementation under test (IUT) of a system is correct w.r.t. a specification. We consider here the conformance test approach advocated in the pioneering work underlying the TGV tool [16]. We give only a brief overview of the theory used by TGV and focus on the algorithmic aspects of test selection, with the objective of reformulating them in terms of BES resolution and diagnostic generation.

The IUT and the specification are modelled as Input-output LTSs (IOLTSs), which distinguish between inputs and outputs: e.g., the actions of the IOLTS of the specification $M = (S^M, A^M, T^M, s_0^M)$ are partitioned into $A^M = A_I^M \cup A_O^M \cup \{\tau\}$, where A_I^M (*resp.* A_O^M) are input (*resp.* output) actions and τ is the internal (unobservable) action. Intuitively, input actions of the IUT are controllable by the environment, whereas output actions are only observable. In practice, tests observe the execution traces consisting of observable actions of the IUT, but can also detect *quiescence*, which can be of three kinds: deadlock (states without successors), outputlock (states without outgoing output actions), and livelock (cycles of internal actions). For an IOLTS M, quiescence is modelled by a *suspension automaton* $\Delta(M)$, an IOLTS which marks quiescent states by adding self-looping transitions labeled by a new output action δ. The traces of $\Delta(M)$ are called suspension traces of M. The conformance relation **ioco** [33] between the IUT and the specification M states that after executing each suspension trace of M, the (suspension automaton of the) IUT exhibits only those outputs and quiescences that are allowed by M.

Test generation requires a determinization of M, since two sequences with the same traces of observable actions cannot be distinguished. Since quiescence must be preserved, determinization must take place after the construction of the suspension automaton $\Delta(M)$.

A *test case* is an IOLTS $TC = (S^{TC}, A^{TC}, T^{TC}, s_0^{TC})$ equipped with three sets of trap states **Pass**∪**Fail**∪**Inconc** $\subseteq S^{TC}$ denoting verdicts. The actions of TC are partitioned into $A^{TC} = A_I^{TC} \cup A_O^{TC}$, where $A_O^{TC} \subseteq A_I^M$ (TC emits only inputs of M) and $A_I^{TC} \subseteq A_O^{IUT} \cup \{\delta\}$ (TC captures outputs and quiescences of the IUT). A test case must satisfy several structural properties, detailed in [16].

The test generation technique of TGV is based upon *test purposes*, which allow to guide the test case selection. A test purpose is a deterministic and complete IOLTS $TP = (S^{TP}, A^{TP}, T^{TP}, s_0^{TP})$, with the same actions as the specification $A^{TP} = A^M$, and equipped with two sets of trap states $Accept^{TP}$ and $Reject^{TP}$, which are used to select targeted behaviours and to cut the exploration of M, respectively. Here we focus on the computation of the *complete test graph* (CTG), which contains all test cases corresponding to a specification and a test purpose, and therefore can serve as a criterion for comparison and performance measures. Controllable test cases can be produced from a CTG by applying specific algorithms [16].

The CTG is produced by TGV as the result of three operations, all performed on-the-fly: (a) computation of the synchronous product $SP = M \times TP$ between the IOLTSs of the specification and the test purpose, in order to mark accepting and refusal states; (b) suspension and determinization of SP, leading to $SP^{vis} = det(\Delta(SP))$, which keeps only visible behaviours and quiescence; (c) selection of the test cases denoting the behaviours of SP^{vis} accepted by TP, which form the CTG. The main operation (c) roughly consists in computing $L2A$ (*lead to accept*), the subset of the states of SP^{vis} from which an accepting state is reachable, checking whether the initial state of SP^{vis} belongs to $L2A$ (which indicates the existence of a test case), and defining, based upon $L2A$, the sets **Pass**, **Fail**, and **Inconc** corresponding to the verdicts. This is the operation we chose to encode as a BES resolution with diagnostic.

Assuming that the accepting states of SP^{vis} are marked by self-looping transitions labeled by an action acc (as it is done in practice), the reachability of an accepting state is denoted by the following μ-calculus formula:

$$\phi_{acc} = \mu Y.(\langle acc \rangle \text{ true} \vee \langle - \rangle Y)$$

The set $L2A$ contains all states satisfying ϕ_{acc}. It can be computed in a backwards manner by using a fixed point iteration to evaluate ϕ_{acc} on SP^{vis}. Since this requires the prior computation of SP^{vis}, we seek another solution suitable for on-the-fly exploration, by considering the formula below:

$$\phi_{l2a} = \nu X.(\phi_{acc} \wedge [-] (\phi_{acc} \Rightarrow X))$$

Formula ϕ_{l2a} has the same interpretation as ϕ_{acc}, meaning that its satisfaction by the initial state of SP^{vis} denotes the existence of a test case. Moreover, the on-the-fly evaluation of ϕ_{l2a} on a state s satisfying ϕ_{acc} requires the inspection of every successor s' of s and, if it satisfies ϕ_{acc}, the recursive evaluation of ϕ_{l2a} on s', etc., until all states in $L2A$ have been explored.

The CTG could be obtained as the diagnostic produced by an on-the-fly model checker (such as EVALUATOR) for the formula ϕ_{l2a}. However, to annotate the CTG with verdict information and to avoid redundancies caused by the two occurrences of ϕ_{acc} present in ϕ_{l2a}, a finer-grained encoding of the problem in terms of a BES resolution with diagnostic is preferred. The corresponding BES denotes the model checking problem of ϕ_{l2a} on SP^{vis}, by applying the translation given in Section 3.1 (s, s' are states of SP^{vis}):

$$\{X_s \overset{\nu}{=} Y_s \wedge \bigwedge_{s \to s'} (Z_{s'} \vee X_{s'})\}, \{Y_s \overset{\mu}{=} \bigvee_{s \overset{acc}{\to} s'} \text{true} \vee \bigvee_{s \to s'} Y_{s'}\},$$

$$\{Z_s \overset{\nu}{=} \bigwedge_{s \overset{acc}{\to} s'} \text{false} \wedge \bigwedge_{s \to s'} Z_{s'}\}$$

If $X_{s_0^{vis}}$ is true, then a positive diagnostic (example) can be exhibited in the form of a boolean subgraph [25] containing, for each conjunctive variable (such as X_s and Z_s), all its successor variables, and for each disjunctive variable (such as Y_s) only one successor which evaluates to true. This diagnostic can be obtained by another forward traversal of the boolean graph portion already explored for evaluating $X_{s_0^{vis}}$. We turn the diagnostic into a CTG in the following manner: we associate a state of the CTG to each variable X_s; we produce an accepting transition going out of X_s only if the first subformula in the right-hand side of the equation defining Y_s is true (i.e., s has an acc-successor); we produce a transition $X_s \xrightarrow{a} X_{s'}$ for each state s' such that $Z_{s'}$ is false. Note that the diagnostic for variables Z_s does not need to be explored. Additional verdict information in the form of refuse and inconclusive transitions is produced in a similar way during diagnostic generation, since the information needed for verdicts in the CTG is local w.r.t. states of $L2A$ [16].

In the discussion above, formula ϕ_{l2a} was evaluated on the IOLTS SP^{vis} obtained after suspension and determinization of SP; however, these two operations can also be performed *after* test case selection. In other words, the BES based generation procedure sketched above can be applied directly on the synchronous product SP between the specification and the test purpose, producing a 'raw' CTG, which is subsequently suspended and determinized to yield the final CTG. This procedure underlies the EXTRACTOR tool we developed within CADP for producing raw CTGs, which are then processed by the DETERMINATOR tool [12], resulting in CTGs strongly bisimilar to those produced by TGV. Although this ordering of operations is not the most efficient one for sequential on-the-fly test case generation (since the IOLTS of the specification can contain large amounts of τ-transitions), it appears to be suitable in the distributed setting, because it leads to large BESs, which are solved efficiently by using MB-DSOLVE.

4   Implementation and Experiments

The model checker EVALUATOR 3.5 [29, 26] and the test case generator EXTRACTOR (see Figure 3) have been developed within CADP [11] by using the generic OPEN/CÆSAR environment [10] for on-the-fly exploration of LTSs.

EVALUATOR (*resp.* EXTRACTOR) consists of two parts: a front-end, responsible for encoding the verification of the L^1_μ formula (*resp.* the test selection guided by the test purpose LTS_2) on LTS_1 as a BES resolution, and for producing a counterexample (*resp.* a CTG) by interpreting the diagnostic provided by the BES resolution; and a back-end, responsible of BES resolution, playing the role of verification engine.

Sequential and distributed versions of EVALUATOR and EXTRACTOR are obtained by using as back-end either the sequential algorithms of the CÆSAR_SOLVE library [26, 28], or the MB-DSOLVE algorithm, respectively.

MB-DSOLVE (15 000 lines of C code) is a conservative extension of the distributed resolution algorithm DSOLVE [18] for single block BESs and was implemented by using the OPEN/CÆSAR environment. The size of the worker and supervisor processes is roughly the double in MB-DSOLVE w.r.t. DSOLVE. For communication, MB-DSOLVE is based on the CÆSAR_NETWORK library of CADP, which offers a set of 40 primitives finely-tuned for verification problems, such as non-blocking asynchronous emission/reception of messages through TCP/IP sockets and explicit memory management by means of bounded communication buffers.

We present in this section experimental measures comparing the distributed versions of EVALUATOR and EXTRACTOR with their sequential counterparts and

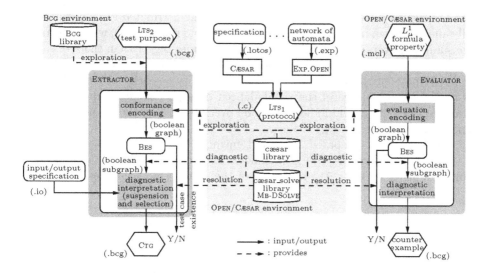

Fig. 3. The distributed on-the-fly tools EVALUATOR and EXTRACTOR

(as regards EXTRACTOR) with the TGV test case generator, and (as regards EVALUATOR) with the UPPDMC distributed model checker.

4.1 Performance of Distributed Model Checking

We begun our experiments by checking two simple properties expressed in modal μ-calculus, namely absence of deadlock $(\nu X.\,(\langle - \rangle\, \mathsf{true} \wedge [-]\,X))$ and presence of livelock $(\mu X.\,(\nu Y.\,(\langle \tau \rangle\, Y) \vee \langle - \rangle\, X))$, on a cluster of 21 XEON 2.4 GHz PCs, with 1.5 GB of RAM, running LINUX, and interconnected by a 1 Gigabit ETHERNET network. These properties were checked on the nine largest LTSs of the VLTS benchmark. Figure 4 shows the speedup (a) and memory ratio (b) between distributed EVALUATOR and its sequential optimized version based on the resolution algorithms for disjunctive/conjunctive BESs present in CÆSAR_SOLVE. Each point on each curve represents the average of ten experiments excluding the minimum and extremum values. The sequential version is very fast in finding counterexamples (e.g., for $vasy\_2581\_11442$, $vasy\_4220\_13944$, $vasy\_4338\_15666$, $vasy\_6120\_11031$, $vasy\_11026\_24660$, and $vasy\_12323\_27667$ which contain deadlocks), as can be observed with the six lower speedup curves close to x-axis on Figure 4 (a). However, when it is necessary to explore the underlying BES entirely (e.g., for cwi_7838_59101 and $vasy\_6020\_19353$ which do not contain deadlocks), the distributed version becomes interesting, allowing close to linear speedups and a good scalability as the number of workers increases.

The (slightly) super linear speedups are due to the use of hash tables for storing sets of boolean variables. Since the balancing of these tables is not perfect, some collision lists tend to become large; the effect of this phenomenon is stronger on the sequential version of the tool (which uses a single large hash table) than on its distributed version (which uses P smaller tables).

The memory overhead (see Figure 4 (b)) of the distributed version is not really affected by an increasing number of workers and remains low, with a memory consumption averaged over all nodes around 5 times bigger than the sequential one. Moreover, we observed almost no idle time, the distributed computation using systematically around 99% of the CPUs capacity on each worker node. This is partly a consequence of the well-balanced data partitioning induced by the static hash function, and indicates a good overlapping between communications and computations.

We have also compared time and memory performances of distributed EVALUATOR against the UPPDMC model checker based on game graphs. Results are given in Table 1, where each of the seven VLTS examples considered

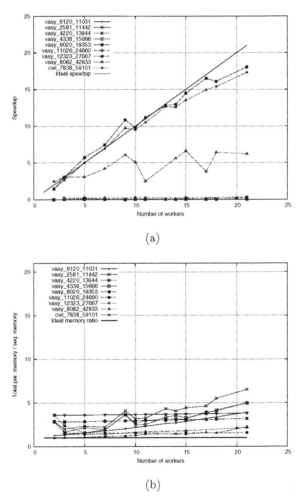

(a)

(b)

Fig. 4. Speedup (a) and memory overhead (b) of distributed w.r.t. sequential EVALUATOR when checking absence of deadlock

Table 1. Execution time (in seconds) and memory consumption (in MB) of two distributed on-the-fly model checkers: UPPDMC (U) with 25 bi-PENTIUM III nodes and EVALUATOR (E) with 21 XEON nodes

EXAMPLE	absence of deadlock				presence of livelock				
	truth	U (s)	U (MB)	E (s)	E (MB)	truth	U (s)	U (MB)	E (s)	E (MB)
vasy_2581_11442	false	44	461	2	272	false	47	n.c.	7	844
vasy_4220_13944	false	56	726	21	294	false	67	n.c.	622	1 149
vasy_4338_15666	false	64	745	2	313	false	64	n.c.	11	1 203
vasy_6020_19353	true	59	1 085	24	1 239	true	125	n.c.	8	1 442
vasy_6120_11031	false	95	947	1	170	false	108	n.c.	13	1 092
cwi_7838_59101	true	149	1 531	46	2 298	true	314	n.c.	16	2 793
vasy_8082_42933	false	162	1 374	2	268	false	134	n.c.	24	2 401

(e.g., *vasy_2581_11442*, an LTS with $2\,581 \cdot 10^3$ states and $11\,442 \cdot 10^3$ transitions) is checked for deadlock and livelock. Distributed EVALUATOR is very fast in detecting counterexamples, which explains most of the improvements in time and memory compared to UPPDMC running two threads on 25 bi-PENTIUM III 500 MHz, with 512 MB of RAM. When the whole BES (*resp.* game graph) has to be explored (e.g., for *vasy_6020_19353*), the execution time is closer to that of UPPDMC, but always remains between 2 and 8 times lower. In this case, the memory consumption of distributed EVALUATOR is slightly greater w.r.t. UPPDMC; this is due to the simple data structures used for storing backward dependencies (linked lists) and could be reduced by using more compact data structures (e.g., packet lists).

We further experimented the scalability of distributed EVALUATOR by considering LTSs of increasing size and more complex properties taken from the CADP demos[2]. For instance, we used the following formula, stating that after a *put* action, either a livelock, or a *get* action will be eventually reached:

$$\nu X. \left([put]\, \mu Y. \left((\nu Z.\, \langle \tau \rangle\, Z \vee (\langle - \rangle\, \mathsf{true} \wedge \overline{[get]}\, \mathsf{false})) \vee (\langle - \rangle\, \mathsf{true} \wedge [-]\, Y) \right) \wedge [-]\, X \right)$$

We checked that this property is satisfied by an LTS named *b256* with 6 067 712 states and 19 505 146 transitions, modelling the behaviour of a communication protocol that exchanges 256 different messages. The sequential version of EVALUATOR (based on the DFS resolution algorithm of CÆSAR_SOLVE) took around 15 minutes to perform the check, whereas the distributed version running on 10 nodes converged in 90 seconds, thus achieving a speedup close to 10.

4.2   Performance of Distributed Conformance Test Case Generation

We experimented the generation of conformance test cases by using a generic test purpose, which states that an accepting state must be reachable after 10 visible actions. Table 2 shows the performance (in time and memory) of TGV and sequential EXTRACTOR for generating CTGs from this test purpose and five LTSs from the VLTS benchmark, together with the LTS *b256* previously used for model checking. The table also gives the size of the resulting CTGs; note that

---

[2] http://www.inrialpes.fr/vasy/cadp/demos.html

Table 2. Performance analysis of TGV and sequential EXTRACTOR on six LTSs with a generic test purpose

EXAMPLE	TGV				(sequential) EXTRACTOR					
	time	MB	states	trans.	time	%	MB	%	states	trans.
vasy_164_1619	15'8s	242	100 319	231 266	3'47s	75	210	13	438 861	2 982 696
vasy_166_651	20'23s	242	170 657	586 602	1'41s	92	113	53	444 542	1 504 985
cwi_371_641	6'5s	1600	125 894	597 445	5'20s	12	310	81	1 912 260	3 163 177
vasy_386_1171	9s	11	3 319	3 892	7s	22	10	9	5 561	6 324
vasy_1112_5290	23s	33	10 827	20 888	13s	44	28	15	15 008	41 225
b256	597'4s	2322	264 194	854 786	139'22s	77	2772	-2	12 139 232	39 020 231

the raw CTGs generated by EXTRACTOR contain τ-transitions, which explains their difference in size w.r.t. the CTGs produced by TGV.

Table 3 gives time and memory measures obtained with distributed EXTRACTOR on the same six LTSs. The raw CTGs generated by this tool are exactly the same as its sequential counterpart, since both tools share the same front-end encoding the problem of test case generation. The raw CTGs are subsequently suspended and determinized using DETERMINATOR [12], yielding final CTGs strongly equivalent to those produced by TGV (this was checked using the BISIMULATOR [4] tool). The table also gives time and memory measures, as well as final CTG sizes obtained by applying DETERMINATOR.

From the measures shown in these two tables, we obtain a speedup of 1.82 of sequential EXTRACTOR combined with DETERMINATOR w.r.t. TGV. However, TGV compares favourably as regards the size of the final CTGs, which is between 30% and 50% smaller. This limitation, although not very significant (the CTGs produced by EXTRACTOR and DETERMINATOR can be subsequently reduced modulo strong equivalence), can be partially overcome by adding on-the-fly reductions, such as compression of τ-cycles [27], during the computation of the synchronous product between the LTS and the test purpose.

Distributed EXTRACTOR exhibits significant speedups w.r.t. its sequential version as regards the resolution of the underlying BES, and also a good scal-

Table 3. Performance analysis of (distributed) EXTRACTOR (7 nodes) and final CTG construction by DETERMINATOR

EXAMPLE	(distributed) EXTRACTOR		DETERMINATOR			
	time	MB	time	MB	states (final)	transitions (final)
vasy_164_1619	4'39s	470	4'40s	55	103 658	975 594
vasy_166_651	2'59s	335	2'27s	50	173 259	801 675
cwi_371_641	12'4s	880	25'8s	185	127 218	777 278
vasy_386_1171	16s	104	15s	6	2 452	3 894
vasy_1112_5290	27s	228	17s	7	8 369	41 225
b256	180'	6127	19'	459	527 875	1 709 058

ability: the resolution on 16 machines of the BES corresponding to the generic test purpose and the LTS $b256$ was done in less than 372 seconds, whereas sequential EXTRACTOR took around 30 minutes (five times slower). This example was handled by TGV in more than 597 minutes, which is four times slower than sequential EXTRACTOR combined with DETERMINATOR.

Finally, some experiments were performed successfully by EXTRACTOR and DETERMINATOR, but not by TGV. Table 4 shows two LTSs from the VLTS benchmark, on which the CTG generation for the generic test purpose using TGV leads to memory shortage (consumption of more than 3 GB of memory). On the contrary, EXTRACTOR concluded in 8 seconds that no test case was present in cwi_214_684 and, together with DETERMINATOR, computed the final (very small) CTG contained in cwi_566_3984.

Table 4. Specification examples on which TGV fails due to memory shortage

EXAMPLE	M states	M trans.	EXTRACTOR + DETERMINATOR
cwi_214_684	214	684	8 s., 19 MB, no test case
cwi_566_3984	566	3 984	1195 s., 145 MB, (32 states, 49 trans.)

5 Conclusion and Future Work

Building efficient and generic verification components is crucial for facilitating the development of robust explicit-state analysis tools. Our MB-DSOLVE algorithm for distributed on-the-fly resolution of multiple block, alternation-free BESs, goes towards this objective. MB-DSOLVE was designed to be compliant with the interface of the BES resolution library CÆSAR_SOLVE [26, 28], thus being directly available as verification back-end for all analysis tools based on CÆSAR_SOLVE. Here we illustrated its application for alternation-free μ-calculus model checking and conformance test generation, as distributed computing engine for the tools EVALUATOR [29, 26] and EXTRACTOR, developed within CADP [11] using the generic OPEN/CÆSAR environment [10] for LTS exploration.

The modular architecture of these tools does not penalize their performance. Our experiments using large state spaces from the VLTS benchmarks have shown that distributed EVALUATOR compares favourably in terms of speed and memory with UPPDMC, the other existing distributed on-the-fly model checker for μ-calculus based on game graphs [13]. Moreover, distributed EVALUATOR exhibits a good speedup and scalability w.r.t. its sequential version, relying on the optimized algorithms of CÆSAR_SOLVE for disjunctive/conjunctive BESs. Distributed EXTRACTOR, to our knowledge the first tool performing distributed on-the-fly conformance test generation, allows to scale up the capabilities of well-established dedicated tools, such as TGV [16].

We plan to continue our work along several directions. First, we will study other distributed resolution strategies, aiming at reducing memory consumption for disjunctive/conjunctive BESs, which occur frequently in practice [26]: one such strategy could combine a distributed breadth-first and a local depth-first exploration of the boolean graph. Next, we will seek distributed solutions to other problems, such as discrete controller synthesis and Horn clause resolution, by investigating their translation in terms of BESs resolution with diagnostic.

References

1. H. R. Andersen. Model checking and boolean graphs. *Th. Comp. Sci.*, 126(1):3–30, April 1994.
2. H. R. Andersen and B. Vergauwen. Efficient Checking of Behavioural Relations and Modal Assertion s using Fixed-Point Inversion. In *Proc. of CAV'95*, LNCS vol. 939, pp. 142–154.
3. J. Barnat, L. Brim, and J. Stribrna. Distributed LTL model-checking in SPIN. In *Proc. of SPIN'01*, LNCS vol. 2057, pp. 200–216.
4. D. Bergamini, N. Descoubes, Ch. Joubert, and R. Mateescu. BISIMULATOR: A Modular Tool for On-the-Fly Equivalence Checking. In *Proc. of Tacas'05*, LNCS vol. 3440, pp. 581–585.
5. B. Bollig, M. Leucker, and M. Weber. Local parallel model checking for the alternation free mu-calculus. In *Proc. of SPIN02*, LNCS vol. 2318, pp. 128–147.
6. E. M. Clarke, E. A. Emerson, and A. P. Sistla. Automatic Verification of Finite-State Concurrent Systems using Temporal Logic Specifications. *ACM Trans. on Prog. Lang. and Systems* 8(2):244–263, 1986.
7. X. Du, S. A. Smolka, and R. Cleaveland. Local Model Checking and Protocol Analysis. *Springer Int. J. on Software Tools for Technology Transfer (STTT)*, 2(3):219–241, 1999.
8. E. A. Emerson and C-L. Lei. Efficient Model Checking in Fragments of the Propositional Mu-Calculus. In *Proc. of the 1st LICS*, pp. 267–278, 1986.
9. M. J. Fischer and R. E. Ladner. Propositional Dynamic Logic of Regular Programs. *J. of Computer and System Sciences*, 18(2):194–211, 1979.
10. H. Garavel. OPEN/CÆSAR: An Open Software Architecture for Verification, Simulation, and Testing. In *Proc. of TACAS'98*, LNCS vol. 1384, pp. 68–84.
11. H. Garavel, F. Lang, and R. Mateescu. An Overview of CADP 2001. *European Assoc. for Software Science and Technology (EASST) Newsletter*, 4:13–24, 2002.
12. H. Hermanns and Ch. Joubert. A Set of Performance and Dependability Analysis Components for CADP. In *Proc. of TACAS'03*, LNCS vol. 2619, pp. 425–430.
13. F. Holmén, M. Leucker, and M. Lindström. UppDMC – A Distributed Model Checker for Fragments of the μ-calculus. In *Proc. of PDMC'04*, ENTCS vol. 128, pp. 91–105.
14. G. Holzmann. *The SPIN Model Checker — Primer and Reference Manual.* Addison-Wesley, 2003.
15. S. T. Huang and P. W. Kao. Detecting Termination of Distributed Computations by External Agents. *J. of Inf. Sci. and Engineering*, 7(2):187–201, 1991.
16. C. Jard and T Jéron. TGV: Theory, Principles and Algorithms. *Springer Int. J. on Software Tools for Technology Transfer (STTT)*, 7(4):297–315, 2005.
17. Ch. Joubert and R. Mateescu. Distributed On-the-Fly Equivalence Checking. In *Proc. of PDMC'04*, ENTCS vol. 128, pp. 47–62.
18. Ch. Joubert and R. Mateescu. Distributed Local Resolution of Boolean Equation Systems. In *Proc. of PDP'05*. IEEE Computer Society Press.

19. D. Kozen. Results on the Propositional μ-calculus. *Th. Comp. Sci.*, 27:333–354, 1983.
20. K. G. Larsen. Proof Systems for Hennessy-Milner logic with Recursion. In *Proc. of CAAP'88*, LNCS vol. 299, pp. 215–230.
21. F. Lerda and R. Sisto. Distributed-memory model checking with SPIN. In *Proc. of SPIN'99*, LNCS vol. 1680, pp. 22–39.
22. M. Leucker, R. Somla, and M. Weber. Parallel Model Checking for LTL, CTL* and L_μ^2. In *Proc. of PDMC'03*, ENTCS vol. 89, pp. 4–16.
23. A. Mader. *Verification of Modal Properties Using Boolean Equation Systems*. VERSAL 8, Bertz Verlag, Berlin, 1997.
24. Z. Manna and A. Pnueli. *The Temporal Logic of Reactive and Concurrent Systems, volume I: Specification*. Springer-Verlag, 1992.
25. R. Mateescu. Efficient Diagnostic Generation for Boolean Equation Systems. In *Proc. of TACAS'00*, LNCS vol. 1785, pp. 251–265.
26. R. Mateescu. A Generic On-the-Fly Solver for Alternation-Free Boolean Equation Systems. In *Proc. of TACAS'03*, LNCS vol. 2619, pp. 81–96.
27. R. Mateescu. On-the-fly state space reductions for weak equivalences. In *Proc. of FMICS'2005*.
28. R. Mateescu. CAESAR_SOLVE: A Generic Library for On-the-Fly Resolution of Alternation-Free Boolean Equation Systems. *Springer Int. J. on Software Tools for Technology Transfer (STTT)*, 2006.
29. R. Mateescu and M. Sighireanu. Efficient On-the-Fly Model-Checking for Regular Alternation-Free Mu-Calculus. *Sci. of Comp. Programming*, 46(3):255–281, 2003.
30. F. Mattern. Algorithms for Distributed Termination Detection. *Distributed Computing*, 2:161–175, 1987.
31. G. Pace, F. Lang, and R. Mateescu. Calculating τ-Confluence Compositionally. In *Proc. of CAV'03*, LNCS vol. 2725, pp. 446–459.
32. P. Stevens and C. Stirling. Practical Model-Checking using Games. In *Proc. of TACAS'98*, LNCS vol. 1384, pp. 85–101.
33. J. Tretmans. Test Generation with Inputs, Outputs and Repetitive Quiescence. *Software - Concepts and Tools*, 17(3):103–120, 1996.

Bounded Model Checking of Software Using SMT Solvers Instead of SAT Solvers

Alessandro Armando, Jacopo Mantovani, and Lorenzo Platania

Artificial Intelligence Laboratory,
DIST, Università degli Studi di Genova,
Viale F. Causa 13, 16145 Genova, Italy
{armando, jacopo, lorenzo}@dist.unige.it

Abstract. C Bounded Model Checking (CBMC) has proven to be a successful approach to automatic software analysis. The key idea is to (*i*) build a propositional formula whose models correspond to program traces (of bounded length) that violate some given property and (*ii*) use state-of-the-art SAT solvers to check the resulting formulae for satisfiability. In this paper we propose a generalisation of the CBMC approach based on an encoding into richer (but still decidable) theories than propositional logic. We show that our approach may lead to considerably more compact formulae than those obtained with CBMC. We have built a prototype implementation of our technique that uses a Satisfiability Modulo Theories (SMT) solver to solve the resulting formulae. Computer experiments indicate that our approach compares favourably with and on some significant problems outperforms CBMC.

1 Introduction

SAT-based Bounded Model Checking (BMC) [1] was originally proposed as a complementary technique to OBDD-based model checking for the automatic analysis of finite state systems (e.g. hardware circuits). The key idea is to build a propositional formula whose models correspond to behaviours of the system that violate a given property.

The application of Bounded Model Checking to software poses new challenges, as most programs are inherently infinite-state and new, non trivial issues such as the handling of (recursive) function calls and the modelling of complex data structures must be properly addressed. An elegant solution to the problem is proposed in [2,3] and implemented in the CBMC (C Bounded Model Checking) model checker. The approach amounts to (*i*) building a propositional formula whose models correspond to program traces (of bounded length) violating some given property and (*ii*) using state-of-the-art SAT solvers to check the resulting formulae for satisfiability.

In this paper we propose a generalisation of the CBMC approach. Instead of encoding the program into a propositional formula, we encode it into a quantifier-free formula to be checked for satisfiability w.r.t. some given decidable theory

A. Valmari (Ed.): SPIN 2006, LNCS 3925, pp. 146–162, 2006.

(henceforth called *background theory*) and use a state-of-the-art SMT (Satisfiability Modulo Theories) solver to perform the satisfiability checking.

We show that our approach may lead to considerably more compact formulae when arrays are involved in the input program. In particular the size of the formulae generated by our approach does not depend on the size of the bit-vector representation of the basic data types nor on the size of the arrays occurring in the program, whereas the encoding technique implemented in CBMC depends on both.

Experimental results obtained with a prototype implementation of our technique, called SMT-CBMC, confirm the effectiveness of our approach: on a number of problems involving complex interactions of arithmetics and arrays manipulation CBMC generates formulae whose size makes the solving phase impractical. On the other hand, SMT-CBMC scales significantly better than CBMC as the size of the arrays occurring in the input program increases.

Structure of the Paper. In the next section (Section 2) we provide a brief introduction to SMT and present a set of decidable theories that we will refer to in the rest of the paper. In Section 3 we present our generalisation to the CBMC approach: we describe the generation of the formula, the different approaches to solve the formula, and how error traces are reconstructed by exploiting the information returned by the SMT solver. In Section 4 we describe our prototype tool SMT-CBMC and present the experimental results. In Section 5 we discuss the related work and finally, in Section 6, we draw some concluding remarks.

2   Satisfiability Modulo Theories

Given a decidable theory T and a quantifier-free formula ϕ in the same language as T, we say that ϕ *is* T-*satisfiable* if and only if there exists a model of T which is also a model of ϕ or, equivalently, if $T \cup \{\phi\}$ is satisfiable. A *SMT solver for* T is a program capable of determining the T-satisfiability of every quantifier-free formula ϕ in the same language as T. Let $\Gamma \cup \{\phi\}$ be a set of formulae in the same language as T, we say that ϕ *is a* T-*consequence of* Γ, in symbols $\Gamma \models_T \phi$, if and only if every model of $T \cup \Gamma$ is a model of ϕ. Obviously, the problem of determining whether $C \models_T \phi$ holds can be reduced to the problem of checking the T-satisfiability of $C \cup \{\neg\phi\}$.

Over the last three decades, a great deal of attention has been paid to solving the SMT problem for a number of (decidable) theories of interest such as, e.g., Linear Arithmetics, the theory of lists, the theory of arrays, and—more recently—the theory of bit-vectors. The practical relevance of these theories in verification cannot be overestimated as arithmetics, lists, arrays, and bit-vectors are ubiquitous in Computer Science. Moreover, since these entities rarely occur in isolation, the problem of building SMT solvers for the combination of two (or more) decidable theories (say $T_1 \cup T_2$) out of SMT solvers for the component theories (say T_1 and T_2) has also been thoroughly investigated and solutions identified [4, 5]. More recently the problem of combining the effectiveness of state-of-the-art SAT solvers with SMT solvers has received growing attention and has led to a new generation of SMT solvers capable of remarkable performance [6].

In the rest of this section we give a brief description of the decidable theories that are relevant for the present paper.

Linear Arithmetics. By Linear Arithmetics we mean standard arithmetics (either over $\mathbb{Z}$, $\mathbb{Q}$, or $\mathbb{R}$) with addition (i.e. $+$) and the usual relational operators (e.g. $=$, $<$, $\leq$, $>$, $\geq$) but without multiplication. Multiplication by a constant, say $n * x$ where n is a numeral, is usually allowed but it is just a notational shorthand for the (linear) expression $x + \cdots + x$ with n occurrences of the variable x.

The Theory of Arrays. Arrays are data structures representing arbitrary associations of elements to a set of indexes. Unlike arrays available in standard programming languages, the arrays modelled by the theory of arrays need not have finite size. Given sorts INDEX, ELEM and ARRAY for indices, elements, and arrays (resp.) and function symbols select : ARRAY × INDEX → ELEM and store : ARRAY × INDEX × ELEM → ARRAY, the standard presentation of the theory of arrays consists of the following two axioms:

$$\forall a, i, e. \qquad \text{select}(\text{store}(a, i, e), i) = e$$
$$\forall a, i, j, e. \ \ (i \neq j \supset \text{select}(\text{store}(a, i, e), j) = \text{select}(a, j))$$

with variable a of sort ARRAY, i and j of sort INDEX, and e of sort ELEM.

SMT solvers for the theory of arrays are described in [7, 8].

The Theory of Records. Records are data structures that aggregate attribute-value pairs. Let $Id = \{id_1, \ldots, id_n\}$ be a set of field identifiers and $T_1, \ldots, T_n$ be types, $\text{REC}(id_1 : T_1, \ldots, id_n : T_n)$, henceforth abbreviated REC, is the sort of records that associate an element of type T_k to the field identifier id_k, for $k = 1, \ldots, n$. The signature of the theory of records consists of a pair of function symbols rselect_k : REC → T_k and rstore_k : REC × T_k → REC for $k = 1, \ldots, n$. The theory is finitely presented by the following axioms:

$$\forall r, e. \qquad \text{rselect}_k(\text{rstore}_k(r, e)) = e \qquad \text{for } k = 1, \ldots, n$$
$$\forall r, e. \ \ \text{rselect}_l(\text{rstore}_k(r, e)) = \text{rselect}_l(r) \ \ \text{for } k, l \text{ such that } 1 \leq k \neq l \leq n$$

where r has sort REC and e has sort T_i.

A SMT solver for the theory of records is described in [9].

The Theory of Bit-Vectors. Similarly to arrays, bit-vectors associate elements to a set of indexes, but unlike arrays the set of indexes is finite. Moreover the element associated to each index is boolean valued. Many theories of bit-vectors have been proposed in the literature [10, 11, 12, 13, 14], the main difference being whether bit-vectors are allowed to have variable size or not. For our purposes, the theory of fixed-size bit-vectors does suffice. The theory we consider has a sort $\text{BV}(n)$ for each positive integer n and a rich family of functions symbols consisting of

- *word-level functions*, e.g. _$[i{:}j]$: $\text{BV}(m) \rightarrow \text{BV}(j - i + 1)$ (bit-vector extraction) for $0 \le i \le j \le m$, @ : $\text{BV}(m) \times \text{BV}(n) \rightarrow \text{BV}(m + n)$ (bit-vector concatenation) for $m, n > 0$;
- *bitwise functions*, e.g. ˜ : $\text{BV}(n) \rightarrow \text{BV}(n)$ (bitwise not), & : $\text{BV}(n) \times \text{BV}(n) \rightarrow \text{BV}(n)$ (bitwise and), | : $\text{BV}(n) \times \text{BV}(n) \rightarrow \text{BV}(n)$ (bitwise or) for $n > 0$;
- *arithmetic functions*, e.g. + : $\text{BV}(n) \times \text{BV}(n) \rightarrow \text{BV}(n)$ (addition modulo 2^n) for $n > 0$.

3   Bounded Model Checking of Sequential Software

As in [2], preliminarily to the generation of the formula, we preprocess the input program (Section 3.1). Given a bound $n > 0$, this amounts to applying a number of transformations which lead to a simplified program whose execution traces have finite length and correspond to the (possibly truncated) traces of the original program. The quantifier-free formula is then obtained by generating a quantifier-free formula for each statement of the resulting program (Section 3.2) and the resulting formula is fed to a SMT solver (Section 3.3). If an execution path leading to a violation of an **assert** statement occurring in the original program is detected, then a corresponding trace is built and returned to the user for inspection (Section 3.4).

In order to simplify the presentation, we assume that = is the only assignment operator occurring in the program and that no pointer variables nor conditional expressions occur in the program. Notice that all these simplifying assumptions can be readily lifted as in [15].

3.1   The Preprocessing Phase

The preprocessing activity starts by replacing **break** and **continue** statements with semantically equivalent **goto** statements. The **switch** construct is replaced by a proper combination of **if** and **goto** statements. Loops are then unwound by reducing them to a sequence of nested **if** statements. For instance, **while** loops are removed by applying the following transformation n times:

$$\texttt{while}(e)\{\ I\ \} \longrightarrow \texttt{if}(e)\{\ I\ \texttt{while}(e)\{\ I\ \}\}$$

The last **while** loop is finally replaced by the statement **assert**$(!\ e)$;, called *unwinding assertion*. The failure of an unwinding assertion indicates that the bound n is not sufficient to model the system and the properties entirely, and that n must be increased.

Non recursive functions are then inlined. Recursive function calls and backward **goto**'s are unwound similarly to loop statements. Forward **goto** statements are transformed into equivalent **if** statements as explained in [1].

Next we put the program in Single Assignment Form [16] by renaming its variables in the following way. Let v be a program variable and i a program location. We define $\alpha(v, i)$ to be the number of assignments made to v prior to location i. Let e be a program expression. With $\varrho(e)$ we denote the expression obtained from e by substituting every variable v in e with $v_{\alpha(v,i)}$. Every assignment to a variable x at a given location i, say $x=e$, is replaced by $x_{\alpha(x,i)+1}=\varrho(e)$. Every assignment to an array element, say $a[e_1]=e_2$, is replaced by $a_{\alpha(a,i)+1}[\varrho(e_1)]=\varrho(e_2)$. Every condition c (also called *guard*) of an if statement is replaced by $\varrho(c)$.

Then we put the program in *conditional normal form* by invoking the normalisation algorithm of Fig. 1 with $G = \texttt{true}$ and by applying to G the usual simplifications. This normalisation step removes the else constructs and pushes the if statements downwards in the abstract syntax tree of the program till they are applied to atomic statements only. An example of the transformation of a program in conditional normal form is given in Fig. 2.

Notice that a program in conditional normal form is a sequence of statements of the form if(c) s; where s is either an assignment or an assert statement.

Let P' be the program that is input to the normalisation algorithm, let n be the number of assert and assignment statements in P', and let m be the maximum number of atomic formulae occurring in the if guards. In the worst

```
procedure NORMALISE(P,G)
    if P is an assignment or an assert statement then
        return if(G) P;
    else if P = (if(c) P₁;) then
        return NORMALISE(P₁,G && c)
    else if P = (if(c) P₁;else P2;) then
        return NORMALISE(P₁,G && c);NORMALISE(P₂,G &&(! c))
    else if P = (P₁; P2) then
        return NORMALISE(P₁,G);NORMALISE(P₂,G)
    end if
end procedure
```

Fig. 1. Turning the program in conditional normal form

```
i = a[0];                    i₁ = a₀[0];
if(x>0){                     if(x₀>0){
    if(x<10)                     if(x₀<10)              if(true) i₁ = a₀[0];
    x=x+1;                       x₁=x₀+1;               if(x₀>0 && x₀<10) x₁=x₀+1;
    else                         else                   if(x₀>0 && !(x₀<10)) x₂=x₁-1;
    x=x-1;                       x₂=x₁-1;               if(true) assert(y₀>0 && y₀<5);
}                            }                          if(true) a₁[y₀]=i₁;
assert(y>0 && y<5);          assert(y₀>0 && y₀<5);
a[y]=i;                      a₁[y₀]=i₁;
         (a)                          (b)                        (c)
```

Fig. 2. Turning a program in conditional normal form: (a) the original program, (b) the renamed program, and (c) the normalised program

case, the program output by the normalisation algorithm contains n **assert** and assignment statements guarded by n **if** guards each of which has at most $m \cdot log_2(n-1)$ atomic formulae. In fact, in the worst case P' is made of n **assert** and assignment statements and $n - 1$ nested **if ... else ...** statements, that is, there are $n - 1$ guards in P', each of which contains m atomic formulae.

3.2   The Encoding Phase

The application of the previous transformations leaves us with a renamed program P in conditional normal form. We now show how to build two sets of quantifier-free formulae C and P such that $C \models_{\mathcal{T}} \bigwedge P$ for some given background theory $\mathcal{T}$ if and only if no computation path of P violates any **assert** statement in P.

For each statement in P of the form **if**(c) v_{j+1}=e; C contains a formula of the form:[1]

$$v_{j+1} = (c' \ ? \ e' \ : \ v_j)$$

where c' and e' are obtained from c and e respectively by replacing every expression of the form $a_l[e]$ with select(a_l, e). Similarly, for each statement in P of the form **if**(c) $a_{j+1}[e_1]$=e_2; C contains a formula of the form:

$$a_{j+1} = (c' \ ? \ \text{store}(a_j, e_1', e_2') \ : \ a_j) \tag{1}$$

where c', e_1', and e_2' are obtained from c, e_1, and e_2 respectively by substituting every expression of the form $a_l[e]$ with select(a_l, e).

The set P contains a formula of the form $(c' \supset e')$ for each statement in P at location i of the form **if**(c) **assert**(e);, where c' and e' are obtained from c and e respectively by replacing every expression of the form $a_l[e]$ with select(a_l, e).

$$
\begin{aligned}
C = \{ \ &i_1 = (\text{TRUE} \ ? \ \text{select}(a_0, 0) \ : \ i_0), \\
&x_1 = ((x_0 > 0 \wedge x_0 < 10) \ ? \ x_0 + 1 \ : \ x_0), \\
&x_2 = ((x_0 > 0 \wedge \neg(x_0 < 10)) \ ? \ x_1 - 1 \ : \ x_1), \\
&a_1 = (\text{TRUE}? \ \text{store}(a_0, y_0, i_1) \ : \ a_0)\} \\
P \ = \ &\{\text{TRUE} \supset (y_0 > 0 \wedge y_0 < 5)\}
\end{aligned}
$$

Fig. 3. The sets of formulae C and P for the program in Fig. 2

---

[1] We use the expression $v = (c \ ? \ e_1 : e_2)$ as an abbreviation for the formula $(c \supset v = e_1) \wedge (\neg c \supset v = e_2)$.

3.3   Solving the Formula

Solving the Formula with a SAT Solver. In [2] this problem is reduced to a propositional satisfiability problem which is then fed to the Chaff SAT solver [17]. This is done by modelling variables of basic data types (e.g. `int` and `float`) as fixed-size bit-vectors and by considering the equations in $\mathcal{C}$ and in $\mathcal{P}$ as bit-vectors equations. Each array variable a is also replaced by $dim(a)$ distinct variables $a^0, \ldots, a^{dim(a)-1}$ and each formula of the form (1) occurring in $\mathcal{C}$ is replaced by the formula

$$\bigwedge_{i=0}^{dim(a)-1} a^i_{j+1} = ((c \wedge e_1 = i) \ ? \ e_2 : a^i_j).$$

Finally each term of the form $select(a_j, e)$ is replaced by a new variable, say x, and the following formulae are added to $\mathcal{C}$

$$\bigwedge_{i=0}^{dim(a)-1} ((e = i) \supset x = a^i_j)$$

The resulting set of bit-vector equations are then turned into a propositional formula. Variables of `struct` types are treated in a similar way. Notice that the size of the propositional formula generated in this way depends *(i)* on the size of the bit-vector representation of the basic data types as well as *(ii)* on the size of the arrays used in the program. It is worth pointing out that if the program contains a multi-dimensional array a with dimensions $d_1, \ldots, d_m$, then the number of added formulae grows as $O(d_1 \cdot d_2 \cdot \ldots \cdot d_m)$.

Solving the Formula with a SMT Solver. The alternative approach proposed in this paper is to use a SMT solver to directly check whether $\mathcal{C} \models_T \bigwedge \mathcal{P}$. By proceeding in this way the size of the formula given as input to the SMT solver does not depend on the size of the bit-vector representation of the basic data types nor on the size of the arrays occurring in the program.[2] Moreover the use of a SMT solver gives us additional freedom in the way we model the basic data types. In fact, program variables with numeric type (e.g. `int`, `float`) can be modelled by variables ranging over bit-vectors or over the corresponding numerical domain (e.g. $\mathbb{Z}$, $\mathbb{R}$, resp.). If the modelling of numeric variables is done through fixed-size bit-vectors, then the result of the analysis is precise but it depends on the specific size considered for the bit-vectors. If, instead, the modelling of numeric variables is done through the corresponding numerical domain, then the result of the analysis is independent from the actual binary representation,

---

[2] It must be said that SMT solvers for the theory of bit-vectors may expand parts of the the formula by a technique known as bit-blasting, however this is usually done as a last resort and in many cases higher level and less expensive techniques are enough to solve the problem at hand [14].

but this comes to the price of losing completeness of the analysis if non linear expressions occur in the program.

In order to check check whether $\mathcal{C} \models_T \bigwedge \mathcal{P}$, we use CVC Lite [18], a decision procedure that determines the validity of quantifier-free first-order formulae over the union of several theories.

3.4 Building the Error Trace

Whenever CVC Lite is asked to determine whether $\Gamma \models_T \phi$, but this does not hold, the tool returns a finite set of formulae $\mathcal{K}$ such that $\Gamma, \mathcal{K} \models_T \neg\phi$. The set of formulae $\mathcal{K}$ is said to be *a counterexample for* $\Gamma \models_T \phi$.

Let $\mathcal{K}$ be a counterexample for $\mathcal{C} \models_T \bigwedge \mathcal{P}$. We have defined a procedure that builds an error trace witnessing the violation of an **assert** statement occurring in the program P. The procedure (shown in Figure 4) traverses the control flow graph G_P of P starting from the first statement of P. Whenever a conditional statement $\texttt{if}(e)$ is met, then the "then" branch is taken if $\mathcal{C}, \mathcal{K} \models_T e$. If instead $\mathcal{C}, \mathcal{K} \models_T \neg e$, then the "else" branch is taken. The *control flow graph* G_P *of* P is a directed graph $G_P = (N_P, Succ_P)$, where $N_P = \{1, \ldots, n\}$ is the set of vertices and $Succ_P : N_P \to 2^{N_P}$ maps each vertex in the set of its successors. For every vertex i such that $1 \leq i \leq n$, s_i denotes the program statement corresponding to i. By convention, node 1 of G_P denotes the first statement of P to be executed. If s_i is a conditional statement (i.e. it is of the form $\texttt{if}(e)$),

```
 1: procedure ERRORTRACE(i, K)
 2:     if sᵢ is an assignment then
 3:         PRINT("Assignment:", sᵢ)
 4:         ERRORTRACE(sSuccₚ(i), K)
 5:     else if sᵢ is if(e) then
 6:         if C, K ⊨_T e then
 7:             ERRORTRACE(TSuccₚ(i), K ∪ {e})
 8:         else if C, K ⊨_T ¬e then
 9:             ERRORTRACE(FSuccₚ(i), K ∪ {¬e})
10:         else
11:             Let ⟨j, c⟩ ∈ {⟨Tsuccₚ(i), e⟩, ⟨Fsuccₚ(i), ¬e⟩}
12:             be non-deterministically chosen.
13:             ERRORTRACE(j, K ∪ {c})
14:         end if
15:     else if sᵢ is assert(e) then
16:         if C, K ⊨_T e then
17:             ERRORTRACE(sSuccₚ(i), K)
18:         else
19:             PRINT("Assertion violated:", assert(e))
20:             HALT
21:         end if
22:     end if
23: end procedure
```

Fig. 4. Building the program trace

then $Succ_P(i) = \{Tsucc_P(i), Fsucc_P(i)\}$, where $Tsucc_P(i)$ $(Fsucc_P(i))$ denotes the successor of i when e evaluates to true (false, resp.). If s_i is an assignment or an assertion statement, $Succ_P(i) = \{j\}$, with $j \in N_P$, and we DEFINE $sSucc_P(i) = j$.

Notice that lines 11–13 of the algorithm allow for the non deterministic selection of a branch of a conditional statement if neither $\mathcal{C}, \mathcal{K} \models_T e$ nor $\mathcal{C}, \mathcal{K} \models_T \neg e$ hold. This is necessary because the counterexample $\mathcal{K}$ might not be sufficient to determine the branch to choose. In this event, the branch can be chosen non deterministically, and any counterexample output by the algorithm is a valid one. Notice that this is a form of "don't care" non-determinism and therefore no backtracking is necessary. As an example of this, it can be noted that in the program of Figure 2 the assertion is violated independently from the value of variables x and i, and therefore also independently from the choice of the branches of the if statements. In fact, CVC Lite outputs a counterexample $\mathcal{K} = \{y_0 \geq 5\}$ for which neither $\mathcal{C}, \mathcal{K} \models_T (x_0 > 0 \wedge x_0 < 10)$ nor $\mathcal{C}, \mathcal{K} \models_T (x_0 > 0 \wedge \neg(x_0 < 10))$ hold.

4   Experimental Results

In order to assess the effectiveness of our approach we have developed a prototype implementation called SMT-CBMC. SMT-CBMC consists of four main modules, implemented in about 5,000 lines of Prolog code. The first module parses the input program, the second carries out the preprocessing, the third builds the quantifier-free formula, and the fourth module solves the formula according to the user options by invoking CVC Lite.[3] The latter module also builds and prints the error trace whenever a counterexample is returned by CVC Lite.

We have run SMT-CBMC against a number of families of C programs. Each family of programs is parametric in a positive integer N and such that both the size of the arrays occurring in the programs and the number of iterations done by the programs depend on N. Therefore the instances become harder as the value of N increases. The benchmark problems considered are:

- BubbleSort.c(N), an implementation of the Bubble Sort algorithm [19],
- SelectSort.c(N), an implementation of the Selection Sort algorithm [19],
- BellmanFord.c(N), an implementation of the Bellman Ford algorithm [20, 21] for computing single-source shortest paths in a weighted graph, and
- Prim.c(N) an implementation of Prim's algorithm [22] for finding a minimum spanning tree for a connected weighted graph.

Notice that these programs are well-known and therefore the result of the analysis is not interesting in itself. However they allow us to carry out a systematic and quantitative assessment of the tools as the size of the arrays involved in

---

[3] Currently SMT-CBMC can represent numeric data types with corresponding numeric domains as well as with fixed-size bit-vectors.

the programs increases. It is also worth pointing out that all the benchmark problems considered involve a tight interplay between arithmetics and array manipulation.

We have run both SMT-CBMC and CBMC on our benchmark programs. We report the total time spent by the tools to tackle each individual instance considered. Times are in seconds. All experiments have been obtained on a Pentium IV 2.4 GHz machine running Linux with the memory limit set to 800MB and the time limit set to 30 minutes. CBMC has been invoked by manually setting the unwinding bound (CBMC --unwind n option) and by disabling simplification (CBMC --no-simplify option).[4]

All the experiments presented in the rest of this section have been obtained by modelling the basic data types using bit-vectors thereby enabling the decision procedure for the theory of bit-vectors available in CVC Lite during the solving phase. Experimental results indicate that similar performances are obtained by modelling the numerical variables with the integers thereby enabling the decision procedure for linear arithmetics available in CVC Lite during the solving phase. In this section we report about testing the tools on safe instances of the benchmarks. Similar results are obtained if unsafe instances are considered.

More information about the experiments is available at URL http://www. ai.dist.unige.it/eureka.

4.1   Sorting Algorithms

The Bubble Sort algorithm (see Figure 5) sorts the array a by using two nested loops that repeatedly swap adjacent elements. The assertion statements at the end of the program check that the array has been sorted. The parameter N here determines the size of the array, as well as the number of unwindings for each loop. Notice that in this case the number of unwindings grows quadratically with N as there are two nested loops.

The experimental results obtained for this family of programs are given in Figure 6. Plot (a) shows the time spent by the tools in analysing the program while plot (b) shows the size (in bytes) of the encodings. In both cases the value of N is on the the the x-axis. CBMC runs out of memory for $N = 17$, while SMT-CBMC can still analyse programs for $N = 35$. A comparison between the formulae sizes of SMT-CBMC and CBMC substantiates our remarks about the size of the encodings: the formula built by SMT-CBMC for $N = 16$ is roughly two orders of magnitude smaller than the one built by CBMC.

Similarly to Bubble Sort, Selection Sort (see Figure 7) counts two nested loops and a swap operation, and the assertions at the end of the program check

---

[4] It is worth pointing out that CBMC features also an (undocumented) option --cvc whose effect is to output the bit-vector equations of the formula in the CVC format [23]. In this way it is possible to reason at the word-level, but still not using the theory of arrays. However this option is still experimental and not yet fully operational and therefore we have been unable to carry out experiments with it.

```
                              void BubbleSort(){
                                int i,j,t;
  int a[N];                     for (j=0;j<N-1;j++){
  void main(){                    for (i = 0; i< N-j-1; i++){
    int i;                      if (a[i]>a[i+1]){
    a={N-1,...,0};              t = a[i];
    BubbleSort();              a[i] = a[i+1];
    for(i=0;i<N;i++)           a[i+1] = t;
      assert(a[i]==i);          }
  }                             }
                              }
```

Fig. 5. Source code of `BubbleSort.c(N)`

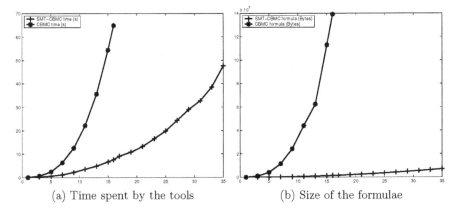

(a) Time spent by the tools   (b) Size of the formulae

Fig. 6. Results on `BubbleSort.c(N)`

that the given array has been sorted. Unlike Bubble Sort, where the swap is guarded by an `if` within the nested loop, the swap operation is done N times, where N is the size of the array, without any guard. Therefore, the encoding grows as $O(N \cdot dim(a))$, where $dim(a)$ is the size of the array. As shown in plot (b) of Figure 8, CBMC runs out of memory already for $N = 21$, whereas SMT-CBMC analyses instances till $N = 35$.

4.2   The Bellman-Ford Algorithm

The problems of the `BellmanFord(N)` family model are implementations of the Bellman Ford algorithm with a graph comprising 5 nodes and N (randomly generated) edges. Each edge is associated with a (randomly generated) positive weight. The instance for $N = 5$ is given in Fig. 9. The edges are represented

```
                            void SelectSort(){
                             int i,j,t,min;
int a[N];                    for (j=0;j<N-1;j++){
void main(){                  min=j;
 int i;                       for (i=j+1; i<N; i++)
 a={N-1,...,0};                if (a[i]>a[min])
 SelectSort();                 min = i;
 for(i=0;i<N;i++)             t = a[j];
   assert(a[i]==i);           a[j] = a[min];
}                             a[min] = t;
                             }
                            }
```

Fig. 7. Source code of `SelectSort.c(N)`

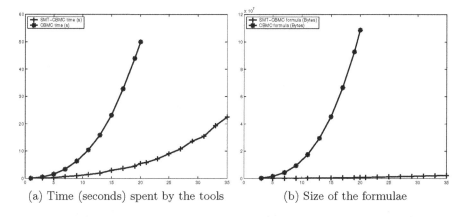

(a) Time (seconds) spent by the tools   (b) Size of the formulae

Fig. 8. Results on `SelectSort.c(N)`

by the arrays `Source` and `Dest`, the weights by the array `Weight`. The `assert` statements at the end on the program check that all the paths originating from the source node (represented by 0) have positive weight.

The results of the experiments are given in the plots of Fig. 10, where the x axis represents the number of edges. Notice that the maximum value for N is 20 in this case as the maximum number of edges in a fully connected directed graph is $k(k-1)$ where k is the number of nodes. Plot (a) displays the time spent by the tools in analysing the problems while plot (b) shows the size of the formulae. Notice that the formula generated by CBMC is already one order of magnitude bigger than the one of SMT-CBMC, for $N = 12$.

```
int INFINITY = 899;
void main(){
  int nodecount = 5;
  int edgecount = 10;
  int source = 0;
  int Source[10] = {0,0,1,0,3,3,0,1,1,3};
  int Dest[10] = {1,1,1,1,2,4,4,2,3,3};
  int Weight[10] = {0,1,2,3,4,5,6,7,8,9};
  int distance[5];
  int x,y,i,j;

  for(i = 0; i < nodecount; i++){
    if(i == source) distance[i] = 0;
    else distance[i] = INFINITY;

  for(i = 0; i < nodecount; i++){
    for(j = 0; j < edgecount; j++){
      x = Dest[j];
      y = Source[j];
      if(distance[x] > distance[y] + Weight[j])
        distance[x] = distance[y] + Weight[j];
      }
  }

  for(i = 0; i < edgecount; i++){
    x = Dest[i];
    y = Source[i];
    if(distance[x] > distance[y] + Weight[i]) return;
  }

  for(i = 0; i < nodecount; i++) assert(distance[i]>=0);
}
```

Fig. 9. Source code of the instance of BellmanFord(N) for $N = 10$

4.3   Prim's Algorithm

Prim's algorithm [22] finds a minimum spanning tree for a connected weighted graph. As in the Bellman-Ford implementation (Fig. 9), three arrays are used to model the attributes of the edges that connect the nodes of the graph. We used instances where the number of nodes of the graph is set to 4 and the number of edges increases according to the parameter N, starting from $N = 4$. As shown in Table 1, already for $N = 4$ the size of the formula output by SMT-CBMC is roughly 37 times smaller than the one of CBMC. For $N = 7$ the difference becomes greater: the formula generated by SMT-CBMC becomes roughly 60 times smaller than the one of CBMC. The generation of compact formulae has an impact on the time spent by SMT-CBMC in resolving them: the formula generated for $N = 7$ is resolved in less than 20 seconds while CBMC takes roughly two minutes, with a difference of one order of magnitude.

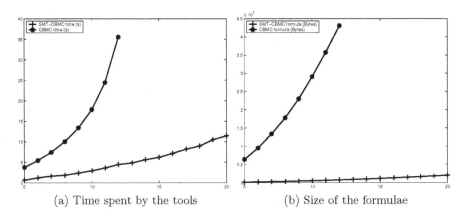

(a) Time spent by the tools   (b) Size of the formulae

Fig. 10. Results on `BellmanFord.c`(N)

Table 1. Performance of SMT-CBMC and CBMC against `Prim`(N)

	Size (Bytes)		Time (s)	
N	SMT-CBMC	CBMC	SMT-CBMC	CBMC
4	381,233	14,269,837	2.99	9.27
5	702,954	31,453,119	5.31	28.08
6	1,170,649	59,675,705	10.81	43.66
7	1,810,798	108,045,992	17.78	151.08

5   Related Work

In the recent years a number of verification procedures and tools have been developed for the analysis of software.

ESC/Java [24] is an effective error-detection tool for Java. User-annotated Java programs are analysed by generating formulae (called *verification conditions*) that represent those initial states from which no execution can violate the given properties. Such formulae are generated according to the semantics of weakest preconditions [25] and checked for validity with the Simplify theorem prover [26]. The use of weakest preconditions to build the verification condition imposes the computation of loop invariants. In order to ensure termination (finding loop invariants is an undecidable problem) several heuristics are employed, but this may lead to possible unsound outcomes of the analysis.

In order to extract error traces from counterexamples, in [27] the authors use *labelling functions* to build particular predicate symbols (labels) that are then added to the verification condition. The labels contain information that can be syntactically and automatically extracted from counterexamples in order to detect the exact position of an error in the source code. Our approach, by directly extracting error traces from counterexamples, does not clutter the formula fed to the SMT solver with extra-logical information. On the other hand it requires the invocation of the SMT solver whenever a condition of a conditional expression is met during the transversal of the control flow graph. However in our experiments the time spent by our tool to carry out this activity is always negligible.

SLAM [28], BLAST [29], and MAGIC [30] extend a symbolic model checking procedure for boolean programs with abstraction and refinement. Their approach has been shown to be very effective on specific application domains such as device drivers programming. However, when they come to reason about arrays they trade precision for efficiency. For instance SLAM and BLAST do not distinguish different elements of an array and this may lead them to report unsound results.

Saturn [31] is an efficient software error-detection tool that, like CBMC, translates C programs into boolean formulae that are then fed to a SAT solver. One of the distinguishing features of Saturn w.r.t. CBMC is the computation of summaries for each analysed function in order to speed up the (interprocedural) analysis. But again efficiency is obtained at the cost of losing soundness: similarly to SLAM and BLAST, Saturn does not distinguish different elements of an array.

Both CBMC and SMT-CBMC treat arrays in a precise way, but they only consider execution traces of bounded length, limitation that can be mitigated by iterating the technique for increasing values of the unwinding bound. As shown in Section 4 SMT-CBMC can be considerably more effective than CBMC when applied to programs involving arrays of non-negligible size. However when no arrays occur in the program or when the arrays have small size CBMC can be more effective than SMT-CBMC. This suggests that the compilation to SMT should be seen as a complement and not as an alternative to the compilation to SAT. An interesting point is to determine syntactic criteria that allow us to determine for any given program which of the two encoding techniques is likely to perform best.

6   Conclusion

We have presented a Bounded Model Checking technique for sequential programs which uses SMT solvers instead of SAT solvers. Our work generalises the one presented in [2] and we have shown that our encoding technique generates considerably more compact formulae than CBMC when arrays are involved in the input program. In particular the size of the formulae generated by our approach does not depend on the size of the bit-vector representation of the basic data types nor on the size of the arrays occurring in the program.

Experimental results confirm the effectiveness of our approach: on problems involving complex interactions of arithmetics and arrays manipulation SMT-CBMC scales significantly better than CBMC as the size of the arrays occurring in the input program increases.

References

1. Biere, A., Cimatti, A., Clarke, E.M., Zhu, Y.: Symbolic model checking without bdds. In Cleaveland, R., ed.: Proceedings of TACAS99. Volume 1579 of Lecture Notes in Computer Science., Springer (1999) 193–207

2. Kroening, D., Clarke, E., Yorav, K.: Behavioral consistency of C and Verilog programs using bounded model checking. In: Proceedings of DAC03, ACM Press (2003) 368–371

3. Clarke, E., Kroening, D., Lerda, F.: A tool for checking ANSI-C programs. In Jensen, K., Podelski, A., eds.: Proceedings of TACAS04. Volume 2988 of LNCS., Springer (2004) 168–176

4. Nelson, G., Oppen, D.: Simplification by Cooperating Decision Procedures. ACM Transactions on Programming Languages and Systems 1 (1979) 245–257

5. Shostak, R.E.: Deciding Combinations of Theories. Journal of ACM 31 (1984) 1–12

6. Barrett, C., de Moura, L., Stump, A.: SMT-COMP: Satisfiability Modulo Theories Competition. In Etessami, K., Rajamani, S., eds.: 17th International Conference on Computer Aided Verification, Springer (2005) 20–23

7. Stump, A., Barrett, C.W., Dill, D.L., Levitt, J.: A Decision Procedure for an Extensional Theory of Arrays. In: Proceedings of LICS01, IEEE (2001)

8. Armando, A., Ranise, S., Rusinowitch, M.: A Rewriting Approach to Satisfiability Procedures. Information and Computation 183 (2003) 140–164

9. Armando, A., Bonacina, M.P., Ranise, S., Schulz, S.: On a rewriting approach to satisfiability procedures: Extension, combination of theories and an experimental appraisal. In Gramlich, B., ed.: Proceedings of FroCoS05. Volume 3717 of Lecture Notes in Computer Science., Springer (2005) 65–80

10. Cyrluk, D., Möller, O., Rueß, H.: An Efficient Decision Procedure for the Theory of Fixed-Sized Bit-Vectors. In: 9th International Conference on Computer Aided Verification (CAV97). Volume 1254 of Lecture Notes in Computer Science., Springer (1997) 60–71

11. Barrett, C.W., Dill, D.L., Levitt, J.R.: A decision procedure for bit-vector arithmetic. In: Proceedings of DAC98. (1998) 522–527

12. Grumberg, O., ed.: Computer Aided Verification, 9th International Conference, CAV '97, Haifa, Israel, June 22-25, 1997, Proceedings. In Grumberg, O., ed.: CAV. Volume 1254 of Lecture Notes in Computer Science., Springer (1997)

13. Möller, O., Rueß, H.: Solving Bit-Vector Equations. In Gopalakrishnan, G., Windley, P., eds.: Formal Methods in Computer-Aided Design (FMCAD '98). Volume 1522 of Lecture Notes in Computer Science., Palo Alto, CA, Springer-Verlag (1998) 36–48

14. Bozzano, M., Bruttomesso, R., Cimatti, A., Franzen, A., Hanna, Z., Khasidashvili, Z., Palti, A., Sebastiani, R.: Encoding RTL Constructs for MATHSAT: a Preliminary Report. In Armando, A., Cimatti, A., eds.: 3rd International Workshop on Pragmatics of Decision Procedures in Automated Reasoning (PDPAR 2005). Volume 144 of Electronic Notes in Theoretical Computer Science. (2005)

15. Clarke, E., Kroening, D., Yorav, K.: Behavioral Consistency of C and Verilog Programs. Technical Report CMU-CS-03-126, Computer Science Department, School of Computer Science, Carnegie Mellon University (2003)

16. Aho, A.V., Sethi, R., Ullman, J.D.: Compilers: Principles, Techniques, and Tools. Addison-Wesley, Reading, MA (1986)

17. Moskewicz, M.W., Madigan, C.F., Zhao, Y., Zhang, L., Malik, S.: Chaff: Engineering an Efficient SAT Solver. In: Proceedings of DAC01, ACM (2001) 530–535
18. Barrett, C., Berezin, S.: CVC Lite: A new implementation of the cooperating validity checker. In Alur, R., Peled, D., eds.: Proceedings of CAV04. Volume 3114 of Lecture Notes in Computer Science., Springer (2004) 515–518
19. Knuth, D.: The Art of Computer Programming, Volume 3: Sorting and Searching. Volume 3. Addison-Wesley (1997)
20. Bellman, R.E.: On a Routing Problem. Quarterly of applied mathematics **16** (1958) 87–90
21. Ford, L.R., Fulkerson, D.R.: Flows in Networks. Princeton University Press (1962)
22. Prim, R.C.: Shortest Connection Networks and Some Generalisations. Bell System Technical Journal **36** (1957) 1389–1401
23. Stump, A., Barrett, C.W., Dill, D.L.: CVC: a Cooperating Validity Checker. In Brinksma, E., Larsen, K.G., eds.: Proceedings of CAV02. Volume 2404 of LNCS., Springer (2002)
24. Flanagan, C., Leino, K.R.M., Lillibridge, M., Nelson, G., Saxe, J.B., Stata, R.: Extended static checking for java. In: PLDI '02: Proceedings of the ACM SIGPLAN 2002 Conference on Programming language design and implementation, New York, NY, USA, ACM Press (2002) 234–245
25. Dijkstra, E.W.: Guarded commands, nondeterminacy and formal derivation of programs. Commun. ACM **18** (1975) 453–457
26. Detlefs, D.L., Nelson, G., Saxe, J.B.: Simplify: a Theorem Prover for Program Checking. Technical Report 148, HP Labs (2003)
27. Leino, K.R.M., Millstein, T.D., Saxe, J.B.: Generating error traces from verification-condition counterexamples. Sci. Comput. Program. **55** (2005) 209–226
28. Ball, T., Rajamani, S.K.: Automatically Validating Temporal Safety Properties of Interfaces. In: Proceedings of SPIN, Springer New York, Inc. (2001) 103–122
29. Henzinger, T., Jhala, R., Majumdar, R., Sutre, G.: Software Verification with Blast. In Ball, T., Rajamani, S.K., eds.: Proceedings of SPIN03. Volume 2648 of LNCS., Springer (2003) 235–239
30. Chaki, S., Clarke, E., Groce, A., Jha, S., Veith, H.: Modular Verification of Software Components in C. In: Proceedings of ICSE03, IEEE Computer Society (2003) 385–395
31. Xie, Y., Aiken, A.: Scalable error detection using boolean satisfiability. In Palsberg, J., Abadi, M., eds.: Proceedings of POPL05, ACM Press (2005) 351–363

Symbolic Execution with Abstract Subsumption Checking

Saswat Anand[1], Corina S. Păsăreanu[2], and Willem Visser[2]

[1] College of Computing, Georgia Institute of Technology
saswat@cc.gatech.edu
[2] QSS and RIACS, NASA Ames Research Center, Moffett Field, CA 94035
{pcorina, wvisser}@email.arc.nasa.gov

Abstract. We address the problem of error detection for programs that take recursive data structures and arrays as input. Previously we proposed a combination of symbolic execution and model checking for the analysis of such programs: we put a *bound* on the size of the program inputs and/or the search depth of the model checker to limit the search state space. Here we look beyond bounded model checking and consider state matching techniques to limit the state space. We describe a method for examining whether a symbolic state that arises during symbolic execution is *subsumed* by another symbolic state. Since subsumption is in general not enough to ensure termination, as the number of symbolic states may be infinite, we also consider abstraction techniques for computing and storing abstract states during symbolic execution. Subsumption checking determines whether an abstract state is being revisited, in which case the model checker backtracks - this enables analysis of an *under-approximation* of the program behaviors. We illustrate the technique with abstractions for lists and arrays. The abstractions encode both the shape of the program heap and the constraints on numeric data. We have implemented the techniques in the Java PathFinder tool and we show their effectiveness on Java programs.

1 Introduction

The problem of finding errors for programs that have heap structures and arrays as inputs is difficult since these programs typically have unbounded state spaces. Among the program analysis techniques that have gained prominence in the past few years are model checking with abstraction, most notably predicate abstraction [3, 11, 4], and static analysis [23, 7]. Both these techniques involve computing a property preserving abstraction that over-approximates all feasible program behaviors. While the techniques are usually used for *proving* properties of software, they are not particularly well suited for error detection – the reported errors may be spurious due to over-approximation, in which case the abstraction needs to be refined. Furthermore, predicate abstraction handles control-dependent properties of a program well, but it is less effective in handling dynamically allocated data structures and arrays [18]. On the other hand,

A. Valmari (Ed.): SPIN 2006, LNCS 3925, pp. 163–181, 2006.

static program analyses, and in particular shape analysis, use powerful *shape* abstractions that are especially designed to model properties of unbounded recursive heap structures and arrays, often ignoring the numeric program data. A drawback is that, unlike model checking, static analyses typically don't report counter-examples exhibiting errors.

We propose an alternative approach that enables discovery of errors in programs that manipulate recursive data structures and arrays, as well as numeric data. The approach uses symbolic execution to execute programs on un-initialized inputs and it uses model checking to systematically explore the program paths and to report counter-examples that are guaranteed to be feasible. We use abstractions to compute *under-approximations* of the feasible program behaviors, hence counter-examples to safety properties are preserved. Our abstractions encode information about the shape of the program heap (as in shape analysis) and the constraints on the numeric data.

We build upon our previous work where we proposed a combination of symbolic execution and model checking for analyzing programs with complex inputs [14, 19]. In that work we put a bound on the input size and (or) the search depth of the model checker. Here we look beyond bounded model checking and we study state matching techniques to limit the state space search. We propose a technique for checking when a symbolic state is subsumed by another symbolic state. The technique handles *un-initialized*, or partially initialized, data structures (e.g. linked lists or trees) as well as arrays. Constraints on numeric program data are handled with the help of an off-the-shelf decision procedure. Subsumption is used to determine when a symbolic state is revisited, in which case the model checker backtracks, thus pruning the state space search.

Even with subsumption, the number of symbolic states may still be unbounded. We therefore define abstraction mappings to be used during state matching. More precisely, for each explored state, the model checker computes and stores an abstract version of the state, as specified by the abstraction mappings. Subsumption checking then determines if an abstract state is being revisited. This effectively explores an under-approximation of the (feasible) paths through the program. We illustrate symbolic execution with abstract subsumption checking for singly linked lists and arrays. Our abstractions are similar to the ones used in shape analysis: they are based on the idea of *summarizing* heap objects that have common properties, for example, summarizing list elements on unshared list segments not pointed to by local variables [18].

To the best of our knowledge, this is the first time shape abstractions are used in software model checking, with the goal of error detection. We summarize our contributions as follows: *(i)* Method for comparing symbolic states, which takes into account uninitialized data. The method handles recursive structures, arrays and constraints on numeric data. The method is incorporated in our framework that performs symbolic execution during model checking. *(ii)* Abstractions for lists and arrays that encode the shape of the heap and the numeric constraints for the data stored in the summarized objects. *(iii)* Implementation in the Java PathFinder tool and examples illustrating the application of the framework on Java programs.

Related Work. Our work follows a recent trend in software model checking, which proposes under-approximation based abstractions for the purpose of *falsification* [1, 2, 12, 21]. These methods are complementary to the usual over-approximation based abstraction techniques, which are geared towards proving properties. There are some important differences between our work and [1, 2, 12, 21]. The works presented in [12, 21] address analysis of closed programs, not programs with inputs as we do here, and use abstraction mappings for state matching during concrete execution, not symbolic execution. Moreover, the approaches presented in [12,21] do not address abstractions for recursive data structures and arrays. The approach presented in [1, 2] uses predicate abstraction to compute under-approximations of programs. In contrast, we use symbolic execution and shape abstractions with the goal of error detection. And unlike [1, 2] and also over-approximation based predicate abstraction techniques, which require the a priori computation of the abstract program transitions, regardless of the size of the reachable state space, our approach uses abstraction only during state matching and it involves only the *reachable* states under analysis.

In previous work [20] we developed a technique for finding guaranteed feasible counter-examples in abstracted Java programs. That work addresses simple numeric abstractions (not shape abstractions as we do here) and it did not use symbolic execution for program analysis.

Program analysis based on symbolic execution has received a lot of attention recently, e.g. [8, 15, 24] - however all these approaches don't address state matching. Symstra [26] uses symbolic execution over numeric data and subsumption checking for test generation; we generalize that work with subsumption for uninitialized complex data; in addition, we use abstraction to further reduce the explored symbolic state space.

The works in [18, 27] propose abstractions for singly linked lists that are similar to the one described in this paper; however, unlike ours, these abstractions don't account for the numeric data stored in the summarized list elements. Recent work for summarizing numeric domains [9, 10] addresses that in the context of arrays and recursive data structures. The work presented in [5] proposes to use predicate abstraction based model checking to programs that manipulate heap structures. However, these approaches use over-approximation based abstractions and it is not clear how to generate feasible counter-examples that expose errors.

2   Background

Java PathFinder. JPF [13, 25] is an explicit-state model checker for Java programs that is built on top of a custom-made Java Virtual Machine (JVM). By default, JPF stores all the explored states, and it backtracks when it visits a previously explored state. Alternatively, the user can customize the search (by forcing the search to backtrack on user-specified conditions) and it can specify what part of the state (if any) to be stored and used for matching. We used these features to implement (abstract) subsumption checking.

Symbolic Execution in Java PathFinder. Symbolic execution [16] allows one to analyze programs with un-initialized inputs. The main idea is to use *symbolic values*, instead of actual (concrete) data, as input values and to represent the values of program variables as symbolic expressions. As a result, the outputs computed by a program are expressed as a function of the symbolic inputs.

The state of a symbolically executed program includes the (symbolic) values of program variables, a *path condition* (PC) and a program counter. The path condition accumulates constraints which the inputs must satisfy in order for an execution to follow the corresponding path.

In previous work [14, 19], we extended JPF to perform symbolic execution for Java programs. The approach handles recursive data structures, arrays, numeric data and concurrency. Programs are instrumented to enable JPF to perform symbolic execution; concrete types are replaced with corresponding symbolic types and concrete operations are replaced with calls to methods that implement corresponding operations on symbolic expressions[1]. Whenever a path condition is updated, it is checked for satisfiability using an appropriate decision procedure. We use the Omega library [22] for linear integer constraints, but other decision procedures can be used. If the path condition is unsatisfiable, the model checker backtracks. Note that if the *satisfiability* of the path condition cannot be determined (i.e., as it may be undecidable), the model checker still backtracks. Therefore, the model checker explores only *feasible* program behaviors, and all counterexamples to safety properties are preserved.

As described in [14], the approach is used for finding counterexamples to safety properties and for test input generation. For every counterexample, the model checker reports the input heap configuration (encoding constraints on reference fields and array indices), the numeric path condition (and a satisfying solution), and thread scheduling, which can be used to reproduce the error.

Lazy Initialization. Symbolic execution of a method is started with inputs that have *un-initialized* fields; *lazy initialization* is used to assign values to these fields, i.e., fields are initialized when they are first accessed during the method's symbolic execution. This allows symbolic execution of methods without requiring an a priori bound on the number of input objects.

When the execution accesses an un-initialized reference field, the algorithm nondeterministically initializes the field to *null*, to a reference to a new object with uninitialized fields, or to a reference of an object created during a prior field initialization; this systematically treats aliasing.

Lazy initialization for arrays proceeds in a similar way. Input arrays are represented by a collection of initialized array cells and a symbolic value representing the array's length. Each cell has a symbolic *index* and a symbolic *elem* value. When symbolic execution accesses an un-initialized cell, it initializes it nondeterministically to a new cell or to a cell that was created during a prior initialization; the path condition is updated with constraints that ensure that

---

[1] The interested reader is referred to [14] for a detailed description of the code instrumentation.

the index is within the array bounds and index of the the cell equals to the index that was accessed.

Method preconditions are used during lazy initialization to ensure that the method is executed only on valid inputs.

3   Example

We illustrate symbolic execution with abstract subsumption checking on the example from Figure 1. Class Node implements singly-linked lists of integers; fields elem and next represent, respectively, the node's value and a reference to the next node in the list. Method find returns the first node in the list whose elem field is greater than v. Let us assume for simplicity that the method has as precondition that the input list (pointed to by this) is non-empty and acyclic. We check if null pointer exceptions can be thrown in this program.

Figure 2 illustrates the paths that are generated during the symbolic execution of method find (we have omitted some intermediate states). Each symbolic state consists of a heap structure and the path condition (PC) accumulated along the execution path. A "cloud" in the figure indicates that the segment of the list pointed to by the next field is not yet initialized. The heap structures represent constraints on program variables and reference fields, e.g. the structure in s_1 represents all the lists that have at least one (non-null) element such that n points to the head of the list.

Branching corresponds to a nondeterministic choice that is introduced to build a path condition or to handle aliasing, during lazy initialization. For example, when the numeric condition at line 3 is executed symbolically there is a branch in execution for each possible outcome of the condition's evaluation (e.g. states s_2 and s_3). As mentioned, branching is also introduced by lazy initialization: for example, at line 4 the next field is accessed for the first time so it is initialized according to all the possible aliasing relationships in the inputs: on one branch, the "cloud" is replaced with a new node, whose next field points

```
    class Node {
      int elem;
      Node next; ...

      Node find( int v ){
1:      Node n = this;
2:      while( n != null ){
3:        if(n.elem > v) return n;
4:        n = n.next;
      }
5:      return null;
    }}
```

Fig. 1. Example illustrating symbolic execution with abstract subsumption checking

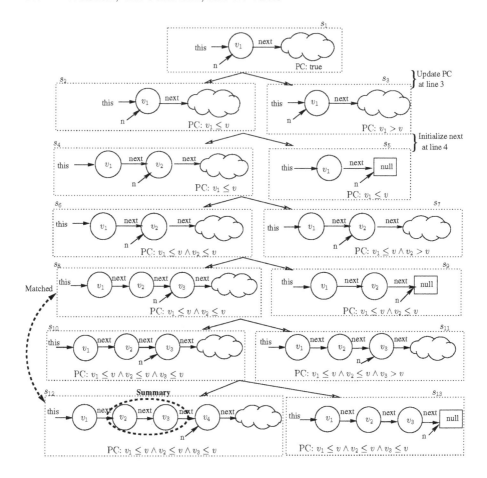

Fig. 2. State space generated during symbolic execution of `find` (excerpts)

to a "cloud", while on the other branch, the cloud is replaced with `null` (e.g. states s_4 and s_5). Note that if we wouldn't have imposed the precondition that the input list is acyclic, there had been a third branch corresponding to `next` pointing to itself.

The (symbolic) state space for this example is infinite and there is no subsumption between the generated symbolic states. However, if we use abstraction, the symbolic state space becomes finite. The list abstraction summarizes contiguous node segments that are not pointed to by local variables into a *summary* node. Since the number of local variables is finite, the number of abstract heap configurations is also finite. For the example, two nodes in state s_{12} are mapped to a summary node. As a result, the abstract state is subsumed by previously stored state s_8, at which point the model checker backtracks. The analysis terminates reporting that there are no null pointer exceptions. Note that due to abstract matching, the model checker might miss feasible behaviors. However, for this example, the abstraction is in fact *exact* – there is no loss of precision due to abstraction (all the successors of s_{12} are abstracted to states that are subsumed by the states depicted in Figure 2).

4   Subsumption for Symbolic States

In this section we describe a method for comparing symbolic states. This method is used in our framework for state matching, during symbolic execution. The method is also used for comparing *abstracted* symbolic states (as described in the next section).

Symbolic states represent multiple concrete states, therefore state matching involves checking *subsumption* between states. A symbolic state s_1 *subsumes* another symbolic state s_2, if the set of concrete states represented by s_1 contains the set of concrete states represented by s_2.

Symbolic State Representation. A symbolic state s consists of a *symbolic heap configuration* H and a path condition PC. The symbolic state also contains the program counter and thread scheduling information, which we ignore here for simplicity. Heap configurations may be partially initialized. Let R and F denote the set of all reference variables and object fields in the program respectively. We also assume that heap configurations are garbage free.

Definition 1. *A symbolic heap configuration H is a graph represented by a tuple (N, E). N is the set of nodes in the graph, where each node corresponds to a heap cell or to a reference program variable. $N = N_O \cup R \cup \{\text{null}, \text{uninit}\}$ where:*

- null *and* uninit *are distinguished nodes that represent respectively,* **null** *and objects not yet initialized.*
- N_O *is the set of nodes representing dynamically allocated objects.*

  E is the set of edges in H such that $E = E_F \cup E_R$ where:

- $E_F \subseteq (N_O \times F \times (N \setminus R))$ *represent selector* field edges. *An edge $(n_1, f, n_2) \in E_F$ denotes that field f of the object represented by n_1 points to the object represented by n_2.*
- $E_R \subseteq (R \times (N_O \cup \{null\}))$ *represent points-to edges. An edge $(r, n_1) \in E_R$ represents the fact that reference variable r points to the object represented by n_1.*

A symbolic heap configuration represents a potentially infinite number of concrete heaps through the *uninit* node. Let $\gamma(H_S)$ denote all the concrete heaps H represented by H_S. For symbolic heaps H_2, H_1: H_2 *subsumes* H_1 iff $\gamma(H_1) \subseteq \gamma(H_2)$.

A symbolic state also includes the *valuation* for the primitive typed fields (described later in this section) and the program counter. We check subsumption only for states that have the same program counter; checking subsumption involves checking (1) subsumption for heap configurations (where we ignore the valuation of the primitive typed fields) and (2) *valid* implication between numeric constraints encoded in the symbolic states.

Data: Heap Configurations $H_1 = (N^{H_1}, E^{H_1}), H_2 = (N^{H_2}, E^{H_2})$
Result: *true* if H_2 subsumes H_1, *false* otherwise; also builds labeling l for
       matched nodes
$wl_1 := \{n$ such that $(r, n) \in E_R^{H_1}\}$, $wl_2 := \{n$ such that $(r, n) \in E_R^{H_2}\}$;
while wl_2 *is not empty* **do**
    if wl_1 *is empty* **then return** false;
    $n_1 := \text{get}(wl_1)$, $n_2 := \text{get}(wl_2)$;
    if $n_2 = uninit$ **then continue**;
    if $n_1 = uninit$ **then return** false;
    if $(l(n_2) \neq null \lor l(n_1) \neq null) \land l(n_2) \neq l(n_1)$ **then return** false;
    /* n_1, n_2 matched before: */
    if $(l(n_2) \neq null \land l(n_1) = l(n_2))$ **then continue**;
    if $n_1 = null \land n_2 = null$ **then continue**;
    if $n_1 \neq null \land n_2 \neq null$ **then**
        $l(n_2) := l(n_1) := new\_label()$;
        add successors of n_1, n_2 to wl_1, wl_2 respectively in the same order;
    end
    else return false;
end
if wl_1 *is not empty* **then return** false;
return *true;*

Algorithm 1. Subsumption for Heap Configurations

Subsumption for Heap Configurations. In order to check if a program
state $s_2 = (H_2, PC_2)$ subsumes another program state $s_1 = (H_1, PC_1)$, we
first check if heap configuration H_2 subsumes heap configuration H_1. Intuitively,
H_2 subsumes H_1 if H_2 is "more general" (i.e., represents more concrete heap
configurations) than H_1. Subsumption for heap configurations is described in
Algorithm 1. The algorithm traverses the two heap graphs at the same time, in
the same order, starting from the *roots* and trying to *match* the nodes in the two
structures. Each of the reference variables from R represents a *root* of the heap.
We impose an order on the reference variables and the heap graph is traversed
from each of the roots in that order. The algorithm maintains two work lists
wl_1 and wl_2 to record the visited nodes; the lists are initialized with the heap
objects pointed to by the variables in R; **get** and **add** are list operations that
remove the first element and add an element to the end of the list, respectively.

The algorithm also *labels* the heap nodes during traversal, such that two
matched nodes have the same *unique* label. These labels are used for checking
state subsumption (as discussed below). Let $l : (N_O^{H_1} \cup N_O^{H_2}) \rightarrow \mathbb{L} \cup \{null\}$,
where $\mathbb{L}$ is a set of labels $\{l_1, l_2, l_3...\}$. If H_2 subsumes H_1 with a labelling l, we
write $H_2 \sqsupseteq^l H_1$. If the algorithm finds two nodes that cannot be matched, it
returns false. Moreover, whenever an uninitialized H_2 node is visited during traversal, the algorithm backtracks, i.e., successors of the node in H_1 that matches
this uninitialized node are not added to the worklist; the intuition is that an
uninitialized node *uninit* in H_2 can be matched with an arbitrary subgraph in
H_1. However, an uninitialized node in H_1 can only match an uninitialized node

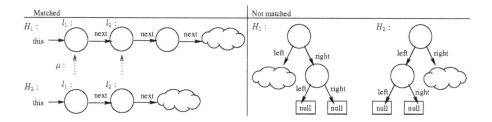

Fig. 3. Matched and unmatched heap configurations; l_1 and l_2 label matched nodes

in H_2. Note that nodes in H_1 which were not visited due to matching with uninitialized nodes are not labeled (i.e. they have *null* labels). As an example, Figure 3 shows the heap configurations for two matched lists and two unmatched binary trees. Figure 3 (left) illustrates the labeling for the two matched lists.

Theorem 1. *If Algorithm 1 returns true and labeling l for inputs H_1 and H_2 then $H_2 \sqsupseteq^l H_1$.*

Note that Algorithm 1 works on shapes represented as graphs that are *deterministic*, i.e. for each node, there is at most one outgoing edge for each selector field. Therefore, the algorithm applies to concrete heap shapes as well as partially initialized symbolic heap shapes (representing, linked lists, trees, etc.). The same algorithm also works on the abstractions for singly linked lists and arrays that we present in the next section (since our abstractions preserve the deterministic nature of the heap).

Checking Validity of Numeric Constraints. Shape subsumption is only a pre-requisite of state subsumption: we also need to compare the numeric data stored in the symbolic states. Let *primfld*(n) denote all the fields of node n that have primitive types. For the purpose of this paper, we consider only integer types, but other primitive types can be handled similarly, provided that we have appropriate decision procedures; $val^S(n, f)$ denotes the (symbolic) value stored in the integer field f of node n in state S.

Definition 2. *The "valuation" of a symbolic state s parameterized by labeling $l : N_O \to \mathbb{N}$ is defined as:*

$$val(s, l) = \bigwedge_{\substack{n \in N_O\, s.t.\, l(n) \neq null \\ f \in primfld(n)}} fn(l(n), f) = val^s(n, f).$$

Where $fn(label, field)$ returns a fresh name that is unique to $(label, field)$ pair.

Let v_s denote all the symbolic names that are used in symbolic state s; this includes both the values stored in the heap and the values that appear in the path condition. In order to check validity for the numeric constraints, we use existential quantifier elimination for these symbolic variables to obtain the numeric constraints for a symbolic state.

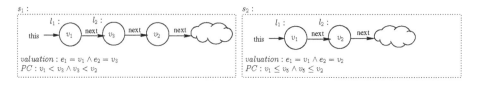

Fig. 4. State Subsumption

We are now ready to describe subsumption checking for symbolic states. A state $s_1 = (H_1, PC_1)$ is subsumed by another state $s_2 = (H_2, PC_2)$ (or s_2 subsumes s_1) if

1. $H_2 \sqsupseteq^l H_1$ and
2. $\exists v_{s_1}.val(s_1, l) \wedge PC_1 \Rightarrow \exists v_{s_2}.val(s_2, l) \wedge PC_2$.

The complexity for one subsumption step includes the complexity of heap traversal ($O(n)$ where n is the size of the heap) and the complexity for checking numeric constraints. While the cost of checking numerical constraints cannot be avoided, we believe that the cost of heap traversal can be somewhat alleviated if it is performed during garbage collection. However we need to experiment further with this idea.

As an example, consider two symbolic states in Figure 4, where s_1 is subsumed by s_2. The corresponding heap configurations were matched and labeled as described before (H_2 subsumes H_1). The valuation encodes the constraints for the numeric fields, e.g. for the first list $e_1 = v_1 \wedge e_2 = v_3$ encodes that the **elem** field of the node labeled by l_1 (denoted by e_1) has symbolic value v_1 while the **elem** field of the node labeled by l_2 (denoted by e_2) has symbolic value v_3. The path condition puts further constraints on the symbolic values v_1 and v_3. The path conditions may contain symbolic values that are not stored in the heap (e.g. v_5 in s_2) according to the program path that led to the symbolic state.

For state comparison, we "normalize" the numeric constraints, i.e., we use the Omega library for existential quantifier elimination – intuitively, for this example, we are only interested in the relative order of the data stored in the matched heap nodes. For s_1 we compute $\exists v_1, v_3, v_2 : e_1 = v_1 \wedge e_2 = v_3 \wedge v_1 < v_3 \wedge v_3 < v_2$ which simplifies to $e_1 < e_2$. Note that since the third node in the list in s_1 was not matched it is not represented in the constraint. Similarly, for s_2, $\exists v_1, v_2, v_5 : e_1 = v_1 \wedge e_2 = v_2 \wedge v_1 \leq v_5 \wedge v_5 \leq v_2$ simplifies to $e_1 \leq e_2$. And as $e_1 < e_2 \Rightarrow e_1 \leq e_2$ is *valid* and H_2 subsumes H_1, s_2 subsumes s_1.

5   Abstractions

5.1   Abstraction for Singly Linked Lists

The abstraction that we have implemented is inspired by [18, 27] and it is based on the idea of summarizing all the nodes in a *maximally uninterrupted* list segment with a *summary* node. The main difference between [18, 27] and the abstraction presented here is that we also keep track of the numeric data stored in the summary nodes and we give special treatment to un-initialized nodes. The numeric data stored in the abstracted list is summarized by setting the valuation for the summary node to be a *disjunction* of the valuations of the summarized symbolic nodes. Intuitively, a summary node stores the *union* of the values stored in the summarized nodes. Subsumption can then be used as before to perform state matching for abstract states (see Algorithm 1 where summary nodes are treated in the same way as the heap object nodes).

Definition 3. *A node n is defined as an interrupting node, or simply an interruption if n satisfies at least one of following conditions:*

1. $n = $ null
2. $n = $ uninit
3. $n \in \{m$ such that $(r, m) \in E_R\}$, *ie. n is pointed to by at least one reference variable.*
4. $\exists n_1, n_2$ such that $(n_1, \mathbf{next}, n), (n_2, \mathbf{next}, n) \in E_F$, *ie. n must be pointed-to by at least two nodes (cyclic list).*

An uninterrupted list segment is a segment of the list that does not contain an interruption. An uninterrupted list segment $[u, v]$ is maximal if, $(a, \mathbf{next}, u) \in E_F \Rightarrow a$ is an interruption and $(v, \mathbf{next}, b) \in E_F \Rightarrow b$ is an interruption.

The abstraction mapping α between symbolic heap configurations replaces all maximally uninterrupted list segments in heap H with a summary node in $\alpha(H)$. If $[u, v]$ is a maximally uninterrupted list segment in H, its abstraction $\alpha(H)$ is computed from H as follows:

1. Add a new *summary* node n_{sum} to the set of nodes N_O^H.
2. If there is an edge $(a, \mathbf{next}, u) \in E_F^H$ replace $(a, \mathbf{next}, u)$ by $(a, \mathbf{next}, n_{sum})$.
3. If there is an edge $(v, \mathbf{next}, b) \in E_F^H$ replace $(v, \mathbf{next}, b)$ by $(n_{sum}, \mathbf{next}, b)$.
4. Remove all nodes m in the list segment $[u, v]$ from N_O^H and all edges incident on m or going out of m.

Note that the edges between the nodes in the list segment, which is replaced by a summary node, are not represented in the abstraction $\alpha(H)$. With this abstraction, Algorithm 1 is used to check subsumption for abstracted heaps.

In order to check validity of numeric constraints, the definition of *valuation* is modified as follows:

Definition 4. *Valuation for an abstract state s, parameterized by labeling l is defined as,*

$$val^{abs}(s, l) = \bigwedge_{\substack{n \in (N_O \setminus N_S) s.t. l(n) \neq null \\ f \in primflds(n)}} fn(l(n), f) = val^s(n, f)$$

$$\bigwedge_{\substack{n_{sum} \in N_S s.t. l(n) \neq null \\ f \in primflds(t)}} \bigvee_{t \in sumnodes(n_{sum})} fn(l(n_{sum}), f) = val^s(t, f)$$

where, $N_S \subseteq N_O$ represents the set of summary nodes in N_O, and sumnodes(n_{sum}) *denotes the set of nodes that are summarized by n_{sum}.*

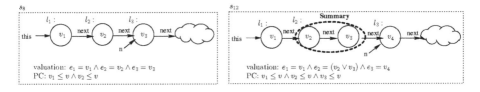

Fig. 5. Abstract subsumption between s_8 and s_{12}

Example. To illustrate the approach, let us go back to the example presented in Section 3. Figure 5 depicts the abstraction for state s_{12} and the valuation for the abstracted heap configuration. The abstracted state is subsumed by state s_8. Note that we don't explicitly summarize list segments of size one (e.g. the second list element in s_8) - in this case, the abstracted and the un-abstracted versions of a symbolic state are in fact the same.

Discussion. Note that the list abstraction ensures that the number of possible abstract heap configurations is finite; however, it is still possible to have an infinite number of different constraints over the numeric data. Also note that the focus here is on abstracting heap structures, more specifically lists, and the numeric data stored in these structures. Therefore we ignored here the numeric values of local program variables, which may also be unbounded (they are currently discarded in the abstracted state). To address these issues, we plan to use predicate abstraction in conjunction with the abstractions presented here. This is the subject of future work.

As mentioned, the list abstraction that we use preserves the deterministic nature of the heap; therefore we can use Algorithm 1 for checking subsumption for abstract heap structures. However, this is not true in general for other abstractions (e.g. in a tree abstraction, a summary node may have multiple outgoing edges for the same selector field). In the future we plan to study the decidability of subsumption checking for more general heap abstractions – see e.g. [17] – and we plan to extend our approach to these cases (e.g. through a conservative approximation of the algorithm for subsumption checking).

5.2   Abstraction for Arrays

We extended our framework with subsumption checking and an abstraction for arrays of integers. The basic idea is to represent symbolic arrays as singly linked lists and to apply the (abstract) subsumption checking methods developed for lists. Specifically, we maintain the arrays as singly linked lists, which are *sorted* according to the relative order of the array indices. Consecutive (initialized) array elements are represented as linked nodes. Summary nodes are introduced between array elements that are not consecutive. These summary nodes model zero or more un-initialized array elements that may possibly exist in the (concrete) array. We must note that this is only one particular abstraction, and there may be others – we adopt this one because in this way we can leverage on our abstraction techniques for lists.

With this list representation we apply subsumption as before. However, the "roots" are now integer program variables that are used to index the array and the special summary nodes are treated as "normal" heap objects that contain unconstrained values. Abstraction is applied in a way similar to abstraction for linked lists. The interruptions are extended to contain the special summary nodes that were introduced to model un-initialized array segments. Note that subsumption becomes "approximate", i.e., we might miss the fact that a state subsumes another, but it is never the case that we say that a state subsumes another state incorrectly.

Array Representation. A symbolic array A is represented by a a collection of array cells and a symbolic value len representing the array length. Each array cell c is a tuple $(index, elem)$: $index$ is a symbolic value representing the index in the array and $elem$ is a symbolic value representing the value stored in the array at position $index$.

The array cells are stored in a singly linked list which is sorted according to the relative order of the indices of the cells. Each list element corresponds to an array cell in A. Given array cell c, let $index(c)$ and $elem(c)$ denote the index and the value of c; also let $next(c)$ denote the cell that is next to c in the list. The following invariants hold for the list.

1. $index$ of first node is greater than or equal to 0.
2. $index$ of last node is less than len.
3. For each array cell c, other than the last cell, $index(c) < index(next(c))$.

Note that our implementation maintains these invariants during lazy initialization, i.e., whenever symbolic execution accesses an un-initialized array cell, it initializes it non-deterministically to a previously created cell or to a new cell to be placed either between two existing cells that may not be consecutive, or at the end or at the beginning of the list. The path condition is also updated to encode this information. As discussed, in order to check subsumption, we further introduce additional summary nodes between nodes that represent non-consecutive array elements.

Algorithm 2 ensures that if two array cells c_1 and c_2 may represent non-adjacent array elements, then they are represented as list nodes separated by special summary nodes (n_*). On the other hand, if c_1 and c_2 represent two consecutive elements, they are connected directly by a **next** link. Similarly, if the first (last) cell of the array may not represent the first(last) element of the array, a special summary node is added before (after) the node.

With this transformation, we can apply subsumption checking as before. However, the "roots" of the heap representing the array now include a variable pointing to the head of the list (that represents the array), and all integer program variables that index array elements. These variables are the analog of the *reference variables* $r \in R$, and are denoted by I. $val^s(i), i \in I$ denotes the (symbolic) value of i.

Abstraction over arrays is very similar to the one used for lists. It summarizes *maximally uninterrupted segments* corresponding to consecutive array elements.

Data: Sorted linked list $H^A = (N, E)$ representing array A
Result: Sorted linked list $H'^A = (N', E')$ that contains additional summary
          nodes representing uninitialized consecutive array elements
foreach c *in* N_O **do**
    add c to N'_O;
    if c *is the first element in* $H^A \wedge PC \Rightarrow index(c) = 0$ *is invalid* **then**
        add a special summary node n_* before c in H'^A;
    end
    if c *is the last element in* $A \wedge PC \Rightarrow index(c) = len - 1$ *is invalid* **then**
        add a special summary node n_* after c in H'^A;
    else
        $next(c) :=$ cell following c in A;
        if $PC \Rightarrow index(c) = index(next(c)) - 1$ *is invalid* **then**
            add a special summary node n_* after c in A';
        end
    end
end

Algorithm 2. Building sorted linked lists representing symbolic arrays

However, the definition for an interruption is slightly different, as it considers the special summary nodes introduced by Algorithm 2 as interruptions.

Definition 5. *A node c in is an interruption if $c = n_*$, or $c=null$, or c represents an array cell such that $\exists i \in I.val^s(i) = index(c)$.*

Abstraction involves replacing all uninterrupted segments with a summary node (similar to list abstraction). Note that this abstraction can be improved further, by mapping all contiguous segments of (summary and non-summary) nodes that are not pointed to by local variables to a (new) summary node.

Example. Consider the symbolic array in Figure 6 (a): $v_0..v_5$ are symbolic values stored in the initialized array elements. The concrete values 0..3 and the symbolic values j and n are array indices. Note that j and n are constrained by the path condition; *len* is a symbolic value representing the array length. Local program variables lo and hi are used to index the array. Figure 6 (b) shows the list representation for the symbolic array. The list is sorted according to the relative order of indices.

In the example the first four array elements are represented by nodes that are directly connected, as they have consecutive indices. However, the 5th array element is separated from the other nodes by two summary nodes (marked with a "*"). Note that unlike *uninit* nodes, these summary nodes are not completely unconstrained (we know their relative order in the array). We use the Omega library to decide if two elements have consecutive indices (in which case they are directly connected in the list). Figure 6 (c) shows the abstracted list, obtained with the method described before, where we consider the two variables lo and hi as interruptions; the "*" nodes are also considered interruptions.

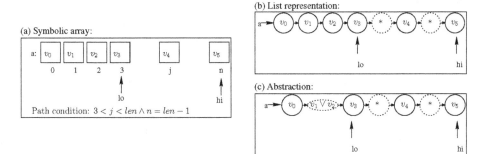

Fig. 6. A symbolic array (a), its list representation (b) and its further abstraction (c)

6 Experiments

We have implemented (abstract) subsumption checking on top of the symbolic execution framework implemented in JPF; the implementation uses the Omega library as a decision procedure. We applied our framework for error detection in two Java programs, that manipulate lists and arrays respectively.

The first program, shown in Fig. 7(a), is a list partition taken from [6]. The method takes as input an acyclic linked list l and an integer v and it removes all the nodes whose **elem** fields are greater than v; the removed elements are stored in a new list, which is pointed to by **newl**. A post-condition of the method is that each element in the list pointed to by l after method's execution must be less than or equal to v. This post-condition is not satisfied for the buggy program.

In order to apply symbolic execution, we first instrumented the code, as shown in Fig. 7(b). Concrete types are replaced with symbolic types (library classes that we provide), and concrete operations are replaced with method calls that implement equivalent symbolic operations. For example, classes **SymList** and **SymNode** implement symbolic **Lists** and **Nodes** respectively, while class **Expression** supports manipulation of symbolic integers.

Method **ifSubsumed** checks for state subsumption. It takes an integer argument that denotes the program counter, and it returns true only if the current program state is subsumed by a state which was observed before at that program point. If **ifSubsumed** returns true, then the model checker backtracks (as instructed by the **Verify.ignoreIf** method); otherwise, the current state is stored for further matching and the search continues. **check()** and its symbolic version **symCheck()** checks if the method's post-condition is satisfied.

Symbolic execution with abstract subsumption checking discovers the bug and it reports a counterexample of 10 steps, for an input list that has two elements, such that the first element is $\leq v$, and the second element is $> v$.

The second program, shown in Fig. 8(a), is an array partition taken from [1]. It is a buggy version of the **partition** function used in the QuickSort algorithm, a classic example used to study test generation. The function permutes the elements of the input array so that the resulting array has two parts: the first

```
class ListPartition{
  List list = new List();
  Node l = list.root;
  Node curr, prev, newl, nextCurr;
  int v;
  public void partition(){
    prev = newl = null;
    curr = l;
    while(curr != null){
      nextCurr = curr.next;
      if( curr.elem > v ){
        //if(prev != null &&
        //  nextCurr != null) //bug
        if(prev != null)        //fix
          prev.next = nextCurr;
        if(curr == l) l = nextCurr;
        curr.next = newl;
        newl = curr;
      }
      else prev = curr;
      curr = nextCurr;
  } check();} }
```

```
class ListPartition{
  SymList list = new SymList();
  SymNode l = list.root();
  SymNode curr, prev, newl, nextCurr;
  Expression v = new SymbolicInteger();
  public void partition(){
    prev = newl = null;
    curr = l;
    while(curr != null){
      Verify.ignoreIf(ifSubsumed(1));
      nextCurr = curr.get_next();
      if(curr.elem()._GT(v)){
        //if(prev != null &&
        //  nextCurr != null)      //bug
        if(prev != null)           //fix
          prev.set_next(nextCurr);
        if(curr == l) l = nextCurr;
        curr.set_next(newl);
        newl = curr;
      }
      else  prev = curr;
      curr = nextCurr;
  } symCheck(); } }
```

(a) Original code   (b) Instrumented code

Fig. 7. List Partition Example

part contains values that are less than or equal to the chosen pivot value a[0];
while the second part has elements that are greater than the pivot value. There
is an array bound check missing in the code at line L2 that can lead to an array
bounds error. The corresponding instrumented code is shown in Fig. 8(b) – class
SymbolicIntArray implements symbolic arrays of integer, while ArrayIndex
implements symbolic integers that are array indexes.

Symbolic execution with abstract subsumption checking reports a counterexample of 30 steps, for an input array that has four elements.

We also analyzed the corrected versions of the two partition programs to
see whether symbolic execution with abstract subsumption checking terminates
when the state-space is infinite, which is the case for the two programs. The
state-exploration indeed terminates without reporting any error. For the list partition the analysis checked subsumption 23 times of which 11 states were found
to be subsumed (12 unique states were stored). For the array partition the respective numbers were: 30 checks, with 17 subsumed and 13 states stored. This
demonstrates the effectiveness of the abstractions in limiting the state space.
We should note that subsumption checking without abstraction is not sufficient
to limit the state space. This is in general the case for looping programs. Although in theory, we should check for subsumption at every program point to
get maximum savings, it may be very expensive. In all our experiments, we
checked for subsumption inside every loop only once, before the body of the
loop is executed.

```
class ArrayPartition{
  int[] a;
  int n, tmp, pivot;
  int lo;
  int hi;
  public void parition(){
    //assume (n > 2);
    pivot = a[0];
    lo = 1;
    hi = n-1;
    while(lo <= hi){
L2:   //while(a[lo] <= pivot) //bug
      while(lo <= hi &&
            a[lo] <= pivot)    //fix
        lo++;
      while(a[hi] > pivot)
        hi--;
      if(lo < hi){
        tmp = a[hi];
        a[hi] = a[lo];
        a[lo] = tmp;
} } } }
```

(a) Original code

```
class ArrayPartition{
  SymbolicIntArray a;
  Expression pivot, n, tmp;
  ArrayIndex lo = new ArrayIndex("lo");
  ArrayIndex hi = new ArrayIndex("hi");

  public void partition(){
    Verify.ignoreIf(n._LE(2));
    pivot = a.get(0);
    lo.assign(new IntegerConstant(1));
    hi.assign(n._minus(1));
    while(lo.index()._LE(hi.index())){
      Verify.ignoreIf(ifSubsumed(1));
L2:   //while(a.get(lo)._LE(pivot)){ //bug
      while(lo.index()._LE(hi.index()) &&
            a.get(lo)._LE(pivot)){    //fix
        Verify.ignoreIf(ifSubsumed(2));
        lo.assign(lo.index()._plus(1));
      }
      while(a.get(hi)._GT(pivot)){
        Verify.ignoreIf(ifSubsumed(3));
        hi.assign(hi.index()._minus(1));
      }
      if(lo.index()._LT(hi.index())){
        Expression tmp = a.get(hi);
        a.set(hi, a.get(lo));
        a.set(lo, tmp);
} } } }
```

(b) Instrumented code

Fig. 8. Array Partition Example

We should note that these simple preliminary experiments show only the feasibility of the approach. A lot more experimentation and engineering is needed to be able to assess the merits of the approach on realistic programs. We should note that even for such small examples, traditional testing methods would not discover the errors easily (e.g. a test-suite which gives 100% statement, or branch coverage might not be able to detect the errors).

7 Conclusion

We described a state space exploration approach that uses symbolic execution and subsumption checking for the analysis of programs that manipulate heap structures and arrays. The approach explores only *feasible* program behaviors. We also defined abstractions for lists and arrays, to further reduce the explored symbolic state space. We implemented the approach in the Java PathFinder tool and we applied it for error detection in Java programs.

The approach presented here is complementary to over-approximation abstraction methods and it can be used in conjunction with such methods, as an efficient way of discovering counter-examples that are guaranteed to be feasible.

We view the integration of the two approaches as an interesting topic for future research. For the future, we plan to investigate how/if our approach extends to other shape abstractions and to use predicate abstraction for the numeric program data. We also plan to use our technique for systematic generation of complex test inputs (similar to [14]) and to characterize when there is loss of precision introduced by abstraction, for automatic abstraction refinement (similar to [21]). Moreover we plan to investigate the use of subsumption checking for *compositional analysis* of large programs. The presented abstractions were used in the context of *falsification*; however, we believe that they have merit in the context of verification - this could be achieved by storing the abstracted state and starting the symbolic execution from this abstracted state.

References

1. T. Ball. A theory of predicate-complete test coverage and generation. *MSR-TR-2004-28*, 2004.
2. T. Ball, O. Kupferman, and G. Yorsh. Abstraction for falsification. In *Proc. of CAV'05*, 2005.
3. T. Ball and S. K. Rajamani. The slam toolkit. In *Proc of CAV '01*, 2001.
4. S. Chaki, E. Clarke, A. Groce, S. Jha, and H. Veith. Modular verification of software components in C. *ACM Trans. Computer Systems*, 30(6):388–402, 2004.
5. D. Dams and K. S. Namjoshi. Shape analysis through predicate abstraction and model checking. In *Proc. VMCAI*, 2003.
6. C. Flanagan and S. Qadeer. Predicate abstraction for software verification. In *Proc. POPL*, 2002.
7. R. Ghiya and L. J. Hendren. Is it a tree, a DAG, or a cyclic graph? a shape analysis for heap-directed pointers in c. In *Proc of POPL*, pages 1–15, 1996.
8. P. Godefroid, N. Klarlund, and K. Sen. Dart: Directed automated random testing. In *Proc. PLDI*, 2005.
9. D. Gopan, F. DiMaio, N. Dor, T. Reps, and M. Sagiv. Numeric domains with summarized dimensions. In *Proc. TACAS*, 2004.
10. D. Gopan, T. Reps, and M. Sagiv. Numeric analysis of arrays operations. In *Proc. 32nd POPL*, 2005.
11. T. A. Henzinger, R. Jhala, R. Majumdar, and G. Sutre. Software verification with blast. In *Proc. of SPIN'03*, volume 2648 of *LNCS*, 2003.
12. G. J. Holzmann and R. Joshi. Model-driven software verification. In *Proc. 11th SPIN Workshop*, volume 2989 of *LNCS*, Barcelona, Spain, 2004.
13. Java PathFinder. +http://javapathfinder.sourceforge.net+.
14. S. Khurshid, C. Pasareanu, and W. Visser. Generalized symbolic execution for model checking and testing. In *Proc. TACAS'03*, Warsaw, Poland, April 2003.
15. S. Khurshid and Y. Suen. Generalizing symbolic execution to library classes. In *Proc. 6th PASTE*, 2005.
16. J. C. King. Symbolic execution and program testing. *Commun. ACM*, 19(7):385–394, 1976.
17. V. Kuncak and M. Rinard. Existential heap abstraction entailment is undecidable. In *Proc. of SAS*, 2003.
18. R. Manevich, E. Yahav, G. Ramalingam, and M. Sagiv. Predicate abstraction and canonical abstraction for singly-linked lists. In *Proc. VMCAI*, Paris, 2005.

19. C. Pasareanu and W. Visser. Verification of java programs using symbolic execution and invariant generation. In *Proc of SPIN'04*, volume 2989 of *LNCS*, 2004.
20. C. S. Păsăreanu, M. B. Dwyer, and W. Visser. Finding feasible abstract counter-examples. *STTT*, 5(1):34–48, November 2003.
21. C. S. Păsăreanu, R. Pelánek, and W. Visser. Concrete model checking with abstract matching and refinement. In *Proc. CAV'05*, 2005.
22. W. Pugh. The Omega test: A fast and practical integer programming algorithm for dependence analysis. *Commun. ACM*, 31(8), Aug. 1992.
23. S. Sagiv, T. W. Reps, and R. Wilhelm. Parametric shape analysis via 3-valued logic. *TOPLAS*, 2002.
24. K. Sen, D. Marinov, and G. Agha. Cute: A concolic unit testing engine for c. In *Proc. 5th ACM Sigsoft ESEC/FSE*, 2005.
25. W. Visser, K. Havelund, G. Brat, S. J. Park, and F. Lerda. Model checking programs. *Automated Software Engineering Journal*, 10(2), April 2003.
26. T. Xie, D. Marinov, W. Schulte, and D. Notkin. Symstra: A framework for generating object-oriented unit tests using symbolic execution. In *Proc. TACAS 2005*, 2005.
27. T. Yavuz-Kahveci and T. Bultan. Automated verification of concurrent linked lists with counters. In *Proc of SAS*, volume 2477 of *LNCS*, 2002.

Abstract Matching for Software Model Checking*

Pedro de la Cámara, María del Mar Gallardo, and Pedro Merino

University of Málaga, Campus de Teatinos s/n,
29071, Málaga, Spain
pedro.delacamara@gmail.com
{gallardo, pedro}@lcc.uma.es

Abstract. Current research in software model checking explores new techniques to handle the storage of visited states (usually called the heap). One approach consists in saving only parts or representations of the states in the heap. This paper presents a new technique to implement sound abstract matching of states. This kind of matching produces a reduction in the number of states and traces explored. With the aim of obtaining a useful result, it is necessary to establish some correctness conditions on the matching scheme. In this paper, we use static analysis to *automatically* construct an abstract matching function which depends on the program and the property to be verified. The soundness of the static analysis guarantees the soundness of verification. This paper describes the overall technique applied to Spin, the correctness issues and some examples which show its efficiency.

Keywords: State Explosion, Model Extraction, Static Analysis.

1 Introduction

Using model checking techniques for software verification usually involves the manual construction of high-level models. This construction process allows designers to exploit many abstraction techniques in order to reduce the size of the model and its complexity. However, it requires a deep understanding of both the real software and the modelling language features. Furthermore, the manual construction process is susceptible to human error due to misunderstandings or simply programming bugs. These errors are especially subtle because they may lead to false results in the process of model checking, thus failing to detect the presence of errors in the program being verified. Recently, many projects are developing automatic *model extraction* techniques, that can contribute to solving this problem with minimal human interaction (see Feaver [8], JPF1 [6] and Bandera [2]). However, extracted models are too cumbersome and have too many implementation details. Therefore, it is desirable to develop further optimization (abstraction) techniques in order to reduce the complexity of the model. This paper is devoted to a new optimization technique which reduces the explored

---

* This work has been supported by the Spanish MEC under grant TIN2004-7943-C04.

state space in models extracted for Spin. The technique is based on the use of abstractions to implement the matching functions to discard visited states, as introduced in [7] and [10]. The main novelty of our *abstract matching* method is the ability to preserve the verification results, due to how the abstract matching function is constructed.

The method proposed in [7] consists in hiding specific C variables in such a way that they are never used to compare global states and decide whether they have been visited or not. However all the variables are always visible when making backtracking or producing new states. The mechanism used to implement this abstraction scheme in [7] is based on a new Promela extension that allows verifier to hide variables when performing the matching of states.

Our approach is an extension of the implementation mechanism in [7], that adds soundness to the verification results for a given class of abstraction functions. In particular, we employ a property-oriented static analysis to locate the set of variables that should be hidden or matched after every execution step. The analysis is a variant of dependency analysis, called *influence analysis*, that produces a set of visible variables for every statement in the model. These variables should be visible after executing the statement (after producing a new global state), in such a way that their values are considered to match the global state.

In our method, the correctness conditions and the algorithm used to carry out the static analysis can be changed depending on the properties to be preserved during verification. In the paper we describe methods for three kinds of properties: a) code reachability, b) safety properties (state properties in Spin) and c) liveness properties (sequence properties in Spin). For all these cases, static analysis is done prior to verification, during the model extraction, producing a Promela model with property-oriented abstract matching. The new model is verified as usual with Spin.

The new approach can be directly implemented for other tools that perform model extraction for Spin (like FeaVer or Bandera), however we are integrating the static analysis in our tool SOCKETMC [3]. This tool is a model extractor focused on verifying *concurrent software with well defined*-APIs. The experimental results with the new optimization are very promising.

Regarding another closely related work, the implementation of abstract matching in [10] is based on applying predicate abstraction to the global states to be compared, in such a way that explicit hiding is not used. Predicate abstraction works matching over-approximations of the states, so the method can produce unsoundness when verifying properties. For that reason, a refinement method, assisted with a theorem prover, is used in order to improve the quality of the analysis.

As far as we know, our work contains valuable contributions compared with [7] and [10]. For example,

1. The method for obtaining the abstraction function based on static analysis can be done automatically
2. Static analysis provides a sound function for each given property.
3. The soundness conditions also allow the verification of liveness properties.

The paper is organized as follows. The preliminary material in Section 2 summarizes the extraction approach in our tool SOCKETMC, which is used as our first target tool to include the new optimization. Section 3 gives an overview of the method and its application to a real example. The soundness of the method is presented in the next two sections. Section 4 explains the static analysis called influence analysis, and Section 5 contains a discussion on the correctness of this approach. Conclusions are given in Section 6.

2   Model Extraction and SocketMC

The aim of tool SOCKETMC is to verify concurrent C applications that make an extensive use of operating system facilities through system calls. We have constructed a Spin oriented model of the behavior of the operating system API. This model is used to automatically obtain a correct abstraction of the software that makes use of this API. Following [8], we have defined a mapping from the original C code to extended Promela. The tool SOCKETMC automatically transforms each API call into Promela code preserving the semantics of the calls. The new Promela model constructed can be verified with standard Spin. Figure 1 shows the main parts of SOCKETMC, the parser and the model generator. The figure also shows the relevant role of the formal semantics given to the operating system API. The semantics is used as a reference to construct a sound Promela version of each API call.

Our basic mapping scheme works as shown in Figure 2. Given a set of C processes (`main()` functions), the mapping from the original code to Promela is done replacing every process (every `main()` function) with a `proctype()` definition. Then, the body of every `proctype()` is filled using the Promela extensions for C code (`c_decl`, `c_state`, `c_expr` and `c_code`). This is done breaking the original C code in the points where a call to API appears. The final Promela

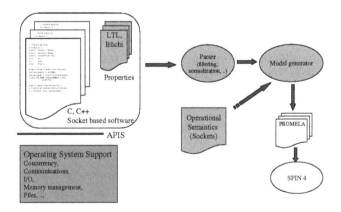

Fig. 1. Extracting models with SocketMC

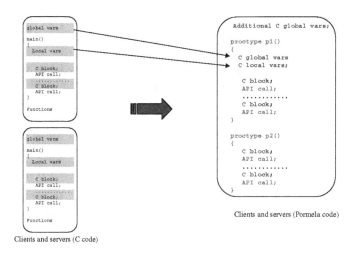

Fig. 2. Mapping scheme in SocketMC

code preserves the sequential execution of every C *block* code between two system calls. Thus, when verifying the model, Spin interleaves blocks and system calls as atomic instructions. The way of implementing the extraction, together with the semantic-driven API implementation, ensures the correctness of our verification model.

By default, the Promela models produced by the first version of the tool contain all the C variables in the original code. The approach presented in the following sections is oriented to automatically reduce the set of variables that should actually be managed to produce the state space. The proposals are implemented as new versions of the two components of SOCKETMC (the parser and the model generator in Figure 1), and the result is a new mapping scheme to extract the final Promela models. It is worth noting, however, that our method to construct abstract matching functions can be applied to other model extraction approaches and even to other model checking tools.

3   Sound Abstract Matching

The technique to include abstract matching in Spin and the problem of how to ensure the validity of abstract matching functions to preserve CTL* was originally presented by Holzmann and Joshi in [7]. The first issue, the implementation approach, is presented in the context of the nested depth-first search algorithm with abstraction described in [1]. The idea is to avoid starting a new search from a given state if an *essentially* equal state has been visited before. In summary, including abstraction when storing visited states works as follows. Given a global state s, abstraction consists in replacing the usual operation "add s to States", that stores it as a visited state, by the new operation "add f(s) to States", where f() represents the abstraction function. Function f()

generates the abstraction of **s** to be matched and stored (note that in [1] and [7], operation **add** has a second argument that does not affect the abstraction process). It is worth noting that function **f()** is only used to cut the search tree, but the exploration is actually realized with the concrete state **s**, without losing information. Observe that when we use abstraction during the model checking process as explained above, we explore a subset of the original state space. Thus, in this case, abstraction produces an *under-approximation* of the original model, in contrast to the usual applications of abstraction which produce *over-approximation*. In order to assure that the explored tree via abstract matching is equivalent to the original one, function **f()** has to satisfy some correctness conditions.

As proposed in [7], a particular version of function **f()** is implemented as a C function which is invoked within a **c_code** construct. The implementation also benefits from the **c_track** primitive to hide the values of C variables from the state-vector. Thus, the abstraction function computes abstract representations of the hidden data and copies the result onto the state-vector.

In [7], the authors do not address any particular method to generate **f()**, however they present necessary conditions to define sound abstract functions that preserve CTL properties. This is the starting point for our work. We provide implementable methods to produce abstraction functions, which are sound and oriented to the property to be checked.

Our Abstraction Approach. In our implementation scheme, abstraction functions are implemented in such a way that they can (automatically) identify the variables to be hidden from the state-vector in every global state, after the execution of every verification step. A simple case shows how it works. Let us consider the following code which can be obtained by a model extractor like the first version of SOCKETMC:

```
proctype p()
{
c_track "&x" "sizeof(int)" "Matched"
c_track "&y" "sizeof(int)" "Matched"
....
L0: initialize();
L1: c_code{x = 1};
L2: c_code{y = x};
...
}
```

Note that in this code variables x and y are visible in the state-vector. Suppose that we extract the model assuming, by default, that C variables do not influence the verification of properties. Following this assumption, both variables x and y are declared as hidden (**UnMatched**). Consider now that we are interested in checking a particular property that needs the precise value of x after executing the code at **L1**. Then, in this case, the model extracted must keep variable x visible after executing the instruction at **L1**, as the following code shows:

```
proctype p()
{
c_track "&x" "sizeof(int)" "UnMatched"
c_track "&y" "sizeof(int)" "UnMatched"
c_track "&x_" "sizeof(int)" "Matched"
c_track "&y_" "sizeof(int)" "Matched"
....
L0: atomic{initialize(); f(L0)};
L1: c_code{x = 1; f(L1)};
L2: c_code{y = x; f(L2)};
...
}
void f(int label)
{
   switch(label)
   {
     ......
     case L0:
            now.x_ = Hide()
            now.y_ = Hide()
     case L1:
            now.x_ = Show(x)
     case L2:
            now.x_ = Hide()
            now.y_ = Hide()
     ....
   }
}
```

This second version calls f() at any point where the global state should be stored. This function uses its argument to check the current execution point in the model. [1] The function updates the variables to be hidden (using Hide()) or updated (using Show()) before matching them with the current set of visited states, depending on the current label. For instance, variable x can be hidden until it is updated in L1. However, it is made visible at L1 because it will be used to update y, and it is again hidden after updating y. The extra variables x_ and y_ are used to store the values of the real (hidden) variables or a representation of their values. We propose to construct f() using the information provided by a static analysis of the model. This construction approach for f() can be extended to models with multiple processes.

Example. We illustrate the use of this technique with a simple case study. In this example, we use a model of a simple server and check the property **P1** which states that *"If the process receives a message END, then it eventually leaves the main loop"*. In Figure 3 (left), it is possible to see the main loop of the server, including those variables which are visible at each control point in order to verify **P1** with abstract matching.

In the example, **READ** and **CREATERESPONSE** are actually non-deterministic selections returning a message from a limited set. **PREPROCESS** and **POSTPROCESS** are loops simulating heavy work between the reception of the message and the response.

---

[1] Note that it would not be necessary to pass the label as an argument of f(), if Promela would allow to access the current label of process p with some code such as `label = now.Pp->_label`

```
do ::c_expr{enter_loop}->
    atomic {
        READ(cRead,sock2,ReadBuf, sizeof(ReadBuf));
        c_code { f(21);};};
Message_Rx:
// P1: ReadBuf and cRead are visible   ----- P2:  ReadBuf and cRead are visible
    atomic {
        PREPROCESS(cRead,ReadBuf);
        c_code { f(22);}; };
// P1: ReadBuf and cRead are visible   ----- P2:  ReadBuf and cRead are visible
    atomic {
        CREATERESPONSE(cResp,ReadBuf,WriteBuf,cRead);
        c_code { f(23);}; };
// P1: WriteBuf and cResp are visible  ----- P2: ReadBuf, WriteBuf and cResp are visible
    atomic {
        POSTPROCESS(cResp, WriteBuf);
        c_code { f(24);}; };
// P1: WriteBuf and cResp are visible  ----- P2: ReadBuf, WriteBuf and cResp are visible
    atomic {
        WRITE(cResp,sock2,WriteBuf,cResp);
        c_code { f(25);};
    };
// P1: cResp is visible                ----- P2: ReadBuf and cResp are visible
    c_code{ enter_loop=(cResp)>0; f(26); };
// P1: enter_loop is visible           ----- P2: ReadBuf and enter_loop are visible
:: else ->
    c_code { f(27);}; break;
od;
```

Fig. 3. Visibility rules for ReadBuf with properties **P1** (left) and **P2** (right)

Variable **ReadBuf** is a receiving buffer that may take multiple non-deterministic values. Suppose that the static analysis to verify **P1** determines that **ReadBuf** is not significant from **CREATERESPONSE** on. Thus, if **ReadBuf** is hidden after executing **CREATERESPONSE**, we avoid multiple re-exploration of the executing paths starting at this point. It is clear that the amount of saved memory (and time) depends on the range of values **ReadBuf** may take. The static analysis decides to hide **ReadBuf** because property **P1** only checks **ReadBuf** at label **Message_Rx**.

Suppose that we modify the property in such a way that we need to check **ReadBuf** at every control point. For example, assume a new property **P2** stating that "**ReadBuf** *never contains a* **RETRY** *message*". In order to verify **P2**, we cannot hide variable **ReadBuf** after **CREATERESPONSE**. Figure 3 (right) shows the result of the new model extracted. Note that the set of visible variables associated to the statements has changed.

Figure 4 shows the performance of our proposal for the previous example. We have assumed that variables **ReadBuf** and **WriteBuf** may take 20 different values, and that loops **PREPROCESS** and **POSTPROCESS** iterate 100 times. The table shows the state space explored in three cases: (1) without abstract matching (2) with abstract matching oriented to property **P1**, and (3) with abstract matching oriented to property **P2**.

Figure 5 explains the different reduction results obtained for the three cases described above. When we do not use abstract matching, we have 20x20 different traces to explore at the end of the loop (left column). If we hide **WriteBuf** after **WRITE**, the number of traces is divided by 20 (right column). Additionally, when

	No Abstract Matching	Abstract Matching. (ReadBuf partial hiding)	Abstract Matching (ReadBuf fully visible)
State-vector	152 bytes	28 bytes	28 bytes
Errors	26753	23	862
States stored	787705	117	1761
Total memory	90.929 MB	2.724MB	5.389 MB
Elapsed time	14:26.44	0:00.72	0:03.33

Fig. 4. Test Results

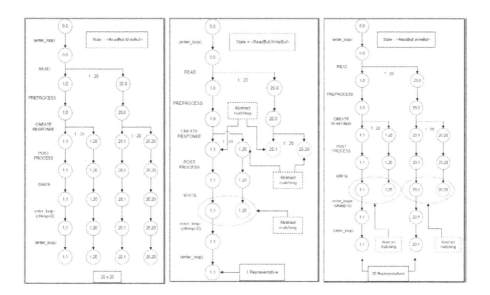

Fig. 5. Reachability trees for the case study

ReadBuf is partially hidden, we have only one representative for all the traces (center column). This phenomenon also happens with other variables and it is the main reason for state reduction.

Optimizations. The actual representation of the visible variables is a bit more complex than shown before. Instead of using duplicate variables (like x_ and y_, in the previous example), we employ a vector as described below.

```
void f(int label) {
    switch (label){
        ...
        case 21:    now.idVector[0]=Hide();
                    now.idVector[1]=ShowVariable(1, sizeof(cRead), &cRead);
                    now.idVector[2]=Hide();
                    ...}
                    break;
        ... }
```

Global variable `idVector` is in fact the abstract representation of the visible variables which are implemented as a vector of identifiers. Auxiliary function `ShowVariable()` computes the identifier associated to the current value of a given variable, while the `Hide()` function returns always a null identifier.

A lookup table allows us to map identifiers to values. This table is dynamically updated in such a way that it always keeps an entry for every reached value. In addition, the table is never included in the usual data structures of the model checker (stack and heap). It can be seen as a global data structure for all execution paths. The results shown in Figure 4 were obtained with this technique.

Experimental results show that our approach to automatically construct abstract functions is very promising, however we still have to discuss about how to ensure soundness. The following sections are devoted to this key issue.

4 Static Analysis

In this section, we describe the static analysis from which we construct sound abstract matching functions. In particular, we develop the so-called *influence analysis* (IA) to annotate each program point with a set of *significant* variables needed to correctly analyze a given property. This static analysis is a refinement of the *live variables analysis* given in [9] (adapted to the case of Promela) where the properties of interest to be verified are taken into account. Our analysis is also related to cone of influence reduction, described in [4], However, as far as we know, the cone-of-influence technique does not take into account that while a given variable could be visible for some states it then could become invisible for successor states of the same trace.

Note that in the analysis we do not distinguish between C variables and pure Promela variables, although currently we have only implemented abstract matching for C variables. In order to simplify the presentation, we only use the traditional Promela syntax for the variables and we have omitted the explicit treatment of some Promela instructions such as those dealing with channels (including rendez-vous).

The *influence analysis* is used to decide which variables should be visible at each program point during the model checking process. It determines for each program control point the variables which *influence* a given set of variables V of interest. The analysis then records the variables which are *alive* wrt a particular property. Thus, if a variable does not affect any variable in V at a given program point, we may hide it since its current value is not relevant for the verification.

Clearly, the most precise analysis is the one attaching the smallest set of variables to each program point. In the following sections, we show different versions of IA. Each extension gives us a different precision degree for the analysis and the abstract matching function induced preserves a different set of program properties. The first analysis IA_1 is the most precise one, it produces the *best* abstract matching function, the one inducing the best state space reduction.

However, IA_1 only preserves the code reachability tree of the original Promela model. In addition, since global variables must be dealt with very carefully, IA_1 assumes that the model under analysis has only local variables. The second analysis IA_2 produces bigger sets of variables, but it preserves *safety properties*. The third analysis IA_3 studies the case of models with global variables, and, finally, IA_4 is the least precise analysis, but in contrast, it preserves *liveness properties*.

4.1   Influence Analysis for Promela Models

Given a Promela program M, the goal of IA is to associate each program point in M with the least set of variables whose value is needed to analyze M.

Let $\mathcal{V}$ be the set of program variables. Informally, given $x, y \in \mathcal{V}$, we say that variable y *influences* variable x at a given program point, if there exists an execution path in M from this point to an assignment $x = exp$ and the current value of y is used to calculate exp, that is, if the current value of y is *needed* to construct the value of x in the future. In Section 5, when we prove the correctness of the analysis, we give a formal definition of the *influence* notion.

In this section, we focus on describing the four above-mentioned IA analyses. We first define the input language and some previous notions.

Let $Inst$ be the set of all valid Promela instructions including the *Basic* statements (boolean expressions, assignments, and input/output instructions over channels), *If, Do, Atomic, Unless* statements, etc. In the sequel, we do not distinguish between C variables and pure Promela variables. We also consider that blocks of C instructions inside c_code are *Basic* instructions, and that the C boolean expressions are managed as pure Promela boolean expressions. In order to simplify the analysis, we assume that *Do* instructions are implemented using *If* and *goto* statements. In addition, we assume that branches of *If* instructions always begin with a boolean expression followed by at least one statement. We use *true* and *skip* to complete the instruction when necessary (for example, see the codes of Figure 6). Finally, when an *else* branch appears, we assume that it

```
active proctype p1(int n) {
  int x = n;
  int y = 1;
  L1:if
    :: x > 0 -> L2: x = x - 1;
              L3: y = 2 * y; goto L1
    :: else -> L4: printf(y); goto End:
  fi;
  End:
}
```

```
active proctype p2() {
  int x1,x2,x3,x4;
  L1:if
    :: true -> L2: x2 = 0;
    :: true -> L3: x2 = 1;
  fi;
  L4: x1 = x2;
  L5: if
    :: x3 < 2 -> L6: x1 = x1 + 1; goto L5;
    :: else -> L7: skip;
      L8: if
        :: true -> L9: x4 = 0;
        :: true -> L10: x4 = -1;
      fi;
      L11: if
        :: x4 >= 0 -> L12: assert(x1 == 2);
        :: else -> L3: skip
      fi
  fi;
  End:
}
```

Fig. 6. Two Promela processes

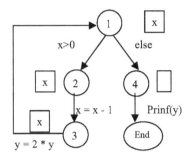

Fig. 7. Result of IA_1 for process p1

has been replaced by the corresponding boolean expression. In the sequel, *Bool-Exp* will denote the set of boolean expressions that can be constructed with the usual arithmetical and boolean operators and with the constant and variables of the model.

As commented above, the first approach IA_1 is focussed on preserving the code reachability tree of M, that is, the abstract matching function induced by IA_1 should preserve each possible execution path in the original model. Since the control flow is determined by boolean expressions and *If* instructions, in order to simulate all the execution paths, we need to record all possible values of the variables appearing in the guards of the control statements.

Let us define the set $\mathcal{I}nit \subseteq \mathcal{V}$ of all program variables appearing in some boolean expression in M. We perform the *influence analysis* IA_1 attaching each program counter of M with the set of program variables influencing some variable in the set $\mathcal{I}nit$.

For instance, set $\mathcal{I}nit$ is respectively defined as $\{x\}$ and $\{x3, x4\}$ for the Promela codes of processes p1 and p2 given in Figure 6. In addition, Figure 7 shows the intended result of IA_1 for p1. For this process, the static analysis associates the set $\{x\}$ with the labels $L1$, $L2$, and $L3$. The usefulness of the analysis is clear. If we are interested in knowing whether a particular label of process p1() is reachable, we only have to store variable x at labels $L1$, $L2$, and $L3$. In particular, variable y may be completely hidden because its value is not relevant for this analysis.

The rest of this section is devoted to formalizing IA_1. Let $M = P_1 || \cdots || P_n$ be the Promela model to be analyzed, where each P_i denotes a concurrent process declared in M. We assume that all instructions of the Promela model M to be analyzed *are labelled*, i.e., each one has the form $L : ins$ where $L \in \mathcal{L}$ is a unique label of the instruction ins. Labels may be defined by the user or automatically assigned. *End* denotes the set of user-defined labels starting with *end*. The code of each process is finished with a label $L \in End$. Note that labels represent program counters of processes. For the sake of simplicity, we assume that labels in each Promela process are different.

Function $I : \mathcal{L} \to Inst$ returns the *basic/If* instruction following a label. For instance, considering the code of process $p2$ of Figure 6, $I(L6) = x1 = x1 + 1$ and $I(L1) = if :: true- > L2 : x2 = 0; :: true- > L3 : x2 = 1; fi;$.

Let us define function $next : \mathcal{L} \to \mathcal{L}$ which associates each label l with the label pointing to the *basic/If* instruction following $I(l)$. For example, in the process $p2$ of Figure 6, $next(L2) = L4$, and $next(L6) = L5$. Function $next$ is well defined because we always apply it to labels pointing to *basic* instructions, although it may return labels pointing to a *basic/If* statement.

Given any expression or instruction, we denote with $var(e) \subseteq \mathcal{V}$ the set of program variables appearing in e. In order to simplify the description, we first define how to apply the static analysis to a simple process P, and then, we extend it to a whole program M composed of several concurrent processes. We also assume that M contains only local variables, and then we again extend the analysis to the case of global variables.

The static analysis $\mathsf{IA_1}$ is formally constructed as the least fixed point of function $F1 : \wp(\mathcal{V})^{\mathcal{L}} \to \wp(\mathcal{V})^{\mathcal{L}}$ which represents a transformation function which transforms vectors of $|\mathcal{L}|$ components, where $|\mathcal{L}|$ is the number of labels in the system. Each component that corresponds to a label is a set of variables.

Given $\overrightarrow{s} = \{s_l | l \in \mathcal{L}\} \in \wp(\mathcal{V})^{\mathcal{L}}$, the l component of $\overrightarrow{s}$ is denoted as $\overrightarrow{s}(l)$ and it corresponds to a subset of variables attached to label l at a given moment during the computation of $\mathsf{IA_1}$. Similarly, we denote the l-component of $F1(\overrightarrow{s})$ as $F1(\overrightarrow{s})(l)$. $F1$ is a backward analysis, that is, it extracts information following the reverse control flow of the program. Thus, to calculate the significant variables at a given label $l \in \mathcal{L}$, we have to collect all variables which are needed by any execution path starting at this point. Recall that a variable is needed at l if its value is needed for executing the next instruction $I(l)$ or for executing any instruction following $I(l)$. Considering this, given $\overrightarrow{s} \in \wp(\mathcal{V})^{\mathcal{L}}$ we construct $F1(\overrightarrow{s})(l)$ making use of function $F1^*$, defined below, as follows:

$$F1(\overrightarrow{s})(l) = F1^*(I(l), \overrightarrow{s}(next(l))) \ if \ I(l) \in Basic \ and$$
$$F1(\overrightarrow{s})(l) = \cup_{i=1}^{n} F1^*(b_i, \overrightarrow{s}(l_i)) if \ I(l) = if :: b_1 \to l_1 : \cdots :: b_n \to l_n : \cdots ; fi$$

where $F1^* : Basic \times \wp(\mathcal{V}) \to \wp(\mathcal{V})$ calculates the significant variables before executing a basic instruction as:

$$F1^*(x = exp, s) = \begin{cases} s & if \ x \notin s \\ s - \{x\} \cup var(exp) & if \ x \in s \end{cases}$$
$$F1^*(bool, s) = s \cup var(bool), bool \ being \ a \ Boolean \ expression$$

That is, assignment $x = exp$ modifies set s only if it has been deduced that x influences some variable in $\mathcal{I}nit$. In that case, the effect of $x = exp$ consists of introducing in s all variables appearing in exp, excluding x because its value is changed in the assignment. In addition, all variables appearing in a boolean expression influence variables in $\mathcal{I}nit$ (in fact, they belong to $\mathcal{I}nit$).

Define $\forall l \in \mathcal{L}.s_l = \emptyset$, and consider the initial vector $\overrightarrow{s_{init}} = \{s_l\}_{l \in \mathcal{L}}$. Then, the static analysis $\mathsf{IA_1} \in \wp(\mathcal{V})^{\mathcal{L}}$ is given by the least fixed point of the equation $\overrightarrow{s} = F1(\overrightarrow{s})$ which can be calculated as the limit of the sequence $\overrightarrow{s_{init}}, F1(\overrightarrow{s_{init}}), \cdots$.

Proposition 1. *The following assertions regarding sequence* $\overrightarrow{s_{init}}, F1(\overrightarrow{s_{init}}), \cdots$ *hold: (1)* $\forall i \in \mathbb{N}, F1^i(\overrightarrow{s_{init}}) \subseteq F1^{i+1}(\overrightarrow{s_{init}}); (2) \exists k \geq 0, F1^k(\overrightarrow{s_{init}}) = F1^{k+1}(\overrightarrow{s_{init}}).$

Now, consider a Promela program $M = P_1 || \cdots || P_n$ involving the concurrent execution of several processes. Let IA_1^i be the vector produced by the *Influence Analysis* for the process P_i. If we denote with $\mathcal{L}_i$ the set of labels appearing in process P_i, then a program point of M may be represented by a tuple $(l_1, \cdots, l_n)$ with $l_i \in \mathcal{L}_i$ being the current program counter of process P_i. Considering this, we define function $\mathsf{IA}_1 : \mathcal{L}_1 \times \cdots \times \mathcal{L}_n \to \wp(\mathcal{V})$ as: $\mathsf{IA}_1(l_1, \cdots, l_n) = \bigcup_{i=1}^n \mathsf{IA}_1^i(l_i)$ That is, the information regarding analysis IA_1 at program counter $(l_1, \cdots, l_n)$ is the union of all variables collected by IA_1 for each process P_i at label l_i.

Example. The following code is a simplified version of the example shown in Fig 3. Observe that when applying analysis IA_1 to this code, variables become visible/unvisible following the rules given by function $F1^*$. For instance, cResp is needed before evaluating the test CResp > 0, but before assignment cResp = WriteBuf is not needed because its value is rewritten. The same rule is applicable to the rest of the variables.

```
do :: enter_loop ->
       ReadBuf = any();
 // ReadBuf is visible
       WriteBuf = ReadBuf;
 // WriteBuf is visible
       cResp = WriteBuf;
 // cResp is visible
       enter_loop = (cResp >0);
   :: else -> break;
od;
```

4.2 Extending the Influence Analysis IA_1

In this section, we propose several refinements of IA_1 which are able to preserve more interesting temporal properties and to take global variables into account. Observe that the construction of IA_1 is based on function $F1^*$, which propagates the information about the needed variables in a bottom-up manner, and on the initial vector $\overrightarrow{s_{init}}$ which is used to start the fixed point computation. The variants of IA_1 presented below are constructed by modifying function $F1^*$ and by considering different initial vectors.

Preserving State Properties. The first extension IA_2 preserves state properties specified using the **assert** statement. For instance, assume that we want to analyze the assertion x1 == 2 of process $p2$ in the right-hand column of Figure 6. It is easy to see that we need to store not only the variables *influencing* the boolean expressions in the code in order to completely simulate the reachability tree, but also those that influence the variables in the **assert** statement (variable x1 in the example). Figure 8 shows the intended result of IA_2 for process $p2$. Observe that variable $x1$ is attached to some labels of the process, since its value is needed at label $L12$. Thus, our purpose is to extend analysis IA_1 to take into account variables appearing in the assertions to be validated in the code

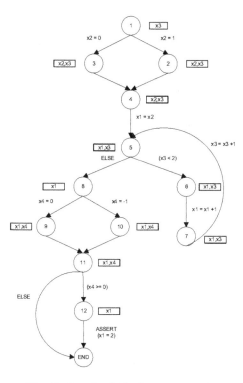

Fig. 8. Result of $|A_2$ for process p2

during execution. It is worth noting that at this point, we are still assuming the model only contains local variables. To extend $|A_1$, it is enough to redefine $F1^*$ as function $F2^*$ defined as:

$$F2^*(x = exp, s) = \begin{cases} s & \text{if } x \notin s \\ s - \{x\} \cup var(exp) & \text{if } x \in s \end{cases}$$
$$F2^*(bool, s) = s \cup var(bool), \text{ bool being a Boolean expression}$$
$$F2^*(assert(b), s) = s \cup var(b), \text{ assert(b) being an assertion expression}$$

Now, we construct $|A_2$ using $F2^*$ as $|A_1$ was defined from function $F1^*$, and considering the same initial vector $\overrightarrow{s_{init}}$. The resulting analysis is able to preserve the assertions as desired.

Dealing with Global Variables. As mentioned above, the previous description is only applicable to models without global variables. It is important to distinguish between global and local variables. Local variables are easier to analyze because their use is localized inside a unique process, and the static analysis follows the control flow of isolated processes. In contrast, the code regarding a global variable may be distributed through many different system processes. Thus, it is possible that some variables used to construct a given global variable in a process are erroneously hidden by the static *local* analysis. In order to solve this problem, we consider the set $\mathcal{G}_M \subseteq \mathcal{V}$ of all global variables appearing in some boolean expression of some process. Now we modify $\overrightarrow{s_{init}}$ and use $\overrightarrow{s_{init}^g}$ defined as $\{s_l | l \in \mathcal{L}\}$ where $\forall l \in \mathcal{L}.s_l = \mathcal{G}_M$.

With this definition for the initial vector, static analysis is able to extract all variables influencing global variables which are critical for the control flow of the model. In the following, we call IA_3 to this extension. Observe that if we consider assertions as boolean expressions, this analysis is also able to preserve the state properties described above.

Preserving Trace Properties. Analysis IA_3 may be extended to IA_4 which is intended to preserve generic temporal properties. Assume that f is a **LTL** property. In order to preserve the evaluation of f we have to make all (global) variables of $var(f)$ *always* significant for the analysis. Thus, since variables appearing in the formula are always saved, the formula may always be correctly checked. Then, function $F4^*$ takes into account variables in the temporal formula f to be checked as follows:

$$F4^*(x = exp, s) = \begin{cases} s & if\ x \notin s \\ s - \{x\} \cup var(exp) & if\ x \in s, x \notin var(f) \\ s \cup var(exp) & if\ x \in s, x \in var(f) \end{cases}$$
$$F4^*(bool, s) = s \cup var(bool),\ bool\ being\ a\ Boolean\ expression$$

Now, define $\overrightarrow{s'_{init}} = \{s'_l | l \in \mathcal{L}\}$ where $\forall l \in \mathcal{L}, s_l = \mathcal{G}_M$. Note that, for practical reasons, we are assuming that all variables in f are global. Thus, analysis IA_4 is constructed following the approach presented in Section 4.1, but using function $F3^*$ and the initial vector $\overrightarrow{s'_{init}}$.

Note that, following the ideas in [11], we can improve the influence analysis by removing variables from the property f when they are not necessary. In that way we can adjust dynamically the visible variables to be taken into account.

5   Correctness Issues

In this section, we formalize the correctness of the static analysis developed in Section 4. We start establishing the semantics of a simplified version of Promela.

5.1   A Simplified Semantics for Promela

Assume that $M = P_1 || \cdots || P_n$ is a Promela system constituted by the concurrent execution of processes $P_i (1 \leq i \leq n)$. If $Value$ represents the set of all possible values for the variables in $\mathcal{V}$, we define the set $Env = \mathcal{V} \rightarrow Value$ of all possible functions giving values to the elements of $\mathcal{V}$. In the sequel, we call environments to the elements of Env. Thus, given $e \in Env$ and $v \in \mathcal{V}$, $e(v)$ denotes the value given to v by the environment e. In addition, $e[n/v]$ denotes the environment that is equal to e for all variables except for v whose value is n.

Given a process P, we define the set of process states $State = \mathcal{L} \times Env$ as the set of pairs $\langle l, e \rangle$ where $l \in \mathcal{L}$ is the program counter of P and $e : \mathcal{V} \rightarrow Value \cup \bot$

BoolExp	$\dfrac{I(l) \in BoolExp, eval(I(l),e)=true}{\langle l,e\rangle \longmapsto_P \langle next(l),e\rangle}$	Assign	$\dfrac{I(l)=x=exp, eval(exp,e)=n}{\langle l,e\rangle \longmapsto_P \langle next(l),e[n/x]\rangle}$

| Non-det | $\dfrac{I(l)=if::b_1 \to l_1 : \cdots ::b_n \to l_n : \cdots ; fi, eval(b_i,e)=true}{\langle l,e\rangle \longmapsto_P \langle l_i,e\rangle}$ |

| IntLeaving | $\dfrac{\langle l_i,e\rangle \longmapsto_P \langle l_i',e'\rangle}{\langle l_1,\cdots,l_i,\cdots,l_n,e\rangle \longmapsto_S \langle l_1,\cdots,l_i',\cdots,l_n,e'\rangle}$ |

Fig. 9. Process-Level and System-Level Rules

is an environment restricted to the variables accessed by P. Thus, $v \in \mathcal{V}$ is given the special value $\perp$ if P cannot access to it (v is local to a different process).

Figure 9 shows a simplified version of the complete semantics for Promela processes. We have included only the most relevant statements for the sake of simplicity. The whole semantics may be found in [5]. The *simplified* transition relation for the process level is defined as $\longmapsto_P \subseteq State \times State$. In the figure, we use the function $eval : Expr \times Env \to Value$ to evaluate expressions, where $Expr$ represents the set of all Boolean and arithmetical expressions that may be constructed with the usual operators and the constants and variables of M.

Given a Promela system $M = P_1 || \cdots || P_n$, we define the set $Conf = \mathcal{L}^n \times Env$ of all global states of M. Thus, a configuration consists of the current program counter of each process in M and the global environment giving the current value to all model variables. Figure 9 also shows the system-level transition relation $\longmapsto_S \subseteq Conf \times Conf$. This rule realizes the interleaving of the system processes in execution.

5.2 Correctness Results for IA_1

In this section, we prove the results showing the usefulness of our proposal. We start by giving some necessary definitions.

Definition 1. *We say that variable $x \in \mathcal{V}$ is redefined at label $l \in \mathcal{L}$, and write it as $redef(x,l)$, iff $I(l) = x = expr$, that is, if x is given a new value at l.*

Definition 2. *Given $x \in \mathcal{V}$ and $l_{1i} \in \mathcal{L}$, we say that x is needed at l_{1i} for IA_1 and write it as $needed_1(x, l_{1i})$ iff there exists a finite path $\langle \cdots, l_{1i}, \cdots, e_1\rangle \longmapsto_S \cdots \longmapsto_S \langle \cdots, l_{ki}, \cdots, e_k\rangle$ such that $\forall 1 \le j \le k. \neg redef(x, l_{ji})$ and it holds that*

1. *$I(l_{ki}) \in BoolExp$ and $x \in var(I(l_{ki}))$*
2. *$I(l_{ki}) = y = exp$, $x \in var(exp)$ and $needed_1(y, l_{ki})$*

That is, variable x is needed by the analysis IA_1 at a given program counter if its current value is used in some boolean expression (case 1) or it is used to calculate some variable further needed by the static analysis (case 2).

Proposition 2 proves that IA_1 attaches each label with all the variables needed at this point.

Proposition 2. *Given $x \in \mathcal{V}$ and $l \in \mathcal{L}$, if $needed_1(x, l)$ then $x \in IA_1(l)$.*

Once we have defined the notion of variable needed at a program location, we may formalize the variables that should be stored at program labels.

Definition 3. *Consider $l \in \mathcal{L}$ such that $I(l)$ is a basic instruction (a Boolean expression or an assignment) or a non-deterministic selection. Then, we define the set $nvar(l) = \{x \in \mathcal{V} | needed_1(x, l)\}$.*

The following proposition proves that the *Influence Analysis* associates each process label with the variables needed (wrt the previous definition) to execute the following instruction.

Proposition 3. *Let P be a Promela process and consider the static analysis for the code reachability tree IA_1^P given in Section 4.1. Let $l \in \mathcal{L}$ be a label of P then $nvar(l) \subseteq IA_1^P(l)$.*

We may extend Proposition 3 to Promela systems as follows:

Corollary 1. *Let $M = P_1 || \cdots || P_n$ be a Promela system and consider the static analysis for the code reachability tree IA_1 given in Section 4.1. Let $(l_1, \cdots, l_n) \in \mathcal{L}^n$ be a program counter of M then $\cup_{i=1}^n nvar(I(l_i)) \subseteq IA_1(l_1, \cdots, l_n)$.*

Given $V \subset \mathcal{V}$, we define the *equivalence relation* $\sim_V \subseteq Env \times Env$ as follows:
$$e_1 \sim_V e_2 \iff \forall v \in V.e_1(v) = e_2(v)$$

Proposition 4. *Consider two environments $e_1, e'_1 \in Env$ and two labels $l, l' \in \mathcal{L}$ such $\langle l, e_1 \rangle \longmapsto_P \langle l', e'_1 \rangle$. Then if $e_1 \sim_{IA_1(l)} e_2$, there exists $e'_2 \in Env$ such that $\langle l, e_2 \rangle \longmapsto_P \langle l', e'_2 \rangle$ and $e'_1 \sim_{IA_1(l')} e'_2$.*

We may extend the previous proposition to system configurations as follows.

Corollary 2. *Consider two environments $e_1, e'_1 \in Env$ and two labels $l_i, l'_i \in \mathcal{L}$ such $\langle l_1, \cdots, l_i, \cdots, l_n, e_1 \rangle \longmapsto_S \langle l_1, \cdots, l'_i, \cdots, l_n, e'_1 \rangle$. Define $\overrightarrow{l} = (l_1, \cdots, l_i, \cdots, l_n)$ and $\overrightarrow{l'} = (l_1, \cdots, l'_i, \cdots, l_n)$. Then if $e_1 \sim_{IA_1(\overrightarrow{l})} e_2$, there exists $e'_2 \in Env$ such that $\langle l_1, \cdots, l_i, \cdots, l_n, e_2 \rangle \longmapsto_S \langle l_1, \cdots, l'_i, \cdots, l_n, e'_2 \rangle$ and $e'_1 \sim_{IA_1(\overrightarrow{l'})} e'_2$.*

The following theorem gives us the desired correctness result for analysis IA_1.

Theorem 1. *Assume that $\langle l_{11}, \cdots, l_{n1}, e_1 \rangle \longmapsto_S \cdots \longmapsto_S \langle l_{1k}, \cdots, l_{nk}, e_k \rangle$ is a finite path. For all $i \leq k$, denote $\overrightarrow{l_i} = (l_{1i}, \cdots, l_{ni})$. Then, if $e'_1 \in Env$ satisfies that $e_1 \sim_{IA_1(\overrightarrow{l_1})} e'_1$, then there exists a finite path $\langle l_{11}, \cdots, l_{n1}, e'_1 \rangle \longmapsto_S \cdots \longmapsto_S \langle l_{1k}, \cdots, l_{nk}, e'_k \rangle$ such that $\forall 1 < j \leq k.e_j \sim_{IA_1(\overrightarrow{l_j})} e'_j$.*

Observe that following Theorem 1, the reachability tree may be pruned. Every new state with visible variables matching one state previously stored is considered as a visited state. The proof of the preservation of properties between the original and the reduced state spaces should take into account the search algorithm, for instance, the algorithm in [1].

5.3   Correctness Results for IA_2, IA_3 and IA_4

In this section, we establish the main results proving the correctness of analysis IA_2, IA_3 and IA_4. The proofs of the corresponding theorems are similar to the ones given for IA_1 in the previous section. Observe that the correctness result for IA_3 does not appear because it is similar to Theorem 1.

Theorem 2 (Correctness for IA_2). *Assume that* $\langle l_{11}, \cdots, l_{n1}, e_1 \rangle \longmapsto_S \cdots \longmapsto_S \langle l_{1k}, \cdots, l_{nk}, e_k \rangle$ *is a finite path. In addition, assume that there exists an index j such that $I(l_{jk}) = assert(b)$ for some boolean expression b. For all $i \leq k$, denote $\overrightarrow{l_i} = (l_{1i}, \cdots, l_{ni})$. Then, if $e'_1 \in Env$ satisfies that $e_1 \sim_{\mathsf{IA}_2(\overrightarrow{l_1})} e'_1$, then there exists a finite path $\langle l_{11}, \cdots, l_{n1}, e'_1 \rangle \longmapsto_S \cdots \longmapsto_S \langle l_{1k}, \cdots, l_{nk}, e'_k \rangle$ such that $\forall 1 < j \leq k.e_j \sim_{\mathsf{IA}_2(\overrightarrow{l_j})} e'_j$ and $eval(b, e_k) = eval(b, e'_k)$.*

Theorem 3 (Correctness for IA_4). *Let f be an LTL formula. Assume that $\sigma = \langle l_{11}, \cdots, l_{n1}, e_1 \rangle \longmapsto_S \langle l_{12}, \cdots, l_{n2}, e_2 \rangle \longmapsto_S \cdots$ is an infinite path from $\langle l_{11}, \cdots, l_{n1}, e_1 \rangle$. For all $i \geq 1$, denote $\overrightarrow{l_i} = (l_{1i}, \cdots, l_{ni})$. Then, if $e'_1 \in Env$ satisfies that $e_1 \sim_{\mathsf{IA}_4(\overrightarrow{l_1})} e'_1$, then there exists a path $\sigma' = \langle l_{11}, \cdots, l_{n1}, e'_1 \rangle \longmapsto_S \langle l_{12}, \cdots, l_{n2}, e'_2 \rangle \longmapsto_S \cdots$ such that $\forall 1 < j.e_j \sim_{\mathsf{IA}_4(\overrightarrow{l_j})} e'_j$ and $\sigma \models f \iff \sigma' \models f$, $\models$ being the standard satisfiability relation defined for evaluating LTL formulas on execution traces.*

6   Conclusions and Future Work

State space explosion in explicit model checking can be partially solved with techniques which change the usual algorithm to identify visited states. Instead of comparing every new global state with the states in the heap, abstract matching is able to compare only parts of the new state. In that way, it is possible to cut some execution paths and reduce the time and memory required to check a particular property. However, the results are only reliable when the abstraction method has been proved to be sound.

In this paper, we have presented the theoretical framework to ensure that static analysis can provide enough information to construct sound abstract functions for a given property. Furthermore, we provide evidence that, in the context of model extraction for Spin, these functions can be automatically produced and included in the final model.

We have obtained the experimental results with the tool SOCKETMC, although static analysis was still done by hand. At the moment, we are implementing these static analysis algorithms as an extension to SOCKETMC. Future work is oriented to integrate the new version of SOCKETMC with our tool for data abstraction αSpin, in such a way that we can make more efficient model checking of C programs.

References

1. D. Bosnacki. *Enhancing State Space Reduction Techniques for Model Checking.* PhD thesis, Eindhoven Univ. of Technology, 2001.
2. J. C. Corbett, M. B. Dwyer, J. Hatcliff, S. Laubach, C. S. Pasareanu, Robby, and H. Zheng. Bandera: Extracting Finite-state Models from Java Source Code. In *Proc. of the 22nd Int. conference on Software engineering*, pages 439–448, 2000. ACM Press.
3. P. de la Cámara, M. M. Gallardo, P. Merino, and D. Sanán. Model Checking Software with Well-Defined APIs: the Socket Case. In *FMICS '05: Proc. of the 10th int. workshop on Formal methods for industrial critical systems*, pages 17–26, 2005. ACM Press.
4. E.M. Clarke, H. Grumberg, and D. Peled. *Model Checking.* 2000.
5. M.M Gallardo, P. Merino, and E. Pimentel. A Generalized Semantics of Promela for Abstract Model Checking. *Formal Aspects of Computing*, 16:166–193, 2004.
6. K. Havelund and T. Pressburger. Model Checking Java Programs using Java Pathfinder. *International Journal of Software Tools for Technology Transfer*, 2(4):366–381, 2000.
7. G. J. Holzmann and R. Joshi. Model-Driven Software Verification. In *SPIN*, pages 76–91, 2004.
8. G. J. Holzmann and M. H. Smith. Software Model Checking: Extracting Verification Models from Source Code. *Software Testing, Verification & Reliability*, 11(2):65–79, 2001.
9. F. Nielson, H. R. Nielson, and C. Hankin. *Principles of Program Analysis.* 1998.
10. C. S. Pasareanu, R. Pelánek, and W. Visser. Concrete Model Checking with Abstract Matching and Refinement. In *CAV*, pages 52–66, 2005.
11. D. Peled, A. Valmari, and I. Kokkarinen. Relaxed Visibility Enhances Partial Order Reduction. *Formal Methods in System Design*, 19(3):275–289, 2001.

A Parametric State Space for the Analysis of the Infinite Class of Stop-and-Wait Protocols*

Guy Edward Gallasch and Jonathan Billington

Computer Systems Engineering Centre, University of South Australia,
Mawson Lakes Campus, SA 5095, Australia
guy.gallasch@postgrads.unisa.edu.au
jonathan.billington@unisa.edu.au

Abstract. The Stop-and-Wait protocol (SWP) has two (unbounded) parameters: the maximum sequence number (MaxSeqNo) and the maximum number of retransmissions (MaxRetrans). This paper presents an algebraic method for analysis of the SWP for all possible values of these parameters. Model checking such a system requires considering an infinite family of models, one for each combination of parameter values, and thus an infinite family of state spaces (reachability graphs). These reachability graphs are represented symbolically by a set of algebraic formulas in MaxSeqNo and MaxRetrans. This result is significant as it provides a complete characterisation of the infinite set of reachability graphs of our SWP model in both parameters, allowing properties to be verified for the infinite class. Verification of a number of properties is described.

Keywords: Stop and Wait Protocols, Infinite Families of Systems, Parametric Reachability Graphs, Coloured Petri Nets.

1 Introduction

Stop-and-Wait is an elementary and well-known form of flow control [20,22] used by communication protocols to prevent buffer overflow in the receiver. In practice Stop-and-Wait is often used with checksums to detect transmission errors and a timeout/retransmission scheme using sequence numbers, such as Automatic Repeat ReQuest [22], for error recovery.

The Stop-and-Wait mechanism forms the basis of many practical data transfer protocols, such as the Internet's Transmission Control Protocol (TCP) [19]. An understanding of how these mechanisms work and how they may fail is thus useful for the verification of more complex protocols like TCP. These protocols have a number of parameters, such as the maximum sequence number (MaxSeqNo) or the maximum number of retransmissions (MaxRetrans). The value of these parameters may vary depending on the application (e.g. TCP has a 32 bit sequence number, whereas others may use a 3 bit sequence number). It is thus of interest to verify these protocols for all values of these parameters.

---

* Partially supported by an Australian Research Council (ARC) Discovery Grant, DP0559927, and a University of South Australia Divisional Small Grant, SP04.

A. Valmari (Ed.): SPIN 2006, LNCS 3925, pp. 201–218, 2006.

Petri nets have proven to be a suitable formal method for protocol verification [2, 3, 6, 15, 17]. A Coloured Petri net (CPN) [14, 16] model of the SWP, parameterised by MaxSeqNo and MaxRetrans, was developed and analysed in [4, 5, 6] following the *protocol verification methodology* presented in [6]. Because the model parameters are unbounded there is an infinite set of CPN models to verify, and state explosion [23] prevents analysis for all but small parameter values. Thus we were motivated to find a way to verify the SWP for any finite (but unbounded) value of the parameters. In [12] we presented a novel technique of representing the reachability graphs (RGs) of the SWP CPN symbolically in the MaxSeqNo parameter (with MaxRetrans=0) using algebraic expressions, and verified a number of properties directly from the expressions, including language equivalence to the service, for all values of the unbounded MaxSeqNo parameter.

Related work on symbolic verification considers only the MaxRetrans parameter. Abdulla et al [1] verify the Alternating Bit Protocol (ABP) (MaxSeqNo=1) with unbounded retransmissions and a variant called the Bounded Retransmission Protocol in which MaxRetrans is modelled nondeterministically. In [7, 8] we used a tool called FAST (Fast Acceleration of Symbolic Transition Systems) [9] to model the SWP and analyse it symbolically. We were successful when MaxRetrans was an unbounded parameter with MaxSeqNo fixed to small values (1 to 5), and when MaxSeqNo was an unbounded parameter but with MaxRetrans fixed to 0. FAST did not return a result when both MaxSeqNo and MaxRetrans were unbounded parameters. In [24] a variant of the ABP with arbitrary MaxRetrans and operating over channels with a capacity of one message only, was verified using Valmari's Chaos-Free-Failures-Divergences (CFFD) equivalence. In contrast, our model operates over unbounded lossy ordered channels (similar to [1]) and explicitly considers any maximum sequence number (not just the alternating bit) and any maximum number of retransmissions.

In this paper, the work in [12] is significantly extended by obtaining algebraic expressions for the infinite set of RGs of the SWP operating over an ordered medium over both the MaxSeqNo and MaxRetrans parameters. A sketch of the proof of correctness is given, details of which can be found in [11]. The contribution of this paper is threefold. Firstly, we further develop the novel algebraic representation method from [12]. Secondly, we provide the aforementioned symbolic representation. Inclusion of the MaxRetrans parameter represents a substantial increase in the complexity of the algebraic expressions. This can be gauged by the size of the RG, which grows linearly in MaxSeqNo but quartically in MaxRetrans [10, 12]. Previous work dealt with the linear growth in MaxSeqNo only, whereas this paper also deals with the quartic growth in MaxRetrans. Thirdly, we sketch the verification of a number of properties directly from the algebraic expressions. The authors are not aware of any previous attempts to obtain an explicit algebraic representation for the family of RGs for arbitrary unbounded values of the MaxSeqNo and MaxRetrans parameters for the class of Stop-and-Wait protocols.

The rest of this paper is organised as follows. Section 2 presents our parametric SWP CPN model. The necessary notational constructs and lemmas regarding model behaviour are presented in Section 3. The parametric algebraic expressions of the RG are presented in Section 4, followed by a description of the verification of a number of properties. Conclusions and future work are presented in Section 5. Familiarity with basic CPN concepts and terminology is assumed. For introductions to CPNs the reader is referred to [14, 16].

2 The Stop-and-Wait Protocol CPN Model

The SWP is modelled using Coloured Petri nets [14, 16], a form of Petri net in which tokens are arbitrarily complex data values. The CPN diagram is shown in

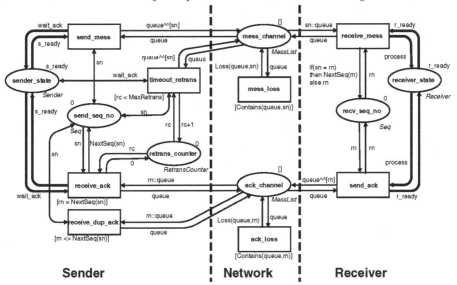

```
val MaxRetrans = 0;
val MaxSeqNo = 1;

color Sender = with s_ready | wait_ack;
color Receiver = with r_ready | process;
color Seq = int with 0..MaxSeqNo;
color RetransCounter = int with 0..MaxRetrans;
color Message = Seq;
color MessList = list Message;

var sn,rn : Seq;
var rc     : RetransCounter;
var queue : MessList;

fun NextSeq(n) = if(n = MaxSeqNo) then 0 else n+1;
fun Contains([],sn) = false
  | Contains(m::queue,sn) = if(sn=m) then true else Contains(queue,sn);
fun Loss(m::queue,sn) = if(sn=m) then queue else m::Loss(queue,sn);
```

Fig. 1. A CPN of the Stop-and-Wait Protocol operating over an in-order medium

Fig. 1 along with all the declarations used in the inscriptions of the CPN diagram. The inscription language is a variant of Standard ML [21]. The two parameters MaxRetrans and MaxSeqNo can be seen at the top of the declarations in Fig. 1. This model is the same as the one presented in [12], with the exception of loss. This change is motivated and described below. (The focus of this paper is not the modelling of SWP with CPNs. A detailed description of the model is given in [12] and hence omitted here.)

The channels are modelled as lists manipulated by the arc inscriptions as First-In-First-Out (FIFO) queues in places mess_channel and ack_channel. Transitions mess_loss and ack_loss model loss, both in the network (buffer overflow in a router) and by discarding messages and acknowledgements with transmission errors (checksum failures). Unlike the model in [12], loss can occur anywhere in the message and acknowledgement queues, not just from the head. This is done via nondeterministic binding of variables sn and rn and the function Contains in the guard of each loss transition, to ensure that sn and rn are only bound to values that are present in the channels. The removal of the message is via function Loss in the arc inscriptions.

Motivation is provided by it being a more general model, suited to the TCP environment, where loss can occur anywhere in the network due to e.g. router congestion, in addition to loss caused by detection of errors. It turns out that this model of loss is easier to formalise in the algebraic expressions in Section 4.

3   Notation and Model Properties

This section introduces notation and proves a number of properties of the SWP CPN model required for the proof of correctness of the algebraic formula presented in Section 4.

3.1   Marking and Arc Notation

We begin by defining the RG of a CPN. In CPN terminology, a reachability graph is often called an *occurrence graph* (OG).

Definition 1 (Reachability Graph). *The* **OG** *of a CPN with initial marking, M_0, and a set of binding elements, BE, is a labelled directed graph $OG = (V,A)$ where*

1. *$V = [M_0\rangle$ is the set of reachable markings of the CPN; and*
2. *$A = \{(M, (t, b), M') \in V \times BE \times V | M[(t, b)\rangle M'\}$ is the set of labelled directed arcs, where $M[(t, b)\rangle M'$ denotes that the marking of the CPN changes from M to M' on the occurrence of transition t with binding b, $(t, b) \in BE$.*

The parameterised CPN and its RG are denoted by $CPN_{(MS,MR)}$ and $OG_{(MS,MR)}$ given by the following definition:

Definition 2 (Parameterised CPN and Reachability Graph). *For* $MS \in$ $\mathbb{N}^+$ *and* $MR \in \mathbb{N}, CPN_{(MS,MR)}$ *is defined as the Stop-and-Wait Protocol CPN of Fig. 1 with* MaxSeqNo $= MS$ *and* MaxRetrans $= MR$. *The reachability graph of* $CPN_{(MS,MR)}$ *is denoted by* $OG_{(MS,MR)} = (V_{(MS,MR)}, A_{(MS,MR)})$.

In order for the notation for markings and arcs defined below to be correct, we must prove that each place in the SWP CPN with initial marking M_0 as illustrated in Fig. 1 always contains exactly one token.

Lemma 1. *For all reachable markings of* $CPN_{(MS,MR)}$ *and all allowable values of* MS *and* MR, *each place in the CPN diagram contains exactly one token, i.e.* $\forall MS \in \mathbb{N}^+, \forall MR \in \mathbb{N}, \forall M \in V_{(MS,MR)}, |M(\mathsf{sender\_state})| = |M(\mathsf{receiver\_state})|$ $= |M(\mathsf{retrans\_counter})| = |M(\mathsf{mess\_channel})| = |M(\mathsf{ack\_channel})| = |M(\mathsf{send\_seq\_no})|$ $= |M(\mathsf{recv\_seq\_no})| = 1$.

Sketch of Proof. Proof is by direct inspection of Fig. 1. Consider the recv_seq_no place. $M_0(\mathsf{recv\_seq\_no}) = 1`0$ and so $|M_0(\mathsf{recv\_seq\_no})| = 1$. The marking of this place can only be changed by transitions receive_mess and send_ack. The occurrence of these transitions either replaces one value by another (the receive_mess transition when $sn=rn$) or does not change the marking (the receive_mess transition when $sn \neq rn$ and the send_ack transition). The value of MS may affect the token value (via function NextSeq) but it does not affect the number of tokens removed or added (always 1). Hence $|M(\mathsf{recv\_seq\_no})| = 1$ for all markings. Similar arguments reveal that this property also holds for the remaining 6 places. $\square$

The following function converts a singleton multiset into its basis element:

Definition 3 (Singleton Multiset to Colour). *Let* S_{MS_1} *be the set of all singleton multisets over a basis set* $S : S_{MS_1} = \{\{(s,1)\}|s \in S\}$. *A function that converts a singleton multiset to its basis element is given by* $f_c : S_{MS_1} \to S$, *where* $f_c(\{(s,1)\}) = s$.

In addition, the following notational conventions are used throughout this paper:

- $M[t\rangle$ is used as shorthand to represent that transition t is enabled by marking M for some binding of variables b, such that $M[(t,b)\rangle, (t,b) \in BE$;
- $|f_c(M(p))|$ is the length of the list on places $p \in \{\mathsf{mess\_channel}, \mathsf{ack\_channel}\}$;
- i^j represents j repetitions of the message (or acknowledgement) with sequence number i in the message (or acknowledgement) channel;
- $\oplus_{MS}$ represents modulo $MS + 1$ addition; and
- $\ominus_{MS}$ represents modulo $MS + 1$ subtraction.

   The markings of our SWP CPN can be classified into *types* based on the four possible combinations of the *major* state of the sender and receiver, i.e. the markings of places sender_state and receiver_state. The relationship between the sender sequence number (ssn) and receiver sequence number (rsn), either $rsn = ssn$ or $rsn = ssn \oplus_{MS} 1$, gives rise to subtypes for two of the four combinations of major state. Thus there are six combinations in total, giving the six types, 1, 2a, 2b, 3a, 3b and 4, shown in Table 1. An explanation of the significance of each type is given in [11].

Table 1. Classification of markings $M \in V_{(MS,MR)}$ into types based on the state of the sender and receiver

M(sender_state)	M(receiver_state)	M(send_seq_no)	M(recv_seq_no)	$Type_{MS}(M)$
1's_ready	1'r_ready	1'sn	1'sn	1
1'wait_ack	1'r_ready	1'sn	1'sn	2a
1'wait_ack	1'r_ready	1'sn	1'$(sn \oplus_{MS} 1)$	2b
1'wait_ack	1'process	1'sn	1'sn	3a
1'wait_ack	1'process	1'sn	1'$(sn \oplus_{MS} 1)$	3b
1's_ready	1'process	1'sn	1'sn	4

Definition 4 (Markings to Types). *We define the family of functions that classifies markings as $Type_{MS} : V_{(MS,MR)} \rightarrow \{1, 2a, 2b, 3a, 3b, 4\}$ where the body of $Type_{MS}$ is given in Table 1.*

In addition, the following assumptions are made about the content of the communication channels, all of which are proved valid at the end of Section 4.1.

Assumption 1. *The content of the message and acknowledgement channels is a list of contiguous integers of the form $i^* j^*$ where $i, j \in \{0, ..., \mathsf{MaxSeqNo}\}$.*

Assumption 2. *The message and acknowledgement channels contain at most two distinct consecutive integers, i.e. of the form $i^* j^*$ where $j = i \oplus_{MS} 1$.*

Assumption 3. *All reachable markings $M \in V_{(MS,MR)}$ of $CPN_{(MS,MR)}$ can be classified into one of the 6 types in Table 1.*

Using Lemma 1, Assumptions 1, 2 and 3, and Table 1, every marking can be encoded and uniquely identified by the following marking notation:

Definition 5 (Shorthand Marking Notation). *For $CPN_{(MS,MR)}$ all markings $M \in V_{(MS,MR)}$ can be uniquely identified and represented by the notation $M^{(MS,MR)}_{(type,ssn),(mo,ao,mn,an,ret)}$ where the superscript contains the parameter values of the SWP CPN and the subscript contains the marking description, where:*

- *$type = Type_{MS}(M)$;*
- *$ssn \in \{0, 1, ..., MS\}$ is the sender sequence number;*
- *$mo \in \mathbb{N}$ is the number of old (duplicate) messages with sequence number $ssn \ominus_{MS} 1$ in the message channel;*
- *$ao \in \mathbb{N}$ is the number of old (duplicate) acknowledgements with sequence number ssn in the acknowledgement channel;*
- *$mn \in \mathbb{N}$ is the number of new (current) messages with sequence number ssn in the message channel;*
- *$an \in \mathbb{N}$ is the number of new (current) acknowledgements with sequence number $ssn \oplus_{MS} 1$ in the acknowledgement channel; and*
- *$ret \in \{0, 1, ..., MR\}$ is the value of the retransmission counter for the currently outstanding (unacknowledged) message;*

so that for a given $M \in V_{(MS,MR)}$ represented by $M_{(type,ssn),(mo,ao,mn,an,ret)}^{(MS,MR)}$ the marking of places sender_state, receiver_state, send_seq_no *and* recv_seq_no *is encoded in the pair $(type, ssn)$ as given by Table 1 and:*

$$M(mess\_channel) \quad = \quad 1`[(ssn \ominus_{MS} 1)^{mo} \quad ssn^{mn}]$$

$$M(ack\_channel) \quad = \quad 1`[ssn^{ao} \quad (ssn \oplus_{MS} 1)^{an}]$$

$$M(retrans\_counter) \quad = \quad 1`ret$$

Analogously, a shorthand notation is defined for arcs in [11].

Sets of markings and sets of arcs are defined as follows:

Definition 6 (Sets of Markings). $V_{(type,ssn)}^{(MS,MR)} = \{M \in V_{(MS,MR)} \mid Type_{MS}(M)$ $= type, M(send\_seq\_no) = 1`ssn\}$ *represents the set of markings in which the sender sequence number is given by ssn, and the sender and receiver states and receiver sequence number are given by the type as specified in Table 1.*

Definition 7 (Sets of Arcs). $A_{(type,ssn)}^{(MS,MR)} = \{(M,(t,b),M') \in A_{(MS,MR)} \mid Type_{MS}(M) = type, M(send\_seq\_no) = 1`ssn\}$ *represents the set of arcs with source nodes in $V_{(type,ssn)}^{(MS,MR)}$.*

3.2   Important Model Properties

There are several important behavioural properties of the SWP CPN model that are needed for the proof of correctness of the algebraic expressions:

Lemma 2. *For all $M \in V_{(MS,MR)}$, the enabling and subsequent firing of each transition is independent of the values of the sequence numbers in the binding.*

Sketch of Proof. (See [11] for the full proof.) Proof is from Lemma 1 and the standard enabling and firing rules of CPNs [14].

From Fig. 1 the enabling conditions of send_mess are: $f_c(M(sender_state)) = $ s_ready; $|M(send\_seq\_no)| > 0$; and $|M(mess\_channel)| > 0$. All three conditions are independent of sequence numbers. send_mess is enabled with binding queue $= f_c(M(mess\_channel))$ and sn $= f_c(M(send\_seq\_no))$. When send_mess occurs, it:

- Removes 1`s_ready from sender_state and returns 1`wait_ack to this place;
- Leaves the marking of place send_seq_no unchanged; and
- Removes 1`queue from place mess_channel and returns 1`queue^^[sn] to this place (append a copy of sn to the end of the message channel queue).

None of these actions depend on or are affected by the particular values of queue or sn in the binding, thus the behaviour of send_mess is independent of the values of the sequence numbers with which it interacts. The same reasoning is used to prove this lemma for the other seven transitions.   □

Lemma 3. *For all $M \in V_{(MS,MR)}$ in which $M(receiver\_state) = 1`r\_ready$ and $|f_c(M(mess\_channel))| > 0$, the message at the head of the queue in the message channel can always be converted into an acknowledgement, i.e. $\exists M', M'' \in V_{(MS,MR)}$ such that $M[receive\_mess\rangle M'[send\_ack\rangle M''$, $|f_c(M''(mess\_channel))| = |f_c(M(mess\_channel))| - 1$ and $|f_c(M''(ack\_channel))| = |f_c(M(ack\_channel))| + 1$.*

Sketch of Proof. (See [11] for the full proof.) Only reachable markings satisfying the enabling conditions of receive_mess need be considered. For each such marking M, Lemma 2 ensures that the enabling and action taken upon firing receive_mess is independent of the values of the sequence numbers involved. When receive_mess occurs from any such M we reach a marking M' in which the receiver state has changed to process and one message has been removed from the message channel. From the CPN diagram in Fig. 1, each such marking M' enables send_ack, the occurrence of which leads to a marking M'' such that the receiver has returned once again to the ready state, the message channel contains one less message than in M and the acknowledgement channel contains one more acknowledgement than in M. Thus the lemma is proved.   □

Lemma 4. $\forall M \in V_{(MS,MR)}, |f_c(M(\text{mess\_channel}))| > 0 \implies \exists M_1 \in V_{(MS,MR)}$
such that $M[\text{mess\_loss}\rangle M_1$ *and* $|f_c(M_1(\text{mess\_channel}))| = |f_c(M(\text{mess\_channel}))| -$
1 *and* $|f_c(M(\text{ack\_channel}))| > 0 \implies \exists M_2 \in V_{(MS,MR)}$ *such that* $M[\text{ack\_loss}\rangle M_2$
and $|f_c(M_2(\text{ack\_channel}))| = |f_c(M(\text{ack\_channel}))| - 1$, *while the marking of all*
other places remains unchanged.

Proof. The proof follows immediately from the CPN in Fig. 1.   □

4   Algebraic Expressions for the SWP CPN RGs

Empirical evidence gathered in [12] for small parameter values reveals a regular structure in the RG that is linear in MaxSeqNo and quartic in MaxRetrans. This also holds true for the model presented in Section 2. Based on the intuition in [12] for the case where MaxRetrans=0, in this paper, we present an algebraic formula representing the family of RGs of our SWP CPN and prove it correct. We then discuss a number of properties that can be proved directly from the algebraic formula. Because of size limitations, only proof sketches are presented (see [11] for details).

4.1   The Algebraic Formula in Both Parameters

When defining the markings and arcs of $OG_{(MS,MR)}$ we specify sets of markings and arcs using the notation from Definitions 5, 6 and 7 and by specifying allowable ranges of the five variables (mo, ao, mn, an, ret). All variables are assumed to be greater than or equal to 0, unless otherwise indicated.

All of the markings of $OG_{(MS,MR)}$ are described in this way in Table 2, by evaluating the expressions in this table for $0 \leq i \leq MS$. The first column gives the name of the set of markings for each subset of the partition according to its type. Column 2 defines the set of markings by specifying the allowed ranges of variable values. If a variable is restricted to a specific value, e.g. 0, we write this directly in the label of the marking. Note that because of the expression $0 \leq mo + ao \leq MR - 1$, the markings of type 3a and type 4 (rows 4 and 6) are defined only when $MR > 0$. Hence $V_{(3a,i)}^{(MS,0)} = V_{(4,i)}^{(MS,0)} = \emptyset$, the empty set, when $MR = 0$.

Table 2. $V_{(type,i)}^{(MS,MR)}$, for $0 \leq i \leq MS$ and $type \in \{1, 2a, 2b, 3a, 3b, 4\}$

Name	Set Definition
$V_{(1,i)}^{(MS,MR)}$	$\{M_{(1,i),(mo,ao,0,0,0)}^{(MS,MR)} \mid 0 \leq mo + ao \leq MR\}$
$V_{(2a,i)}^{(MS,MR)}$	$\{M_{(2a,i),(mo,ao,mn,0,ret)}^{(MS,MR)} \mid 0 \leq mo + ao \leq MR, 0 \leq ret \leq MR,$ $0 \leq mn \leq ret + 1\}$
$V_{(2b,i)}^{(MS,MR)}$	$\{M_{(2b,i),(0,ao,mn,an,ret)}^{(MS,MR)} \mid 0 \leq ao \leq MR, 0 \leq ret \leq MR, 0 \leq mn \leq ret,$ $0 \leq mn + an \leq ret + 1\}$
$V_{(3a,i)}^{(MS,MR)}$	$\{\}$, for $MR = 0$; or $\{M_{(3a,i),(mo,ao,mn,0,ret)}^{(MS,MR)} \mid 0 \leq mo + ao \leq MR - 1, 0 \leq ret \leq MR,$ $0 \leq mn \leq ret + 1\}$, for $MR > 0$.
$V_{(3b,i)}^{(MS,MR)}$	$\{M_{(3b,i),(0,ao,mn,an,ret)}^{(MS,MR)} \mid 0 \leq ao \leq MR, 0 \leq ret \leq MR, 0 \leq mn + an \leq ret\}$
$V_{(4,i)}^{(MS,MR)}$	$\{\}$, for $MR = 0$; or $\{M_{(4,i),(mo,ao,0,0,0)}^{(MS,MR)} \mid 0 \leq mo + ao \leq MR - 1\}$, for $MR > 0$.

All of the arcs of $OG_{(MS,MR)}$ are described in Tables 3 to 8 by evaluating each table for $0 \leq i \leq MS$. There is one table of arcs per set of markings (i.e. per row) in Table 2, describing the set of outgoing arcs of that set of markings. Correspondingly, $A_{(3a,i)}^{(MS,0)}$ and $A_{(4,i)}^{(MS,0)} = \emptyset$ when $MR = 0$. The first column of each arc table gives any additional restrictions that must be placed on the variables mo, ao, mn, an and ret. For example, loss of an old message cannot occur when $mo = 0$. The second, third and fourth columns list the source marking, binding element and destination marking respectively.

We now state the theorem for our parametric RG over both parameters and prove its correctness.

Theorem 1. *For all $MS \in \mathbb{N}^+, MR \in \mathbb{N}$ and for $Type = \{1, 2a, 2b, 3a, 3b, 4\}$, $OG_{(MS,MR)} = (V_{(MS,MR)}, A_{(MS,MR)})$ where*

$$V_{(MS,MR)} = \bigcup_{\substack{0 \leq i \leq MS \\ t \in Type}} V_{(t,i)}^{(MS,MR)}$$

and

$$A_{(MS,MR)} = \bigcup_{\substack{0 \leq i \leq MS \\ t \in Type}} A_{(t,i)}^{(MS,MR)}$$

where all nodes and arcs are defined in Tables 2 to 8.

Proof. The proof is in two parts. The first part proves that all states in $V_{(MS,MR)}$ are reachable from the initial marking using a connected spanning graph. The second part proves that every arc from every state in $V_{(MS,MR)}$ leads to a state in $V_{(MS,MR)}$ and that this set of arcs equals $A_{(MS,MR)}$. The two parts of the proof each describe a necessary condition, which together are sufficient to show that Theorem 1 is correct.

Table 3. The set of arcs $A_{(1,i)}^{(MS,MR)}$ with source markings in $V_{(1,i)}^{(MS,MR)}$

Condition	Source Marking	Binding Element	Destination Marking
none	$M_{(1,i),(mo,ao,0,0,0)}^{(MS,MR)}$	send_mess<queue = $[(i \ominus_{MS} 1)^{mo}]$, sn=$i$>	$M_{(2a,i),(mo,ao,1,0,0)}^{(MS,MR)}$
$mo \geq 1$	$M_{(1,i),(mo,ao,0,0,0)}^{(MS,MR)}$	mess_loss<queue = $[(i \ominus_{MS} 1)^{mo}]$, sn=$i \ominus_{MS} 1$>	$M_{(1,i),(mo-1,ao,0,0,0)}^{(MS,MR)}$
$mo \geq 1$	$M_{(1,i),(mo,ao,0,0,0)}^{(MS,MR)}$	receive_mess<queue = $[(i \ominus_{MS} 1)^{mo-1}]$, sn=$i \ominus_{MS} 1$, rn=$i$>	$M_{(4,i),(mo-1,ao,0,0,0)}^{(MS,MR)}$
$ao \geq 1$	$M_{(1,i),(mo,ao,0,0,0)}^{(MS,MR)}$	ack_loss<queue = $[i^{ao}]$, rn=i>	$M_{(1,i),(mo,ao-1,0,0,0)}^{(MS,MR)}$
$ao \geq 1$	$M_{(1,i),(mo,ao,0,0,0)}^{(MS,MR)}$	receive_dup_ack<queue = $[i^{ao-1}]$, sn=i, rn=i>	$M_{(1,i),(mo,ao-1,0,0,0)}^{(MS,MR)}$

Table 4. The set of arcs $A_{(2a,i)}^{(MS,MR)}$ with source markings in $V_{(2a,i)}^{(MS,MR)}$

Condition	Source Marking	Binding Element	Destination Marking
$ret < MR$	$M_{(2a,i),(mo,ao,mn,0,ret)}^{(MS,MR)}$	timeout_retrans<queue = $[(i \ominus_{MS} 1)^{mo} i^{mn}]$, sn=$i$, rc=$ret$>	$M_{(2a,i),(mo,ao,mn+1,0,ret+1)}^{(MS,MR)}$
$mo \geq 1$	$M_{(2a,i),(mo,ao,mn,0,ret)}^{(MS,MR)}$	mess_loss<queue = $[(i \ominus_{MS} 1)^{mo} i^{mn}]$, sn=$i \ominus_{MS} 1$>	$M_{(2a,i),(mo-1,ao,mn,0,ret)}^{(MS,MR)}$
$mn \geq 1$	$M_{(2a,i),(mo,ao,mn,0,ret)}^{(MS,MR)}$	mess_loss<queue = $[(i \ominus_{MS} 1)^{mo} i^{mn}]$, sn=$i$>	$M_{(2a,i),(mo,ao,mn-1,0,ret)}^{(MS,MR)}$
$mo \geq 1$	$M_{(2a,i),(mo,ao,mn,0,ret)}^{(MS,MR)}$	receive_mess<queue = $[(i \ominus_{MS} 1)^{mo-1} i^{mn}]$, sn=$i \ominus_{MS} 1$, rn=$i$>	$M_{(3a,i),(mo-1,ao,mn,0,ret)}^{(MS,MR)}$
$mn \geq 1$	$M_{(2a,i),(0,ao,mn,0,ret)}^{(MS,MR)}$	receive_mess<queue = $[i^{mn-1}]$, sn=i, rn=i>	$M_{(3b,i),(0,ao,mn-1,0,ret)}^{(MS,MR)}$
$ao \geq 1$	$M_{(2a,i),(mo,ao,mn,0,ret)}^{(MS,MR)}$	ack_loss<queue = $[i^{ao}]$, sn=i, rn=i>	$M_{(2a,i),(mo,ao-1,mn,0,ret)}^{(MS,MR)}$
$ao \geq 1$	$M_{(2a,i),(mo,ao,mn,0,ret)}^{(MS,MR)}$	receive_dup_ack<queue = $[i^{ao-1}]$, sn=i, rn=i>	$M_{(2a,i),(mo,ao-1,mn,0,ret)}^{(MS,MR)}$

Table 5. The set of arcs $A^{(MS,MR)}_{(2b,i)}$ with source markings in $V^{(MS,MR)}_{(2b,i)}$

Condition	Source Marking	Binding Element	Destination Marking
$ret<MR$	$M^{(MS,MR)}_{(2b,i),(0,ao,mn,an,ret)}$	timeout_retrans<queue = $[i^{mn}]$, sn=i,rc=ret>	$M^{(MS,MR)}_{(2b,i),(0,ao,mn+1,an,ret+1)}$
$mn \geq 1$	$M^{(MS,MR)}_{(2b,i),(0,ao,mn,an,ret)}$	mess_loss<queue = $[i^{mn}]$, sn=i>	$M^{(MS,MR)}_{(2b,i),(0,ao,mn-1,an,ret)}$
$mn \geq 1$	$M^{(MS,MR)}_{(2b,i),(0,ao,mn,an,ret)}$	receive_mess<queue = $[i^{mn-1}]$,sn=i, rm=$i\oplus_{MS}1$>	$M^{(MS,MR)}_{(3b,i),(0,ao,mn-1,an,ret)}$
$ao \geq 1$	$M^{(MS,MR)}_{(2b,i),(0,ao,mn,an,ret)}$	ack_loss<queue = $[i^{ao}(i\oplus_{MS}1)^{an}]$, rm=$i$>	$M^{(MS,MR)}_{(2b,i),(0,ao-1,mn,an,ret)}$
$an \geq 1$	$M^{(MS,MR)}_{(2b,i),(0,ao,mn,an,ret)}$	ack_loss<queue = $[i^{ao}(i\oplus_{MS}1)^{an}]$, rm=$i\oplus_{MS}1$>	$M^{(MS,MR)}_{(2b,i),(0,ao,mn,an-1,ret)}$
$ao \geq 1$	$M^{(MS,MR)}_{(2b,i),(0,ao,mn,an,ret)}$	receive_dup_ack<queue = $[i^{ao-1}(i\oplus_{MS}1)^{an}]$, sn=$i$, rm=$i$>	$M^{(MS,MR)}_{(2b,i),(0,ao,mn,an-1,ret)}$
$an \geq 1$	$M^{(MS,MR)}_{(2b,i),(0,0,mn,an,ret)}$	receive_ack<queue = $[(i\oplus_{MS}1)^{an-1}]$, sn=i, rm=$i\oplus_{MS}1$, rc = ret>	$M^{(MS,MR)}_{(1,i\oplus_{MS}1),(mn,an-1,0,0,0)}$

Table 6. The set of arcs $A^{(MS,MR)}_{(3a,i)}$ with source markings in $V^{(MS,MR)}_{(3a,i)}$, for $MR > 0$

Condition	Source Marking	Binding Element	Destination Marking
$ret<MR$	$M^{(MS,MR)}_{(3a,i),(mo,ao,mn,0,ret)}$	timeout_retrans<queue = $[(i\ominus_{MS}1)^{mo}i^{mn}]$,sn=$i$,rc=$ret$>	$M^{(MS,MR)}_{(3a,i),(mo,ao,mn+1,0,ret+1)}$
$mo \geq 1$	$M^{(MS,MR)}_{(3a,i),(mo,ao,mn,0,ret)}$	mess_loss<queue = $[(i\ominus_{MS}1)^{mo}i^{mn}]$, sn=$i\ominus_{MS}1$>	$M^{(MS,MR)}_{(3a,i),(mo-1,ao,mn,0,ret)}$
$mn \geq 1$	$M^{(MS,MR)}_{(3a,i),(mo,ao,mn,0,ret)}$	mess_loss<queue = $[(i\ominus_{MS}1)^{mo}i^{mn}]$, sn=$i$>	$M^{(MS,MR)}_{(3a,i),(mo,ao,mn-1,0,ret)}$
$ao \geq 1$	$M^{(MS,MR)}_{(3a,i),(mo,ao,mn,0,ret)}$	ack_loss<queue = $[i^{ao}]$, rm=i>	$M^{(MS,MR)}_{(3a,i),(mo,ao-1,mn,0,ret)}$
$ao \geq 1$	$M^{(MS,MR)}_{(3a,i),(mo,ao,mn,0,ret)}$	receive_dup_ack<queue = $[i^{ao-1}]$, sn=i, rm=i>	$M^{(MS,MR)}_{(3a,i),(mo,ao-1,mn,0,ret)}$
none	$M^{(MS,MR)}_{(3a,i),(mo,ao,mn,0,ret)}$	send_ack<queue = $[i^{ao}]$, rm=i>	$M^{(MS,MR)}_{(2a,i),(mo,ao+1,mn,0,ret)}$

Table 7. The set of arcs $A_{(3b,i)}^{(MS,MR)}$ with source markings in $V_{(3b,i)}^{(MS,MR)}$

Condition	Source Marking	Binding Element	Destination Marking
$ret<MR$	$M_{(3b,i),(0,ao,mn,an,ret)}^{(MS,MR)}$	timeout_retrans<queue = $[i^{mn}]$, sn=i, rc=ret>	$M_{(3b,i),(0,ao,mn+1,an,ret+1)}^{(MS,MR)}$
$mn \geq 1$	$M_{(3b,i),(0,ao,mn,an,ret)}^{(MS,MR)}$	mess_loss<queue = $[i^{mn}]$, sn=i>	$M_{(3b,i),(0,ao,mn-1,an,ret)}^{(MS,MR)}$
$ao \geq 1$	$M_{(3b,i),(0,ao,mn,an,ret)}^{(MS,MR)}$	ack_loss<queue = $[i^{ao} (i \oplus_{MS} 1)^{an}]$, rn=$i$>	$M_{(3b,i),(0,ao-1,mn,an,ret)}^{(MS,MR)}$
$an \geq 1$	$M_{(3b,i),(0,ao,mn,an,ret)}^{(MS,MR)}$	ack_loss<queue = $[i^{ao} (i \oplus_{MS} 1)^{an}]$, rn=$i \oplus_{MS} 1$>	$M_{(3b,i),(0,ao,mn,an-1,ret)}^{(MS,MR)}$
$ao \geq 1$	$M_{(3b,i),(0,ao,mn,an,ret)}^{(MS,MR)}$	receive_dup_ack<queue = $[i^{ao-1} (i \oplus_{MS} 1)^{an}]$, sn=$i$,rm=$i$>	$M_{(3b,i),(0,ao-1,mn,an,ret)}^{(MS,MR)}$
$an \geq 1$	$M_{(3b,i),(0,ao,mn,an,ret)}^{(MS,MR)}$	receive_ack<queue = $[(i \oplus_{MS} 1)^{an-1}]$, sn=$i$,rm=$i \oplus_{MS} 1$, rc $= ret$>	$M_{(4,i \oplus_{MS} 1),(mn,an-1,0,0,0)}^{(MS,MR)}$
none	$M_{(3b,i),(0,ao,mn,an,ret)}^{(MS,MR)}$	send_ack<queue = $[i^{ao} (i \oplus_{MS} 1)^{an}]$, rm=$i \oplus_{MS} 1$>	$M_{(2b,i),(0,ao,mn,an+1,ret)}^{(MS,MR)}$

Table 8. The set of arcs $A_{(4,i)}^{(MS,MR)}$ with source markings in $V_{(4,i)}^{(MS,MR)}$, for $MR > 0$

Condition	Source Marking	Binding Element	Destination Marking
none	$M_{(4,i),(mo,ao,0,0,0)}^{(MS,MR)}$	send_mess<queue = $[(i \oplus_{MS} 1)^{mo}]$, sn=i>	$M_{(3a,i),(mo,ao,1,0,0)}^{(MS,MR)}$
$mo \geq 1$	$M_{(4,i),(mo,ao,0,0,0)}^{(MS,MR)}$	mess_loss<queue = $[(i \oplus_{MS} 1)^{mo}]$, sn=$i \oplus_{MS} 1$>	$M_{(4,i),(mo-1,ao,0,0,0)}^{(MS,MR)}$
$ao \geq 1$	$M_{(4,i),(mo,ao,0,0,0)}^{(MS,MR)}$	ack_loss<queue = $[i^{ao}]$, rm=i>	$M_{(4,i),(mo,ao-1,0,0,0)}^{(MS,MR)}$
$ao \geq 1$	$M_{(4,i),(mo,ao,0,0,0)}^{(MS,MR)}$	receive_dup_ack<queue = $[i^{ao-1}]$, sn=i, rm=i>	$M_{(4,i),(mo,ao-1,0,0,0)}^{(MS,MR)}$
none	$M_{(4,i),(mo,ao,0,0,0)}^{(MS,MR)}$	send_ack<queue = $[i^{ao}]$, rm=i>	$M_{(1,i),(mo,ao+1,0,0,0)}^{(MS,MR)}$

Lemma 5. Spanning Lemma. *For $MR \in \mathbb{N}$ and $MS \in \mathbb{N}^+$, and for $0 \le i \le MS$, and for $Type = \{1, 2a, 2b, 3a, 3b, 4\}$, all markings in $\cup_{t \in Type}(V_{(t,i)}^{(MS,MR)}) \cup \{M_{(1,i \oplus_{MS} 1),(MR,0,0,0,0)}^{(MS,MR)}\}$ are reachable from $M_{(1,i),(MR,0,0,0,0)}^{(MS,MR)}$.*

Sketch of Proof. (See [11] for the full proof.) Lemma 2 allows this lemma to be proved directly, for any value of $i \in \{0, ..., MS\}$, rather than inductively over MS. The marking $M_{(1,i),(MR,0,0,0,0)}^{(MS,MR)}$, identical to the initial marking but for MR old duplicate messages with sequence number MS in the message channel, is chosen as the starting point, rather than the initial marking $M_{(1,i),(0,0,0,0,0)}^{(MS,MR)}$. This is because, as it turns out, it is easier to show that $M_{(1,i),(MR,0,0,0,0)}^{(MS,MR)}$ can reach all markings in $V_{(1,i)}^{(MS,MR)}$. (Had we started with the initial marking, we would need to complete a full cycle of the sequence number space in order to get old messages in the message channel when $ssn = 0$.)

Application of Lemma 3 MR number of times shows that $M_{(1,i),(MR,0,0,0,0)}^{(MS,MR)}$ can reach all markings in $V_{span1} = \{M_{(1,i),(mo,MR-mo,0,0,0)}^{(MS,MR)} \mid 0 \le mo \le MR\}$. Then by application of Lemma 4, V_{span1} can reach the markings in

$$V_{span2} = \{M_{(1,i),(mo',ao,0,0,0)}^{(MS,MR)} \mid M_{(1,i),(mo,MR-mo,0,0,0)}^{(MS,MR)} \in V_{span1},$$
$$0 \le mo' \le mo, 0 \le ao \le MR - mo\}$$

By a process of simplification of the inequalities in the set definition, we determine that V_{span2} equals $V_{(1,i)}^{(MS,MR)}$ (see Table 2).

From inspection of the CPN diagram in Fig. 1, $M_{(1,i),(MR,0,0,0,0)}^{(MS,MR)} \in V_{(1,i)}^{(MS,MR)}$ can reach $M_{(2a,i),(MR,0,1,0,0)}^{(MS,MR)}$ via occurrence of send_mess, regardless of the value of i. A similar process is then followed for marking $M_{(2a,i),(MR,0,1,0,0)}^{(MS,MR)}$ as was followed for $M_{(1,i),(MR,0,0,0,0)}^{(MS,MR)}$, to prove that $M_{(2a,i),(MR,0,1,0,0)}^{(MS,MR)}$ can reach all other markings in $V_{(2a,i)}^{(MS,MR)}$. This process continues for the markings in $V_{(2b,i)}^{(MS,MR)}$, $V_{(3a,i)}^{(MS,MR)}$, $V_{(3b,i)}^{(MS,MR)}$ and $V_{(4,i)}^{(MS,MR)}$, and for reachability from one set to another. The procedure for determining a spanning of markings in $V_{(type,i)}^{(MS,MR)}$ for $type \in \{2a, 2b, 3a, 3b\}$ is slightly more complicated, due to the fact that retransmissions can occur from these markings when $ret < MR$.

Finally, $M_{(1,i \oplus_{MS} 1),(MR,0,0,0,0)}^{(MS,MR)}$ can be reached from $M_{(2b,i),(0,0,MR,1,MR)}^{(MS,MR)} \in V_{(2b,i)}^{(MS,MR)}$ by firing the receive_ack transition. (The MR new messages become MR old messages because ssn has incremented.) Thus the lemma is proved. □

Corollary 1. *All markings in $V_{(MS,MR)}$ are reachable from $M_{(1,0),(MR,0,0,0,0)}^{(MS,MR)}$. This follows directly from the Spanning Lemma by a trivial induction over MS.*

To complete the final step in the proof that all markings in $V_{(MS,MR)}$ are accessible from the initial marking, it is sufficient to show that the initial marking

$M_{(1,0),(0,0,0,0,0)}^{(MS,MR)}$ can reach one of the markings in $\{M_{(1,i),(MR,0,0,0,0)}^{(MS,MR)} \mid 0 \leq i \leq MS\}$. By repeated application of Lemma 5 this can reach $M_{(1,0),(MR,0,0,0,0)}^{(MS,MR)}$, which in turn, by Corollary 1, can reach all markings in $V_{(MS,MR)}$. The marking $M_{(1,1),(MR,0,0,0,0)}^{(MS,MR)}$ is chosen as it is the first suitable marking that can be reached from the initial marking. This is proved in the following lemma.

Lemma 6. $M_{(1,1),(MR,0,0,0,0)}^{(MS,MR)}$ *is reachable from* $M_{(1,0),(0,0,0,0,0)}^{(MS,MR)}$.

Sketch of Proof. (See [11] for the full proof.) Proof is by direct inspection of the CPN diagram in Fig. 1. The initial marking enables transition send_mess with binding $<queue = [], sn = 0>$. This results in the marking $M_{(2a,0),(0,0,1,0,0)}^{(MS,MR)}$. From this marking, transition timeout_retrans can occur consecutively MR number of times. The resulting marking is $M_{(2a,0),(0,0,MR+1,0,MR)}^{(MS,MR)}$ in which $MR+1$ copies of the message with sequence number 0 are in the message channel. From this marking, receive_mess can occur, leading to marking $M_{(3b,0),(0,0,MR,0,MR)}^{(MS,MR)}$. From this marking, send_ack can occur, leading to $M_{(2b,0),(0,0,MR,1,MR)}^{(MS,MR)}$. The single acknowledgement with sequence number 1 is the acknowledgement for which the sender is waiting. The occurrence of receive_ack with binding $<queue = [], sn = 0, rn = 1, rc = MR>$ results in marking $M_{(1,1),(MR,0,0,0,0)}^{(MS,MR)}$. (Again, the new messages are now old messages because ssn has incremented.) Thus $M_{(1,0),(0,0,0,0,0)}^{(MS,MR)}$ can reach $M_{(1,1),(MR,0,0,0,0)}^{(MS,MR)}$ and the lemma is proved. □

From Corollary 1 and Lemma 6, all markings in $V_{(MS,MR)}$ are reachable from $M_{(1,0),(0,0,0,0,0)}^{(MS,MR)}$ and Part A of the proof of Theorem 1 is proved.

Part B of the proof of Theorem 1 is proved by the Successor Lemma:

Lemma 7. Successor Lemma. *For all* $MR \in \mathbb{N}$, $MS \in \mathbb{N}^+$, $i \in \{0, ..., MS\}$ *and* $t \in \{1, 2a, 2b, 3a, 3b, 4\}$, $A_{(t,i)}^{(MS,MR)}$ *describes exactly the enabled binding elements of all markings in* $V_{(t,i)}^{(MS,MR)}$ *and the destination marking of every arc in* $A_{(t,i)}^{(MS,MR)}$ *is in* $V_{(MS,MR)}$.

Sketch of Proof. (See [11] for a full proof.) Lemma 2 allows this lemma to be proved correct for any value of $i \in \{0, ..., MS\}$. Consider the markings in $V_{(1,i)}^{(MS,MR)}$ defined in row 1 of Table 2. From the CPN diagram in Fig. 1 and standard enabling rules of CPNs [14], all enabled binding elements (and thus associated arcs) can be identified. The send_mess transition is enabled by all markings in $V_{(1,i)}^{(MS,MR)}$. The mess_loss and receive_mess transitions are enabled only by markings in the subset of $V_{(1,i)}^{(MS,MR)}$ in which the message channel is non-empty. The ack_loss and receive_dup_ack transitions are enabled only by the subset of $V_{(1,i)}^{(MS,MR)}$ in which the acknowledgement channel is non-empty. No other transitions are enabled by any markings in $V_{(1,i)}^{(MS,MR)}$.

By systematically determining the destination marking for each pair of source marking and binding element, all arcs with source nodes in $V_{(1,i)}^{(MS,MR)}$ can be determined. For example, the occurrence of transition send_mess from marking $M_{(1,i),(mo,ao,0,0,0)}^{(MS,MR)} \in V_{(1,i)}^{(MS,MR)}$ with binding $< queue = [(i \ominus_{MS} 1)^{mo}], sn = 1 >$ leads to a marking $M_{(2a,i),(mo,ao,1,0,0)}^{(MS,MR)} \in V_{(2a,i)}^{(MS,MR)}$, for all $i \in \{0, ..., MS\}$. This corresponds to row 1 of Table 3. Rows 2 to 5 can be obtained by a similar procedure for the other enabled transitions.

This procedure can then be repeated for all markings in the other five sets of nodes defined in Table 2. This shows that all arcs with source markings in $V_{(MS,MR)}$ also have destination markings in $V_{(MS,MR)}$ and that these arcs correspond exactly to those defined in Tables 3 to 8. Thus the lemma is proved.   □

For all $MS \in \mathbb{N}^+$ and all $MR \in \mathbb{N}$, Lemmas 5, 6 and 7 and Corollary 1 show that the markings in $V_{(MS,MR)}$ defined by Table 2 correspond exactly to the markings reachable from the initial marking. Lemma 7 also shows that the arcs captured by Tables 3 to 8 correspond exactly to the set of arcs with source markings in $V_{(MS,MR)}$. Thus, for all $MS \in \mathbb{N}^+$ and all $MR \in \mathbb{N}$, $OG_{(MS,MR)} = (V_{(MS,MR)}, A_{(MS,MR)})$ and hence Theorem 1 is proved.   □

The validity of the three assumptions made in Section 3.1 is confirmed by the correctness of the algebraic expressions. No marking can be reached that violates any of the three assumptions, i.e. every marking has channel content of the form $i^* j^*$ where $i, j \in \{0, ..., MS\}$ and $j = i \oplus_{MS} 1$, and every reachable marking can be classified into one of the 6 types in Table 1.

4.2   Analysis Results

Absence of Unexpected Deadlocks. Dead markings can be detected by subtracting from the corresponding set of markings in Table 2 the sets of markings defined as source markings in each table of arcs.

For all $MR \in \mathbb{N}$ and $MS \in \mathbb{N}^+$, the dead markings are $V_{dead}^{(MS,MR)} = \cup_{0 \le i \le MS} \{M_{(2a,i),(0,0,0,0,MR)}^{(MS,MR)}, M_{(2b,i),(0,0,0,0,MR)}^{(MS,MR)}\}$. All dead markings occur because of loss and a bounded retransmission scheme, and all are expected.

Channel Bounds. Channel bounds can be determined by direct examination of the set definitions in the rows of Table 2. Maximising $mo + mn$ gives the message channel bound for the markings in each row. The message channel bound of the SWP becomes the maximum of $mo + mn$ taken over all 6 rows. Similarly, the acknowledgement channel bound is found by maximising $ao + an$. The bound for both channels is $2MR + 1$, from row 2 (message channel) and row 3 (acknowledgement channel). These bounds are imposed by the SWP itself.

Size of the Reachability Graph. By direct inspection of Table 2 and Tables 3 to 8, Theorem 2 for the size of the RG in both parameters can be proved.

Theorem 2. *For $MR \in \mathbb{N}$ and $MS \in \mathbb{N}^+$, the number of nodes and arcs in $OG_{(MS,MR)}$ is given by*

$$|V_{(MS,MR)}| = ((MS+1)/6)(5MR^4 + 38MR^3 + 97MR^2 + 100MR + 36)$$

and

$$|A_{(MS,MR)}| = ((MS+1)/6)(30MR^4 + 175MR^3 + 306MR^2 + 179MR + 36).$$

Sketch of Proof. The nodes in $V_{(1,i)}^{(MS,MR)}$ and $V_{(4,i)}^{(MS,MR)}$ actually form a triangular structure, where the base contains the nodes where $mo + ao = MR$ and the apex is the node where $mo = ao = 0$. Using the formula for the nth triangular number, $n(n+1)/2$, for $n = MR$ and $n = MR - 1$ respectively, we obtain $|V_{(1,i)}^{(MS,MR)}| = (MR^2 + 3MR + 2)/2$ and $|V_{(4,i)}^{(MS,MR)}| = (MR^2 + MR)/2$, for each value of $i \in \{0, ..., MS\}$.

The nodes in the other four sets have a more complicated structure. Take $V_{(2a,i)}^{(MS,MR)}$ for example. The structure can be visualised as a succession of triangular structures over mo and ao, one for each value of $mn \in \{0, ..., ret\}$. A summation over $0 \le ret \le MR$ obtains $|V_{(2a,i)}^{(MS,MR)}| = (MR^4 + 8MR^3 + 21MR^2 + 22MR + 8)/4$. Similar techniques are used to obtain the size of the other node sets. The total number of markings is given by a summation over all values of $i \in \{0, ..., MS\}$ and the result $V_{(MS,MR)} = (MS+1)(5MR^4 + 38MR^3 + 97MR^2 + 100MR + 36)/6$ is obtained.

Determining the number of arcs requires a more complicated approach. The number of source markings for which each arc is defined is determined for each row in Tables 3 to 8. To do this in a way that prevents excessively copious summations, for each row, the number of markings that do not satisfy the conditions in column 1 of each arc table is determined. This is then subtracted from the total number of markings defined by the corresponding set in Table 2. The total number of arcs is then the summation over all rows in all arc tables of the number of arcs defined by each row. The result is as stated in the theorem. $\square$

This theorem confirms our empirical results for small parameter values and matches RG size expressions obtained using methods to fit polynomials to data.

5   Conclusions and Future Work

We have proved a theorem which gives an algebraic expression for the infinite family of RGs of a parameterised CPN model of the class of Stop-and-Wait protocols. The parameters, MaxSeqNo and MaxRetrans, are both unbounded and the protocol operates over a lossy unbounded in-order medium. This is a considerable advance over previous work [12], which was restricted to the case where MaxRetrans $= 0$, and automatic verification attempts using the tool FAST [9] which were only successful when MaxRetrans was an unbounded parameter with MaxSeqNo restricted to small concrete values (1 to 5) [8], and when MaxSeqNo was an unbounded parameter with MaxRetrans fixed to 0 [7].

These symbolic expressions can be used for protocol verification. For example, we have shown how deadlocked states can be identified from the arc expressions as those markings that never appear as source nodes. Further, we have shown that the node table (Table 2) can be used to determine upper bounds on the channel capacity. This result (2MaxRetrans+1) confirms that previously obtained using a hand proof on the CPN in [5,6], but is much simpler (once the algebraic expressions are known). We have also derived formulae for the number of nodes and arcs in the state space as a function of the two parameters, proving they are linear in MaxSeqNo and quartic in MaxRetrans, an interesting complexity result. Proving language equivalence to a service of alternating send and receive events [6], as was done in [12] for the restricted case of MaxRetrans = 0, is currently being undertaken for the general case.

In the future, we would like to automate the procedure for obtaining algebraic expressions for the RGs of parametric systems based on finding structural regularities as a function of the parameters. Our experience with modelling other systems, including the Capability Exchange Signalling service [18] and TCP's data transfer service [13], also reveals repeating patterns in their RGs from which symbolic RGs representing the infinite family have been obtained. This provides evidence that our new parametric approach is promising and may be generalised to a larger class of systems.

References

1. P. Aziz Abdulla, A. Collomb-Annichini, A. Bouajjani, and B. Jonsson. Using Forward Reachability Analysis for Verification of Lossy Channel Systems. *Formal Methods in System Design*, 25(1):39–65, 2004.
2. J. Billington. Formal specification of protocols: Protocol Engineering. In *Encyclopedia of Microcomputers*, volume 7, pages 299–314. Marcel Dekker, New York, 1991.
3. J. Billington, M. Diaz, and G. Rozenberg, editors. *Application of Petri Nets to Communication Networks*, volume 1605 of *Lecture Notes in Computer Science*. Springer-Verlag, 1999.
4. J. Billington and G. E. Gallasch. How Stop and Wait Protocols Can Fail Over The Internet. In *Proceedings of FORTE'03*, volume 2767 of *Lecture Notes in Computer Science*, pages 209–223. Springer-Verlag, 2003. (invited paper).
5. J. Billington and G. E. Gallasch. An Investigation of the Properties of Stop-and-Wait Protocols over Channels which can Re-order messages. Technical Report CSEC-15, Computer Systems Engineering Centre Report Series, University of South Australia, May 2004.
6. J. Billington, G. E. Gallasch, and B. Han. A Coloured Petri Net Approach to Protocol Verification. In *Lectures on Concurrency and Petri Nets, Advances in Petri Nets*, volume 3098 of *Lecture Notes in Computer Science*, pages 210–290. Springer-Verlag, 2004.
7. J. Billington, G.E. Gallasch, and L. Petrucci. FAST Verification of the Class of Stop-and-Wait Protocols modelled by Coloured Petri Nets. *Nordic Journal of Computing*, Vol. 12(3):251–274, 2005.

8. J. Billington, G.E. Gallasch, and L. Petrucci. Transforming Coloured Petri Nets to Counter Systems for Parametric Verification: A Stop-and-Wait Protocol Case Study. In *Proceedings of 2nd International Workshop on Model-Based Methodologies for Pervasive and Embedded Software (MOMPES'05), Rennes, France*, TUCS General Publication, No. 39, pages 37–55, May 2005.

9. FAST - Fast Acceleration of Symbolic Transition systems. http://www.lsv.ens-cachan.fr/fast/.

10. G. E. Gallasch and J. Billington. Towards the Parametric Verification of the Class of Stop-and-Wait Protocols over Ordered Channels. Technical Report CSEC-21, Computer Systems Engineering Centre Report Series, University of South Australia, March 2005, revised June 2005.

11. G. E. Gallasch and J. Billington. Parametric Verification of the Class of Stop-and-Wait Protocols over Ordered Channels. Technical Report CSEC-23, Computer Systems Engineering Centre Report Series, University of South Australia, Draft of January 2006.

12. G.E. Gallasch and J. Billington. Using Parametric Automata for the Verification of the Stop-and-Wait Class of Protocols. In *Proceedings of ATVA 2005*, volume 3707 of *Lecture Notes in Computer Science*, pages 457–473. Springer-Verlag, 2005.

13. B. Han. *Formal Specification of the TCP Service and Verification of TCP Connection Management*. PhD thesis, Computer Systems Engineering Centre, School of Electrical and Information Engineering, University of South Australia, Adelaide, Australia, December 2004.

14. K. Jensen. *Coloured Petri Nets: Basic Concepts, Analysis Methods and Practical Use. Vol. 1, Basic Concepts*. Springer-Verlag, 2nd edition, 1997.

15. K. Jensen. *Coloured Petri Nets: Basic Concepts, Analysis Methods and Practical Use. Vol. 3, Practical Use*. Springer-Verlag, 1997.

16. L.M. Kristensen, S. Christensen, and K. Jensen. The Practitioner's Guide to Coloured Petri Nets. *International Journal on Software Tools for Technology Transfer*, 2(2):98–132, 1998.

17. L.M. Kristensen, M. Westergaard, and Peder Christian Nørgaard. Model-Based Prototyping of an Interoperability Protocol for Mobile Ad-Hoc Networks. In *Proceedings of IFM 2005*, volume 3771 of *Lecture Notes in Computer Science*, pages 266–286. Springer-Verlag, 2005.

18. L. Liu and J. Billington. Tackling the Infinite State Space of a Multimedia Control Protocol Service Specification. In *Proceedings of ICATPN'02*, volume 2360 of *Lecture Notes in Computer Science*, pages 273–293. Springer-Verlag, 2002.

19. J. Postel. Transmission Control Protocol. RFC 793, September 1981.

20. W. Stallings. *Data and Computer Communications*. Prentice Hall, 7th edition, 2004.

21. Standard ML of New Jersey. http://cm.bell-labs.com/cm/cs/what/smlnj/.

22. A. Tanenbaum. *Computer Networks*. Prentice Hall, 4th edition, 2003.

23. A. Valmari. The State Explosion Problem. In *Lectures on Petri Nets I: Basic Models*, volume 1491 of *Lecture Notes in Computer Science*, pages 429–528. Springer-Verlag, 1998.

24. A. Valmari and I. Kokkarinen. Unbounded Verification Results by Finite-State Compositional Techniques: 10^{any} States and Beyond. In *Proceedings of International Conference on Application of Concurrency to System Design*, pages 75–85. IEEE Computer Society, March 1998.

Verification of Medical Guidelines by Model Checking – A Case Study

Simon Bäumler, Michael Balser, Andriy Dunets,
Wolfgang Reif, and Jonathan Schmitt

Lehrstuhl für Softwaretechnik und Programmiersprachen,
Institut für Informatik, Universität Augsburg,
Augsburg, 86135 Germany
{baeumler, balser, dunets, reif, schmitt}@informatik.uni-augsburg.de
http://www.informatik.uni-augsburg.de/lehrstuehle/swt/se/

Abstract. This paper presents a case study on how to apply formal modeling and verification in the context of quality improvement in medical healthcare. The aim is to verify quality requirements of medical guidelines and clinical treatment protocols that are used to standardize patient care both for general practitioners and hospitals. This research is supported by the European Commission's IST program and brings together experts from computer science, artificial intelligence in medicine, hospitals, and the Dutch Institute for Healthcare Improvement (CBO). We present the process of formal modeling and verification of guidelines using the modeling language Asbru, temporal logic for expressing the quality requirements, and model checking for proof and error detection. The approach is illustrated with a case study on a guideline from the American Association for Pediatrics on "Jaundice in healthy Newborns"[1].

Keywords: Model checking, verification, formal methods, Asbru, abstraction, medical guidelines.

1 Introduction

Over the last decade, the approach of evidence-based medicine has increased the application of clinical guidelines in medical practice. Medical guidelines provide clinicians with healthcare recommendations based on valid and up-to-date empirical evidence. Usually they consist of "systematically developed statements to assist hospital staff with appropriate healthcare decisions" [12]. Application of guidelines improves the quality of medical treatment and it has been proven that adherence to guidelines and protocols may reduce healthcare costs up to 25%.

Many practical guidelines and protocols still contain ambiguous, incomplete or even inconsistent elements. Recent efforts have tried to address quality improvement of guidelines [21]. Our general approach to verification of guidelines is based

---

[1] This work has been partially supported by the European Commission's IST program, under contract number IST-FP6-508794 Protocure II.

A. Valmari (Ed.): SPIN 2006, LNCS 3925, pp. 219–233, 2006.

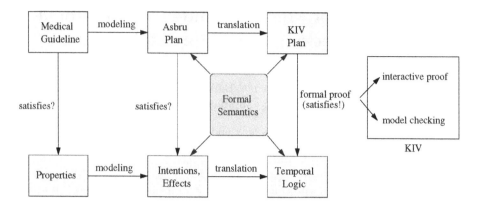

Fig. 1. Formalization and verification of protocols in the Protocure project

on the observation that guidelines can be viewed as parallel programs. Therefore the classical formal methods for the quality assurance of software can be applied for the case of medical guidelines, especially because guidelines are highly-structured, systematic documents that are amenable for formal verification.

Because most parts of a guideline consist of informal plain text an appropriate representation language with clear and well-defined semantics is required. For this purpose we use Asbru[19]. Asbru is a temporal, skeletal plan-representation language which was especially designed for the medical domain. The most important advantage of using Asbru as a modelling language is its formal semantics[3]. Figure 1 shows the flow of documents in the overall verification process. The original guideline is depicted in the upper left corner of Fig. 1. It is modeled as Asbru plan using the knowledge-representation language Asbru.

The Asbru model is the basis for further tasks, e.g. to build decision support systems. For these tasks it is necessary to ensure the quality of the model. Thus, we are interested in tools to efficiently debug the model, e.g. to ensure its consistency. [10] defines a number of structural properties which should be fulfilled by a good quality Asbru model. Some of these properties can be checked by syntactic analysis. Other properties require formal analysis. Furthermore, we are interested in the formal verification of more complex medical properties such as medical indicators. Complex, infinite state properties in general require interactive theorem proving. For structural and simple medical properties we aim for efficient techniques which can be automatically applied. For this, we automatically translate the model into a formal representation for an interactive theorem prover KIV[2]. In order to apply model checking, we further translate the model into the input language of SMV model checker[18]. In this paper, we focus on model checking of properties.

Simultaneously to the above transformation, in Figure 1, a number of interesting properties have been identified while analyzing both the original protocol and its Asbru model. We distinguish between *Medical Properties* and *Structural Properties* (see 3.2).

To evaluate our approach we have considered the medical guideline for "Jaundice in healthy newborns", a medical guideline from the American Association of Pediatrics, that covers various features of Asbru. We will use the jaundice protocol in the following sections as running example for our paper.

The identified properties do not depend on timing constraints. Therefore, it has been possible to abstract away from time which reduces the complexity of the model. For the verification of these properties, we have chosen SMV as a model checker, because to our knowledge this is one of the most efficient tools to verify large models without complex timing constraints. For real-time properties, the use of timed model checkers, e.g. UPPAAL[22], will be of interest.

We have used Cadence SMV version 10-11-02 with default settings on a computer with a 3 GHz Pentium processor and 2 GB of RAM.

Our main contributions are: (i) a validated formal model of a concrete medical guideline where the quality has been assured by automatic techniques, (ii) tool support for automatic verification of all of the properties from [10], (iii) case study to assess the possibilities of light-weight model checking techniques to verify structural or simple medical properties of medical guidelines; this case study could serve as a reference case study for other model checkers and other automatic techniques in the field of medical guidelines. We do not present new strategies for model checking SMV models in general.

The paper is organized as follows. Section 2 gives a short overview of the Jaundice guideline and the Asbru language with its formal semantics. Section 3 gives a description of a concrete infinite state model of the jaundice protocol and describes its reduction to a finite state model using an abstraction. In section 4 we summarize our experiences from this case study and describe possible improvements of the current process planned for future work.

2   Asbru: A Knowledge Representation Language for Protocols

We describe Asbru and its use by a simple example. Details on Asbru can be found in [19].

2.1   The Jaundice Protocol

Jaundice, or hyperbilirubinemia, is a common disease in newborns which is caused by increased bilirubin levels in blood. Under certain circumstances, high bilirubin levels may have destructive neurological effects and thus must be accurately treated. Often jaundice disappears without treatment, but sometimes a phototherapy is needed to reduce the level of total serum bilirubin(TSB). In a few cases, however, jaundice is a sign of a severe disease, which must be treated appropriately.

The jaundice reference guideline[1] is a 10 pages document which contains various notations: the main text; a list of factors to be considered when assessing a jaundiced newborn; two tables - one for the management of the healthy term newborns and another for the treatment options for jaundiced breast-fed ones; and a flowchart describing the steps in the protocol. The Protocol consists of two parts performed sequentially: diagnosis and treatment. Treatment is performed if disease symptoms are detected. During the application of the protocol, as soon as the possibility of a more serious disease is uncovered, the recommendation is to exit without any further action. The further treatment is not considered in the guideline.

2.2 Modeling the Jaundice Protocol in Asbru

Medical guidelines are represented as hierarchical skeletal **plans**, i.e. plans with subplans. Figure 2 shows the hierarchy of plans representing the Asbru model of jaundice protocol. It is made up of about 40 plans. Two phases in the protocol control flow clearly emerge: diagnostics and treatment parts which are executed sequentially. Three "Check-for-..." plans model two check-ups at specific time intervals and a continuous monitoring of the TSB level. We focus here on the treatment phase, which is more interesting from the verification point of view. It consists of two parallel plans, namely the actual treatment and a cyclical plan asking for the input of new TSB and age values every 12 to 24 hours. Depending on the current bilirubin level, either the *regular-treatments* or an *exchange-transfusion* can take place. The plan-body of regular-treatments plan contains two subplans which are executed in parallel without any ordering. The

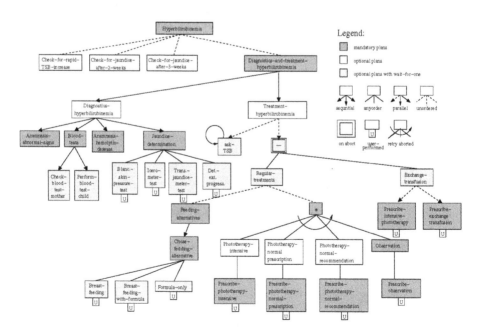

Fig. 2. Asbru plans modeling jaundice protocol

regular-treatments* subplan (which is abbreviated with * in Figure 2) represents a group of therapies, which are executed sequentially without any order. All of the therapy plans are optional with the exception of the *observation* plan which must complete for the successful completion of the parent plan. Any of these therapies can be restarted, in case if it is eventually aborted.

Figure 3 shows an example of two Asbru plans from the jaundice guideline. An Asbru model of a plan contains the definitions of different descriptive elements like intentions, conditions, plan body and control structures. In the following we describe these main elements.

The **intentions** are the high-level goals of a plan. Intentions can be expressed in terms of achieving, maintaining or avoiding certain states or actions. The states or actions to which intentions refer can be intermediate or final.

```
plan regular-treatments
intentions ...
conditions ...
plan-body type=unordered, wait-for all
    feeding-alternatives
    /* implicit subplan regular-treatments*: */
    do type=any-order, retry-aborted-subplans=yes, wait-for observation
        phototherapy-intensive
        phototherapy-normal-prescription
        phototherapy-normal-recommendation
        observation


plan phototherapy-intensive
intentions
    achieve-overall-state: (bilirubin=observation)
    maintain-intermediate-state:
            (and(TSB-decrease=yes in [[4h,-],[-,6h],[-,-]] SELF)
                (TSB-change>1 in [[4h,-],[-,6h],[-,-]] SELF))
conditions
    setup-condition: (or(bilirubin=phototherapy-intensive in NOW)
                        (normal-phototherapy-failure))
    abort-condition: (or(and(bilirubin!=phototherapy-intensive)
                            (not normal-phototherapy-failure))
                        (intensive-phototherapy-failure))
    intensive-phototherapy-failure:
            (and(bilirubin=phototherapy-intensive in NOW)
                (or(and(TSB-decrease=yes in [[4h,-],[-,6h],[-,-]] SELF)
                    (TSB-change<1 in [[4h,-],[-,6h],[-,-]] SELF))
                    (TSB-decrease=no in [[4h,-],[-,6h],[-,-]] SELF)))
plan-body
    prescribe-intensive-phototherapy
```

Fig. 3. Regular-treatments and Phototherapy-intensive plans

Thus, the intention label "maintain-intermediate-state" means that always during the execution of the plan a certain condition must be satisfied. Generally there are twelve possible forms of intention: [achieve/maintain/avoid] [intermediate/overall] [state/action]. Most of the medical properties we considered in the verification are gained from the intentions (see Sec. 3.2). For example, one of the intentions of the phototherapy-intensive plan (see Fig. 3) is to maintain a certain intermediate state, i.e. in all cases in 4 to 6 hours after the activation of the plan the bilirubin level decreases. As all intentions of the jaundice guideline this is an universal property.

Every **plan-body** contains the actions to be performed by the plan and/or subplans to be executed as part of the plan. A wide variety of **control** structures can be used to specify the execution order of the actions in the plan-body. There are the following types of plan-bodies in Asbru:

- user-performed: an action to be performed by the user, which requires user interaction and thus is not modeled further
- single step: an action which can be either an activation of a subplan, an assignment of a variable, or request for an input value
- subplans: a set of steps to be performed in a given order. The possible execution orders are: **sequential**, **parallel**, in any possible sequential order(**anyorder**) and in parallel without any restrictions on the synchronization (**unordered**)
- cyclical plan: a repetition of actions over time periods

When a plan-body contains subplans it is possible to define the completion of some (or all) subplans as a necessary precondition for the successful completion of the parent plan. For example **wait-for-all** type of the plan-body means, that the successful completion of parent plan requires successful completion of all of its subplans. Similarly **wait-for-one** or **wait-for someplan** can be defined.

The *regular-treatments* plan (Fig. 3) is a good example for a more complicated structure of the plan-body. It has an unordered plan-body with wait-for-all option and two subplans: *feedings-alternatives* and *regular-treatments**. The implicit plan *regular-treatments** consists of several different therapies executed in any order (see Fig. 2 and Fig. 3). Its subplan *phototherapy-intensive* (Fig. 3), for instance, describes one of the therapies. Its plan-body simply contains the activation of the subplan *prescribe-intensive-phototherapy*.

A variety of **conditions** can be associated with a plan, which influence control of an execution of the plan. The most important types of conditions are the following: filter-, setup-, activate-, abort-, and complete-condition. The meaning of these conditions is described more closely in the section 2.3. Conditions can not only specify a set of satisfying current states[2] but also they can be monitored over time, if they are formulated using time annotations, e.g. in 4 to 6 hours after the activation of plan the bilirubin level change decrease is greater then 1.

---

[2] An Asbru state is composed of the state of execution of all plans and the state of the patient. Further we have the Asbru history which is defined as a mapping from the Asbru clock to an Asbru state and allows to specify time annotated conditions.

Time annotations can occur in conditions. They specify the time period where a parameter condition used in the time annotation is monitored. A time annotation is defined by the following eight entities: reference point *(REF)*, earliest starting shift *(ESS)*, latest starting shift *(LSS)*, earliest finishing shift *(EFS)*, latest finishing shift *(LFS)*, minimum duration *(MinDu)*, maximum duration *(MaxDu)* and parameter proposition *ParamProp*. These components are combined in the data structure:

$$(ParamProp \textbf{ in } [[ESS,LSS], [EFS,LFS], [MinDu,MaxDu]] \; REF)$$

Reference points like *NOW* (current time) and *SELF* (time of activation of this plan) are commonly used. Consequently a time annotation defines a set of time intervals (also called *set of possible occurrences*). A time annotation is *TRUE* if and only if there exist a time interval in the set of possible occurrences where the condition *ParamProp* is evaluated to *TRUE* in all time points within this interval.

As example consider the following time annotation from the phototherapy-intensive plan:

$$(TSB\text{-}decrease = yes \textbf{ in } [[4h,\text{-}], [\text{-},6h], [\text{-},\text{-}]] \; SELF)$$

This time annotation monitors the bilirubin level on the time interval between 4 to 6 hours after the plan start. It is evaluated to TRUE if there is a new bilirubin measurement with a value smaller than the latest measured value before the plan started. It has the following meaning: there exist time interval (or point as special case of interval) with earliest starting at 4h after the plan activation and latest finishing at 6h after activation where *TSB-decrease=yes* is true. The predicate *TSB-decrease=yes* is evaluated to *TRUE* on the given interval if and only if for all time point t_0 on this interval the bilirubin value is smaller than bilirubin value at the time of plan activation.

2.3   Formal Semantics of Asbru

We use the formal semantics of Asbru defined in [3]. The semantics follows two goals: first it should document Asbru and be understandable for users; on the other hand it should be formal enough. We use the example of *regular-treatments** plan to explain the semantics here.

The operational semantics of Asbru is defined using statecharts. It uses the formal semantics of statecharts defined in [9]. Asbru plans are modeled as statecharts which run in parallel and communicate via shared variables and signals. Asbru conditions are monitored over time. The evaluated conditions trigger transitions of the statecharts. The evaluation of conditions depends on the data inputs from the environment usually describing dynamics of patient. Shared variables like patient parameters or state of other plans can also influence the evaluation of Asbru conditions. For example the abort-condition of phototherapy-intensive plan (see Fig. 3) triggers the abort of the plan as soon as it fails to reduce bilirubin level in 4 to 6 hours after the plan activation.

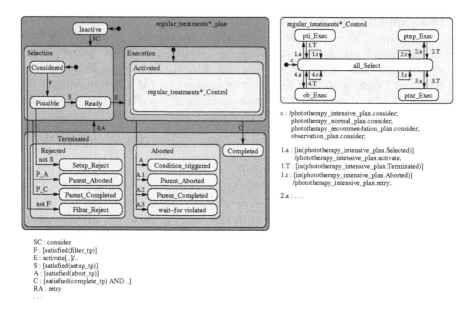

Fig. 4. Statecharts modeling regular-treatments* plan

The *regular-treatments** plan is an implicit subplan of the *regular-treatments* plan (see Fig. 2 and Fig. 3). The behavior of the *regular-treatments** plan is defined by the statechart in Figure 4. This statechart is divided into a *Selection* phase and an *Execution* phase. Initial state of the plan is *Inactive*. An external signal *consider* triggers the selection phase (transition SC). In the state *Considered* the condition *filter_tp* is checked. In case this condition is satisfied, the plan changes to the state *Possible* and so on. In the state *Activated* the subplans are executed. The execution of subplans is controlled by the *regular_treatments*_Control* statechart (Fig. 4), which models an anyorder control of subplans. It is responsible for the generation of the *consider-*, *activate-* or *retry*-signals, which control the execution of subplans. All subplans are selected in parallel (transition *c*) and executed such that at most one subplan is active at the same time (transitions *i.a*). If the activated plan terminates(transitions *i.T*) another one can be activated. If several subplans reach state *Selected* simultaneously, one of them is activated nondeterministically. If parameter flag "retry-aborted" is set, then the transition *i.r* initiates a restart.

The original infinite state model of the system is a composition of statecharts running in parallel and reacting on environment inputs. Interaction with the environment happens in micro- and macro-steps. One macro-step consists of many micro-steps which describe reactions of the system on certain environment input. When a system achieves a stable state the corresponding macro-step is completed and in the first micro-step of the next macro-step new input from the environment is read. This model corresponds to the assumption that the system, which models the guideline, always reacts quick enough to changes of the environment. It is also intuitively the proper modeling for medical plans,

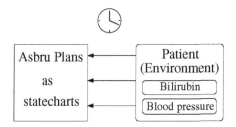

Fig. 5. Original infinite state model of medical guideline

i.e. control of plans does not take time to activate or cancel some plans. The notion of time is defined using macro-steps. Time passes only at the begin of every macro-step.

In Asbru we have no explicit model of the patient, i.e. we do not model specific patient behavior. We assume that the patient has chaotic behavior, i.e. parameter values blood pressure, bilirubin level in blood, etc., change arbitrarily over time. This allows us to investigate whether the medical protocol reacts adequately in all possible cases. Consequently the infinite state concrete model is the composition of statecharts modeling medical plans, the environment and the Asbru clock modeling current time, see Figure 5. This model resembles somehow the model of parallel processes communicating using shared variables.

3 Model Checking Process

The crucial point in model checking and verification in general is computing an optimal abstraction of the examined system. Much research has concentrated on tackling the state explosion problem. A variety of abstraction techniques have been developed, for example [15], [16], [4], [14] and [8]. The basis for these investigations is an important observation: there are various aspects of the concrete model that have no impact on the checked property and can be abstracted in such a way that the size of the model is drastically reduced, but the property is still safely verified, i.e. the satisfaction of a property over an abstract model implies satisfaction over the concrete model. Methods that derive an abstract model directly from some high-level description of the system are needed.

3.1 Abstract Finite State Model

Generally, it is a hard task to construct a correct abstract finite state model for the generic Asbru model completely automatically, since Asbru is a very expressive language.

The infinite parameters describing the patient (or environment) can be abstracted to finite state variables using data abstraction [4], [17]. The more problematic issue is time, which usually requires some kind of history variable. All plans, in order to proceed, must know whether their setup-, filter-, abort- or complete-condition is satisfied or not. Some of these conditions contain time annotations, as for example the abort-condition of *phototherapy-intensive* plan does (see Fig. 3). In order to evaluate time annotated conditions an Asbru plan must access its history.

Our goal is an abstraction which can be constructed automatically for the given Asbru model. In order to construct a finite state model an appropriate abstraction which eliminates time and history is needed. We use a simple abstraction that maps all time annotations to atomic propositions whose logical value is randomly assigned in every macro step. Those random inputs can eventually generate behavior in the abstract model that is not present in the concrete model. This abstraction preserves only ACTL[3] properties, as it is an over-approximation, which adds extra behavior to the abstract model. Nevertheless, this is not a problem for us, because most interesting properties we aim to verify are intentions, which are ACTL properties.

The main weakness of this abstraction is the generation of false negatives during the verification of properties. On the other hand the important advantage is its automatic generation. By this abstraction we shift the complexity of time and history to the environment. According to the statechart semantics inputs from the environment happen in the first micro-step of every macro-step and provide the required information about the patient needed for the controls of plans, e.g. up-to-date value of blood pressure or information about change of the bilirubin level in blood over the period of 6 hours after the start of the plan.

For the generation of the SMV model we translate the statecharts from the Asbru semantics into an equivalent flat state transition system, which can be directly encoded in the SMV input language. This part models the control flow of the guideline. On the other hand, data flow and time is modeled using the abstraction techniques described above.

3.2 Properties

The results from the verification of properties should help to improve the quality of medical guideline. Structural properties specify the general correctness requirements, which must be satisfied by every Asbru protocol, regardless of its content. For example, every plan should eventually terminate, every plan must have a chance to execute or be able to complete. Our experiences from the jaundice case study has shown that verification of structural properties helps to discover errors produced during the translation of informal medical guideline into the formal Asbru model. The following structural properties have been considered: termination (Asbru plans should always terminate), every plan can eventually be activated (completed), there are no redundant conditions (i.e. every condition can eventually have influence on the control flow of plans) and all wait states are eventually quitted. These properties have been formalized as CTL formulas and are automatically generated for every Asbru plan as SMV specifications. Most of them are originally not ACTL properties, but their verification can be indirectly accomplished by the verification of the corresponding

---

[3] The logic ACTL is the set of all well-formed state formulas from CTL[11] containing no existential operators (EX and EU).

```
term_pti_plan: SPEC AG(!ptip_state = inactive ->
                       AF(ptip_state = completed |
                          ptip_state = rejected |
                          ptip_state = aborted))
satisf_abort_pti_plan: SPEC AG(!(ptip_state=activated &
                               ptip_abort_condition))
reach_activated_pti_plan: SPEC AG(!(ptip_state=activated))
wait_possible_pti_plan: SPEC AG(ptip_state = possible ->
                               AF(ptip_setup_condition |
                                  ptip_is_terminated))
```

Fig. 6. SMV specification of structural properties for Phototherapy-intensive plan

ACTL properties, as described in Section 3.3. For example, the corresponding ACTL properties (in SMV syntax) for the plan *photatherapy intensive(pti)* are depicted in Figure 6. The property **term_pti_plan** formulates a termination property, i.e. every plan that was previously selected always terminates in the future. By the **satisf_abort_pti_plan** property we try to verify whether the abort-condition of the phototherapy-intensive plan is redundant or not. In case we find a non-spurious counter-example for **satisf_abort_pti_plan** we know that abort-condition is not redundant, i.e. it has an influence on the plan execution. Similar properties can be formulated for all other Asbru conditions. Reachability of important states is tested by properties like **reach_activated_pti_plan**. The property **wait_possible_pti_plan** tests whether wait state *possible* is eventually quitted.

In contrast to structural properties medical properties address high level aspects of medical protocols, such as relevant clinical parameters or general safety requirements concerning actions of physicians or overall intentions of the guideline. As an example, when treating jaundice, it is required that 6 hours after application of phototherapy the bilirubin level must drop significantly. In the jaundice case study we considered only plan intentions as conceptual properties. For instance, plan *phototherapy-intensive* has two intentions, which can be specified as ACTL properties, as Figure 7 shows. With the *intermediate state* in the second property we mean only stable states, i.e. states in which the reaction of the plan on the environment inputs is completed. Therefore, the variable *tick*

```
--achieve overall state: bilirubin = observation
SPEC AG(ptip_state = completed -> AF AG bilirubin = observation)

--maintain intermediate state: tsb_decrease = yes & tsb_change>=1
SPEC AG((ptip_state = activated & tick) ->
        (pti_tsb_decrease_yes_signal &
        !pti_tsb_change_less_one_signal))
```

Fig. 7. SMV specification of medical properties for Phototherapy-intensive plan

is used to describe the *activated* state of the *pti* plan where it is *stable*, i.e. no transitions of the corresponding statechart are activated.

3.3 Verification Process

The abstraction we use is described in 3.1. It allows us to generate the SMV model fully automatically. On the other hand it can introduce unrealistic behavior, which has an impact on the verification process. Figure 8 illustrates the general scheme of verification. Due to property preservation considerations we examine only ACTL properties although it is also indirectly possible to verify ECTL properties. The medical properties we considered are the intentions of the plans, which are formulated as ACTL formulas.

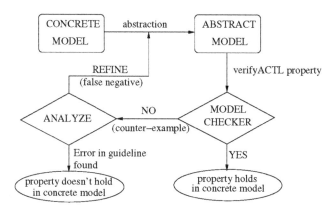

Fig. 8. Verification scheme

IF ACTL property is proved to be false the corresponding counter example is generated. In the next step we have to analyze this trace to find out whether it is a real bug in the concrete model or just some unrealistic trace added by the over-approximation. We also have to verify ECTL properties since most implementation level (structural) properties are existential properties, e.g. satisfiability of Asbru conditions or non-redundancy of plans. If, for instance, a ECTL formula $EF\phi$ must be verified, we first verify the ACTL formula $AG\neg\phi$. If it is *true* then original formula is *false*. On the other hand, if a counter example is found then we analyze whether it is realistic one. If the found counter example trace is realistic then the original formula is *true* and the generated counter example is the trace that satisfies the original formula.

3.4 Results and Experiences from Verification of Jaundice

The abstracted model of the jaundice guideline was constructed in the SMV language and model checking was used to verify different properties. In particular we verified structural and medical properties of approximately 30 Asbru

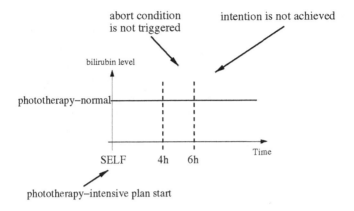

Fig. 9. Counter example visualization

plans from the jaundice hierarchy of plans. Automatic generation of the SMV model consisting of 3000 lines of code and including 360 structural and 40 medical properties has accelerated the whole process. Checking one property takes about 2 minutes on average whereby 2×10^6 BDD-nodes were allocated. Complete verification of circa 400 properties lasted 3.5 hours and 4×10^6 BDD-nodes were allocated.

In the whole verification process the manual effort of analyzing the counter examples and refining the abstract model was rather small and acceptable. The verification of structural properties uncovered several nontrivial modelling errors and therefore helped immensely to gain more confidence in the formal Asbru model.

During the process of formalization and verification of the medical properties, a number of errors and ambiguities were discovered. We have found special cases of treatment that violate plan intentions. These special cases have been overlooked by the Asbru modelers and were consequently not appropriately considered in the Asbru model. Figure 9 illustrates a possible execution sequence that violates the intention of the photptherapy-intensive plan, see Figure 3. The intention postulates that in 4 to 6 hours after plan start the bilirubin level must decrease in the other case plan must abort. As we see in Figure 9 bilirubin level does not decrease in the corresponding time interval and the plan does not abort. The reason for the violation of the plan intention is that the abort-condition was two weak and did not consider all possible cases. Using model checking verification method we have discovered many other similar "forgotten" cases in the overall plan hierarchy containing 30 plans.

4 Summary and Outlook

In this paper we have described the automated verification of medical guidelines using the jaundice case study as an example. The simple abstraction we applied yielded surprisingly good results in the jaundice case study. In fact only few refinements and fine tuning were needed while verifying properties. This simple abstraction allows us to construct the SMV model fully automatically, which is an important advantage as we plan to apply this method on further case studies. The approach as a whole is not completely automatic but partly an interactive one (see Fig. 8) because our abstraction is over-approximation. Due to the high expressiveness of the Asbru modeling language it is practically not possible to construct a correct abstraction for the general case of an Asbru-model automatically without any user interaction. Nonetheless the degree of automation of this process is very high.

The first errors we have found were consequence of too coarse abstraction. In some cases our first verification experiments have shown that the used abstraction is too coarse. Therefore, to avoid the interactive component *ANALYZE* in the process, see Figure 8, we plan to construct the correct abstraction. We see this as promising direction for further work on verification of Asbru. Further we plan to use the KIV theorem prover to show the correctness of the constructed abstraction by proving the corresponding bisimulation equivalence. Another profitable improvement can be a visualization of model checking results. The graphical interpretation of counter examples can make verification more efficient as it makes the interpretation of traces easier.

Our approach to verify simple properties of medical guidelines by model checking were surprisingly successful. Therefore, it is promising to also apply other automatic techniques to the verification of more complex properties, e.g. real-time properties, and larger guidelines.

Currently, we are applying our method on a second guideline, which describes the treatment of breast cancer. This guideline is considerably larger but our first experiences with it are very promising.

References

1. American Academy of Pediatrics, Provisional Committee for Quality Improvement and Subcommittee on Hyperbilirubinemia. Practice parameter: management of hyperbilirubinemia in the healthy term newborn *Pediatrics,* 94:558-565, 1994.
2. M. Balser, W. Reif, G. Schellhorn, K. Stenzel, A. Thums. Formal system development with KIV. In T.Maibaum, editor, *Fundamental Approaches to Software Engineering*, number 1783 in LNCS. Springer, 2000.
3. M. Balser, C. Duelli, W. Reif. Formal Semantics of Asbru - An Overview *In Proc. of the 6th World Conference on Integrated Design and Process Technology(IDPT-02)*, June 2002.
4. E.M. Clarke, O. Grumberg, D.E. Long. Model checking and abstraction. *ACM Transactions on Programming Languages and Systems,* 16(5):1512-1542, September 1994.
5. E.M. Clarke, O. Grumberg, D. Peled. Model Checking. *MIT Press,* 2000.
6. P. Cousot, R. Cousot. Abstract interpretation : A unified lattice model for static analysis of programs by construction or approximation of fixpoints. *ACM Symposium of Programming Language,* pages 238-252, 1977.
7. D. Dams. Abstract Interpretation and Partition Refinement for Model Checking. *PhD Thesis,* Eindhoven University of Technology, 1996.

8. D. Dams, R. Gerth, O. Grumberg. Abstract interpretation of reactive systems. *ACM Transactions on Programming Languages and Systems,* 19(2):253-291,1997.

9. A. Pnueli, B. Josko, H. Hungar, W. Damm. A Compositional Real-time Semantics of STATEMATE Designs. *Lecture Notes in Computer Science,* pages 186-238, Springer Verlag, Berlin, Proceedings COMPOS'97.

10. G. Duftschmid, S. Miksch. Knowledge-based verification of clinical guidelines by detection of anomalies *OEGAI Journal* 1999, pages 37 – 39.

11. E. Allen Emerson. Temporal and Modal Logic. *Handbook of Theoretical Computer Science, Volume B: Formal Models and Sematics 1990,* J. van Leeuwen, ed., North-Holland Pub. Co./MIT Press, Pages 995-1072.

12. M.J. Field, K.N. Lohr. *Clinical Practice Guidelines: Directions for a New Program.* National Academy Press, Washington D.C., USA, 1992.

13. J. Fox, N. Johns, C. Lyons, A. Rahmanzadeh, R. Thomson, P. Wilson. PROforma: a general technology for clinical decision support systems. *Computer Methods and Programs in Biomedicine,* 54:59-67, 1997.

14. P. Godefroid, M. Huth, R. Jagadeesan. Abstraction-based Model Checking using Modal Transition Systems. *Proceedings of CONCUR'2001,* Aalborg, August 2001. Lecture Notes in Computer Science, vol. 2154, pages 426-440, Springer-Verlag.

15. O. Grumberg. Abstractions and Reductions in Model Checking. *Nato Science Series,* Vol. 62, Marktoberdorf summer school, 2001.

16. S. Graf, H. Saidi. Construction of abstract state graphs with PVS. In *Computer aided verification,* volume 1254 of LNCS, pages 72-83, June 1997.

17. D.E. Long. Model checking, Abstraction, and Compositional Reasoning. *PhD Thesis,* Carnegie Mellon University, 1993.

18. K.L. McMillan. Symbolic Model Checking: An Approach to the State Explosion Problem. *Kluwer Academic,* 1993.

19. Y. Shahar, S. Miksch and P. Johnson. The Asgaard project: a task-specific framework for the application and critiquing of time-oriented clinical guidelines. *Artificial Intelligence in Medicine* 1998, pages 29 – 51.

20. R. Milner. A Calculus of Communicating Systems. Springer, 1980.

21. A. ten Teije, M. Marcos, M. Balser, J. van Croonenborg, C. Duelli, F. van Harmelem, P. Lucas, S. Miksch, W. Reif, K. Rosenbrand, A. Seyfang, J. Coltel, A. Jovell. Supporting the development of medical protocols through formal methods. *In Proc. of the Symposium on Computerized Guidelines and Protocols (CGP-04), IOS Press, 2004.*

22. K.G. Larsen, P. Peterson, Wang Yi. UPPAL in a nutshell. *Journal of Software Tools for Technology Transfer, 1(1-2):134-152, 1997.*

Towards a Compositional SPIN

Corina S. Păsăreanu and Dimitra Giannakopoulou

QSS and RIACS, NASA Ames Research Center, Moffett Field, CA 94035, USA
{pcorina, dimitra}@email.arc.nasa.gov

Abstract. This paper discusses our initial experience with introducing automated assume-guarantee verification based on learning in the SPIN tool. We believe that compositional verification techniques such as assume-guarantee reasoning could complement the state-reduction techniques that SPIN already supports, thus increasing the size of systems that SPIN can handle. We present a "light-weight" approach to evaluating the benefits of learning-based assume-guarantee reasoning in the context of SPIN: we turn our previous implementation of learning into a main program that externally invokes SPIN to provide the model checking-related answers. Despite its performance overheads (which mandate a future implementation within SPIN itself), this approach provides accurate information about the savings in memory. We have experimented with several versions of learning-based assume guarantee reasoning, including a novel heuristic introduced here for generating component assumptions when their environment is unavailable. We illustrate the benefits of learning-based assume-guarantee reasoning in SPIN through the example of a resource arbiter for a spacecraft.

Keywords: Assume-guarantee reasoning, model checking, learning.

1   Introduction

This paper describes work performed in the context of a NASA project called Reliable Software Systems Development. The aim of the project is to improve the reliability and safety of software systems to support human and robotic exploration of space. The emphasis is on tool support for the development of verifiable software - tools will be applicable at all stages of the software development, and will target the C language for implementation. For design, the tool that will be supported is SPIN [18] for the following two main reasons. SPIN has been used extensively and successfully for industrial applications. Moreover, SPIN enables embedding of C code, which allows to combine designs with implementations. The users of the tool are offered the convenience of using a single environment for verification when transitioning between different phases of the software development.

We present here a component of this project which aims at investigating whether/how compositional techniques can benefit SPIN in dealing with software designs. The compositional techniques that we investigate are based on automated assumption generation for assume-guarantee reasoning, as presented

A. Valmari (Ed.): SPIN 2006, LNCS 3925, pp. 234–251, 2006.

in [4, 9, 13]. The techniques were implemented in the LTSA tool [12] for the analysis of design models encoded as *finite state* labelled transition systems with blocking communication. Although these techniques have proven effective in the LTSA [25], there is no guarantee that they will be (as) successful in the context of other model checkers. For example, as seen in [14], the savings obtained with automated assume-guarantee reasoning at the design level with LTSA were more pronounced than those obtained at the (Java) code level with the Java PathFinder model checker [30]. The LTSA is by nature a compositional tool, which means that any component in isolation can be targeted for analysis, without the need to provide an environment to turn it into a "closed" system, which is the case for a Java component. Moreover, the amount of detail at the code level makes state spaces larger and may "hide" the size of the savings obtained from a particular approach. SPIN lies somewhere in between the two tools: SPIN's input language – Promela – is closer to a programming language than the input language of the LTSA, but it is still a modeling language, which allows to abstract away implementation details that may hamper verification.

The work reported here is a first study of the issues and benefits of introducing compositional techniques into SPIN (which is not inherently a compositional tool). Our approach has been to make such an evaluation in a "light-weight" fashion, that is, to avoid re-implementing our algorithms within SPIN itself. We will describe how we turned our existing implementations into a main program that invokes SPIN to provide answers to specific model checking questions. As will be discussed later, such an approach has a number of disadvantages, as for example high time overheads. However, we claim that it provides a good way for researchers to make a quick evaluation of the potential benefits of compositional techniques in their model-checking environment. After all, the main interest in model checking is to obtain savings in memory, and these can be evaluated accurately with the framework that we propose.

We will discuss the technical details involved in the implementation of our "light-weight" compositional framework for SPIN. For simplicity, we only look into Promela programs where components communicate in a "rendez-vous" fashion (i.e., Promela channels of size 0). Our evaluations also include a novel heuristic presented in this paper for generating component interface specifications using learning. The description of our approach is given in terms of a running example of a client-server system. We then discuss the application of our techniques to the larger case study of a resource arbiter for a spacecraft, where learning-based assume-guarantee reasoning achieved significant memory gains.

To summarize, the contributions of this paper are: 1) an approach for fast and easy evaluation of the benefits that compositional verification techniques based on learning can bring in the context of any model checker, 2) a description of the technical details involved in the implementation of this approach using SPIN, 3) the discussion of a novel heuristic for learning assumptions of components in isolation, and 4) the application of our approach to a realistic resource arbiter for a spacecraft, for which it achieved significant memory gains over traditional monolithic (non-compositional) model checking.

The remainder of the paper is organized as follows. We give background on assume-guarantee reasoning and learning in Section 2. A description of our proposed approach is provided in Section 3, with the technical details of its implementation using SPIN presented in Section 4. Section 5 discusses our experience with applying our approach to the resource arbiter case study. Finally, Section 6 presents related work and Section 7 concludes the paper.

2   Background

2.1   Assume Guarantee Reasoning

We address the problem of checking *design models* expressed as finite state labeled transition systems. We use compositional techniques for increased scalability. For simplicity, let us consider two software components M_1 and M_2 and a *safety* property P (expressed as a finite state automaton). Reasoning about more than two components will be discussed later in Section 3.

The goal is to check if the two components operate correctly together to achieve the desired property, i.e. to check $M_1 \| M_2 \models P$ using model checking techniques. Here, the parallel composition operator $\|$ denotes the product construction for finite state automata, where the behavior of two components is combined by synchronization of common actions and interleaving of remaining actions. Property P encodes the desired *interactions* between components. Checking $M_1 \| M_2 \models P$ directly may be too expensive (there may not be enough time and memory resources to complete the computation), so we break-up the verification into two smaller sub-problems, i.e. we check M_1 and M_2 separately, using *assume-guarantee reasoning*.

In the assume-guarantee paradigm a formula is a triple $\langle A \rangle\ M\ \langle P \rangle$, where M is a component, P is a property, and A is an assumption about M's environment. The formula is true if whenever M is part of a system satisfying A, then the system must also guarantee P.

The simplest assume-guarantee proof rule shows that if $\langle A \rangle\ M_1\ \langle P \rangle$ and $\langle true \rangle\ M_2\ \langle A \rangle$ hold, then $\langle true \rangle\ M_1\ \|\ M_2\ \langle P \rangle$ also holds. This proof strategy can also be expressed as an inference rule as follows:

$$\frac{(\text{Premise 1})\ \langle A \rangle\ M_1\ \langle P \rangle \qquad (\text{Premise 2})\ \langle true \rangle\ M_2\ \langle A \rangle}{\langle true \rangle\ M_1\ \|\ M_2\ \langle P \rangle}$$

Thus, using this rule we can show that P holds on $M_1\ \|\ M_2$, by checking $\langle A \rangle\ M_1\ \langle P \rangle$ and $\langle true \rangle\ M_2\ \langle A \rangle$ separately. More elaborate rules can be used for this style of reasoning [4]. The underlying aim for all such rules is to make model checking of their premises cheaper, in terms of time and in particular consumed memory, than non-compositional verification. To achieve this, the assumptions have to be *much smaller* than the analyzed components. Coming up with appropriate assumptions is traditionally a difficult, manual process.

In previous work we proposed to use an off-the-shelf learning algorithm, L*, to derive appropriate assumptions *automatically*. Initial approximate assumptions are gradually refined by means of learning from counterexample traces obtained by model checking assume guarantee triples.

2.2   The L* Learning Algorithm

The learning algorithm used by our approach was developed by Angluin and later improved by Rivest and Schapire. We refer to the *improved* version by the name of the original algorithm, L*. L* learns an unknown regular language and produces a DFA that accepts it – see Figure 1. Let U be an unknown regular language over some alphabet Σ. In order to learn U, L* needs to interact with a *Minimally Adequate Teacher*. The Teacher must be able to correctly answer two types of questions from L*. The first type is a *membership query*, consisting of a string $s \in \Sigma^*$; the answer is *true* if $s \in U$, and *false* otherwise. For the second type of question, the learning algorithm generates a *conjecture*, i.e., a candidate DFA A whose language the algorithm believes to be identical to U. The answer is *true* if $\mathcal{L}(A) = U$. Otherwise the Teacher returns a counterexample, which is a string s in the symmetric difference of $\mathcal{L}(A)$ and U.

At a higher level, L* creates a table where it incrementally records whether strings in Σ^* belong to U. It does this by making membership queries to the teacher. At various stages L* decides to make a conjecture. It constructs a candidate automaton A based on the information contained in the table and asks the Teacher whether the conjecture is correct. If it is, the algorithm terminates. Otherwise, L* uses the counterexample returned by the Teacher to extend the table with strings that witness differences between $\mathcal{L}(A)$ and U.

Characteristics of L*. L* is guaranteed to terminate with a minimal automaton A for the unknown language U. The conjectures made by L* strictly increase in size; each conjecture is smaller than the next one, and all incorrect

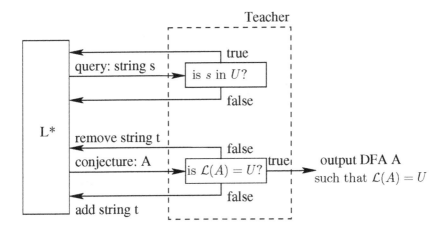

Fig. 1. The L* learning algorithm

conjectures are smaller than A. Therefore, if A has n states, L* makes at most $n - 1$ incorrect conjectures. The number of membership queries made by L* is $\mathcal{O}\left(kn^2 + n\log m\right)$, where k is the size of the alphabet of U, n is the number of states in the minimal DFA for U, and m is the length of the longest counterexample returned when a conjecture is made.

3   Tool Architecture

We present here an initial study for a tool-based approach to compositional verification, that uses the L* algorithm to build assumptions and the SPIN model checking tool to check assume guarantee triples. Although using learning to automate assume guarantee reasoning was introduced in our previous work, there are some novel ideas that we propose here:

- We present a *generic* tool architecture that uses learning for automated assume guarantee reasoning for multiple components. By generic, we mean that the tool can be instantiated with different model checking tools for checking assume guarantee triples; we discuss the use of SPIN here.
- The tool can be used for checking different assume guarantee rules (as before), but in addition we present a novel heuristic that allows us to derive the *interface specification* for a component M_1, in the absence of a specification of its environment (i.e. M_2). This interface specification can be used to check if the component M_1 behaves correctly in multiple contexts. In the past, we have experimented with an approach that uses conformance checking [9]. Instead of using this expensive approach, we present a light-weight heuristic that enables cheaper generation of precise interface specifications.

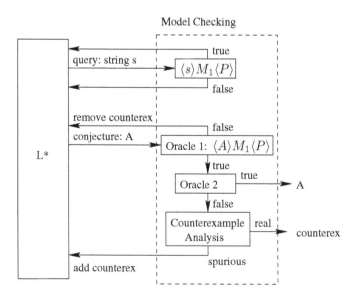

Fig. 2. Tool Architecture

The architecture of the compositional verification tool is illustrated in Figure 2. The architecture is derived from our previous work on compositional verification [9]. The goal is to use learning to derive an assumption A such that the assume guarantee triple $\langle A \rangle\ M_1\ \langle P \rangle$ evaluates to *true*. The *weakest assumption* A_w under which M_1 satisfies P is such that, for any environment component E, $\langle true \rangle\ M_1\ \|\ E\ \langle P \rangle$ if and only if $\langle true \rangle\ E\ \langle A_w \rangle$. In our framework, L* attempts to build A_w through iterative learning. For L* to learn A_w, we need to provide a Teacher that is able to answer the two different kinds of questions that L* asks. Our approach uses model checking to implement such a Teacher.

Membership Queries. To answer a membership query for s the Teacher simulates s to check if it may lead to a violation. For simplicity, our current implementation for SPIN reduces the simulation to model checking $\langle s \rangle\ M_1\ \langle P \rangle$ (here we abuse the notation and we let s denote also the automaton that accepts string s). If there is no violation, it means that $s \in \mathcal{L}(A_w)$, because M_1 does not violate P in the context of s, so the Teacher returns true. Otherwise, the answer to the membership query is false.

Conjectures. Our framework uses the conjectures returned by L* as intermediate candidate assumptions A. The teacher uses two *oracles*: *Oracle 1* guides L* towards a conjecture that is strong enough to make $\langle A \rangle\ M_1\ \langle P \rangle$ true. Once this is accomplished, the resulting conjecture may be too strong, in which case our framework uses *Oracle 2* to guide L* towards a *weaker* conjecture. There are many options for implementing *Oracle 2*, and we discuss some of them below.

Oracle 1 checks $\langle A \rangle\ M_1\ \langle P \rangle$. If this does not hold, the model checker returns a counterexample. The Teacher informs L* that its conjecture A is not correct and provides the counterexample to witness this fact. If, instead, $\langle A \rangle\ M_1\ \langle P \rangle$ holds, the Teacher forwards A to Oracle 2.

Oracle 2 needs to ensure that the candidate assumption is indeed the *weakest*. In the context of this work, we have implemented different versions for this oracle.

- If component M_2 is available then the oracle checks $\langle true \rangle\ M_2\ \langle A \rangle$ (as in our previous work). If the result of model checking is true, then, according to the assume-guarantee rule, P holds on $M_1 \| M_2$. The teacher therefore returns true, whether A represents the weakest assumption or not, because the computed assumption (smaller or equal in size to A_w) is good enough to prove that the property holds. If model checking returns a counterexample, our implementation performs counterexample analysis. If the counterexample indicates a real error, the framework stops and the error is reported to the user. Otherwise, the counterexample indicates that the candidate assumption needs to be refined and it is returned to guide L*. Our implementation has been extended to reasoning for n components $M_1 \| M_2 \| ... \| M_n$. The system is decomposed into two parts M_1 and $M_2' = M_2 \| ... \| M_n$ and the learning algorithm is invoked recursively for checking the second premise of the rule.
- We have implemented a different version of *Oracle 2* (described in detail below), which leads to the generation of the *interface specification* of M_1, and it does not use M_2.

3.1   Generation of Interface Specifications

As discussed, Oracle 2 is responsible for ensuring that an assumption A, shown strong enough by Oracle 1, is not too strong. In other words, the assumption should include all traces over the alphabet of the assumption, in the context of which M_1 satisfies the property P. By alphabet we mean the set of events that are involved in a state machine.

We discuss here the case where the alphabet of the property and the alphabet of the assumption are the same. We restrict ourselves to this case for simplicity, but also because it covers all the examples that we discuss in this paper. We are currently studying different cases and plan on extending the proposed heuristic heuristic for those.

Let T_A denote the set of all traces over the alphabet of the assumption A. Then A should include all traces in T_A that satisfy the property; if some trace $t \in T_A$ that satisfies P is not in the current candidate assumption A, then A is too imprecise, so t is returned to the learning algorithm for the assumption to be refined. The above check can be formulated as $P \models A$, and can be performed by a model checker, with the counterexamples returned to the learning algorithm. Our proposed heuristic for Oracle 2 for generating interface specifications is to therefore implement $P \models A$.

Note that our heuristic is not always accurate, meaning that it may fail to report traces that the assumption does not include even though it should. The traces that it may miss are traces that violate P but that will never be exercised in the context of the component M_1. These traces are the traces of $!M_1 \| !P$, where $!M_1$ denotes the complement of M_1, and similarly for P. Computing the complement of M_1 involves determinization, which may increase the state-space of M_1 exponentially, in the worst case. For this reason, we do not include this check in our heuristic. One may argue that many components do not exhibit this worst-case complexity. For such components, however, rather than computing $!M_1 \| !P$, it would make more sense to construct the assumption directly, using the algorithm presented in our previous work [13]. Learning was introduced in [9] in order to avoid the potential complexity of the computation presented in [13].

It is worth mentioning that, although our heuristic as currently implemented may not always compute the weakest assumption, our experiments discussed later in the paper demonstrate that it is quite effective in practice.

4   Implementation

Our implementation makes use of our previous Java implementation of L* in the context of the LTSA tool [9, 12]. The implementation supports the analysis of multiple components through recursive invocation and the new heuristic for Oracle 2. Moreover, the learning now runs as a stand-alone application that invokes SPIN (from within Java) to answer queries and conjectures.

We consider here only a subset of Promela, where components are Promela processes that communicate through rendezvous channels. We consider safety

```
mtype = {u1, u2, Nobody};
chan request = [0] of {mtype};
chan cancel = [0] of {mtype};
chan grant = [0] of {mtype};
chan deny = [0] of {mtype};

active proctype server() {
 mtype resUser = Nobody;
 mtype u;
 S0: if
     :: request?u ->
          if
          :: (resUser == Nobody) -> grant!u; resUser = u; goto S0;
          :: else -> deny!u; goto S0;
          fi;
     :: cancel?u ->
          if
          :: (resUser == u) ->  resUser = Nobody;  goto S0;
          :: else -> goto S0;
          fi;
     fi;
}
```

Fig. 3. Promela code for server

```
proctype client (mtype u) {          |   trace {
  Init:    if                        |   Q0: if
           :: request!u              |       ::grant?u2 -> goto Q4;
           fi;                       |       ::grant?u1 -> goto Q5;
  PendingReservation:                |       fi;
           if                        |   Q4: if
           ::grant?eval(u)           |       ::cancel?u2 -> goto Q0;
           ::deny?eval(u) -> goto Init; |     fi;
           fi;                       |   Q5: if
  PendingCancel:                     |       ::cancel?u1 -> goto Q0;
           if                        |       fi;
           :: cancel!u -> goto Init  |   }
           fi;                       |
  }                                  |
```

Fig. 4. Promela code for client (left) and mutual exclusion property (right)

properties that refer to the rendezvous communication between components. We leave for future work the extension of the approach to handling the full Promela language. We selected this subset of Promela because it bears a close correspondence to the type of models that we analyze in the context of LTSA. Moreover, several systems can be described in this subset. For example, the work presented in [10, 27] shows how abstracted Java and Ada programs can be translated into this exact subset of Promela.

We illustrate the implementation on a simple Promela model for a client server application – see Figure 3 and Figure 4 (left). The model has a *server* and two *clients* that communicate through global rendezvous channels. Note that the MER case study is a more complex version of this type of system.

The clients send *requests* to make a reservation for using a common resource, they wait for the server to *grant* the reservation, they use the resource, after which they *cancel* the reservation. The server can *grant* or *deny* a *request*, such that the resource is used only by one client at a time. We analyzed a property stating that the resource shall be used mutually exclusive.

There are many ways of encoding (safety) properties in SPIN: i.e. as basic assertions, never claims or trace assertions [19]. We chose to encode properties as *trace assertions*: the types of safety properties that we typically encounter refer to valid sequences of channel operations, and trace assertions are specifically designed for formulating such sequences. In Section 5 we discuss other formalisms for encoding assume guarantee triples. Figure 4 (right) shows the trace assertion for the mutual exclusion property. The assertion specifies the correctness requirement that receive operations on channel **grant** with **u1** and **u2** alternate with receive operations on **cancel** with **u1** and **u2**, respectively. In other words, for mutual exclusion to be guaranteed, when a user is granted the resource, then this user needs to cancel it before it gets granted to a different user. The trace assertion defines an automaton that monitors the system execution (it changes state when a channel operation that is within its scope is executed).

In order to analyze this model using our learning based implementation, we first brake up the system into its components, i.e. processes **client(u1)**, **client(u2)** and **server()**. We also need to provide the *alphabet* of actions for the candidate assumptions. As discussed in Section 3.1, we set the alphabet of the assumptions to be the same as the alphabet of properties.

Checking Assume Guarantee Triples. In our approach, we use SPIN to answer queries and oracles, which are encoded as assume guarantee triples of the form $\langle A \rangle\ M\ \langle P \rangle$. Here A denotes a deterministic finite state automaton that may encode traces (in the case of queries) or candidate assumptions generated by L*. Property P is also a deterministic finite state automaton (encoded as a trace assertion). The assumptions define execution *environments* for the components under analysis. We therefore encode them as Promela processes that run in parallel with the analyzed components (and thus restrict their behavior). The assumption A and the property P are used to examine the component M and to check whether behaviors that are allowed by the assumption may lead to a property violation.

To check an assume guarantee triple, the teacher first creates a file that encodes the assumption as a Promela process and the property as a trace assertion, and it invokes SPIN i.e., it executes the following commands:

```
spin -a M1.promela
cc -o pan pan.c -DSAFETY
./pan -E
```

The teacher waits for the verification to complete and it parses the output of the verification process to check if there were any assertion violations, in which case

```
active proctype query () {          active proctype CandidateAssumption(){
  grant!u1;                         Q0:     if
  grant!u2;                                 :: grant!u1-> goto Q2;
}                                           :: grant!u2-> goto Q3;
                                            :: cancel?u1-> goto Q1;
active proctype UniversalEnv() {            fi;
  do /* actions unmatched in U1||A */  Q1:     if
  :: request?u1                             :: grant!u1-> goto Q1;
  :: deny!u1                                :: grant!u2-> goto Q1;
                                            :: cancel?u1-> goto Q1;
  /* actions of other users */              :: cancel?u2-> goto Q1;
  :: grant?u2                               fi;
  :: cancel!u2                      Q2:     if
  :: grant?u3                               :: grant!u1-> goto Q1;
  :: cancel!u3                              :: cancel?u1-> goto Q0;
  :: grant?u4                               fi;
  :: cancel!u4                     Q3:     if
  :: grant?u5                               :: cancel?u1-> goto Q1;
  :: cancel!u5                              :: cancel?u2-> goto Q0;
  od                                        fi;
}                                   }
```

Fig. 5. Promela code for a query, an assumption and the universal environment

it returns *false* (together with the counterexample reported by SPIN) to the L*
algorithm; otherwise, it returns *true*. All these steps are automated.

As an example, Figure 5 shows the Promela process for checking a query on
component client(u1) for string "grant!u1; grant!u2;". Figure 5 also shows
the Promela process for a CandidateAssumption for client(u1).

We should note that both properties and assumptions are *global*, i.e. they may
refer to actions that are not local to the component under analysis. In order to
check in isolation whether a component violates a global property, we need to
provide an environment that substitutes the rest of the system, as typically performed in model checking. In the context of checking assume-guarantee triples,
the environment is the universal environment as restricted by the assumption. To
simulate that, we provide for each component a universal environment for those
rendezvous actions that are not matched with actions in the provided assumption. For example, Figure 5 shows such a closing environment for client(u1) –
in an infinite loop, the process performs rendezvous for the actions that are unmatched by client(u1) and by the process encoding the assumption. Note that
the same universal environment is used for checking all the queries and oracles
for one particular component (and one property).

5   Analysis of a Resource Arbiter

5.1   Description

We experimented with our approach in the context of a model derived from a
component of the flight software for JPL's Mars Exploration Rovers (MER) (see

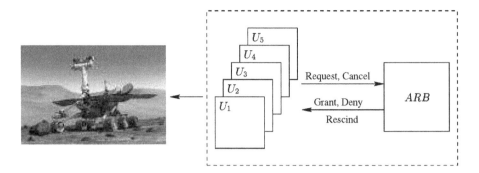

Fig. 6. Arbiter Architecture

Figure 6). The MER software contains 11 user threads (U_i). Each thread serves one specific application, such as imaging, controlling the robot arm, communicating with earth, and driving. There are 15 shared resources on the rover, to which access is controlled by an arbiter module (ARB). The arbiter module prevents potential conflicts between resource requests, and enforces priorities. For instance, it would not make sense to start a communication session with earth while the rover is driving. The system has been analyzed with SPIN before, in a non-compositional way - a detailed description can be found in [20].

5.2 Analysis

We present here the results of applying compositional analysis for a subproblem with 5 user threads and 5 shared resources. A design-level Promela model of the system was created based on available documentation (3000 lines of Promela code) and was used to check several properties. We report here the results for checking a mutual exclusion property (P) stating that communication and driving can not happen at the same time.

The compositional techniques discussed in this paper work on a specific ordering of the components in the system. For the analyzed system, we ordered the user components first as $(U_1 \ldots U_5)$ and the arbiter module last as (ARB). As described in [7], compositional techniques tend to be sensitive to different decompositions of a system. The reason we selected this particular ordering was that part of the project involved experimenting with generating assumptions in the absence of an arbiter component.

Table 1. Arbiter Analysis Results

Analysis	MEM	State Space	Time: $t_{model} + t_{compile} + t_{run}$	Assumption Size
Monolithic	544.019 MB	$3.91653e + 06$	$0.021s + 0.854s + 33.745s$	N/A
Recursive	2.622 MB	1002	$0.038s + 1.142s + 0.032s$	6 .. 12
Heuristic	2.622 MB	2941	$0.044s + 1.392s + 0.021s$	12

We then used the learning tool described in Section 3 to generate automatically assumptions $A_1 \ldots A_5$ such that:

$$\langle A_1 \rangle \ U_1 \ \langle P \rangle$$
$$\langle A_2 \rangle \ U_2 \ \langle A_1 \rangle$$
$$\langle A_3 \rangle \ U_3 \ \langle A_2 \rangle$$
$$\langle A_4 \rangle \ U_4 \ \langle A_3 \rangle$$
$$\langle A_5 \rangle \ U_5 \ \langle A_4 \rangle$$
$$\langle true \rangle \ ARB \ \langle A_5 \rangle$$

For this purpose, we manually created environments that exercise each component, as described in the previous section. We also specified the alphabet of interface actions to be used for building the assumptions. We experimented with the recursive technique that we have implemented for handling multiple components and with the heuristic approach, that analyzes one component at a time. In both cases we were able to compute assumptions for the above premises to hold. Hence, according to the compositional rule presented in Section 2, we concluded that the system $U_1\|U_2\|U_3\|U_4\|U_5\|ARB$ indeed satisfies P.

The results of the analysis applied to the arbiter system are shown in Table 1. We used a 2.2 GHz dual processor Pentium with 1 Gb of memory running Red Hat Enterprise Linux WS. In the table, row "Monolithic" reports the results obtained from the verification of the system in a non-compositional way, and rows "Recursive" and "Heuristic" report the results obtained by the application of the recursive learning scheme and the heuristic described in Section 3.1, respectively. Specifically, we report the memory and time consumed for verification of the system. For the compositional techniques, the reported time and memory refer to the maximum time or memory consumed to for checking a single premise. They do not include the process of generating the assumptions (reported in Table 2), but rather the process of applying the assume-guarantee premises once the assumptions are available.

The reported times are divided into three parts: t_{model} is the time to create a C model from a Promela model, $t_{compile}$ is the compilation time, and t_{run} is the time to run the specific verification task in SPIN. We also report the size of the assumptions used for compositional verification. Using the recursive algorithm yields assumptions that have 12 states (A_1, A_2 and A_3) and 6 states (A_4 and A_5) while the heuristic approach yields assumptions of size 12 for each component (for this case study, all the assumptions generated using the heuristic approach are the weakest). We need to study further the trade-offs between the two learning approaches: the heuristic approach has the advantage that it can be used for the analysis of a component in isolation (in the absence of the rest of the over-all system, and maybe even before it is available), while the recursive approach may yield smaller assumptions (as it is the case here). This is expected to happen for some systems, because the recursive approach has knowledge of the environment of each component, and may therefore produce stronger (and smaller) assumptions.

The results indicate that compositional verification can achieve significant memory savings over non-compositional verification.

Table 2. Cost of Assumption Generation

Analysis	queries	oracle 1	oracle 2	$t_{SPIN} + t_{Learn}$	MEM_{Learn}	t_{LTSA}	MEM_{LTSA}
Recursive	4884	48	1	5646.365s	1743 K	42.87 s	20400K
Heuristic (A_1)	852	12	1	818.213s	508 K	3.076 s	4845K

Cost of Assumption Generation. Table 1 reports the results of compositional analysis using assumptions that are already available. Let us now analyze the cost of building these assumptions using learning based techniques. Table 2 reports the results of running the two learning approaches for assumption generation: for the recursive approach, we report the number of queries, the number of oracle invocations and the total time for running the algorithm (this includes t_{Learn} – the time of running the Java implementation that makes external calls to SPIN – plus t_{SPIN} – the total time of running SPIN multiple times for answering queries and conjectures). For interface generation, we report the same data for the generation of an assumption for *only one* component (U_1) – the results for the rest of the components are similar. Therefore, the total time of generating all five interface specifications is approximately 4095 s (5 times 819 s). Table 2 also reports MEM_{Learn} – the memory consumed by our Java implementation (this does not include the memory consumed by a SPIN run – which is reported in Table 1).

Our experiments indicate a serious time overhead, where a dominant factor is the compilation time for queries. For example, there are 852 queries made for the generation of the interface specification of component U_1, and the cost of running a query is $0.045s + 1.283s + 0.011s$, where the compilation time $1.283s$ clearly dominates.

Therefore we looked into ways of reducing the compilation time overhead for queries. In particular, we experimented with an alternative way of encoding queries – as never claims – in order to take advantage of the SPIN's feature that allows for the *separate compilation* of a model and of properties (written as never claims). Note that never claims can be used not only to define correctness properties, but also to *restrict* the search of the verifier to a user-defined subset of the system [19]. It is in the latter fashion that we use never-claims to attempt more efficient checking of queries.

As an example, Figure 7 shows the never claim used for checking a query "grant!u1; grant!u2;" (the analog of the query in Figure 5). Here **grant_u1**, **grant_u2**, **cancel_u1** and **cancel_u2** are global boolean flags added to the Promela model of a component. They are set to true whenever a corresponding rendezvous occurs and are reset to false on any other action. For example, **grant_u1** is set to true (while all the other flags are reset to false) atomically with **grant?u1**. The reason we use these flags is that SPIN does not allow rendezvous actions in never claims. The effect is that the never claim restricts a verification run to all the states that conform to the trace (note that the flags need to be reset after every system step execution, to make sure that the never claim restricts correctly the system). For technical reasons (SPIN does not allow never claims and trace assertions to be checked at the same time), we changed the encoding

```
never {
 do
 :: grant_u1 -> break
 :: !grant_u1 && !grant_u2 && !cancel_u1 && !cancel_u2
 od;
 do
 :: grant_u2 -> break
 :: !grant_u1 && !grant_u2 && !cancel_u1 && !cancel_u2
 od;
 do
 :: !grant_u1 && !grant_u2 && !cancel_u1 && !cancel_u2
 od;
}
```

Fig. 7. A query encoded as a never claim

for properties (as monitors). The encoding of queries as never claims allows us to compile the component model combined with the property only once and to compile separately the never claims for each query. Note that the same approach can be used for encoding assumptions.

With this new encoding, we obtained a significant reduction in running time. For example, the cost of heuristic interface generation for U_1 was reduced by a factor of 4 (from $818.213s$ to $185.185s$). We expect a similar reduction to be obtained for running the recursive algorithm, and even further reduction for the separate compilation of assumptions.

5.3 Discussion

The implementation described is a first step towards introducing learning-based assume guarantee reasoning in the SPIN model checker. The purpose of this work is fast experimentation with the algorithms in the context of examples encoded in Promela. We intend to explore several directions for improving the performance of this approach in future stages of the project.

The current implementation invokes SPIN for each query and for the two oracles. This involves creating appropriate Promela files, compiling them and running the verification at each step. While this approach works well for small examples, for realistic (large) examples, parsing and compiling the Promela files at each step is costly in terms of time. We believe that a first step towards a better integration will be the creation of specialized algorithms for efficient trace simulation (for checking queries) and for checking properties in the presence of restricting assumptions; these algorithms should allow for separate compilation of models, assumptions and properties.

We should note that we encountered similar timing overheads with the implementation of the learning assume-guarantee approach as a plugin for the LTSA model checker [12], as compared to our initial implementation within the core of the LTSA tool [9]. In that implementation, we encountered a significant performance overhead due to the fact that the plugin communicates with the LTSA by placing descriptions of the models in the Edit tab. As a result, each query or conjecture would require parsing and computing the component model. The avenue we took to solve the problem was to implement our techniques in the core of the LTSA and expose them to the LTSA plugins, while keeping the interfacing for our assume-guarantee reasoning as an LTSA plugin. As a result, the running time of our iterative learning algorithms is low.

For example, the last two columns in Table 2 show the results of running the LTSA implementation for the arbiter case study. The results indicate that an implementation directly in SPIN is likely to similarly improve the performance significantly. Note that part of the gain of having the learning algorithms run within LTSA is that the LTSA can store the results of a particular composition (for a component, for example) and use it in the analysis of multiple properties. The impact can be great in the evaluation of queries, and it may be worth adding this capability in SPIN, for cases where that would be appropriate (when, for example, the component state space is manageable).

A nice feature that the LTSA supports is that the plugin can extend the user interface of the tool, and can be invoked from the LTSA's graphical user interface. As a result, the user can easily customize their assume-guarantee problem, i.e., select the modules and properties that participate in a compositional proof, as well as the rule that is to be applied. In the future, we would like to take a similar approach in integrating our techniques using XSpin. To achieve this, we need to understand better what mechanisms are available or can be added for achieving Spin/XSpin extensions. Ideally, we would like to display all the components (i.e. processes) in a Promela specification, and to allow the user to choose which components to analyze using assume guarantee reasoning.

6   Related Work

Assume-guarantee reasoning [8, 16, 22, 28] is based on the observation that large systems are being build from components and that this composition can be leveraged to improve the performance of analysis techniques. To reason formally about components in isolation, some form of assumption (either implicit or explicit) about the interaction with, or interference from, the environment has to be made. Several frameworks have been proposed to support this style of reasoning. For example, the Calvin tool [11] provides support for assume guarantee reasoning for the analysis of Java programs, while the Mocha toolkit [2] provides support for modular verification of components with requirement specifications based on the Alternating-time Temporal logic. However, the practical impact of these previous approaches has been limited because they require non-trivial human input in defining appropriate assumptions.

As mentioned, in previous work [9, 13], we have developed techniques for performing assume-guarantee reasoning of software in a *fully automated* fashion. Our techniques target components with message-passing communication - a paradigm used in NASA mission critical software (e.g. MER code). The approach presented in [9] uses L* to build incrementally appropriate assumption, and it forms the basis of the work presented in this paper. Since then, several assume guarantee reasoning frameworks that use L* for learning assumptions have been developed – [3] (see also [1]) presents a symbolic approach to assumption leaning, while [5, 6] use learning based assume guarantee verification for communicating finite state automata specifications extracted from C code. The work presented here is a first attempt to introduce *automated* assume guarantee reasoning in SPIN. In the past [27] we have studied the use of assume guarantee reasoning in the context of SPIN – however, in that work, the assumptions were provided manually by the user.

A related effort [17] includes a framework for thread-modular abstraction refinement, in which assumptions and guarantees are both refined in an iterative fashion. The framework applies to programs that communicate through shared variables, and uses predicate abstraction techniques for the iterative construction of assumptions.

The problem of generating an assumption for a component is similar to the problem of generating component interfaces to deal with intermediate state explosion in compositional reachability analysis. Several approaches have been defined for automatically abstracting a component's environment to obtain interfaces [7, 23]. These approaches do not address the incremental refinement of interfaces.

A number of machine learning approaches has been investigated recently in the context of software verification, with a goal different then ours. One approach uses learning for computing the set of reachable states in regular model checking [29]. The work in [15] uses the L* to generate a model of a software system in a black box fashion; the model then be fed to a model checker for analysis. Similarly, [21] presents learning techniques for building software models for verification, while a recent approach [24] uses inductive learning to build precise abstractions for program analysis.

7 Conclusions and Future Work

In this paper we discussed our initial experience with automated assume guarantee verification based on learning in the context of SPIN. We presented a light-weight tool that uses learning to build assumptions incrementally and that makes external calls to SPIN to provide all the model checking related answers. We discussed the application of the tool for the verification of a realistic software system – the resource arbiter for a space craft – which resulted in significant memory gains as compared to traditional monolithic model checking.

While this light-weight implementation allows for a quick evaluation of the merits of learning based assume guarantee reasoning in SPIN, it may result in serious performance overheads and we discussed in the paper ways of improving our implementation. In the future, we plan to work towards a tighter integration in SPIN and to investigate how we can further improve the performance of our approach. One possible way is to run in parallel the checks for multiple queries. We also plan to study how our algorithms extend to alternative communication mechanisms (buffered message passing) and to handling liveness properties – the work on learning infinitary regular sets [26] may be a good start in this direction. Another issue that we want to investigate is to make a finer distinction in our algorithms between the interface actions of a component (i.e. to distinguish channel read and write operations) and to study how this affects our approach.

Acknowledgements

The authors would like to thank Gerard Holzmann for his invaluable support and guidance throughout this project.

References

1. R. Alur, P. Cerny, P. Madhusudan, and W. Nam:. Synthesis of interface specifications for java classes. In *Proc. of 32nd POPL*, pages 98–109, 2005.
2. R. Alur, T. A. Henzinger, F. Y. C. Mang, S. Qadeer, S. K. Rajamani, and S. Tasiran. MOCHA: Modularity in model checking. In *Proc. of the Tenth Int. Conf. on Comp.-Aided Verification (CAV)*, pages 521–525, June 28–July 2, 1998.
3. R. Alur, P. Madhusudan, and W. Nam. Symbolic compositional verification by learning assumptions. In *Proc. of 17th International Conference CAV*, pages 548–562, 2005.
4. H. Barringer, D. Giannakopoulou, and C. S. Păsăreanu. Proof rules for automated compositional verification through learning. In *Int. Workshop on Specification and Verification of Component-Based Sys.*, Sept. 2003.
5. S. Chaki, E. Clarke, D. Giannakopoulou, and C. Pasareanu. Abstraction and assume-guarantee reasoning for automated software verification. Technical report, RIACS, 2004.
6. S. Chaki, E. M. Clarke, N. Sinha, and P. Thati. Automated assume-guarantee reasoning for simulation conformance. In *Proc. of 17th International Conference CAV*, pages 534–547, 2005.
7. S. C. Cheung and J. Kramer. Context constraints for compositional reachability analysis. *ACM Trans. on Soft. Eng. and Methodology*, 5(4):334–377, Oct. 1996.
8. E. M. Clarke, D. E. Long, and K. L. McMillan. Compositional model checking. In *Proc. of the Fourth Symp. on Logic in Comp. Sci.*, pages 353–362, June 1989.
9. J. M. Cobleigh, D. Giannakopoulou, and C. S. Păsăreanu. Learning assumptions for compositional verification. In *9th International Conference for the Construction and Analysis of Systems (TACAS 2003)*, volume 2619 of *LNCS*, Warsaw, Poland, 2003. Springer.
10. J. C. Corbett, M. B. Dwyer, J. Hatcliff, S. Laubach, C. S. Păsăreanu, Robby, and H. Zheng. Bandera: Extracting finite-state models from Java source code. In *Proc. of the 22nd Int. Conf. on Soft. Eng.*, June 2000.
11. C. Flanagan, S. N. Freund, and S. Qadeer. Thread-modular verification for shared-memory programs. In *Proc. of the Eleventh European Symp. on Prog.*, pages 262–277, Apr. 2002.
12. D. Giannakopoulou and C. S. Păsăreanu. Learning-based assume-guarantee verification (tool presentation). In *Proc. of SPIN'05 Workshop*, volume 3639 of *Lecture Notes in Computer Science*. Springer, 2005.

13. D. Giannakopoulou, C. S. Păsăreanu, and H. Barringer. Assumption generation for software component verification. In *Proc. of the Seventeenth IEEE Int. Conf. on Auto. Soft. Eng.*, Sept. 2002.

14. D. Giannakopoulou, C. S. Păsăreanu, and J. M. Cobleigh. Assume-guarantee verification of source code with design-level assumptions. In *Int. Conf. on Soft. Eng.*, pages 211–220, May 2004.

15. A. Groce, D. Peled, and M. Yannakakis. Adaptive model checking. In *Proc. of the Eighth Int. Conf. on Tools and Alg. for the Construction and Analysis of Sys.*, pages 357–370, Apr. 2002.

16. O. Grumberg and D. E. Long. Model checking and modular verification. In *Proc. of the Second Int. Conf. on Concurrency Theory*, pages 250–265, Aug. 1991.

17. T. A. Henzinger, R. Jhala, and R. Majumdar. Race checking by context inference. In *Proc. of PLDI*, pages 1–13, 2004.

18. G. J. Holzmann. The model checker SPIN. *IEEE Trans. on Soft. Eng.*, 23(5):279–295, May 1997.

19. G. J. Holzmann. *The SPIN Model Checker : Primer and Reference Manual.* Addison-Wesley Publ., 2003.

20. G. J. Holzmann and R. Joshi. Model driven software verification. In *Proc. of 11th International SPIN Workshop*, pages 76–91, Oct. 2004.

21. H. Hungar, O. Niese, and B. Steffen. Domain-specific optimization in automata learning. In *Proc. of 15th International Conference CAV*, pages 315–327, 2003.

22. C. B. Jones. Specification and design of (parallel) programs. In R. Mason, editor, *Information Processing 83: Proceedings of the IFIP 9th World Congress*, pages 321–332. IFIP: North Holland, 1983.

23. J.-P. Krimm and L. Mounier. Compositional state space generation from Lotos programs. In *Proc. of the Third Int. Workshop on Tools and Alg. for the Construction and Analysis of Sys.*, pages 239–258, Apr. 1997.

24. A. Loginov, T. W. Reps, and S. Sagiv. Abstraction refinement via inductive learning. In *Proc. of 17th International Conference CAV*, pages 519–533, 2005.

25. J. Magee and J. Kramer. *Concurrency: State Models & Java Programs.* John Wiley & Sons, 1999.

26. O. Maler and A. Pnueli. On the Learnability of Infinitary Regular Sets. *Information and Computation*, 118(2), 1995.

27. C. S. Păsăreanu, M. B. Dwyer, and M. Huth. Assume-guarantee model checking of software: A comparative case study. In D. Dams, R. Gerth, S. Leue, and M. Massink, editors, *Theoretical and Practical Aspects of SPIN Model Checking*, volume 1680 of *Lecture Notes in Comp. Sci.*, pages 168–183. Springer-Verlag, Sept. 1999.

28. A. Pnueli. In transition from global to modular temporal reasoning about programs. In K. Apt, editor, *Logic and Models of Concurrent Systems*, volume 13, pages 123–144, New York, 1984. Springer-Verlag.

29. A. Vardhan, K. Sen, M. Viswanathan, and G. Agha. Using language inference to verify omega-regular properties. In *Proc. of 11th International Conference TACAS*, pages 45–60, 2005.

30. W. Visser, K. Havelund, G. Brat, and S.-J. Park. Model checking programs. In *Proc. of the Fifteenth IEEE Int. Conf. on Auto. Soft. Eng.*, pages 3–12, Sept. 2000.

Exploiting Symmetry and Transactions for Partial Order Reduction of Rule Based Specifications[*]

Ritwik Bhattacharya[1], Steven M. German[2], and Ganesh Gopalakrishnan[1]

[1] School of Computing, University of Utah
{ritwik, ganesh}@cs.utah.edu
[2] IBM T.J. Watson Research Center
german@watson.ibm.com

Abstract. Rule based specifications are popular for specifying protocols, such as cache coherence protocols specified in TLA+, Murphi, or
the BlueSpec language. Specifications in these notations are a collection
of unordered *rules* of the form *guard* → *atomic_updates*. There is no
notion of a sequential process with local scope or specialized communication channels, and each rule tends to update multiple fields of the
global state. It is believed that partial order (PO) reduction, a powerful
state space reduction technique, is difficult to achieve in such a setting.
Partial order reductions attempt to visit a smaller set of states by selec-
tively exploring a subset of all enabled transitions at each state, based
on the *independence* of transitions. In earlier work, we have reported a
suitable algorithm for this purpose, where the independence relation is
computed using symbolic analysis and SAT. In this paper, we expand
on this algorithm and show how to exploit some commonly seen characteristics of rule based specifications. First, many of these systems have
a *transactional* nature, such as the request/grant transactions of cache
coherence protocols. We show how to use this information while picking
subsets of transitions at each state. Second, many of these systems are
parameterized, and also exhibit *symmetry*. We show that, for such systems, the SAT-based computation of the *independence* relation between
rules can be performed once and for all in a manner that is accurate for
all parameterized instances of the protocol. Third, we show that sharpening the SAT-based independence computation through local invariants
can aid PO reduction. Here, we propose a way by which users may *guess*
these invariants: we can check these invariants *and* the property of interest in one combined phase under PO reduction (we prove that there is no
circularity in this process). Our results indicate that with the above measures, rule based systems can have efficient and effective PO reduction
algorithms.

[*] This work was supported in part by NSF Award CCR-0219805, and SRC Contract
2005-TJ-1318.

A. Valmari (Ed.): SPIN 2006, LNCS 3925, pp. 252–270, 2006.

1   Introduction

Rule-style specification of protocols are widely employed. They are often written in languages such as Murphi [6], TLA+ [14], or BlueSpec [1], and are often used for modeling cache coherence, file systems, message networks, and solutions to similar locking/concurrency problems. Protocols specified in these notations are a collection of unordered rules of the form *guard(state)* → *atomic_updates*. The state of systems modeled in such notations can be a global aggregate datatype such as a record of arrays of simpler types or other records. There is no notion of a sequential process with local scope or FIFO channels[1], and each rule tends to update multiple fields of the global state. Such specifications are natural to write for domains such as cache coherency, where designers prefer a declarative approach to modeling using an unordered collection of rules.

Hardware systems and protocols often have a very large degree of concurrency, and it is natural to view this concurrency in terms of collections of rules, where many rules may update the same part of the global state space. A similar effect can be achieved in process based paradigms such as Promela/SPIN [10], for example by implementing each rule as a process. However, where the division of state variables into global and local components is either not apparent, or not possible, the process based approach has no advantages, and presents the same difficulties and challenges to state space reduction as rule based systems.

Also, such unordered collection of rules are often automatically compiled into the underlying cache coherency engine [1]; from this perspective, the unordered and declarative nature of the rules leads to concurrent hardware that can be modularly understood.

SAT Based Independence Computation, Exploiting Local Invariants: Given these differences in specification style, however, it is clear that one of the main weapons to combat state explosion of these protocol models during enumerative model checking—namely *partial order reduction* (PO reduction or POR)—becomes difficult to realize for rule based systems. Partial order reductions [9, 22] are based on avoiding redundant interleavings that are explored by explicit state enumeration model checkers to preserve concurrency semantics. Computing the *independence relation* over transitions is a crucial aspect of partial order techniques. Independence of a pair of transitions formalizes the notion that they don't interfere with each other's enabledness at a state, and result in the same state no matter which order they're executed in. In general, the greater the number of pairwise independent transitions in a system, the greater is the reduction achievable using partial order techniques.

Traditional partial order reduction algorithms rely on a syntactic check of transitions for references to (global) state variables, in order to compute the

---

[1] While FIFO channels are convenient for modeling, and help obtain the benefits of PO reduction, (i) rule based languages we know about do not support channels, and (ii) designers often want something other than any one of the standard varieties of channels such as FIFO, sorted, lossy, etc., such as reordering queues in the case of the Wildfire protocol [15].

independence relation. The rationale is that transitions that refer to disjoint
sets of state variables can safely be marked independent of each other. However,
in the presence of high-level data structures, especially arrays, this approach can
be overly conservative. For example, consider the two guard::action pairs below:

1. $((i >= 0) :: a[i + 1] :=$ True$)$
2. $((i <= 0) :: a[i + 2] :=$ False$)$

A syntax-based PO reduction approach (such as used in SPIN [10]) would classify
rules 1 and 2, which both access the same array variable, as dependent. Our
symbolic simulation based approach would, on the other hand, determine that
the rules are independent, since in all states where both rules are enabled, the
rules access different indices of the array a. In particular, our independence
computation based on SAT will, as most used definitions of independence require
(e.g., [5, Chapter 10]), (i) start the system from a general symbolic state s (all
states are broken into the individual bits), (ii) pick a pair of rules r_1 and r_2,
(iii) determine whether, whenever r_1 and r_2 are enabled in s, firing one rule
leaves the other enabled, and (iv) determine whether $r_1(r_2(s)) = r_2(r_1(s))$ ($r_1(s)$
denotes the state that results from executing the action of rule r_1 at state s).
All this is performed by symbolically simulating the actions of rules, and then
performing SAT checks on the resulting propositional expressions. For example,
the last step is realized by seeing whether $r_1(r_2(s)) \neq r_2(r_1(s))$ can be satisfied.

Obviously, doing this analysis starting from a general starting state can result in pessimal independence information. Later we show how *local invariants*
can help sharpen the analysis to states that contain reachable states but exclude
certain unreachable states. One of our main results is that the kinds of invariants
that tend to give sharp results regarding independence are *not* those that we are
proving at the top level (e.g., cache coherence), but those that (i) provide some
information about which rules might follow which other rules, and (ii) those that
tend to capture relationships between different global variables. More specifically,
we observe from the available list of benchmark protocols written by others that
one often employs more variables than necessary in a protocol for modeling convenience. Our observation is that often it is necessary to pin down relationships
that might exist between these variables. In any case, once a local invariant g_1
is obtained, a rule such as $g \to action$ is strengthened into $g \wedge g_1 \to action$. We
show that such strengthened rules yield a better (larger) independence relation.

Clearly, we do not wish that the solving the problem of POR lead to another
hard problem, namely that of invariant discovery! Here, we have found a simpler,
but often equally effective approach. We show a method by which designers can
(i) guess these invariants (even if they are incorrect, we will be safe, as we show
below), (ii) perform the independence check with respect to modified rules of the
form $g \wedge g_1 \to action$, *but* (iii) while performing model checking using our POR
algorithm (that of course enjoys the benefit of the larger independence relation),
be checking not merely *original_property* but actually *original_property* $\wedge (g \Rightarrow
g_1)$. If there are more guards than one strengthened in this way, for each such
g and its strengthening g_i, we would have the conjunct $g \Rightarrow g_i$ in the top-level
property being verified. This way, if any of the g_i excludes a state that g includes,

it will be detected while verifying the modified property that includes $g \Rightarrow g_i$. A similar approach is presented in [20], but they only consider invariants related to synchronization.

Symmetry and Carry-over of Independence Computation: We observe that many of the protocol descriptions in languages such as Murphi employ scalarsets [12]. Scalarsets are a specialized data type that, by restricting the types of operations permitted on elements of the type, guarantee *symmetry* of systems with respect to permutations over elements of the scalarset type. Furthermore, the variables that are of scalarset type participate in *ruleset* constructs inside protocols. Rulesets of Murphi model parametric sets of rules. For example, if a cache coherence protocol has N nodes, it is quite likely that there is a ruleset collectively modeling each node's behavior. In the Murphi model checker, rulesets defined over scalar set parameters are handled as follows: (i) the user picks a number (*e.g.* 4) for the size parameter of the rule set, (ii) the model-checker creates four copies of the rules, and (iii) while model checking, these four rules are non-deterministically fired in all possible ways (this is necessary, as each rule instance may be, for example, modeling the behavior of a different caching node), (iv) after each state is generated, Murphi's symmetry algorithm performs *state canonicalization* [12], thus generating representative states out of each.

Our approach to exploit the scalarset symmetry is as follows: we demonstrate that under certain conditions, we can, for the purposes of SAT-based independence computation, analyze an instance of size N but model-check an instance $M > N$. This way, the number of rules analyzed as well as the data structures involved in the analysis (e.g., if the data structure sizes were determined by N) would be much smaller. Later, the user may model-check an instance M that is much bigger than N, because currently parameterized proofs are hard to obtain and the designer takes the approach of flushing out bugs in as high an instance as they can. However, in model checking the M-sized instance, the user can employ the same independence relation as calculated on the basis of an N-sized instance.

Ample Set Computation Exploiting Transactions: In *ample set* based POR algorithms (e.g., [5, Chapter 10]), computing the independence relation is only part of the story; ample set formation is a run-time activity where independence comes into play. The search algorithm computes at each state in the search space a set of transitions called an ample set. The ample set is a subset of the enabled transitions, and the search algorithm only generates next states via the transitions in the ample set. Ample sets are minimal (subject to certain sufficient conditions) subsets of the set of enabled transitions at a state, and act as a locally optimal heuristic to maximize global state space reduction. Naturally, smaller ample sets are preferred over larger ones. In our approach, ample sets are computed by picking a *seed* transition and performing a least-fixed-point computation based on the dependence relation. We then check to ensure that the set thus obtained satisfies a set of sufficient conditions **C0 - C3**[5, Chapter 10] (see Appendix A). Picking the seed transition turns out to be an important factor in forming small ample sets, and we have discovered that the *transactional* nature of many of the systems modeled using the rule-based paradigm allows for a particularly effective choice of the *seed transition*. These transactional systems often operate in fairly sequential phases of requests, intermediate processing, and grants. Thus, detecting the phase of the transaction in progress allows us to pick, as seed transitions, transitions that will take the current transaction forward, in effect delaying the "scheduling" of new transactions as long as possible. The sequential nature of transactions means that only a very few (often just one) transitions are enabled at any given point in the transaction, resulting in small ample sets.

Roadmap: Section 2 goes over the notations and definitions. In Section 3, we introduce the notion of exploiting scalarset symmetry, and how it can be used to extrapolate independence results for parameterized systems. We also state and prove our main theorem regarding this result. Section 4 discusses the use of *transactions* to form more effective ample sets, and Section 5 proposes a novel technique called *guard strengthening* to soundly refine rule-based systems to achieve higher independence between transitions. Section 6 discusses experiments and results. Related work and conclusions are in Section 7.

2   Background, Notations and Definitions

A labeled finite state transition system $\mathcal{F}$ is a 5-tuple $\langle S, T, I, P, L \rangle$ where S is a finite set of *states*, T is a finite set of deterministic *transitions*, such that every $t \in T$ is a partial function $t : S \mapsto S$, $I \subseteq S$ is the set of initial states, P is a set of atomic propositions, and $L : S \mapsto 2^P$ labels each state with a set of propositions that are true in the state. Without loss of generality, we assume that T includes a transition from every state to itself. A *labeled path* of a finite state system is an infinite sequence starting with a state and then alternating transitions and states,

$$s_0, t_0, s_1, t_1, s_2, t_2, \ldots,$$

where $\forall i \geq 0 : t_i(s_i) = s_{i+1}$. A labeled path is called a labeled *run* if it starts with a state in I. For any labeled path p of a system, we define the predicate **before**(p, t_1, t_2) to be true when t_1 occurs before the earliest occurrence of t_2 in p, or t_2 does not occur in p. Let the set of all labelled paths of a finite state system be $\mathcal{P}$. The *restriction* of $\mathcal{P}$ with respect to a state s, written $\mathcal{P}_{|s}$, is the set of all labelled paths in $\mathcal{P}$ starting from the state s. A transition t is said to be *enabled* at a state s if $\exists s' \in S : t(s) = s'$. We define the predicate **en**(s, t) that is true exactly when t is enabled at s. We also define the predicate **enabled**$(s) = \{t \in T \mid \textbf{en}(s, t)\}$. Two transitions t_1 and t_2 are *independent* iff the following conditions hold:

- *Enabledness*(En): $\forall s \in S : \textbf{en}(s, t_1) \wedge \textbf{en}(s, t_2) \Rightarrow \textbf{en}(t_1(s), t_2) \wedge \textbf{en}(t_2(s), t_1)$
- *Commutativity*(Co): $\forall s \in S : \textbf{en}(s, t_1) \wedge \textbf{en}(s, t_2) \Rightarrow t_1(t_2(s)) = t_2(t_1(s))$

We define the predicate **ind**(t_1, t_2), that is true exactly when t_1 and t_2 are independent, and **dep**$(t_1, t_2) = \neg\textbf{ind}(t_1, t_2)$. Independence is a symmetric, irreflexive relation. A *property* π of a system is a formula in next-time free *linear* *temporal logic* [17] (LTL$_{-X}$), such that the set of propositions in the logic is P. In this paper, however, we restrict our attention to *invariant* properties, which are properties that must hold at every reachable state of the system. For any property π, we define **props**$(\pi) \in 2^P$ as the set of propositions occurring in π. A transition t is *invisible* with respect to a property π, written as **inv**$_\pi(t)$, iff:

$$\forall s_1, s_2 \in S : t(s_1) = s_2 \Rightarrow L(s_1) \cap \mathbf{props}(\pi) = L(s_2) \cap \mathbf{props}(\pi)$$

Our partial order reduction algorithm has two phases, *static* and *dynamic*. In the first, static phase, we compute the truth values of the **dep** relation for each pair of transitions of the system. For rule based systems (and Murphi in particular, on which our implementation is based), as mentioned earlier, transitions are described as *rules*, each of which is a guard/action pair. To compute the **dep** relation for a pair of rules, we symbolically simulate the effect of each rule's action, to build propositional expressions representing the enabledness and commutativity conditions. Murphi also allows the parametric definition of *rulesets*, as mentioned earlier. When computing the **dep** relation for a pair of rules from rulesets, we employ various techniques to avoid the combinatorial explosion that would occur if we were to actually instantiate every parameterized rule with every possible value. For example, for a pair of rules from different rulesets, we build propositional expressions that leave the symbolic variables representing the parameters totally unconstrained. When checked by a SAT solver, this effectively corresponds to checking every pair of instances of the two rules. Of course, this is conservative, because if the SAT solver finds a satisfying assignment to one of these expressions, it only means that two *particular* rule instances (corresponding to the values assigned to the parameter variables by the satisfying assignment) are dependent. Our algorithm, however, will mark *every* pair of rule instances dependent, in this case. Similar techniques are also applied when computing the **dep** relation for rules from the same ruleset, as well as for a single rule and a rule from a ruleset.

When the static phase terminates, we have obtained a complete **dep** relation, for every pair of rule instances of the system. In the dynamic phase of POR, ample sets are constructed at each state visited, during a *depth first* traversal of the state graph. At each state, we pick an arbitrary enabled transition called *seed*, and form an ample set around it, as follows. We first obtain the *dependency closure* of all transitions that are dependent on *seed*. Now we are left with *enabled independent* transitions, and *disabled dependents* (clearly, another possible category, namely *disabled independent* transitions are completely inconsequential for ample-set formation). We have to ensure (as condition C1 of [5, Chapter 10] requires) that there is no transition in the *unreduced* state graph such that one of these disabled dependent transitions could fire **before** one of the transitions in the current ample set. This could easily happen if one of the *enabled independent* transitions could fire and "wake up" one of the disabled dependent transitions. We have experimented with two schemes, the second of which gives better performance:

Approach 1: If the *disabled dependent* set is empty, **then** the ample set is the dependency closure set (thus it leaves out the enabled independent transitions), **else** all enabled transitions are in ample.

Approach 2: If there are any *disabled dependent* transitions, ensure that they can fire *only* as a result of any one of the transitions in the dependency closure set firing (thus precluding that they may occur **before** one of the ample set transitions). This information can be computed and stored in the static phase of the POR algorithm, thus avoiding a run-time cost.

In Section 4, we discuss how these seed transitions are picked according to the weighing scheme described earlier. We do have implementations of the other checks, namely C0, C2, and C3, as [5] requires. In particular, for the C3 condition which avoids *ignoring*, we have an implementation that implements an on-the-fly *in-stack* check. Details of these checks are omitted, but can be found in [3].

3   Computing Independence for Parametric Systems

A Murphi system description is considered to be *parameterized* if the state variables and transitions are indexed over one or more parameters. In this paper, we only consider parameterized systems with one parameter. In the absence of a general method for verification of parameterized systems, it is common to verify a system for multiple instances of the parameter. However, realistic system sizes increase greatly with an increase in parameter size, and so does the complexity

```
CONST
  num_clients : 3;
TYPE
  message : enum{empty, req_shared, req_exclusive,
                invalidate, invalidate_ack,
                grant_shared, grant_exclusive};
  cache_state : enum{invalid, shared, exclusive};
  client: scalarset(num_clients);
VAR
  channel1: array[client] of message;
  cache: array[client] of cache_state;
RULESET cl: client do
  RULE "client requests shared access"
    cache[cl] = invalid & channel1[cl] = empty ==>
    BEGIN channel1[cl] := req_shared END;
  RULE "client requests exclusive access"
    (cache[cl] = invalid | cache[cl] = shared )
    & channel1[cl] = empty ==>
    BEGIN channel1[cl] := req_exclusive END;
END;
```

Fig. 1. A simple parameterized Murphi system outline

of computing the independence relation. We show that for such parameterized systems, it is sufficient to compute the independence relation for a small parameter size. Model checking can be performed for higher parameter sizes using this independence relation.

As a simple example, consider the Murphi system outline of Figure 1. This is an extract from the parameterized German protocol, and shows the two transitions responsible for making new requests for access to a cache line, in either the shared or exclusive mode. The parameter of this system is the number of clients, represented by num_clients. The first thing to note is that there are actually multiple instances of each transition (rule) in the system, for any value of num_clients. In this case, there are 3 instances of each rule, corresponding to the range of the variable cl. Theoretically, therefore, we need to check 9 pairs of rules for dependence (each of the 3 instances of the first rule against each of the 3 instances of the second rule). However, as we show in [3], it suffices to check a pair where the indices have the same value, and a pair where they have different values, and conservatively extrapolate the results to all pairs. So in the given system, we might choose to check rule $1[\mathtt{cl} \leftarrow cl_1]$ (the instance of the first rule with cl set to cl_1) against rule $2[\mathtt{cl} \leftarrow cl_1]$ (a pair with the same index value), and rule $1[\mathtt{cl} \leftarrow cl_1]$ against rule $2[\mathtt{cl} \leftarrow cl_2]$ (a pair with different index values). Here, cl_1 and cl_2 are symbolic values that are left unconstrained in the propositional expressions that are passed to the SAT solver. In the first case, if the SAT solver is unable to find a satisfying assignment, this implies that none of the rule instances with the same parameter value are dependent, since we left the parameter value unconstrained. In the second case, our algorithm conjoins to the propositional expressions representing enabledness and commutativity, a clause that constrains cl_1 and cl_2 to be different from each other. Thus, if the SAT solver is unable to find a satisfying assignment, it is evident that none of the rule instances with different parameter values are dependent on each other.

What does the truth of the above checks for one value of num_clients tell us about the truth of the corresponding checks for a different value of num_clients? Consider first the case of the two rules with the same value for the ruleset parameter cl. Obviously, these two rules are dependent, for they pass neither the enabledness check nor the commutativity check. This is because they are essentially requests from the same node, and therefore each request disables the other. In this case, it would not make any difference what the range of the index variable cl was, since the rules do not count the range in any manner, and only refer to state variables that are directly indexed over cl, which we have already instantiated to a particular value. Therefore, for these particular rules, it is sufficient to check independence for a particular instance, to be able to conclude that for every instance of the parameterized system, instantiations of these rules with the same index value will never be independent. Now consider the case of the two rules with different values for the parameter cl. In this case, the rules involve entirely disjoint sets of state variables, and hence the rules are independent. However, this is true as long as the values of cl are different for the two rules, irrespective of what *particular* values they are. Therefore, here too, it is sufficient to check independence for one instance, and infer independence for all instances.

In the following sections, we develop a framework for describing independence among rules of parameterized systems, and show that under certain assumptions, independence of rules is indeed unaffected by parameter size. Section 3.1 introduces the notation and definitions used, and in Section 3.2 we state and prove the main theorem that relates independence of rules across different instances of a parameterized system.

3.1 Notations and Definitions

Recall that a *scalarset* variable in Murphi is a variable such that the system description is completely symmetric with respect to permutations of the elements of the domain of the scalarset variable. A parameterized Murphi specification, with a single scalarset parameter N, can be described in terms of a first order language over the set of variables of the specification. Following Pnueli *et al*'s notion of *bounded data systems* [18], we partition the set of variables into three broad classes, as follows:

- $\mathcal{V}_1 = \{x_1, x_2, \ldots x_a\}$ where x_i is interpreted over $\mathbb{B}$, the boolean domain, and $a \in \mathbb{N}$, the set of natural numbers.
- $\mathcal{V}_2 = \{y_1, y_2, \ldots y_b\}$ where each y_i is a *scalarset* variable interpreted over the integer subrange $[1 \ldots N]$, and $b \in \mathbb{N}$.
- $\mathcal{V}_3 = \{ar_1, ar_2, \ldots ar_c\}$ where each ar_i is an array with index type $[1 \ldots N]$, each array's cell type is interpreted over $\mathbb{B}$, and $c \in \mathbb{N}$.

The terms of the language are the boolean constants **True** and **False**, variables of type $\mathcal{V}_1$ or $\mathcal{V}_2$, and array references of the form $ar_i[y_j]$, where $y_j \in \mathcal{V}_2$ and $ar_i \in \mathcal{V}_3$. The valid atomic formulas of our language are partitioned into the set of *ordinary* atomic formulas $\mathcal{O}$ and *quantified* atomic formulas $\mathcal{Q}$, where: $\mathcal{O} = \{x_i \mid x_i \in \mathcal{V}_1\} \cup \{ar_i[y_j] \mid ar_i \in \mathcal{V}_3, y_j \in \mathcal{V}_2\} \cup \{y_i = y_j \mid y_i, y_j \in \mathcal{V}_2\}$, and $\mathcal{Q} = \{\forall x \in 1 \ldots N.ar_i[x] \mid ar_i \in \mathcal{V}_3\} \cup \{\forall x \in 1 \ldots N.\neg ar_i[x] \mid ar_i \in \mathcal{V}_3\} \cup \{\exists x \in 1 \ldots N.ar_i[x] \mid ar_i \in \mathcal{V}_3\} \cup \{\exists x \in 1 \ldots N.\neg ar_i[x] \mid ar_i \in \mathcal{V}_3\}$. The set of formulas is then the standard extension of the atomic formulas using the boolean connectives $\wedge$, $\vee$ and $\neg$. We say that the set of all formulas over a set of variables $\mathcal{V}$, $\mathcal{L}(\mathcal{V})$ is the *language* of our logic.

A Murphi system description, which consists of a set of variable declarations, and a set of transitions (rules) defined as *guard/action* pairs, can be mapped into our first order language by mapping the variable definitions to the variables of the language, mapping guards to formulas of the language, and mapping actions as sets of substitutions of variables by terms or formulas of the language. Since the variables in $\mathcal{V}_1$ and $\mathcal{V}_3$ are of boolean type, they can be assigned any valid formula of the language, because Murphi allows arbitrary boolean expressions as rvalues in assignments. For a complete description of the allowed substitutions, and the corresponding Murphi constructs, see [2]. A state of a Murphi system can thus be seen as an interpretation of the variables of the logic. We denote the set of all states of a system as S, and, in particular, the set of all states of a *parameterized* system with parameter N as $S(N)$.

In bounded data systems, both states (interpretations) and the satisfaction of formulas, are *symmetric* with respect to any permutation of the indices [18]. This is enforced in Murphi syntax by declaring the parameter range to be a *scalarset* type.

3.2 The Carry over Theorem

We now show that in the above setting, we can compute the dependence relation between transitions for all parameter sizes $N > 1$, by computing the relation for a small size, calculated as described below.

Enabledness: Given a pair of rules $\langle g_1, a_1 \rangle$ and $\langle g_2, a_2 \rangle$, they satisfy the enabledness condition when:

$$g_1(s) \wedge g_2(s) \Rightarrow g_1(a_2(s)) \wedge g_2(a_1(s)) \tag{3.1}$$

is valid over $S(N)$, the set of all states (interpretations) s, $g_1(s)$ denotes the evaluation of the formula g_1, given the interpretation s of the variables, $a_1(s)$ (with a slight abuse of notation) denotes the application of the substitutions represented by a_1 to the variables, followed by an evaluation of the resulting terms over the interpretation s. Similarly for g_2 and a_2.

We would like to find a bound, $\widehat{N}$, such that 3.1 is valid over $S(N)$ for all N, $N > 1$ iff it is valid over $S(N)$ for all N, $1 < N \leq \widehat{N}$. To arrive at such a bound, we proceed as follows: in formula 3.1, we push negations inside atomic formulas of type $\mathcal{Q}$ (ie, a formula $\neg \forall i.ar_j[i]$ is converted into the equivalent formula $\exists i.\neg ar_j[i]$, and so on for every atomic formula of type $\mathcal{Q}$). Let the cardinality of the set $\mathcal{V}_2$ be k, the number of *existentially quantified* atomic formulas of type $\mathcal{Q}$ in a guard g_i be e_i, and the number of *universally quantified* atomic formulas of type $\mathcal{Q}$ in g_i be u_i.

Theorem 1. *3.1 is valid over $S(N)$ for all N, $N > 1$ iff it is valid over $S(N)$ for all N, $1 < N \leq \widehat{N}$, where $\widehat{N} = k + 2 \times (\max\{e_1, e_2\} + \max\{u_1, u_2\})$.*

Proof (sketch)[2]: To show this, it is sufficient to show that the negation of 3.1:

$$g_1(s) \wedge g_2(s) \wedge (\neg g_1(a_2(s)) \vee \neg g_2(a_1(s))) \tag{3.2}$$

is satisfiable for $N > \widehat{N}$ iff it is satisfiable for some N, $1 < N \leq \widehat{N}$. To show this, moreover, it is sufficient to show that if 3.2 is satisfiable over $S(N)$, for $N > \widehat{N}$, it is satisfiable over $S(\widehat{N})$.

By counting the number of existentially quantified atomic formulas of the forms $\exists x.ar_i[x]$ or $\exists x.\neg ar_i[x]$ in 3.2, which can be equivalently written as $ar_i[p]$ and $\neg ar_i[q]$ respectively, where p and q are fresh variables of type $\mathcal{V}_2$, we can show that the total number of variables of type $\mathcal{V}_2$ is bounded by $\widehat{N}$. Thus, given an interpretation s over $S(N)$ that satisfies 3.2, it can assign at most $\alpha \leq \widehat{N}$ different values to these variables. Without loss of generality, assume

---

[2] The proof is very similar to, and follows closely, the proof of **Claim 3** in [18, Section 4].

that these values are $v_1 < v_2 < \cdots < v_\alpha$. Since the system is symmetric, there is a permutation over the indices $[1..N]$ that maps v_k to k, for every $k \in 1..\alpha$. Let $\tilde{s}$ be the state derived from s by applying this permutation-induced transformation to the set of variables above. Clearly, $\tilde{s}$ is also an interpretation that satisfies 3.2. To construct the interpretation $\hat{s} \in \hat{N}$ that satisfies 3.2, we let $\tilde{s}$ and $\hat{s}$ agree on the interpretation of the variables in V_1 and V_2. For the remaining variables $ar_1, ar_2, \ldots ar_c$, we let $\tilde{s}$ and $\hat{s}$ agree on the values of all $ar_i[k]$, for $k \leq \alpha$. After replacing existentials by new variables, the formula 3.2 is a formula over the variables in V_1 and V_2, and universally (over the parameter size) quantified expressions over V_3. Since $\tilde{s}$ and $\hat{s}$ agree on the interpretation of all of the above, $\hat{s}$ satisfies 3.2 over $S(\hat{N})$. By similar reasoning, we can also compute bounds on the commutativity condition. Taken together, these provide an overall bound on the size of the system for which independence checks need to be performed for partial order reduction.

4 Transaction-Based Priorities for Ample Set Construction

For many of the kinds of systems that are typically described using the rule-based paradigm (e.g., protocols of various types), it is often the case that the system proceeds along fairly sequential paths called *transactions*. For example, consider a typical directory-based cache coherence protocol. Most activities in such protocols begin with the cache controller making a request for a line. This request travels to the directory controller which typically evicts other caches from the sharing group by sending invalidations. Thereafter, the directory controller sends the line back to the requesting node. Modeled in Murphi, we can say that (i) this whole activity consists of a *transaction* (refer to [16] for somewhat related notions of a transaction), and (ii) there are Murphi rules that begin a transaction, there are rules that are somewhere in the "middle" of transactions (e.g., invalidation rules), and finally there are rules that end transactions. One can often obtain the situation of a rule—whether it is at the beginning, middle, or end of a transaction—through concrete execution on small instances of the protocol. Most designers also clearly know the situation of rules within a transaction. Clearly, a transaction can involve actions of multiple components (the requesting node and the directory controller in the example above). This is a slightly different notion than the notion of a transaction as a sequence of actions within a single thread (or component), as presented in [19], for example. In any case, we *weigh* each rule as follows: (i) rules that begin transactions are weighed "low," (ii) the rules that end transactions are weighed "high," (iii) rules that are in the middle of transactions are weighed "medium." We need not be exact in how we assign numeric values to "low, medium, and high." Users can be completely wrong in these weight assignments—the only consequence being poorer ample sets but never incorrect execution.

Given a set of weights for the transitions, we use them to pick the *seed* transition during ample set computations. Enabled transitions that have the highest priority are picked as seed transitions at each state. Effectively, this results in "scheduling" ongoing transactions with greater priority, and postponing the start of new transactions as long as possible. Note that this is completely sound, because we will only be able to postpone the start of a new transaction as long as the transition that starts it is independent of transitions that belong to the ongoing transaction. The results of applying this heuristic while computing ample sets are discussed in Section 6.

5   Strengthening Guards

It is often the case that a pair of rules is independent at all reachable states, but dependent at some unreachable state(s). Our analysis, as described so far, marks such rules dependent, since it starts from an entirely general symbolic state. To be able to use the independence of these rules during partial order reduction, a simple idea is to find potential *strengthenings* for guards, that don't change the enabledness of rules in reachable states, and extend the independence of rules to *all* states, both reachable and unreachable. This is useful while checking the **C1** condition, since the fewer the dependent transitions, the smaller the likelihood of there being disabled transitions dependent on the ample set.

To actually discover these strengthenings requires a deep understanding of the protocol involved, and we discuss some intuitions in Section 6.

Once we have strengthened the guards of transitions, it is necessary to show that these strengthenings are sound, and do indeed preserve the semantics of the original transitions. We now show that it is sufficient to model check the strengthened system with a modified property, to be able to prove the soundness of the strengthenings.

Since Murphi transitions are guard action pairs (g_i, a_i), strengthening the guards corresponds to adding predicates p_i to the guards of transitions t_i. Define the *strengthening operator* Θ over transitions such that:

$$\Theta(\langle g_i, a_i \rangle) = \begin{cases} \langle g_i \wedge p_i, a_i \rangle & \text{if } t_i \text{ is strengthened} \\ \langle g_i, a_i \rangle & \text{otherwise} \end{cases}$$

We extend Θ to apply to runs $\sigma = \langle s_1, t_1, s_2, \ldots, s_k, \ldots \rangle$ so that $\Theta(\sigma)$ results in the sequence (not necessarily a run) $\langle s_1, \Theta(t_1), s_2, \ldots, s_k, \ldots \rangle$. Let the original system be $\mathcal{F}$, and the modified system $\mathcal{F}'$. Note that both systems have the same set of states, and the same initial state predicate I. Assume that the property to be verified of the original system was P. We model check the new system with the property $P \wedge Str$, where:

$$Str = (g_{i_1} \rightarrow p_{i_1}) \wedge (g_{i_2} \rightarrow p_{i_2}) \wedge \ldots \wedge (g_{i_k} \rightarrow p_{i_k})$$

$g_{i_1} \ldots g_{i_k}$ are the k guards of the original system that have been strengthened with the predicates $p_{i_1} \ldots p_{i_k}$.

Definition. A run $\sigma = \langle s_1, s_2, \ldots, \rangle$ of a system satisfies an invariant property P, written as $\sigma \models P$, iff the property is true at every state in the run.

Definition. A system $\mathcal{M}$ satisfies an invariant property P, written as $\mathcal{M} \models P$, iff every run of the system satisfies the property.

Theorem 2.
$$\mathcal{F}' \models P \wedge Str \Rightarrow \mathcal{F} \models P$$

Proof. By contradiction. Assume that the antecedent of the theorem is true, and assume that there is a run $r = \langle s_1, t_1, s_2, t_2, \ldots, s_m, \ldots \rangle$ of $\mathcal{F}$ that does not satisfy the property P. Without loss of generality, we assume that $s_1, s_2, \ldots s_{m-1} \models P$, and $s_m \not\models P$. If $\Theta(r)$ is a run of $\mathcal{F}'$, $s_m \models P \wedge Str$, which implies that $s_m \models P$, contradicting our assumption. Therefore, assume that $\Theta(r)$ is not a run of $\mathcal{F}'$. Then, there is a t_k, such that $\Theta(t_k)$ is not enabled at s_k, and $\Theta(\langle s_1, t_1, s_2, \ldots s_k \rangle)$ is a valid prefix of a run of $\mathcal{F}'$, such that $s_1, s_2, \ldots s_k \models P \wedge Str$. Since r is a run of $\mathcal{F}$, t_k is enabled at s_k.

$\quad$ *Case 1:* $\Theta(t_k) = \langle g_k, a_k \rangle$. In this case, since $\Theta(t_k)$ is not enabled at s_k, this implies that $s_k \not\models g_k$. But we know that t_k is enabled at s_k. That is, $s_k \models g_k$, leading to a contradiction.

$\quad$ *Case 2:* $\Theta(t_k) = \langle g_k \wedge p_k, a_k \rangle$. In this case, we have $s_k \not\models g_k \wedge p_k$. However, we know that $s_k \models g_k$. Also, $s_k \models P \wedge Str$. That is, $s_k \models g_k \rightarrow p_k$. Therefore, $s_k \models g_k \wedge p_k$, leading to a contradiction.

$\quad$ Thus, in every case, we arrive at a contradiction, and hence, the theorem is true, and, by model checking the strengthened system for the property $P \wedge Str$, we can prove that the strengthenings of the guards are sound.

$\quad$ If the model check fails, on the other hand, we have to manually examine the error trail to determine whether the property failed, or whether one of the strengthenings does not hold, and rerun the model check after making the necessary changes, in the latter case.

6   Experimental Results, and Analysis

We have run **POeM** on a number of examples of different sizes, and Table 1 shows our overall results on some mutual exclusion algorithms and a cache coherence protocol. *The experiments in Table 1 were performed with Murphi's symmetry reduction turned on, whenever scalar sets were employed.* This is safe because symmetry and partial order reductions are orthogonal to each other, and can be combined for safety property verification[7]. Guard strengthening and transaction-based weights were not employed in these examples, and are discussed later. In the table, the columns under "Unreduced" represent the number of states explored, and the time taken for the verification to complete, without any partial order reduction. The columns under "Static PO" represent the same figures for the case where a static, syntax-based analysis was used to determine the independence relation (this was our initial prototype version of POeM before we moved on to the use of SAT for independence computation). The columns under "Symbolic PO" represent the figures for **POeM**. The final column, "Analysis Time", is the time taken by **POeM**'s symbolic evaluation based module to compute the independence relation. In cases where we've used the

Table 1. Performance of partial order reduction algorithm

Example	Unreduced		Static PO		Symbolic PO		Analysis
	States	Time	States	Time	States	Time	Time
Bakery	157	0.1	157	0.1	119	0.1	8.9
Burns	82010	1.83	82010	3.65	69815	11.67	52.9
Dekker	100	0.13	100	0.13	90	0.13	11.6
Dijkstra6	11664	0.57	11664	0.88	4900	1.17	17.9
Dijkstra8	139968	4.32	139968	8.81	33286	8.98	CO
Dijkstra10	>1.5M	>1000.0	>1.5M	>1000.0	202248	82.6	CO
DP6	1152	0.32	1152	0.36	90	0.31	0
DP10	125952	7.44	125952	7.86	823	0.48	0
DP14	>1.0M	>800.0	>1.0M	>800.0	7395	2.6	0
Peterson2	26	0.15	26	0.15	24	0.15	4.6
Peterson4	22281	0.3	22281	0.53	14721	0.58	CO
German6	7378	1.31	7378	1.36	2542	0.83	32.4
German8	42717	14.6	42717	15.23	10827	4.6	CO
German10	193790	127.24	193790	131.83	36606	24.91	CO
Leader1	683	0.32	683	0.36	21	0.10	8.5
Leader2	12651	0.20	12651	0.33	12651	0.33	4.6

carry over theorem of Section 3, the entry for higher instances is marked CO, and represents the fact that the results were carried over from the analysis of the smallest instance in the table. The experiments were run on a dual processor Xeon 3GHz machine with 1GB of RAM. As can be seen, **POeM** is most effective on large examples, where the overhead of performing the symbolic analysis, and computing an ample set at each state, is outweighed by the savings that result from a far fewer number of states being explored.

Assessing Guard Strengthenings: We experimented with guard strengthenings on the German protocol, as well as the Stanford FLASH [13] cache coherence protocol, and these results are now discussed. The German cache coherence protocol is a directory-based protocol for maintaining coherence among shared memory multiprocessors, proposed by Steven German [8] The Murphi description of the protocol only models a single address/cache line, and a parameterized number of processors.

Our technique for generating predicates to strengthen guards is to first run **POeM** directly on the protocol, and analyze the resulting dependency matrix. For pairs of rules that **POeM** marks dependent, we examine the test(s) that failed (enabledness, dependency, or both), and try to reason about predicates that, if added, would make the rules independent, without violating the properties we wish the protocol to hold. If we are able to come up with such predicates, we add them to the guard, and add the corresponding implication predicate to the invariant to be proved.

Run directly on the German protocol, **POeM** concludes that the rule "home sends invalidate message" is dependent on the rule "home sends reply to client-exclusive".

The guards for the two rules are:

```
rule "home sends invalidate message"
    (home_current_command = req_shared & home_exclusive_granted
    | home_current_command = req_exclusive)
    & home_invalidate_list[cl]
    & channel2_4[cl] = empty

rule "home sends reply to client -- exclusive"
    home_current_command = req_exclusive
    & client_requests[home_current_client]
    & forall i: client do home_sharer_list[i] = false endforall
    & channel2_4[home_current_client] = empty
```

It is evident that the two rules ought never to be enabled together, and therefore, marked independent. However, it is not apparent what predicate is to be added to enforce this. It is clear from the existing guards that, if the rules are to be simultaneously enabled, **home_current_command = req_exclusive** must be true. Looking at the rule "home picks new request", which sets this variable, leads to the realization that, in the case of a request for exclusive access, the home node copies the **home_sharer_list** to the **home_invalidate_list**. The protocol then clears an entry in the invalidate list once it sends out the invalidate message to that client, and clears the entry in the sharer list once the client has sent the acknowledgment to the invalidate. This means that, at the time the home node sends out an invalidate message to a client, that client must be on the sharer *and* invalidate lists. Therefore, we can add the predicate **home_sharer_list[cl]** to the guard for the rule "home sends invalidate message":

```
rule "home sends invalidate message"
    (home_current_command = req_shared & home_exclusive_granted
    | home_current_command = req_exclusive)
    & home_invalidate_list[cl]
    & channel2_4[cl] = empty
    & home_sharer_list[cl]
```

Similar reasoning is used to strengthen the guards of other pairs of rules that we determine to have been falsely marked dependent by **POeM**.

As is evident, the ability to effectively strengthen the guards of a given protocol depends on a good understanding of the workings of the protocol, which we possess for the German protocol. From a practical perspective, however, industrial design groups possess a deep understanding of their protocols, and we have reasons to believe that designers will, when presented with *false* entries in the independence matrix, be able to identify guard strengthenings as discussed above. Our results on the FLASH coherence protocol further demonstrate the effectiveness of this approach, yielding over 60% reduction for 4 nodes, although, with over 30 rules, and many auxiliary variables, it is a much more complex protocol and guard strengthenings were only performed for the most obvious cases.

Table 2. Advantages of Guard Strengthening

Example	Without Strengthening				With Strengthening			
	Unreduced		POeM		Unreduced		POeM	
	States	Time	States	Time	States	Time	States	Time
German6	13270	2.68	4485	1.29	7378	1.42	2542	0.74
German8	81413	30.28	20104	8.87	42717	14.5	10827	4.56
German10	378236	260.96	69613	49.04	193790	126.6	36606	24.72
FLASH	6336	0.78	6336	1.46	2888	0.46	2146	0.64

Table 2 shows the results of running the protocols with and without strengthened guards.

Assessing Transaction-Based Priorities: The next set of experiments run on the German protocol were aimed at testing the significance of user-defined priorities for rules, over the automatically computed priorities, which are based on the number of variable references. Table 3 shows the comparison between the two methods of assigning priorities to rules. Lower weights translate into a higher priority for the rule to be picked as the seed transition.

The user defined priorities were assigned in such a fashion as to give higher priority to rules that complete transactions, the transactions in this case being the requests for exclusive or shared access to a line. Rules that represent the intermediate steps of a transaction were given medium priority, and rules that represent the start of a transaction were given the lowest priority.

In the case of the German protocol, user-defined priorities gave a distinct performance boost to **POeM**, resulting in upto an 80% reduction over the already reduced state space explored by **POeM** using the regular variable reference count based priorities. This confirms our intuitions that user-defined priorities are a good way to select the seed transition around which to form ample sets.

Recently [4], we have built an experimental variant of Murphi that records the sequence of rules fired with respect to user-identified *request* rules and *completion* rules. From this experimental version of Murphi, we observe that rule weights can be computed with reasonable accuracy based on concrete executions of small instances of the protocol.

Table 3. Transaction-based priorities vs. Variable reference based priorities (G=German)

Ex	Without Strengthening				With Strengthening			
	Trans. based wts		Var based wts		Trans. based wts		Var based wts	
	States	Time	States	Time	States	Time	States	Time
G6	2521	0.66	4485	1.29	1166	0.36	2542	0.74
G8	8098	2.75	20104	8.87	2851	0.94	10827	4.56
G10	20968	10.52	69613	49.04	5890	2.57	36606	24.72

6.1   Protocols That Yield Low Reductions with POeM

Our partial order reduction algorithm yields large reductions on many complex protocols, but also fails to yield significant reductions on some others. An example in Table 1 is the leader election protocol from [5](Leader2). This example is of a network of nodes in a ring topology running an algorithm to determine the node with the largest id. The algorithm involves exchanging messages through buffers, and POeM's independence computation, relying on the *primary* and *alternate* checks, concludes that all the message-passing transitions of each node are dependent on those of *all* of the other nodes, although each node's transitions only depend on its *neighbor*'s transitions (since neighboring nodes read and write a common message buffer). This indicates that rule-based systems might benefit from making buffers/queues first-class data structures in their language, allowing partial order reduction algorithms to take advantage of the orchestrated fashion in which these buffers operate. This example also lacks scalarset symmetry, and it might be possible to improve our algorithm by examining other kinds of specialized symmetries, such as the ring symmetry of this example. On the other hand, POeM is very successful on the other leader election example studied (Leader1), since that example employs a single-cell buffer, and thus forces the nodes to proceed in lock-step fashion. This also makes the case that the specification style can often influence the amount of reduction achievable.

7   Conclusions and Future Directions

In this paper, we have described in detail a number of heuristics and techniques to further improve the efficiency of partial order reduction algorithms for rule-based systems, and demonstrated the advantages of our heuristics over conventional, static analysis based partial order reduction algorithms for these types of systems.

An interesting experiment to perform might be to replace our SAT-based backend with a more powerful solver such as CVC [21], which combines decision procedures for fragments of arithmetic, theories for uninterpreted functions, etc. It might also be possible to automatically generate candidate predicates to strengthen guards, based on the satisfying assignment returned by the SAT solver/decision procedure, in case two rules are found to be dependent.

References

1. Arvind. Bluespec: A language for hardware design, simulation, synthesis and verification, Invited Talk. In *MEMOCODE*, pages 249–249, 2003.
2. Ritwik Bhattacharya. http://www.cs.utah.edu/~ritwik/carryover.html.
3. Ritwik Bhattacharya, Steven German, and Ganesh Gopalakrishnan. A symbolic partial order reduction algorithm for rule based transition systems. Technical Report UUCS-03-028, School of Computing, University of Utah, 2003.
4. Xiaofang Chen. personal communication.

5. Edmund M. Clarke, Orna Grumberg, and Doron Peled. *Model Checking*. MIT Press, December 1999.
6. David Dill. The Stanford Murphi Verifier. In *CAV '96*, pages 390–393, 1996.
7. E. Allen Emerson, Somesh Jha, and Doron Peled. Combining partial order and symmetry reductions. In *TACAS '97*, pages 19–34, 1997.
8. Steven German. http://www.cs.utah.edu/~ritwik/poem/german_cache.m.
9. Patrice Godefroid. Using partial orders to improve automatic verification methods. In *CAV '90*, pages 176–185, 1990.
10. G. J. Holzmann. The model checker SPIN. *IEEE Transactions on Software Engineering*, 23(5):279–295, May 1997. Special issue on Formal Methods in Software Practice.
11. G.J. Holzmann, P. Godefroid, and D. Pirottin. Coverage preserving reduction strategies for reachability analysis. In *Proc. 12th Int. Conf on Protocol Specification, Testing, and Verification, INWG/IFIP*, 1992.
12. C. Norris Ip and David L. Dill. Better verification through symmetry. In *CHDL '93*, pages 87–100, 1993.
13. J. Kuskin and D. Ofelt et al. The Stanford FLASH multiprocessor. In *SIGARCH94*, pages 302–313, May 1994.
14. L. Lamport. Specifying concurrent systems with TLA+. In *Calculational System Design*, 1999.
15. Leslie Lamport. The wildfire challenge problem. http://research.microsoft.com/users/lamport/tla/wildfire-challenge.html.
16. Vladimir Levin, Robert Palmer, Shaz Qadeer, and Sriram K. Rajamani. Sound transaction-based reduction without cycle detection. In *SPIN '05*, pages 106–122, 2005.
17. Amir Pnueli. A temporal logic of concurrent programs. In *Theoretical Computer Science*, pages 45–60, 1977.
18. Amir Pnueli, Sitvanit Ruah, and Lenore D. Zuck. Automatic deductive verification with invisible invariants. In *TACAS '01*, pages 82–97, 2001.
19. S. Qadeer, S. Rajamani, and J. Rehof. Summarizing procedures in concurrent programs. In *Proceedings of the ACM Symposium on the Principles of Programming Languages*, 2004.
20. Scott D. Stoller and Ernie Cohen. Optimistic synchronization-based state-space reduction. In *TACAS '03*, pages 489–504, 2003.
21. Aaron Stump, Clark W. Barrett, and David L. Dill. CVC: A Cooperating Validity Checker. In *CAV '02*, pages 500–504, 2002.
22. Antti Valmari. A stubborn attack on state explosion. In *CAV '90*, pages 156–165, 1990.

APPENDIX

A   Sufficient Conditions for Ample Set Construction

Adapted from [5, Chapter 10], the sufficient conditions **C0-C3** for constructing valid ample sets are:

- **C0** : $\forall s \in S : \mathbf{ample}(s) = \phi \Leftrightarrow \mathbf{enabled}(s) = \phi$. An ample set is empty if and only if there are no enabled transitions.

- **C1:** $\forall s \in S : \forall t_1, t_2 \in T : t_1 \in \mathbf{ample}(s) \wedge t_2 \notin \mathbf{ample}(s) \wedge \mathbf{dep}(t_1, t_2) \Rightarrow \forall p \in \mathcal{P}_{|s} : \exists t_3 \in \mathbf{ample}(s) : \mathbf{before}(p, t_3, t_2)$ Along every path in the full state graph that starts at state s, the following must hold - if there is an enabled transition that depends on a transition in the ample set, it is not taken before some transition from the ample set is taken.
- **C2** $: \forall s \in S : \mathbf{ample}(s) \neq \mathbf{enabled}(s) \Rightarrow \forall t \in \mathbf{ample}(s) : \mathbf{inv}_\pi(t)$. If a state is not fully expanded, then every transition in the ample set is invisible.
- **C3**[3] $: \forall s \in S : \mathbf{ample}(s) \neq \mathbf{enabled}(s) \Rightarrow \exists t \in \mathbf{ample}(s) : t(s) \notin \mathbf{onstack}(s)$ There is no transition t that is enabled in a state that is part of a cycle, and is not in the ample set of any state in that cycle.

---

[3] For a proof of the sufficiency of this form of the condition see [11].

Partial-Order Reduction for General State Exploring Algorithms

Dragan Bošnački[1], Stefan Leue[2], and Alberto Lluch Lafuente[3]

[1] Eindhoven University of Technology,
Den Dolech 2, P.O. Box 513,
5612 MB Eindhoven, The Netherlands
[2] Department of Computer and Information Science,
University of Konstanz,
D-78457 Konstanz, Germany
[3] Via del Giardino A 58,
I 50053 Empoli (FI), Italy

Abstract. An important component of partial-order based reduction algorithms is the condition that prevents action ignoring, commonly known as the cycle proviso. In this paper we give a new version of this proviso that is applicable to a general search algorithm skeleton also known as the General State Expanding Algorithm (GSEA). GSEA maintains a set of open (visited but not expanded) states from which states are iteratively selected for exploration and moved to a closed set of states (visited and expanded). Depending on the open set data structure used, GSEA can be instantiated as depth-first, breadth-first, or a directed search algorithm. The proviso is characterized by reference to the open and closed set of states in GSEA. As a result the proviso can be computed in an efficient manner during the search based on local information. We implemented partial-order reduction for GSEA based on our proposed proviso in the tool HSF-SPIN, which is an extension of the model checker SPIN for directed model checking. We evaluate the state space reduction achieved by partial-order reduction according to the proviso that we propose by comparing it on a set of benchmark problems to other reduction approaches. We also compare the use of breadth-first search and A*, two algorithms ensuring that counterexamples of minimal length will be found, together with the proviso that we propose.

1 Introduction

Partial-Order Reduction (POR) [4, 8, 22, 23, 25, 26] is one of the main techniques used to tackle the state explosion problem in model checking. An important component of partial-order based reduction algorithms is the condition that prevents action ignoring, commonly known as the cycle proviso. In this paper we give a new version of this proviso that is applicable to a general state search algorithm skeleton also known as the General State Exploring Algorithm (GSEA) which maintains a set of open (visited but not expanded) states from which states

A. Valmari (Ed.): SPIN 2006, LNCS 3925, pp. 271–287, 2006.

are iteratively selected for exploration and moved to a closed set of states (visited and expanded).

Unlike the full state space exploration, POR expands only a subset of the enabled actions in a given state, called the ample set. The actions outside the ample set are temporarily ignored. However, if one is not careful, an action could be permanently ignored along some cycle in the reduced state space. Consider a state s that appears in both the full and the reduced state spaces. An action a is (permanently) ignored if it is executed in s in the full state space, but it is ignored along all execution sequences starting at s in the reduced state space.

To prevent this, we require that the following condition (which we call *open set proviso*) is satisfied: at least one state s which is directly reachable via an action from the ample set has not been visited before or it is in the set of open states. Otherwise the ample set consists of all enabled transitions. For simplicity, in the remainder of this introductory section we treat the newly generated unvisited states also as open states since they will eventually be entered in the open set.

The intuition behind the open set proviso is that the ignoring problem is postponed until state s is expanded later. As the ignored actions are independent of the actions in the ample set, they stay enabled in the open state. Thus, they will be either selected in the ample set of s and as such executed, or they will be delayed for another open state reachable from s. Under the assumption that the GSEA algorithm terminates one can show that this postponement will eventually stop. This is because the set of open states will eventually become empty.

Such a proviso is a generalization of the cycle proviso for partial-order reduction with breadth-first search (BFS) [2] implemented in the model checker SPIN. The BFS POR proviso in turn was inspired by the algorithm presented in [1] for the application of POR in symbolic state space exploration.

Being characterized by means of the open set of states in GSEA, the open set proviso can be computed in an efficient manner during the search based on local information, i.e., information about the currently expanded state and its successors. Further, depending on the data structure which is used to represent the open set, GSEA can be instantiated as a depth-first, a breadth-first, or a directed search algorithm. As it was shown in [5], the latter can significantly improve the error-detection capabilities of explicit state model checking.

We implemented partial-order reduction for GSEA based on our proposed proviso in the tool HSF-SPIN, which is an extension of the model checker SPIN for directed model checking. We evaluate the state space reduction achieved by partial-order reduction according to the proviso that we propose by comparing it on a set of benchmark problems to other reduction approaches.

With the development of a proviso that is applicable to BFS as well as A*, which is an optimal directed heuristic search algorithm if an admissible heuristics is used, we can experimentally address a further relevant issue. When checking safety properties both BFS and A* are capable of returning counterexamples of minimal length if an erroneous state is found in the state space. The usage of BFS without partial order reduction is often impossible due to the memory needs of this algorithm. But this obstacle to its application is partially remedied by the availability of an efficient partial order reduction, which this paper (as well as some previous papers) offers. It will hence be interesting to see how both optimal algorithms perform when used to find errors with the proposed proviso.

Related Work. The POR algorithm of [1] is for symbolic state space exploration and as such it is based on BFS. Unlike the POR version of GSEA (and the open set proviso, as a part of it) which is presented in this paper, the algorithm proposed in [1] is not dealing with reopening of states. Further, the practical side of the theory in [1] hinges on the concept of history function which assigns to each state a set of states.

The states in the history can be seen as potentially "dangerous" because they can lead to a cycle. By requiring that at least one action leads outside the "dangerous" set, i.e., at least one successor state does not belong to the history, one ensures that at least one action from the ample set does not close a cycle. (Therefore, the temporarily ignored transitions can safely be postponed.) In order to be useful in practice, there should be a simple criterion to define such history sets. For example, in the context of explicit state model checking, assuming depth-first search (DFS) exploration, the history set of the currently expanded state s consists of the states which are on the DFS stack. If at least one of the successors is not on the DFS stack we are sure that at least one transition from the ample set does not close a cycle.

To avoid cycles, the definition of history requires that for no two states s, s', s belongs to the history of s' and, vice versa, s' is in the history of s. Because of the reopening of states that GSEA performs, a direct application of the history concept is not possible since the set of open states does not satisfy such a requirement. Our approach, however, results in an efficiently checkable condition which is still expressed in terms of the set of open (closed) states.

In [5] a simple proviso is proposed. It requires that at least one newly generated state is not one of the already visited states. As the set of open states is a subset of the visited states, the open set proviso is weaker than the visited proviso. As a result reductions which are refuted by the visited proviso are allowed by the open set proviso. Our experiments show that this leads to significantly better results than the ones presented in [5].

In another work [14], the authors exploit the fact that the concurrent systems we work with are defined by a parallel composition of sequential processes. This leads to the formulation of a static version of the cycle proviso. This variant of the proviso does not depend on the search status but on information regarding control flow cycles of component processes that is gathered at compile-time. This static proviso is in general much stronger than the previously discussed provisos. Nonetheless, as our experiments showed, in practice it tends to be less efficient than the open set proviso that we introduce in this paper.

Alternatives for the cycle proviso are presented in [17] and [16]. Both references assume DFS exploration of the state space and are therefore not directly applicable to our setting. Shortly before the submission of this paper we were made aware of an adaptation for breadth-first search of the algorithm in [17] described in [20]. The very short description of the POR algorithm in [20] does not provide sufficient detail to allow for a meaningful comparison with our approach. However, reconciling this approach with ours might be an interesting subject for future research.

Paper Outline. In Section 2 we review the foundations of labeled transition systems, partial-order reduction and directed model checking. Our approach towards an efficient partial-order reduction for general state space exploring algorithms is introduced in Section 3. We describe our experimental results in Section 4 and conclude in Section 5.

2 Preliminaries

2.1 Transition Systems

Our approach mainly targets the verification of asynchronous systems where the global system is constructed as an asynchronous product of a set of local component processes. We assume an interleaving model of execution. To reason formally about such systems, we introduce the notion of a *labeled transition system*.[1]

Definition 1 (Labeled transition system). *A labeled transition system (LTS), is a 6-tuple $(S, \hat{s}, A, \tau)$, where S is a finite set of* states, $\hat{s} \in S$ *is the* initial *state, A is a finite set of* actions, *and $\tau : S \times A \to S$ is a (partial) transition function.*

Let $\mathcal{T} = (S, \hat{s}, A, \tau)$ be an LTS. An action $a \in A$ is said to be $\mathcal{T}$-*enabled* in state $s \in S$, denoted $s \xrightarrow{a}_{\mathcal{T}}$ iff $\tau(s, a)$ is defined. The set of all actions $a \in A$ enabled in state $s \in S$ is denoted $enabled_{\mathcal{T}}(s)$; that is, for any $s \in S$, $enabled_{\mathcal{T}}(s) = \{a \in A \mid s \xrightarrow{a}_{\mathcal{T}}\}$. When the LTS is clear from the context we omit the $\mathcal{T}$ subscript. A state $s \in S$ is a *deadlock* state iff $enabled(s) = \emptyset$.

The transition function τ of LTS $\mathcal{T}$ induces a set $T \subseteq S \times A \times S$ of transitions defined as $T = \{(s, a, s') \mid s, s' \in S \wedge a \in A \wedge s' = \tau(s, a)\}$. To improve readability, we write $s \xrightarrow{a} s'$ for $(s, a, s') \in T$. We also say that s' is a *successor* of s.

The transition function τ implies that the LTSs are deterministic in the sense that in a given state s an action a cannot result in more than one state. However, this is not a restriction from a practical point of view, as we shall now argue. Note that in practice the labels of the transitions correspond to program statements (see [11], for instance). Consider first two statements which are the same but belong to two different processes. As an example, this is the case if we have two instances of the same statement that belong to different instances of the same concurrent process (proctype, in SPIN). If the statement does not change the program (location) counter, then the theoretical condition

---

[1] Labeled Transition Systems with state propositions, like the ones used in this paper, are sometimes named "Labeled Kripke structures" or "Doubly labeled transition systems".

that $\tau(s, a)$ always results in the same state is trivially satisfied. Suppose that in a given (global) state s the execution of the statement that corresponds to action a changes the program (location) counter of the process to which it belongs. Then, since the program counters are part of the state vector, the execution of each statement results in a different global state. In case we have non-determinism within the same process, it does not make much sense to have statements with the same name within the same non-deterministic choice. For instance, consider the following code in Promela, the input language of Spin:

```
if
:: a=1
:: a=1
fi
```

Depending on the implementation, in such a case each statement would either have a unique identifier or the statements would automatically be merged into one statement, such as this would be done in Spin. A similar argument can be made regarding non-determinism in other contexts, like process algebra. As an example consider non-observable actions obtained as a result of hiding. Translated into Promela they become *skip* actions that only affect the program counter. An analogous argument as above also applies to this case.

   An *execution sequence* of an LTS $\mathcal{T}$ is a (finite) sequence of consecutive transitions in T. For any natural number $n \in \mathbb{N}$, states $s_i \in S$ and actions $a_i \in A$ with $i \in \mathbb{N}$ and $0 \le i < n$, $s_0 \xrightarrow{a_0} s_1 \xrightarrow{a_1} \ldots s_{n-1} \xrightarrow{a_{n-1}} s_n$ is called an execution sequence of length n of $\mathcal{T}$ iff $s_i \xrightarrow{a_i} s_{i+1}$ for all $i \in \mathbb{N}$ with $0 \le i < n$. State s_n is said to be *reachable* from state s_0. A state is said to be reachable in $\mathcal{T}$ iff it is reachable from $\hat{s}$.

2.2   Partial-Order Reduction

The basic idea of state space reduction is to restrict the part of the state space of a concurrent system that is explored during verification in such a way that all properties of interest are preserved. *Partial-order* reduction exploits the independence of properties from the many possible interleavings of the individual actions of a concurrent system. In our experimental context, actions correspond to statements of Promela (the model specification language of SPIN and HSF-SPIN).

   To be practically useful, a reduction of the state space must be achieved on-the-fly, during the construction and traversal of the state space. This means that it must be decided *per state* which transitions, and hence which subsequent states, must be considered. Let $\mathcal{T} = (S, \hat{s}, A, \tau)$ be some LTS.

Definition 2 (Reduction). *For any* reduction *function* $r : S \to 2^A$, *we define the (partial-order)* reduction *of* $\mathcal{T}$ *with respect to* r *as the smallest LTS* $\mathcal{T}_r = (S_r, \hat{s}_r, A, \tau_r)$ *satisfying the following conditions:*

 - $S_r \subseteq S$, $\hat{s}_r = \hat{s}$
 - *for every* $s \in S_r$ *and* $a \in r(s)$ *such that* $\tau(s, a)$ *is defined,* $\tau_r(s, a) = \tau(s, a)$.

Note that the definition implies that, for every $s \in S_r$ and $a \in A$, if $\tau_r(s, a)$ is defined, then also $\tau(s, a)$ is defined and $\tau_r(s, a) = \tau(s, a)$. Formally, if the function $r(s)$ is fixed in advance, the reduced LTS $\mathcal{T}_r$ is independent of the particular algorithm with which it is generated. In practice $r(s)$ is computed on-the-fly during the generation of $\mathcal{T}_r$, so the latter may depend on the algorithm.

Not all reductions preserve all properties of interest. Depending on the properties that a reduction must preserve, we have to define additional restrictions on r. To this end, we need to formally capture the notion of independence. Actions occurring in different processes can easily influence each other, for example, when they access global variables. The following notion of independence defines the absence of such mutual influence: two independent actions neither disable nor enable one another and they are commutative.

Definition 3 (Independence of actions). *Actions $a, b \in A$ with $a \neq b$ are independent in a given state $s \in S$ iff the following holds:*

- *if $a \in enabled(s)$ then $b \in enabled(s)$ iff $b \in enabled(\tau(s, a))$,*
- *if $b \in enabled(s)$ then $a \in enabled(s)$ iff $a \in enabled(\tau(s, b))$, and*
- *$\tau(\tau(s, a), b) = \tau(\tau(s, b), a)$*

Actions that are not independent are called dependent. The following conditions are sufficient for preservation of deadlocks [8, 9, 19, 24]:

- C0a: if $a \in r(s)$ then $a \in enabled(s)$
- C0b: $r(s) = \emptyset$ iff $enabled(s) = \emptyset$.
- C1 (persistence): For any $s \in S$ and execution sequence $s_0 \overset{a_0}{\to} s_1 \overset{a_1}{\to} \ldots \overset{a_{n-1}}{\to}$ s_n of length $n \in \mathbb{N} \setminus \{0\}$ such that $s_0 = s$ and $a_i \notin r(s)$ for all $i \in \mathbb{N}$ with $0 \leq i < n$, it holds: action a_{n-1} is independent in s_{n-1} with all actions in $r(s)$.

In this paper we focus on subclasses of safety properties that include Promela assertions [11] (annotations stating the truth of a predicate). (See also the comments in the paragraph after Theorem 1 below.)

The main obstacle in the verification of safety properties is the *action ignoring problem* which was identified for the first time in [25]. Informally, the ignoring problem occurs when a reduction of a state space ignores the actions of an entire process. For instance, if there is a cyclic process in the system which contains only globally independent actions, i.e., does not interact with the rest of the system, the reduction algorithm could ignore the rest of the system by choosing only actions of this process in $r(s)$. An action a is ignored in a state $s \in S_r$ iff $a \in enabled_{\mathcal{T}}(s)$ and for all s' which are reachable in $\mathcal{T}_r$ from s it holds $a \notin enabled_{\mathcal{T}_r}(s')$. An action is ignored in $\mathcal{T}_r$ iff it is ignored in some state $s \in S_r$. So, the following condition prevents action ignoring:

- C2ai: For every $s \in S_r$ and every $a \in A$, if $a \in enabled_{\mathcal{T}}(s)$, then there exists an execution sequence $s_0 \overset{a_0}{\to} s_1 \overset{a_1}{\to} \ldots s_{n-1} \overset{a_{n-1}}{\to} s_n$ such that $s = s_0$ and which is in the reduced state space $\mathcal{T}_r$ (i.e., $s_i \in S_r$ for $1 \leq i \leq n$ and $a_i \in r(s_i)$ for $0 \leq i \leq n - 1$) and $a \in r(s_n)$.

In other words, each delayed transition in s must be eventually executed in a state reachable from s.

Condition C2ai implies that each execution sequence (of the original state space) σ starting in s has a representative in the reduced state space. A representative violates the safety property iff the sequence in the non-reduced state space violates the property (e.g. [1]). If we see the execution sequence as a sequence of actions, this representative is a permutation of an action sequence obtained by extending σ with another (possibly empty) action sequence σ' from the original state space. More formally, the claim is given by the following theorem:

Theorem 1. *Given an LTS $\mathcal{T}$ and a reduction function r that satisfies C0a, C0b, C1, and C2ai, let $s_0 \xrightarrow{a_0} s_1 \xrightarrow{a_1} \ldots s_{n-1} \xrightarrow{a_{n-1}} s_n$ be a finite execution sequence of $\mathcal{T}$, such that $s_0 \in S_r$. Then there exists (in $\mathcal{T}$) an execution sequence $s_n \xrightarrow{a_n} s_1 \xrightarrow{a_{n+1}} \ldots s_{n+k-1} \xrightarrow{a_{n+k-1}} s_{n+k}$, $(k \geq 0)$, such that in $\mathcal{T}_r$ there exists an execution sequence $s_0 \xrightarrow{a_{\pi(0)}} s'_1 \xrightarrow{a_{\pi(1)}} \ldots s'_{n+k-1} \xrightarrow{a_{\pi(n+k-1)}} s_{n+k}$, where $a_{\pi(0)}, a_{\pi(1)}, \ldots, a_{\pi(n+k-1)}$ is a permutation of $a_0, a_1, \ldots, a_{n+k-1}$.*

Proof of the above theorem can be found in [25]. Analogous results were proven previously using different versions of the condition that prevents action ignoring (e.g. [8]). Theorem 1 is a meeting point of almost all existing POR-like techniques. It implies preservation of various classes of safety properties (for instance, see [26] for an overview). Among them are also Promela assertions that can be fitted in a straightforward way in one of the existing approaches like assertions in the sense of [8, 12], fact transitions of [25], or local properties of [1].

2.3 Directed Model Checking

Explicit-state model checking is primarily state space search. For memory efficiency reasons, the most commonly used algorithms are DFS for safety property verification and nested DFS for liveness property checking. The verification of safety properties can be performed with BFS, which is rather memory inefficient in comparison with DFS. To be able to reconstruct paths to states, BFS needs to store a predecessor link with each state. In addition, the search horizon in BFS grows exponentially with the depth while only linearly in DFS. See [15] for further details. However, BFS guarantees to find an error on an optimally short path. Since short paths into property violating states are helpful in debugging, the authors of [5] suggested the use of heuristically guided search algorithms such as best-first search (BF) and A* in the state space search, an approach to which they refer to as directed model checking (DMC). Such algorithms hold the potential of locating safety property violating states on short or even optimally short error paths while requiring less states to be stored than BFS. They accomplish this by functions that heuristically assign to each state a value representing the desirability of exploring it. Typical heuristics, for instance, estimate the distance of a state to the set of error states. The heuristic function takes structural properties of the state space as well as properties of the requirements specification into account.

```
(1)     procedure GSEA(s)
(2)         Closed ← ∅; Open ← {s}
(3)         while not Open.empty() do
(4)             u ← Open.extract(); Closed.insert(u);
(5)             if goal(u) then return solution;
(6)             for each a ∈ enabled_T do
(7)                 v ← τ(u, a); process(v);
(8)                 if reopenOK(v) then Closed.delete(v);
(9)                 if v ∉ Closed and v ∉ Open then Open.insert(v);
```

Fig. 1. A general state expanding search algorithm

In this paper we base the construction of a cycle proviso for partial-order reduction on a general search algorithm skeleton that we refer to as general state expanding algorithm (GSEA), c.f. Figure 1. This algorithm divides the set of system states S into three mutually disjoint sets: the set $Open$ of visited but not yet expanded states, the set $Closed$ of visited and expanded states, and the set of unvisited states. The algorithm performs the search by extracting states from $Open$ and moving them into $Closed$. States extracted from $Open$ are expanded, i.e., the respective successor states are generated. If a successor of an expanded state is neither in $Open$ nor in $Closed$ it is added to $Open$. Based on the processing done by function $reopenOK$ (line 8) a state can be reopened, i.e., after it is deleted from $Closed$ (line 8) it is reinserted in $Open$ (line 9). DFS (respectively, BFS) can be defined as an instance of the general algorithm presented above, that do not perform reopening of states and where $Open$ is implemented as a stack (resp., queue). Notice that GSEA is not guaranteed to terminate. The termination depends on the state reopening policy, i.e., on the function $reopenOK$. However, in the sequel we consider only instances for which the termination is guaranteed.

Successful heuristic search algorithms include the non-optimal algorithm BF and the optimal algorithm A* [10]. We present a variant of A* suitable to verify safety properties in Figure 2. It can also be considered a variant of GSEA if one interprets $Open$ as a priority queue in which the priority of a state v is determined by a value f. The f–value for a state v is computed as the sum of i) the length $v.g$ of the currently shortest path from the start state to v and ii) the estimated distance $h(v)$ from v to a goal state. A* can perform a reopening of states. This means that it can move states from $Closed$ to $Open$ when they are reached along a path that is shorter than any path that they were reached on earlier. It is necessary to reopen states in order to guarantee that the algorithm will find the shortest path to the goal state when non-monotone heuristics are used. Monotone heuristics satisfy the property that for each state u and each successor v of u the difference between $h(u)$ and $h(v)$ is less than or equal to the cost of the transition that goes from u to v. Note that we usually consider that each transition has a unit cost of 1, corresponding to the step distance between adjacent states. However, our algorithmic framework can easily handle non unit costs as well. If

```
( 1)    procedure A *(s)
( 2)    begin
( 3)      Closed ← ∅; Open ← ∅; s.f ← h(s); s.g ← 0; Open.insert(s);
( 4)      while not Open.empty() do
( 5)        u ← Open.extractmin(); Closed.insert(u);
( 6)        if goal(u) then return solution;
( 7)        for each a ∈ enabled_T(u) do
( 8)          v ← τ(u,a); v.g ← u.g + cost(a); f' ← v.g + h(v);
( 9)          if v ∈ Open then
(10)            if (f' < v.f) then v.f ← f';
(11)          else if v ∈ Closed then
(12)            if (f' < v.f) then v.f ← f'; Closed.delete(v); Open.insert(v);
(13)          else v.f ← f'; Open.insert(v);
```

Fig. 2. A* search algorithm

non-monotone heuristics are applied, the number of reopenings can be exponential in the size of the state space. However, even if many of the heuristics that we use cannot be proven to be monotone, experimental experience has shown that in practical protocol validation examples states are very rarely reopened [6]. An interesting property of A* is that if h is a lower bound of the distance to a goal state, then A* will always return the shortest path to a goal state [18].

A key challenge in directed model checking is determining appropriate heuristics. In precursory work, heuristics based on the structure of the property specification, in particular on the syntactic structure of LTL formulae, on local state machine distances as well as property specific heuristics, for instance for deadlock detection, were developed and experimentally evaluated. For more information on directed model checking, as well as the tool HSF-SPIN we refer to the papers [5,6].

When applying partial-order reduction in the context of directed model checking one is faced with two challenges: a) The pruning of a part of the state space leads to suboptimality of the combined method since optimal error traces may be cut away by the reduction. Experimental results [6] show that in practical examples the sub-optimal solutions are very close to the optimal solutions, if a discrepancy can be detected at all. b) Algorithms such as BF and A* lack a search stack, hence a stack based action prevention condition, such as it is used when implementing partial-order reduction for DFS based state space exploration, cannot be used. The authors of [6] therefore applied two independent over-approximations of the cycle proviso that do not rely on the presence of a search stack, c.f. our discussion in Section 3.

3   Action Ignoring Prevention Condition for General Space Exploration

Condition C2ai from Section 2.2 is stated as a global property of the state space and as such it is expensive to check. Therefore, for practical purposes it is important to have a possibly stronger condition (which implies C2ai), but which can be locally checked in an efficient way. For particular state expanding strategies such stronger versions of the ignoring condition exist. For instance for DFS there exists a simple locally checkable condition. For each expanded state s in the reduced state space we require that there exists at least one action a in the reduced action set $r(s)$ and a state $s' \in S_r$ such that $s \xrightarrow{a} s'$ and s' is not on the DFS stack. In other words, at least one transition from $r(s)$ must lead to a transition outside the stack, i.e., must not close a cycle. Otherwise, $r(s) = enabled_T(s)$. An analogous version of this condition exists also for BFS [2].

The partial-order reduction version of the general state expanding algorithm (POR GSEA) differs from the original of Figure 1 in line 6 only, where $enabled_T(u)$ is substituted by $r(u)$. We now put the emphasis on the new version of the action ignoring prevention condition.

The conditions that ensure persistence of r, C0a, C0b and C1, do not depend on the search order, as is argued in [5]. Consequently, they may remain unchanged. Only the condition for ignoring prevention should be adjusted to comply with the general search.

To prevent action ignoring we require that for the currently expanded state s at least one action of $r(s)$ leads to a state s' that will be processed later by the algorithm. This means that s' is unvisited or it has been visited already but it is in the *Open* set. The intuition is that the solution to the ignoring problem is postponed until state s' is expanded later. The actions which are temporarily ignored in s remain enabled in s'. This is because by the persistence condition they are independent from the actions in $r(s)$ and therefore they cannot be disabled. Under the assumption that the algorithm terminates, i.e., that the *Open* set eventually becomes empty, such a postponement will eventually stop. This is because we will eventually arrive at a state for which all transitions lead to states outside *Open*. For such a state our condition does not hold and therefore the set of explored actions cannot be reduced since at that point we are guaranteed that all possibly postponed actions will be explored.

So, we require that the reduced set (reduction function) $r(u)$, besides conditions C0a, C0b and C1, has to satisfy for each state $u \in S_r$ immediately before its use in the algorithm (the line in POR GSEA corresponding to line 6 of the original algorithm depicted in Figure 1) also the following condition:

– C2c (closed): There exists at least one action $a \in r(u)$ and a state $v \in S_r$ such that $u \xrightarrow{a} v$ and $v \notin Closed$. Otherwise, $r(u) = enabled_T(u)$.

We show below that C2c implies that the ignoring prevention condition C2ai is satisfied too by the reduced state space, which further entails (via Theorem 1) preservation of safety properties by the POR GSEA algorithm.

Lemma 1. *Let* $T = (S, \hat{s}, A, \tau)$ *be an LTS with a reduction function r that satisfies conditions C0a, C0b, C1, and C2c. Further, let us assume that the POR*

GSEA algorithm terminates when applied on the initial state $\hat{s}$ and produces the reduction T_r. Then r satisfies the ignoring prevention condition C2ai.

Proof. The proof is by induction on the (decreasing) order in which the states are removed from *Open*. As in general each state can be reinserted in *Open* several times, we establish the ordering based on the *last removal* of the state. To this end we assign to each state a number $n \in \mathbb{N}$, which we call the *removal order of the state*. The state which is removed as the very last is assigned the number $|S_r| - 1$, where $|S_r|$ is the number of states in S_r, while the one which is removed first is assigned 0. Such an ordering is always possible because of the assumption that POR GSEA terminates. As a consequence, the set *Open* eventually becomes empty and there exists some state s which is removed last from the *Open* set.

Base case: Let s be the state with the highest removal order, i.e., s is removed as the last from *Open*. Consider the very last removal of s from *Open*. Since *Open* is empty, all successors of s must be in *Closed*. (If they were new they would have been inserted in *Open* which is a contradiction.) So, by condition C2c, $r(s) = enabled_T(s)$, i.e., all enabled actions will be explored. The prevention condition C2ai holds trivially.

Inductive step: Let s be the state with removal order n. We assume that for each state s'' with removal order greater than n, i.e., which is removed for the last time from *Open* after s is removed for the last time, the following holds: for each $a \notin r(s'')$, there exists a state s' reachable via an execution sequence in the reduced state space such that $a \in r(s')$. Consider the very last removal of s from *Open*. If $r(s) = enabled_T(s)$ C2ai holds trivially. So, let us assume that $r(s)$ is a proper subset of $enabled_T(s)$. By condition C2c there exists at least one action $b \in r(s)$ and a state $s'' \in S_r$ such that $s \xrightarrow{b} s''$ and $s'' \notin Closed$. This implies that s'' is either a new unvisited state and it will be inserted in *Open* or it is already in *Open*. As by our assumption s is already removed (before it is expanded) for the last time from *Open* (line 4 of the POR GSEA algorithm) we are sure that s'' will be removed from *Open* for the last time after s. Let a be an action which is not in $r(s)$, i.e., it is postponed. By the persistence condition C1 actions a and b are independent and therefore a is enabled in s''. By the induction hypothesis there exists a state s' reachable from s'' via a transition sequence in the reduced state space. The concatenation of $s \xrightarrow{a} s''$ and the execution sequence from s'' to s' gives the desired execution sequence from s to s'.   □

After proving the termination of the concrete version of the POR GSEA algorithm, its correctness follows by Lemma 1 and further by Theorem 1. Evidently, termination of the concrete version of the POR GSEA algorithm depends on the reopening strategy. Practical strategies, however, guarantee termination. For a deeper discusion, proofs of termination of A^* and similar directed search algorithms discussed in Section 2.3 can be found in Section 3.1.2 of [21]. As the POR versions of those algorithms work on a subset of the original state space it is trivial to adapt the argument from [21] to the case of the state space reduced by partial-order reduction. Another argument for the termination of the instances of (POR) GSEA is given in [3].

In full analogy with the DFS case [22, 13], accompanied with some additional restrictions on r [7, 23], a stronger version of the open set proviso that preserves LTL_{-X} and CTL^*_{-X}(e.g. [4]) can be defined:

- C2cl: (closed liveness) For all actions $a \in r(s)$ and states $s' \in S_r$ such that $s \xrightarrow{a} s'$, $s' \notin Closed$.

We refer the reader to [3] for further details.

We now turn to the problem of finding efficiently computable cycle provisos for A*. Using the observation made in [14] to prevent global cycles one has to break all local cycles of the involved concurrent processes, in [6] a *static* POR method was adapted to the A* based directed model checking setting. The method relies on marking one action in every local control cycle as "sticky". It is then enforced that no sticky action is allowed in an ample set of a state if the state is not fully expanded. The resulting proviso c2s is defined as the following condition (for the details we refer to the literature) on the reduced set $r(s)$ of a state s state being expanded.

- C2s (static): There exists no sticky action $a \in r(s)$ such that $s \xrightarrow{a} s'$. Otherwise, $r(s) = enabled_T(s)$.

A second idea proposed in [6] was to enforce breaking cycles by requiring that at least one transition in the ample set does not lead to a previously visited state, which lead to the following condition:

- C2v (visited): There exists at least one action $a \in r(s)$ and a state $s' \in S_r$ such that $s \xrightarrow{a} s'$ and $s' \notin Closed \cup Open$. Otherwise, $r(s) = enabled_T(s)$.

It is worth noting that our proviso is better than the visited proviso described in the previous section. This is simply because C2c trivially implies C2v. In the experimental section we will show that, in practice, C2c performs significantly better than C2v.

For safety properties it was shown that C2s and C2v entail the original cycle proviso [6]. Further, while strictly weaker than condition C2ai, experimental results show that still significant reductions could be achieved with these conditions.

4   Experiments

This section presents experimental results that evaluate the performance of the proposed proviso. We implemented the approach described in our paper in the tool HSF-SPIN [5] and performed various experiments in which we compare our proposed proviso with the performance of other, previously proposed provisos for BFS and A*. Experiments were performed under Linux on a PC with an AMD Athlon 1.8 Ghz processor. We use various models in our experiments: A leader election algorithm (**leader**) that solves the problem of finding a leader in a ring topology, a model of a concurrent program that solves the stable marriage problem (`marriers(n)`), the CORBA GIOP protocol (`giop(n,m)`) which is a key component of the OMG's Common Object Request Broker Architecture (CORBA) specification, and the preliminary design of a Plain Old Telephony System (`pots`). A description of these models can be found in [5]. Note that these models have been used in benchmarking partial order reductions before, and that the GIOP and POTS models have real-life system complexities. For parameterized scalable models we indicate the instantiated parameters using brackets after the name of the protocol.

Our first set of experiments is devoted to a specific case of the GSEA, namely BFS. None of the previous works on BFS with PO [2, 5] presents a comparison with the newly proposed proviso (C2c). The results of [5], which do not consider C2c, show that none between the visited proviso (C2v) [5] and the static proviso (C2s) [14] is better than the other. In contrast, the results of [2] do not consider C2s but show that an instance of C2c for BFS is significantly better than C2v. The main question to investigate is therefore how C2c performs in comparison to C2s. Table 1 depicts results obtained by completely exploring the state space of some models using BFS as search algorithm in combination with various reduction methods: no partial-order reduction at all (no), no action ignoring prevention (C2i), C2v, C2s and C2c. Note that C2i leads to an unsound reduction. We introduce it only in order to assess the other provisos in terms of the number of ample sets that they refuse. For each experiment we present the size of the state space (s), the amount of memory required (m), and the running time (r).

The first thing we observe is that C2c performs better than C2v. This, for instance, becomes especially obvious in the case of the `giop` model where C2c explores about three times less states. Regarding the comparison with the C2s approach, the C2c based reduction performs better in all cases. Here, the `leader` model is the most significant example since C2c explores almost four times less states. Finally, by comparing the colums C2c and C2i we observe that C2c

Table 1. Completely exploring state spaces with BFS and several reduction methods

marriers(3)

	BFS+no	BFS+C2i	BFS+C2v	BFS+C2s	BFS+C2c
s	96,295	29,501	56,345	57,067	29,501
m	12 MB	6 MB	8 MB	8 MB	6 MB
r	1.13 s	0.21 s	0.58 s	0.54 s	0.23 s

leader(6)

	BFS+no	BFS+C2i	BFS+C2v	BFS+C2s	BFS+C2c
s	445,776	3,160	5,209	11,921	3,160
m	147 MB	3 MB	4 MB	6 MB	3 MB
r	34.48 s	0.07 s	0.18 s	0.19	0.08 s

giop(2,1)

	BFS+no	BFS+C2i	BFS+C2v	BFS+C2s	BFS+C2c
s	664,376	65,964	209,382	231,102	66,160
m	384 MB	39 MB	122 MB	134 MB	39 MB
r	16.42 s	1.12 s	4.76 s	4.44 s	1.23 s

refuses ample sets in the `giop` model only. Note that when the exploration with C2c results in equal state spaces as when ignoring the proviso, there is a small difference in the running time that can be traced to the overhead caused by computing the proviso.

We continue the evaluation of our C2c proviso in a different setting, namely where the goal is error detection and directed model checking algorithms like A* are used. We also performed additional experiment with other DMC algorithms like best-first search leading to similar results. The results of [5] show no clear winner between C2v and the C2s. Hence, the first question to answer is whether C2c outperforms C2s. Second we would like to find out to what degree C2c is actually superior to C2v.

To answer this last question we basically extend the results presented in [5] with C2c. Table 2 depicts the results. As in the previous set of experiments, C2c performs significantly better than C2v. Consider, for instance, the models `marriers` and `giop`, where the number of states explored with C2c is only about half the number explored with C2v. On the other hand, there is no clear winner between C2c and C2s approach. For instance, the best reduction is achieved with C2s in model `marriers` and with C2c in model `giop`. In the rest of the models both provisos work equally well.

By comparing the two previous sets of experiments we observe the following phenomenon: in the `marriers` model, algorithm BFS with C2c explores as many states as BFS with C2i (Table 1), while A* with C2c explores almost twice as many states as A* with C2i (Table 2). In other words, the C2c proviso is refuting

Table 2. Finding a safety violation with A* and BFS with several reduction methods

marriers(4)

	A*+no	A*+C2i	A*+C2v	A*+C2s	A*+C2c	BFS+C2c
s	225,404	37,220	100,278	37,220	58,500	155,894
m	31 MB	7 MB	15 MB	7 MB	6 MB	22 MB
r	5.15 s	0.31 s	2.99s	0.36 s	0.73 s	7.17 s

pots

	A*+no	A*+C2i	A*+C2v	A*+C2s	A*+C2c	BFS+C2c
s	6,654	5,429	5,574	5,429	5,429	22,786
m	5 MB	4 MB	4 MB	4 MB	4 MB	12 MB
r	0.18 s	0.15 s	0.15 s	0.15 s	0.15 s	0.78 s

leader(8)

	A*+no	A*+C2i	A*+C2v	A*+C2s	A*+C2c	BFS+C2c
s	558,214	104	104	104	104	128
m	265 MB	2 MB	2 MB	2 MB	2 MB	2 MB
r	30.54 s	0.01 s	0.01 s	0.01 s	0.01 s	0.01 s

giop(3,1)

	A*+no	A*+C2i	A*+C2v	A*+C2s	A*+C2c	BFS+C2c
s	485,907	90,412	314,964	191,805	117,846	120,132
m	291 MB	55 MB	189 MB	116 MB	72 MB	73 MB
r	20.09 s	2.82 s	12.41 s	6.60 s	3.98 s	2,52

ample sets when the search algorithm is A* but not when it is BFS. What happens is that the new proviso, as well as the rest of the provisos, depends on the order in which states are explored. This phenomenon can be illustrated by a simple example. Assume the following state space:

$$s_0 \overset{c}{\underset{d}{\rightrightarrows}} s_1 \xrightarrow{a} s_2$$
$$\quad \searrow \quad \downarrow b \quad \overset{a}{\underset{}{}} \quad \downarrow b$$
$$\qquad s_3 \xrightarrow{a} s_4$$

Suppose that $\hat{s} = s_0$ and that actions a,b are unconditionally independent and that we use BFS with our proviso to explore the state space. First, state s_0 is extracted from the open set and its successors s_1, s_3 are inserted into $Open$ (we assume that no reduction is possible at s_0). Assume that the order in which they are inserted is s_1 first and then s_3. At the next iteration of BFS, state s_1 is selected for expansion. Now, $\{b\}$ is selected as ample set since it satisfies all the conditions. In the last step state s_4 is explored. The algorithm, hence, explores all states but s_2.

Consider now that s_3 is inserted in $Open$ first and s_1 second. Now, state s_3 is extracted from the $Open$ set and s_4 is inserted in it. In the next step, state s_2 is selected for expansion, but this time set $\{b\}$ is refused by C2c since state s_3 is no more in the open set. Thus, the search is forced to visit state s_4. In sum, the whole state space is visited.

We have performed some experiments in which the exhaustive exploration is performed randomly. This was done by using the A* algorithm and a random heuristic function. The result leads to larger state spaces than with BFS. At this point an interesting question arises. While previous work presents the benefits of using directed search algorithms over BFS, can BFS when used with C2c take advantage of the exploration order phenomenon so as to become more memory efficient than A* with C2c? This is particularly relevant since partial-order reduction holds the potential of containing the state space explosion that BFS is particularly vulnerable to. To answer this question we included experiments with BFS and C2c in Table 2. With the C2c proviso A* explores less states than BFS with C2c. While in the **pots** and **marriers** models the improvement is significant, in **giop** the small difference together with the overhead introduced by heuristics leads to slightly longer running times for A*.

5   Conclusions

In this paper we presented a partial-order reduction for general state exploring algorithms. The main novelty in the algorithm lies in the condition for avoiding action ignoring, which we call open set proviso, which is basically a generalization of the queue proviso proposed for SPIN's BFS based partial-order reduction in [2]. During the state space exploration this condition can be checked locally and in an efficient way. We implemented the open set proviso for some directed model checking algorithms which are special instances of the general search algorithm. The experimental results show that the new proviso leads to a significant performance improvement of the directed model checking algorithms in comparison to previously known provisos. The experiments also showed that A* together with the open list proviso is performing superior in terms of explored states and memory consuption over BFS with partial-order reduction and this new proviso.

We notice that the efficiency of the proviso can depend on the order in which the actions in the reduced state set are selected. In addition, further experiments we have performed evidence that when there are various valid ample sets the choice amongst them influencences size of the reduced state space. It could be interesting to see if this can be exploited to further improve POR algorithms. In particular, we propose to investigate whether heuristics, possibly exploiting the property being verified, can be defined to select amongst different prossibleample sets in order to improve efficiency of the reduction. Another interesting topic for future work will be to apply the ideas of this paper in the realm of symbolic model checking, for instance, for the verification of liveness properties.

References

1. R. Alur, R.K. Brayton, T.A. Henzinger, S. Qadeer, and S.K. Rajamani, *Partial-order reduction in symbolic state-space exploration*, *Formal Methods in System Design*, 18:97-116, 2001. A preliminary version appeared in Proc. of the 9th International Conference on Computer-aided Verification, CAV '97, LNCS 1254, pp. 340–351, Springer, 1997.
2. D. Bošnački, G.J. Holzmann, *Improving Spin's Partial-Order Reduction for Breadth-First Search*, Model Checking Software: 12th International SPIN Workshop, SPIN 2005, LNCS 3639, pp.91-105, Springer, 2005.
3. D. Bošnački, S. Leue, A. Lluch Lafuente, *Partial-Order Reduction for General State Exploring Algorithms*, Technical Report soft-05-02, Chair for Software Engineering, University of Konstanz, 2005.
   http://www.inf.uni-konstanz.de/soft/research/publications/pdf/soft-05-01.pdf
4. E. Clarke, O. Grumberg, D.A. Peled, *Model Checking* MIT Press, 2000.
5. S. Edelkamp, A. Lluch Lafuente and S. Leue, *Directed explicit-state model checking in the validation of communication protocols*, Software Tools for Technology Transfer, vol. 5, pp. 247-267, 2004.
6. S. Edelkamp, S. Leue and A. Lluch Lafuente, *Partial-order reduction and trail improvement in directed model checking*, International Journal on Software Tools for Technology Transfer, vol. 6, nr. 4, pp. 277-301, 2004.
7. R. Gerth, R. Kuiper, D. Peled, W. Penczek, *A Partial-Order Approach to Branching Time Logic Model Checking*, Information and Computation 150(2): 132-152, 1999.
8. P. Godefroid, *Partial-Order Methods for the Verification of Concurrent Systems: An Approach to the State Space Explosion*, LNCS 1032, Springer, 1996.
9. P. Godefroid, P. Wolper, *Using Partial-Orders for the Efficient Verification of Deadlock Freedom and Safety Properties*, Computer Added Verification, CAV '91, LNCS 575, pp. 332-342, Springer, 1991.
10. P.E. Hart, N.J. Nilsson and B. Raphael, *A formal basis for heuristic determination of minimum path costs*, IEEE Transactions on Systems Science and Cybernetics, 4:100-107, 1968.

11. G.J. Holzmann, *The SPIN Model Checker: Primer and Reference Manual*, Addison Wesley, 2003.
12. G.J. Holzmann, P. Godefroid, D. Pirottin, *Coverage Preserving Reduction Strategies for Reachability Analysis*, in Proc. 12th IFIP WG 6.1. International Symposium on Protocol Specification, Testing, and Validation, FORTE/PSTV '92, pp.349-363, North-Holland, 1992.
13. G.J. Holzmann, D. Peled, *An Improvement in Formal Verification*, FORTE 1994, Bern, Switzerland, 1994.
14. R.P. Kurshan, V. Levin, M. Minea, D. Peled, H. Yenigün, *Static Partial-Order Reduction*, in Tools and Algorithms for Construction and Analysis of Systems TACAS '98, LNCS 1384, pp. 345-357, 1998.
15. A. Lluch-Lafuente, S. Edelkamp, S. Leue, *Directed Search for the Verification of Communication Protocols*, PhD Thesis, Freiburger Dokument Server, Institute of Computer Science, University of Freiburg, June 2003.
16. V. Levin, R. Palmer, S. Qadeer, S.K. Rajamani, *Sound Transaction-Based Reduction Without Cycle Detection*, Model Checking Software: 12th International SPIN Workshop, SPIN 2005, LNCS 3639, pp.106-121, Springer, 2005.
17. R. Nalumasu, G. Gopalakrishnan, *An Efficient Partial-Order Reduction Algorithm with an Alternative Proviso Implementation*, Formal Methods in System Design 20(3): 231-247, 2002.
18. N.J. Nilsson, *Principles of Artificial Intelligence*, Tioga Publishing Co. Palo Alto, California, 1980.
19. W.T. Overman, Verification of Concurrent Systems: Function and Timing, Ph.D. Thesis, UCLA, Los Angeles, California, 1981.
20. R. Palmer, G. Gopalakrishnan, *A Distributed Partial Order Reduction Algorithm*, Formal Techniques for Networked and Distributed Systems FORTE 2002, LNCS 2529, p.370, 2002.
21. J. Pearl, *Heuristics*, Addison-Wesley, 1985
22. D.A. Peled, *Combining Partial-Order Reductions with On-the-Fly Model Checking*, Formal Methods on Systems Design, 8: 39-64, 1996. A previous version appeared in Computer Aided Verification 1994, LCNS 818, pp. 377-390, 1994.
23. B. Willems, P. Wolper, *Partial-Order Models for Model Checking: From Linear to Branching Time*, Proc. of 11 Symposium of Logics in Computer Science, LICS 96, New Brunswick, pp. 294-303, 1996.
24. A. Valmari, *Eliminating Redundant Interleavings during Concurrent Program Verification*, Proc. of Parallel Architectures and Languages Europe '89, vol. 2, LNCS 366, pp. 89-103, Springer, 1989.
25. A. Valmari, *A Stubborn Attack on State Explosion*, in Advances in Petri Nets, LNCS 531, pp. 156-165, Springer, 1991.
26. A. Valmari, *The State Explosion Problem*, Lectures on Petri Nets I: Basic Models, LNCS Tutorials, LNCS 1491, pp. 429-528, Springer, 1998.

A Counterexample-Guided Refinement Tool for Open Procedural Programs*

Aleksandar Dimovski[1], Dan R. Ghica[2], and Ranko Lazić[1,**]

[1] Department of Computer Science, Univ. of Warwick, Coventry, CV4 7AL, UK
[2] School of Computer Science, Univ. of Birmingham, Birmingham, B15 2TT, UK

Abstract. We present a model checking tool based on game semantics and CSP for verifying safety properties of software, such as assertion violations or array-out-of-bounds errors. The tool implements a data-abstraction refinement procedure applicable to open programs with infinite integer types. The procedure is guaranteed to terminate for unsafe inputs.

Keywords: software model checking, abstraction refinement, game semantics, CSP, FDR.

1 Introduction

The traditional approach to building models of software is based on representations of *program state* and the way it changes in the course of execution. A different approach to constructing models of software is by looking at the ways in which a term can observably *interact* with its context. This modelling technique, known as *game semantics*, has been shown to provide useful algorithms for software model checking [1]. In this framework, computation is seen as a game between two players, the environment and the program, and the model of a program is given as a *strategy* for the second player. Strategies can be then given concrete representations using various automata or process theoretic formalisms, thus providing direct support for model checking.

This approach has several benefits compared with the state-based approach. First, it can be applied to open program fragments with higher-order procedures. Second, game semantics is defined recursively on syntax, therefore the model of a term is constructed from the models of its subterms, using a notion of strategy composition. Third, the generated models are fully abstract, i.e., two terms have the same models if and only if they cannot be distinguished with respect to operational tests such as abnormal termination in any program context. Finally, game models are often much smaller than state-based models because details of local-state manipulation are hidden during strategy composition.

The traditional, state-based, approach to software model checking has been applied successfully to verifying realistic industrial software. At the heart of

---

* This research was supported by the EPSRC (GR/S52759/01).
** Supported by a grant from the Intel Corporation. Also affiliated to the Mathematical Institute, Serbian Academy of Sciences and Arts, Belgrade.

A. Valmari (Ed.): SPIN 2006, LNCS 3925, pp. 288–292, 2006.

many successful tools such as SLAM [2] and BLAST [6] are algorithms based on abstract-check-refine loops [3]. Recently, it has been shown how counterexample-guided refinement ideas can be adapted to the setting of game-semantic models [5]. However, implementing the procedure in [5] is non-trivial because the semi-algorithm, as described, is highly inefficient.

In this paper, we describe GAMECHECKER, a tool which implements efficiently an abstraction refinement procedure for checking whether a program fragment is unsafe, i.e. it *may* execute the designated unsafe command abort. Using this special command, we can easily perform various code-level checks for errors such as buffer overruns or assertion violations. Semantically, this corresponds to reachability, in the model, of the designated unsafe move *abort*.

GAMECHECKER adds abstraction annotations to the source code, to approximate infinite integer data types by partitionings. Any partitioning consists of finitely many partitions, which are called *abstracted integers*. Any abstracted integer is thus a set of integers. Terms which use abstracted rather than actual integers are called *abstracted terms*. Operationally, abstracted terms behave just like their concrete counterparts, but first they nondeterministically instantiate any abstracted integer argument a by choosing nondeterministically some concrete integer $n \in a$, then abstract the concrete integer result n' to the partition $a' \ni n'$ to which it belongs. As shown in [5], this is a conservative approximation. By quotienting over abstracted integers, the models become finite and can be model-checked.

Within GAMECHECKER, an abstracted term is compiled into a process in the CSP process algebra (e.g. [7]), whose finite-traces set represents the quotiented game-semantic model of the term. The resulting process is then verified for safety using the FDR refinement checker, which is based on explicit state enumeration.[1] If no counterexample is found by FDR, the procedure terminates with answer SAFE. Otherwise, the counterexamples are analysed and classified as either genuine or (potentially) spurious. If genuine counterexamples exist the program is deemed UNSAFE, otherwise the spurious counterexamples are used to refine the abstractions, by splitting some of their partitions. The procedure is then repeated on the refined term.

The abstraction refinement procedure is a semi-algorithm: it terminates and reports a genuine error trace for unsafe terms, but it may diverge for safe terms.

GAMECHECKER is available from:
http://www.dcs.warwick.ac.uk/~aleks/gamechecker.htm.

2   The Programming Language and Its Game Semantics

The input is any program fragment of an expressive programming language combining imperative features, locally-scoped variables and (call-by-name) procedures. The actual language on which GAMECHECKER works also incorporates abstraction annotations, which are managed automatically by the tool. The data

---

[1] FDR is a commercial product of Formal Systems (Europe) Ltd. It is available free of charge for academic use. See http://www.fsel.com

types are booleans and abstracted integers ($\tau ::= \mathsf{bool} \mid \mathsf{int}_\pi$). The phrase types are types of expressions, variables and commands ($\sigma ::= \mathsf{exp}\,\tau \mid \mathsf{var}\,\tau \mid \mathsf{com}$), and 1st-order functions types ($\theta ::= \sigma \mid \sigma \to \theta$).

The abstractions π range over computable finite partitionings of the integers $\mathbb{Z}$. The tool currently uses the following abstractions:

$$[] = \{\mathbb{Z}\} \quad [n,m] = \{<n, \{n\}, \{n+1\}, \ldots, \{0\}, \ldots, \{m-1\}, \{m\}, >m\}$$

where $<n = \{n' \mid n' < n\}$ and $>n = \{n' \mid n' > n\}$. Instead of $\{n\}$, we may write just n. Abstractions are refined by *splitting* abstract values: $[]$ is refined to $[0,0]$ by splitting $\mathbb{Z}$; $[n,m]$ to $[n-1,m]$ by splitting $<n$, or to $[n,m+1]$ by splitting $>m$.

We write $\Gamma \vdash M : \theta$ to indicate that term M with free identifiers in Γ has type θ. (The typing rules can be found in [5].) A context (i.e. term-with-hole) is *safe* if it does not contain the **abort** command. A term is *unsafe* if there exists a closed program formed from a safe context and the term, which may execute **abort**. Otherwise, we say that a term is *safe*.

GAMECHECKER includes a compiler from any abstracted term $\Gamma \vdash M : \theta$ to a CSP process $[\![\Gamma \vdash M : \theta]\!]$ whose set of finite traces **traces**$[\![\Gamma \vdash M : \theta]\!]$ is the set of all plays of the game strategy for the term. Those processes are defined compositionally, by induction on the structure of terms (see [4]).

The abstraction refinement procedure described in [5] requires models consisting of *fully revealed plays*, i.e., models in which semantic composition of strategies does not involve *hiding* of the moves involved in composition. The fully revealed plays allow us to discern between genuine and spurious counterexamples by identifying the precise subterms that produce abstracted moves. However, fully revealed models are much larger and therefore impractical. In GAMECHECKER, this is overcome as follows: first we use special marker moves to identify points in plays at which abstraction gives rise to nondeterminism, then we use a special debugging feature of FDR that lets us reveal only those plays which are counterexamples rather than full models.

Nondeterminism due to abstraction happens when an arithmetic/logic operation produces more than one result. In such an instance, the operation necessarily has at least one abstracted integer operand which is not a singleton, i.e. which abstracts more than one integer. The game strategy for the operation then performs a special marker move $nd.a$, where a is such an operand. Those moves are propagated through strategy compositions, so for any term $\Gamma \vdash M : \theta$, they appear in **traces**$[\![\Gamma \vdash M : \theta]\!]$ at the points where nondeterminism due to abstraction occurs.

Example 1. Consider $[\![x : \mathsf{var}\,\mathsf{int}_{[0,4]} \vdash x := x + 1 : \mathsf{com}]\!]$. If the abstract value <0 is read from x, $x + 1$ can evaluate to both 0 and <0. The following trace corresponds to choosing the result 0: *run* $read_x$ $<0_x$ $nd.(<0)$ $write(0)_x$ ok_x ok. The move $nd.(<0)$ records the non-singleton abstracted integer operand <0.

FDR offers a number of state-space reduction algorithms which preserve finite-trace sets, and which are thus compositional. The processes representing the game strategies are particularly amenable to such reductions, because moves which are hidden through composition of strategies become internal (τ) process transitions. The compiler within GAMECHECKER inserts calls to FDR's state-space reduction algorithms within the process scripts it outputs.

It was established in [5] that the game semantic models are fully abstract for the language of concrete and abstracted terms. This result ensures that, for any term $\Gamma \vdash M : \theta$, model-checking the process $[\![\Gamma \vdash M : \theta]\!]$ for safety (i.e. for unreachability of the *abort* event) is equivalent to checking whether $\Gamma \vdash M : \theta$ is safe.

3   Abstraction Refinement Procedure

GAMECHECKER checks safety of a given term $\Gamma \vdash M : \theta$ (with infinite integer data types) by performing a sequence of iterations. The initial abstracted term $\Gamma_0 \vdash M_0 : \theta_0$ uses the coarsest abstraction $\mathbb{Z}$ for any free identifier or local variable, and the abstraction $[0, n]$ or $[n, 0]$ for constants n. Other abstractions (such as those for integer expression subterms) are determined from the former by inference.

Each iteration consists of model checking (by calling the FDR tool), slicing, and refining abstractions. Only abstractions which occur in types of free identifiers or local variables are explicitly refined, and others are obtained by inference. That yields a refined abstracted term $\Gamma_{i+1} \vdash M_{i+1} : \theta_{i+1}$, which is passed to the next iteration.

The following are the steps of any iteration. If t is a trace which contains at least one special move marking a nondeterminism, let $\mathbf{pick}(t) = a$, where $nd.a$ is the first such move.[2] For ordering non-singleton abstracted integers, we use a bijection r to the natural numbers: $r(\mathbb{Z}) = 0$, $r(<n) = 2|n| + 2$, and $r(>n) = 2n + 1$. This has the property that $r(a) < r(a')$ whenever $a' \subseteq a$.

1. If $[\![\Gamma_i \vdash M_i : \theta_i]\!] \setminus \{|nd|\}$ is unsafe, terminate with answer UNSAFE.
2. If $[\![\Gamma_i \vdash M_i : \theta_i]\!]$ is safe, terminate with answer SAFE.
3. Among the counterexamples (i.e. traces of $[\![\Gamma_i \vdash M_i : \theta_i]\!]$ which end with *abort*), select t such that $r(\mathbf{pick}(t))$ is minimal.
4. Apply the FDR trace-reveal feature to t, obtaining a fully revealed trace s.
5. Call a slicing procedure to determine a set S of all occurences of non-singleton abstracted integers which were involved in causing the first $nd.a$ move in s.
6. For any data type int_π of a free identifier or a local variable which corresponds to an occurence of an abstracted integer b in S, refine π by splitting b.

Steps **2** and **3** are implemented as follows. The process $[\![\Gamma_i \vdash M_i : \theta_i]\!]$ is composed in parallel with an auxiliary process *Rank_of_pick* which, once the first move of the form $nd.a$ has occured, keeps in its state the value $r(a)$. FDR is called to model check that parallel composition, and for any reachable state which has

---

[2] This definition of $\mathbf{pick}(t)$ is currently implemented, but other definitions are possible. The crucial property is that, if t is used to refine abstractions, then one of the refinements will split $\mathbf{pick}(t)$.

an *abort* transition, to return a trace which reaches it. By step **1**, any such trace must contain an *nd.a* move. The parallel composition with *Rank_of_pick* ensures that, for any possible value of $r(\mathbf{pick}(t))$ with t a counterexample, at least one such counterexample is returned by FDR.

Theorem 1. *If the abstraction refinement procedure terminates, its answer is correct. Moreover, it terminates for any unsafe term.*

Proof. UNSAFE answers are correct because any trace which contains no special moves marking nondeterminism corresponds to a concrete trace. Correctness of SAFE answers is a consequence of the conservativity of abstraction. (See [5].)

Suppose $\Gamma \vdash M : \theta$ is unsafe. Let u be a fully revealed play of the game strategy for $\Gamma \vdash M : \theta$ which ends with *abort*, and let m be an integer in u with maximum absolute value. For any non-singleton abstracted integer a, we define $d(a) = 2|m| + 1 - r(a)$. Then $d(a) > 0$ whenever $|n| \leq |m|$ for some $n \in a$.

For any iteration i, let D_i be the sum of all positive $d(a)$ as a ranges over the non-singleton equivalence classes of all abstractions in $\Gamma_i \vdash M_i : \theta_i$. Steps **3–6** ensure that $D_0 > D_1 > \cdots$, so the procedure must terminate.   □

4   Conclusion

This paper presents the first software model checker based on game semantics and counterexample-guided abstraction refinement. By combining the two theories, it can handle arbitrary open program fragments with infinite integer data types. The tool is a prototype implementation, which has been tested on a variety of academic examples.

Possibilities for future work include extensions to programs with concurrency, recursion and 2nd-order procedures, as well as to abstractions by arbitrary predicates. The goal is a tool which uses game semantics to achieve compositional verification of practical programs.

References

1. S. Abramsky, D.R. Ghica, A. Murawski and C.-H.L. Ong. Applying Game Semantics to Compositional Software Modeling and Verification. In Proceedings of *TACAS*, LNCS **2988**, (2004), 421–435.
2. T. Ball and S.K. Rajamani. The SLAM Toolkit. In Proceedings of *CAV*, LNCS **2102**, (2001), 260–264.
3. E.M. Clarke, O. Grumberg, S. Jha, Y. Lu and H. Veith. Counterexample-Guided Abstraction Refinement for Symbolic Model Checking. J. ACM **50**(5), (2003), 752–794.
4. A. Dimovski and R. Lazić. CSP Representation of Game Semantics for Second-Order Idealized Algol. In Proceedings of *ICFEM*, LNCS **3308**, (2004), 146–161.
5. A. Dimovski, D.R. Ghica and R. Lazić. Data-Abstraction Refinement: A Game Semantic Approach. In Proceedings of *SAS*, LNCS **3672**, (2005), 102–117.
6. T.A. Henzinger, R. Jhala, R. Majumdar and G. Sutre. Software Verification with Blast. In Proceedings of *SPIN*, LNCS **2648**, (2003), 235–239.
7. A.W. Roscoe. Theory and Practice of Concurrency. Prentice Hall, 1998.

jMosel: A Stand-Alone Tool and jABC Plugin for M2L(Str)

Christian Topnik[1], Eva Wilhelm[1], Tiziana Margaria[2], and Bernhard Steffen[1]

[1] Universität Dortmund, FB Informatik, Lehrstuhl 5, Germany
{christian.topnik, eva.wilhelm}@uni-dortmund.de
steffen@cs.uni-dortmund.de
[2] Universität Göttingen, Service Engineering for Distributed Systems, Germany
margaria@cs.uni-goettingen.de

Abstract. *jMosel* is a tool-set for the analysis and verification of linear parametric systems in monadic second-order logic on strings. In this paper we give a short introduction to the underlying concepts, as well as an overview of the implementation and the usage of *jMosel*.

1 Introduction

Monadic second-order logic on strings (M2L(Str)) was proposed as an appropriate formalism for reasoning about bit vector sequences by A. Church in the 1960's [3]. It is expressive enough to capture parametric finite-state systems and it is also decidable, though in non-elementary time. However, many relevant practical problems have proved to be solvable in reasonable time.

M2L has been used for the specification and verification of classes of parametric hardware systems [2, 7, 9] and software systems [8, 11], in which the logic can serve, for example, as a description language for model-based analysis.

This paper introduces *jMosel*, a new tool-set for handling M2L(Str) formulas, i.e. constructing the automata[1] representing the desired semantics and providing the means to further work with them in different contexts.

It is developed as the successor to the MoSeL tool-set from the 1990's, but using current technologies like Java and XML. The emphasis is placed on flexibility, to allow the customisation of many aspects of the tool's properties. Currently there are two interfaces to access *jMosel's* functionality: a command line tool and a plugin to the *jABC* framework [12]. Both versions are presented in this paper.

2 The jMosel Concept

2.1 Design Principles

jMosel supports flexible adaptation and extension to new input or output formalisms, as well as the interchange of many components, including the most

---

[1] The semantics of a *jMosel* formula is defined via finite-state automata.

A. Valmari (Ed.): SPIN 2006, LNCS 3925, pp. 293–298, 2006.

crucial algorithms and libraries. This allows the user to experiment with a great variety of technologies. The aim is that the best-fitting incarnation of the tool for a specific application area may be put together at need from the collection of existing components. The following components can be customised:

BDD libraries: The performance of the operations on BDDs[2], which label the edges of a *jMosel* automaton, has a great impact on the overall performance of the compilation process. To encourage the user to compare different implementations, *jMosel* already supports the use of the following BDD libraries: CUDD [15], BuDDy [6], CAL BDD [14], JavaBDD (Java port of BuDDy) [17], JavaBDD Micro (Java port of BuDDy) [17], JDD [16]. Switching bet-ween these libraries can be done easily by changing the corresponding *lib* parameter of the command line tool.

Algorithms: Even such fundamental compiler parts like the algorithms for determinisation and minimisation can be easily changed or replaced.

Output formats: The support of various output formats allows the use of different visualisation tools, like Graphviz or our own *jABC* libraries for graph layout and rendering.

2.2 The Syntax

The syntax is given in Fig. 1. It contains the non-terminal symbols F (formula), T (second-order term[3]) and A (atomic formula); the start symbol is F.

There are two special second-order variables: **empty**, which represents the string only containing 0's, and **all**, which represents the string only consisting

```
T ::= Id  |  all  |  empty  |  union(T,T)  |  inter(T,T)  |
      comp(T)  |  (T)
A ::= sing(T)      |  ~sing(T)      |  subset(T,T)    |  ~subset(T,T)  |
      subseteq(T,T)  |  ~subseteq(T,T)  |  T = T     |  T ~= T  |
      shifteq(T,T)   |  ~shifteq(T,T)   |  T < T     |  T <= T  |
      roteq(T,T)     |  ~roteq(T,T)     |
      0 in T  |  0 ~in T  |  $ in T  |  $ ~in T
F ::= true  |  false  |  F & F  |  F | F  |  F -> F  |
      F <-> F  |  F ^ F  |  Id(T,...,T)  |  ~Id(T,...,T)  |
      ex Id,...,Id: F  |  ~ex Id,...,Id: F  |
      "<aut_file>"(T,...,T)  |  ~"<aut_file>"(T,...,T)  |
      let Id(Id,...,Id) in F  |  A  |  (F)
```

Fig. 1. The syntax of *jMosel*

---

[2] Binary decision diagrams, see for example [4].

[3] Second-order terms can be identified with parametric bit-strings as well as sets.

of 1's. Since second-order variables can be identified with sets, the usual set operations (union, inter, comp) can be applied.

The atomic formula sing(T) specifies a second-order variable T to be singleton, subset(T,T) and subseteq(T,T) define subset relations between the two second-order arguments, the formulas T=T, T~=T, T<T, T<=T allow us to compare second-order terms as binary numbers, the formulas 0 in T and $ in T test if the positions 0 (first position) and $ (last position) are elements of the set of positions denoted by the second-order term T, and shifteq(T,T) and roteq(T,T) compare two second-order terms after bit-shift and bit-rotation respectively. Every atomic formula has a negated counterpart with a leading ~.

The set of formulas contains the elementary formulas true and false, the operations conjunction &, disjunction |, implication ->, equivalence <-> and exclusive or ^. Furthermore the syntax offers existential quantification, the specification of user-defined predicates by the let-construct and the reuse of precomputed automata.

2.3   The Semantics

The *jMosel* formulas are transformed into complete and deterministic finite-state automata in such a way that the language recognized by an automaton corresponds to the interpretation of the represented formula. All automata for atomic formulas are pre-compiled to accelerate the compilation process.

As an example, Fig. 2 shows the semantics of sing(x). The accepting state of the automaton can only be reached if the second-order term x contains exactly one 1-bit.

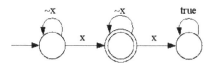

Fig. 2. Semantics of sing(x)

3   Implementation

jMosel is implemented in Java, for easy maintainance of the code and to make the tool instantly available on nearly every important hardware and operating system. Only for the most crucial and time consuming part, the potentially complex edge labels represented by BDDs, C++ libraries can be referenced, to ensure fast calculations with minimum overhead. At need, the same mechanism can be used to access packages written in other languages or in assembler - but this would then reintroduce platform-dependence.

The architecture of *jMosel* is shown in Fig. 3. An input formula is parsed into a syntax tree. The compiler traverses the tree to create the automaton representing the formula's semantics, which is finally translated into the desired output format.

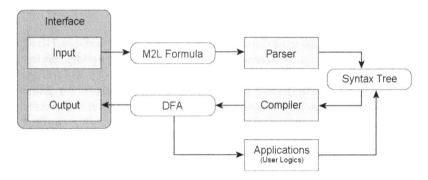

Fig. 3. The architecture of *jMosel*

The modular design of *jMosel* allows the input and ouput mechanisms to be exchanged or extended easily. Currently two implementations of such interfaces are available:

The command line tool jMoselC offers text-based input and output of formulas and automata. For visualisation, external tools are supported, e.g. Graphviz. Figure 4 shows the result of a combined use of jMoselC, Graphviz and a picture viewer. The automaton represents the semantics of the formula `subseteq(x,y) & x~=empty & y~=all`, which has been entered on the command line (see the upper left part of the figure).

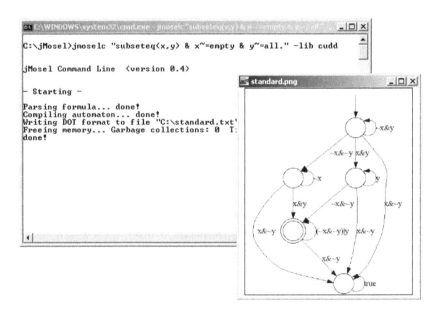

Fig. 4. Command line tool with Graphviz output

The jABC plugin enables the user to construct more sophisticated workflows, that may for example include the graphical construction of formulas with the *Formula Builder* plugin [5] and the custom layout of automata. Figure 5 shows an example session during which an automaton has been compiled and layouted. The corresponding formula `let fa(x) = 0 ~in x | x=all in fa(x) ^ fa(y)` can be seen in the *jMosel* input field on the left side of the figure.

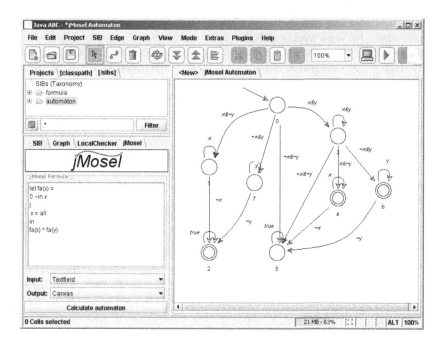

Fig. 5. *jABC* plugin example session

4   Ongoing Work

The main emphasis of the development within the *jMosel* group is placed on the following tasks:

- The *jETI System* [10, 13] will enable *jMosel* to be remotely executed over the internet as a WebService.
- An extension of the input logic will contain first-order and bit variables, e.g. as arguments to quantifiers.
- A new PSL [1] logic layer will offer means for the formulation and verification of PSL assertions based on regular expressions.
- An exhaustive library of hardware circuits will allow the intuitive description and verification of parametric hardware systems at register-transfer and gate level. This approach abstracts from the underlying logic layers and therefore is accessible for users unfamiliar with M2L(Str).

References

1. Accellera Organization, Inc. *Accellera Property Specification Language 1.1 Reference Manual*, 2004.
2. David A. Basin and Nils Klarlund. Hardware Verification using Monadic Second-Order Logic. In *Proc. CAV'95*, volume 939 of *Lecture Notes in Computer Science*, pages 31–41. Springer Verlag, 1995.
3. Alonzo Church. Logic, arithmetic and automata. In *Proc. Intern. Congr. Math.*, pages 23–35. Almqvist and Wiksells, 1963.
4. Rolf Drechsler and Bernd Becker. *Binary Decision Diagrams: Theory and Implementation*. Springer Verlag, 1998.
5. S. Jörges, T. Margaria, and B. Steffen. FormulaBuilder: A Tool for Graph-based Modelling and Generation of Formulae. 2006. To be published in ICSE '06: Proceedings of the 28th international conference on Software engineering.
6. Jørn Lind-Nielsen. BuDDy. http://sourceforge.net/projects/buddy. 18. 01. 2006.
7. Tiziana Margaria. Fully Automatic Verification and Error Detection for Parameterized Iterative Sequential Circuits. In *Proc. TACAS '96*, volume 1055 of *Lecture Notes in Computer Science*, pages 258–277. Springer Verlag, 1996.
8. Tiziana Margaria and Michael Mendler. Model-based Automatic Synthesis and Analysis in Second-Order Monadic Logic. In *Proceedings AAS'97, ACM/SIGPLAN Int. Worksh. on Automated Analysis of Software*, pages 99–112, 1997.
9. Tiziana Margaria, Michael Mendler, and Claudia Gsottberger. Modelling and Verification of Unbounded Length Systolic Arrays in Monadic Second Order Logic. In *Proc. Infinity'98 - Int. Workshop on Infinite State Systems, satellite to ICALP98, SFB-Bericht 342/09/98A*, pages 9–23. TU Munich, 1998.
10. Tiziana Margaria, Ralf Nagel, and Bernhard Steffen. Remote Integration and Coordination of Verification Tools in jETI. In *Proc. ECBS 2005, 12th IEEE Int. Conf. on the Engineering of Computer Based Systems*, pages 431–436. IEEE Computer Soc. Press, 2005.
11. Anders Møller. Program Verification with Monadic Second-Order Logic & Languages for Web Service Development. Technical report, Brics, Daimi, 2002. PhD thesis.
12. Ralf Nagel. jABC. http://jabc.cs.uni-dortmund.de. 18. 01. 2006.
13. Ralf Nagel. jETI. http://jeti.cs.uni-dortmund.de. 18. 01. 2006.
14. Rajeev Ranjan. CAL BDD. http://www-cad.eecs.berkeley.edu/Research/cal_bdd/. 18. 01. 2006.
15. Fabio Somenzi. CUDD. http://vlsi.colorado.edu/ fabio/CUDD/cuddIntro.html 18. 01. 2006.
16. Arash Vahidi. JDD. http://javaddlib.sourceforge.net/jdd/index.html. 18. 01. 2006.
17. John Whaley. JavaBDD. http://javabdd.sourceforge.net/. 18. 01. 2006.

Model Checking Dynamic States in GROOVE

Harmen Kastenberg* and Arend Rensink

Department of Computer Science, University of Twente,
P.O. Box 217, AE 7500, Enschede, The Netherlands
{h.kastenberg, rensink}@cs.utwente.nl

Abstract. Much research has been done in the field of model-checking complex systems (either hardware or software). Approaches that use explicit state modelling mostly use bit vectors to represent the states of such systems. Unfortunately, that kind of representation does not extend smoothly to systems in which the states contain values from a domain other than primitive types, such as reference values commonly used in object-oriented systems.

In this paper we report preliminary results on applying CTL model checking on state spaces generated using graph transformations. The states of such state spaces have an internal graph structure which makes it possible to represent complex system states without the need to know the exact structure beforehand as when using bit vectors.

1 Introduction

Verifying complex systems is a big field of research. For hardware systems, model checking techniques have proven to be quite successful. Lately, researchers are trying to also apply model-checking techniques for the verification of software systems.

In the Groove-project we focus on the use of model checking techniques for verifying object-oriented systems, where the states of the system are modelled as *graphs*, instead of bit vectors as in most explicit state representing approaches. We think this approach creates new opportunities to specify and verify systems in which the states mainly depend on a set of reference values instead of values of primitive types (with a finite domain) only. Due to frequent (de)allocation of reference values, the states of such systems are highly dynamic, due to their *variable size*. Graphs provide a natural way of representing the states of such systems and specifying interesting properties.

The state spaces on which we perform the model checking process are generated from so-called graph production systems using the GROOVE Simulator [9]. This results in a so-called graph transition system. These are then translated to ordinary Kripke structures after which we are able apply standard CTL model checking.

---

* The author is employed in the GROOVE project funded by the Dutch NWO (project number 612.000.314).

A. Valmari (Ed.): SPIN 2006, LNCS 3925, pp. 299–305, 2006.

2   State Space Generation

In our approach we model systems by representing their states as graphs and
their behaviour as graph transformations [13]. In this work, a *graph* G consists
of a finite set N of *nodes* and a finite set $E \subseteq N \times L \times N$ of *edges* (where L is
a global set of labels). We use $\mathcal{G}$ to denote the set of all graphs, ranged over by
G, H. Fig. 2.1 shows an example graph representing a specific state of a circular
buffer containing three cells.[1]

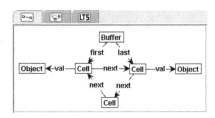

Fig. 2.1. A circular buffer having 2 filled cells out of 3

The state space representing the entire behaviour of the system can be generated from a *graph production system* (GPS), which consists of a graph I representing the initial state of the system and a set of *graph transformation rules*
$\mathcal{R}$. A graph transformation rule specifies how the system evolves when going
from one state to another. A graph transformation rule $p \in \mathcal{R}$ is identified by
its *name* ($N_p \in \mathcal{N}$, where $\mathcal{N}$ is a global set of rule names) and consists of a
left-hand-side graph (L_p), a *right-hand side graph* (R_p), and a set of so-called
negative application conditions (NAC_p, which are supergraphs of L_p) [4]. The
application of a graph transformation rule p transforms a graph G, the *source
graph*, into a graph H, the *target graph*, by looking for an occurrence of L_p in G
(specified by a graph matching m that cannot be extended to an occurrence of
any graph in NAC_p) and then replacing that occurrence with R_p, resulting in H.
Such a rule application is denoted as $G \xrightarrow{p,m} H$. A precise technical specification
of the graph transformation process can be found in [13, 4].

Fig. 2.2 shows three screen-shots from our tool (see below) displaying three
graph transformation rules: put for inserting a newly created object into the
buffer, get for getting an object out of the buffer (and deleting it), and extend
for enlarging the capacity of the buffer with one. Note that these transformation
rules specify the behaviour of a circular buffer. This means that performing a
put and get operation subsequently, moves both the first and the last pointer one
cell further. Performing an equal number of puts and gets (without extending
the buffer) results in isomorphic states (which are identified within the tool).

The different shapes (and colours) of the nodes and edges refer to the different
roles of the elements within the rule. The thin solid elements (black in a coloured

---

[1] In order to improve the readability of the graphs, we show the labels of self-edges as
labels of the corresponding nodes.

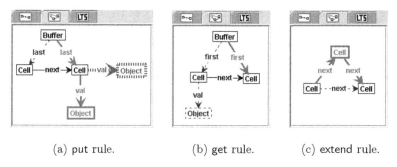

(a) put rule.   (b) get rule.   (c) extend rule.

Fig. 2.2. Graph transformation rules specifying the behaviour of the circular buffer

print-out) are part of both L and R. They need to be present in the source graph in order for the rule to apply and will be preserved during transformation. The thin dashed elements (blue) are also part of L but not of R, and will be removed. The solid fat gray elements (green) are part of R but not of L and will be created. The dashed fat gray elements (red) represent the NACs, whose presence in the source graph prevent the rule from being applied.

Each GPS $P = \langle \mathcal{R}, I \rangle$ specifies a (possibly infinite) state space which can be generated by repeatedly applying the graph transformation rules on the states, starting from the initial state I. This results in a *graph transition system* (GTS):

Definition 1 (graph transition system). *The graph transition system $T = \langle S, \rightarrow, I \rangle$ generated by $P = \langle \mathcal{R}, I \rangle$ consists of a set S of states, which are actually graphs $(S \subseteq \mathcal{G})$; a transition relation $\rightarrow \subseteq S \times \mathcal{R} \times [\mathcal{G} \rightarrow \mathcal{G}] \times S$, such that $\langle G, p, m, H \rangle \in \rightarrow$ iff there is a rule application $G \xrightarrow{p,m} H'$ with H' isomorphic to H; and an initial state $I \in S$.*

The graph transformation process is implemented in the Groove Simulator [9]. This tool is implemented in Java, and currently consists of 18 packages comprising approximately 400 classes, and 75,000 lines of code. The tool can handle arbitrary

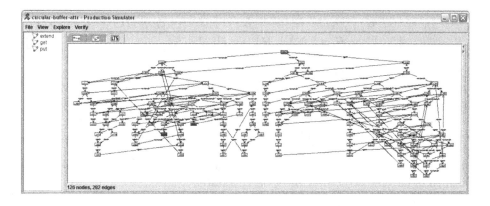

Fig. 2.3. State space of a circular buffer with capacity extending to 5

GPSs, but can obviously only generate a finite part of the corresponding graph transition system. Some performance figures were reported in [11]; as an indication, in its current form the tool can handle up to 200,000 states for average graph size of 50 nodes. Two intrinsically complex parts of the state space generation are: finding occurrences of left hand sides, and determining isomorphism of states.

Fig. 2.3 shows a finite part of the graph transition system for the transformation rules from Fig. 2.2 and the initial graph of Fig. 2.1, where the states are limited to those where the number of buffer cells is 5. The resulting state space consists of 126 states and 282 transitions.

3   CTL Model Checking

In the approach reported here, we have chosen to express properties in the temporal logic CTL [3]. The main reason for choosing CTL and not, for example, LTL, is the simplicity of the former, both in terms of complexity (the model checking problem for CTL is well known to be linear in both the size of the state space and the size of the formula) and in terms of the actual algorithm.

In order to perform model checking on the graph transition systems generated in the previous section we need to translate them to *Kripke structures*, which are defined over a finite set AP of *atomic propositions*.

Definition 2 (Kripke structure). *A Kripke structure $K = \langle S, \rightarrow, I, L \rangle$ consists of a set S of states, a total transition relation $\rightarrow \subseteq S \times S$, a set $I \subseteq S$ of initial states, and a labelling function $L : S \rightarrow 2^{AP}$, which maps each state to the subset of atomic propositions holding in that state.*

When translating a GTS T to a Kripke structure K_T, two issues need to be taken care of: (1) $\rightarrow_T$ must be made *total* (if this is not yet the case) and (2) the labelling function L_K must be defined. As atomic propositions we use the rule names, $\mathcal{N}$. Thus, a GTS T gives rise to a Kripke structure K_T such that:

$$S_K = S_T$$
$$I_K = \{S_I\}$$
$$\rightarrow_K = \{\langle G, H \rangle \mid \exists p, m : G \xrightarrow{p,m}_T H\} \cup \{\langle G, G \rangle \mid \nexists p, m, H : G \xrightarrow{p,m}_T H\}$$
$$L_K(G) = \{N_p \mid \exists m, H : G \xrightarrow{p,m}_T H\}, \text{ for all } G \in S_K$$

From the construction process described above it becomes clear that the labelling function of the resulting Kripke structure, in graph transformation terms, actually maps each state on the set of names of the graph transformation rules that were applicable in that state. This means that for each transformation rule p, L_p and NAC_p constitute a property of graphs that can be used as an atomic proposition named N_p[2]. In the special case where L_p and R_p are identical, the rule actually specifies a *state property* instead of a graph transformation, since such rules have no structural effect on any state.

---

[2] In [10] we show that properties specified this way may correspond precisely to a certain fragment of First-Order logic.

Two example properties to check for on the circular buffer example are:

$$AG(\neg gap) \qquad (1)$$

$$AG(EF(empty)) \qquad (2)$$

Property 1 is a safety property specifying that the buffer may not contain a *gap*, which is an empty cell following a non-empty cell that is not the last cell of the buffer. Fig. 3.1 (a) specifies the gap-proposition in the form of a rule (with identical left and right hand side). Property 2 is a liveness property specifying that the state representing the empty buffer must reachable infinitely often. The buffer is empty when the first cell does not contain a value, as shown in Fig. 3.1 (b).

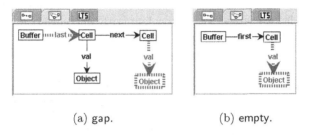

(a) gap.   (b) empty.

Fig. 3.1. Graph structures as properties

It turns out that the system of Fig. 2.3 actually does *not* satisfy Property 1. This is because we have not specified the extend-rule correctly: it puts no constraints on the places where the buffer may be extended, and hence may well introduce a gap. After fixing this, the system indeed satisfies both properties.

Results. In order to compare our tool with existing ones, we also implemented our running example as a (more or less) equivalent SPIN-program [7]. A naive translation results in a SPIN-program using a bit-array (with the maximum allowed capacity as its length) storing 1's (representing full cells) and 0's (representing empty cells). A more sophisticated SPIN-program can use the built-in channels to store the buffer values. Note that this no longer is a real circular buffer. In both cases we implement the possible operations as being atomic. In the naive implementation, the first and last pointer travel along the array resulting in many more states. In the sophisticated implementation there is no need for a first and last pointer.

Statistics about the state spaces generated by the three programs are given in Table 3.2. In this table we list for each implementation the number states, the state space generation time (GT) and the memory needed to store the states. From this table we can conclude that GROOVE cannot compete with SPIN regarding time-performance. The main reason for this is because checking for isomorphic graphs and constructing the graph matchings is very expensive; indeed, for the buffer of 200 cells, over 90% of the time is spent in isomorphism checking. However, isomorphism does result in automatic symmetry reduction, as can be seen be comparing the numbers of states in the GROOVE and naive SPIN implementations. Concerning memory usage for state storage, both tools perform

Table 3.2. Performance statistics

Max cap.	GROOVE			SPIN naive			SPIN smart		
	States	GT (s)	Memory (MB)	States	GT (s)	Memory (MB)	States	GT (s)	Memory (MB)
25	345	1.5	< 1	5,845	< 1	0.2	345	< 1	< 1
50	1,320	6.9	< 10	44,195	< 1	3.1	1,320	< 1	< 1
100	5,145	60.6	< 20	343,395	< 1	42.6	5,145	< 1	0.6
200	20,295	636.5	< 20	2.7+e6	20	606.3	20,295	< 1	4.5

comparable. From the object-oriented point of view, the example showed that GROOVE provides a natural way of dealing with reference-pointers, whereas the encoding in SPIN resorts to built-in static data types.

As mentioned before, we have implemented the standard CTL algorithm (with backwards state traversal). Currently, the verification process is performed sequentially after the state space generation. By combining both phases, so called *on-the-fly* model checking, we could also run the algorithm on graph production systems that yield potentially infinite state spaces, and get a result if it can be computed on a finitely representable fragment of the graph transition system.

4 Conclusion

We have shown how to apply CTL model checking on state spaces generated from graph production systems. The innovation in this approach lies not in the model checking itself but in the use of graphs for explicit dynamic state representation, which, as we have argued before, gives rise to an alternative to bit vectors that is potentially more flexible. We have shown some statistics on how our tool performs when compared to SPIN. The choice of CTL is not important in this respect.

Within the area of software model checking, a large number of other software verification tools have been developed, e.g. Java PathFinder [5], BLAST [6], SLAM [1], and MAGIC [2]. The last three focus on the verification of C programs instead of OO-systems like our tool and Java PathFinder. Representing states as graphs, instead of using arrays and lists, as is done in Java PathFinder, provides a more natural way of dealing with reference values, and symmetry reduction boils down to checking for isomorphic graphs. While Java PathFinder uses the byte code of a program, we represent the source code as graphs, taking the abstract syntax of the language as a starting point [8].

In the future we plan to do more experiments using the technique described in this paper. Next to that, there is a lot of further work to be done on improving the state space generation part. For one thing, currently no advantage is taken whatsoever of the potential for partial order reduction. In the running example of this paper, partial order reduction would already pay off, because the put-and get-rules are actually provably *confluent*. Alternatively, in [12] we describe an *abstraction* technique for graph transformation that results in smaller (in fact, finite) state spaces, at the price of false negatives in the model checking phase.

Acknowledgements

We would like to thank the anonymous referees for their detailed comments and constructive suggestions.

References

1. T. Ball and S. K. Rajamani. The SLAM project: Debugging system software via static analysis. In *29th Annual ACM SIGPLAN - SIGACT Symposium on Principles of Programming Languages (POPL)*, pages 1–3. ACM Press, 2002.
2. S. Chaki, E. Clarke, A. Groce, S. Jha, and H. Veith. Modular verification of software components in C. *IEEE Trans. Softw. Eng.*, 30(6):388–402, 2004.
3. E. M. Clarke and E. A. Emerson. Design and synthesis of synchronization skeletons using branching time temporal logic. In *Proceedings of the IBM Workshop on Logics of Programs*, volume 131 of *Lecture Notes in Computer Science*, pages 52–71. Springer, 1982.
4. A. Habel, R. Heckel, and G. Taentzer. Graph grammars with negative application conditions. *Fundamenta Informaticae*, 26(3-4):287–313, 1996.
5. K. Havelund and T. Pressburger. Model checking Java programs using Java PathFinder. *International Journal on Software Tools for Technology Transfer*, 2(4), 2000.
6. T. A. Henzinger, R. Jhala, R. Majumdar, and G. Sutre. Software verification with BLAST. In T. Ball and S. K. Rajamani, editors, *SPIN Workshop on Model Checking Software*, volume 2648 of *Lecture Notes in Computer Science*, pages 235–239. Springer, 2003.
7. G. J. Holzmann. *The Spin Model Checker - Primer and Reference Manual*. Addison-Wesley, 2003.
8. H. Kastenberg, A. Kleppe, and A. Rensink. Engineering object-oriented semantics using graph transformations. Technical report, Department of Computer Science, University of Twente, 2005. Pre-final version available at http://www.cs.utwente.nl/~rensink/papers/taal-draft.pdf.
9. A. Rensink. The GROOVE Simulator: A tool for state space generation. In J. L. Pfaltz, M. Nagl, and B. Böhlen, editors, *Applications of Graph Transformations with Industrial Relevance (AGTIVE)*, volume 3062 of *Lecture Notes in Computer Science*, pages 479–485. Springer, 2004.
10. A. Rensink. Representing first-order logic using graphs. In H. Ehrig, G. Engels, F. Parisi-Presicce, and G. Rozenberg, editors, *International Conference on Graph Transformations (ICGT)*, volume 3256 of *Lecture Notes in Computer Science*, pages 319–335. Springer, 2004.
11. A. Rensink. Time and space issues in the generation of graph transition systems. In *International Workshop on Graph-Based Tools (GraBaTs)*, volume 127 of *Electronic Notes in Theoretical Computer Science*, pages 127–139, 2005.
12. A. Rensink and D. Distefano. Abstract graph transformation. In *International Workshop on Software Verification and Validation (SVV)*, Electronic Notes in Theoretical Computer Science, 2005. To appear. Technical report version: CTIT TR–CTIT–05–04, University of Twente.
13. G. Rozenberg, editor. *Handbook of Graph Grammars and Computing by Graph Transformation*, volume 1: Foundations. World Scientific, 1997.

Author Index

Lecture Notes in Computer Science

For information about Vols. 1–3813

please contact your bookseller or Springer

Vol. 3860: D. Pointcheval (Ed.), Topics in Cryptology – CT-RSA 2006. XI, 365 pages. 2006.

Vol. 3858: A. Valdes, D. Zamboni (Eds.), Recent Advances in Intrusion Detection. X, 351 pages. 2006.

Vol. 3857: M.P.C. Fossorier, H. Imai, S. Lin, A. Poli (Eds.), Applied Algebra, Algebraic Algorithms and Error-Correcting Codes. XI, 350 pages. 2006.

Vol. 3855: E. A. Emerson, K.S. Namjoshi (Eds.), Verification, Model Checking, and Abstract Interpretation. XI, 443 pages. 2005.

Vol. 3854: I. Stavrakakis, M. Smirnov (Eds.), Autonomic Communication. XIII, 303 pages. 2006.

Vol. 3853: A.J. Ijspeert, T. Masuzawa, S. Kusumoto (Eds.), Biologically Inspired Approaches to Advanced Information Technology. XIV, 388 pages. 2006.

Vol. 3852: P.J. Narayanan, S.K. Nayar, H.-Y. Shum (Eds.), Computer Vision – ACCV 2006, Part II. XXXI, 977 pages. 2006.

Vol. 3851: P.J. Narayanan, S.K. Nayar, H.-Y. Shum (Eds.), Computer Vision – ACCV 2006, Part I. XXXI, 973 pages. 2006.

Vol. 3850: R. Freund, G. Păun, G. Rozenberg, A. Salomaa (Eds.), Membrane Computing. IX, 371 pages. 2006.

Vol. 3849: I. Bloch, A. Petrosino, A.G.B. Tettamanzi (Eds.), Fuzzy Logic and Applications. XIV, 438 pages. 2006. (Sublibrary LNAI).

Vol. 3848: J.-F. Boulicaut, L. De Raedt, H. Mannila (Eds.), Constraint-Based Mining and Inductive Databases. X, 401 pages. 2006. (Sublibrary LNAI).

Vol. 3847: K.P. Jantke, A. Lunzer, N. Spyratos, Y. Tanaka (Eds.), Federation over the Web. X, 215 pages. 2006. (Sublibrary LNAI).

Vol. 3846: H. J. van den Herik, Y. Björnsson, N.S. Netanyahu (Eds.), Computers and Games. XIV, 333 pages. 2006.

Vol. 3845: J. Farré, I. Litovsky, S. Schmitz (Eds.), Implementation and Application of Automata. XIII, 360 pages. 2006.

Vol. 3844: J.-M. Bruel (Ed.), Satellite Events at the MoDELS 2005 Conference. XIII, 360 pages. 2006.

Vol. 3843: P. Healy, N.S. Nikolov (Eds.), Graph Drawing. XVII, 536 pages. 2006.

Vol. 3842: H.T. Shen, J. Li, M. Li, J. Ni, W. Wang (Eds.), Advanced Web and Network Technologies, and Applications. XXVII, 1057 pages. 2006.

Vol. 3841: X. Zhou, J. Li, H.T. Shen, M. Kitsuregawa, Y. Zhang (Eds.), Frontiers of WWW Research and Development - APWeb 2006. XXIV, 1223 pages. 2006.

Vol. 3840: M. Li, B. Boehm, L.J. Osterweil (Eds.), Unifying the Software Process Spectrum. XVI, 522 pages. 2006.

Vol. 3839: J.-C. Filliâtre, C. Paulin-Mohring, B. Werner (Eds.), Types for Proofs and Programs. VIII, 275 pages. 2006.

Vol. 3838: A. Middeldorp, V. van Oostrom, F. van Raamsdonk, R. de Vrijer (Eds.), Processes, Terms and Cycles: Steps on the Road to Infinity. XVIII, 639 pages. 2005.

Vol. 3837: K. Cho, P. Jacquet (Eds.), Technologies for Advanced Heterogeneous Networks. IX, 307 pages. 2005.

Vol. 3836: J.-M. Pierson (Ed.), Data Management in Grids. X, 143 pages. 2006.

Vol. 3835: G. Sutcliffe, A. Voronkov (Eds.), Logic for Programming, Artificial Intelligence, and Reasoning. XIV, 744 pages. 2005. (Sublibrary LNAI).

Vol. 3834: D.G. Feitelson, E. Frachtenberg, L. Rudolph, U. Schwiegelshohn (Eds.), Job Scheduling Strategies for Parallel Processing. VIII, 283 pages. 2005.

Vol. 3833: K.-J. Li, C. Vangenot (Eds.), Web and Wireless Geographical Information Systems. XI, 309 pages. 2005.

Vol. 3832: D. Zhang, A.K. Jain (Eds.), Advances in Biometrics. XX, 796 pages. 2005.

Vol. 3831: J. Wiedermann, G. Tel, J. Pokorný, M. Bieliková, J. Štuller (Eds.), SOFSEM 2006: Theory and Practice of Computer Science. XV, 576 pages. 2006.

Vol. 3830: D. Weyns, H. V.D. Parunak, F. Michel (Eds.), Environments for Multi-Agent Systems II. VIII, 291 pages. 2006. (Sublibrary LNAI).

Vol. 3829: P. Pettersson, W. Yi (Eds.), Formal Modeling and Analysis of Timed Systems. IX, 305 pages. 2005.

Vol. 3828: X. Deng, Y. Ye (Eds.), Internet and Network Economics. XVII, 1106 pages. 2005.

Vol. 3827: X. Deng, D.-Z. Du (Eds.), Algorithms and Computation. XX, 1190 pages. 2005.

Vol. 3826: B. Benatallah, F. Casati, P. Traverso (Eds.), Service-Oriented Computing - ICSOC 2005. XVIII, 597 pages. 2005.

Vol. 3824: L.T. Yang, M. Amamiya, Z. Liu, M. Guo, F.J. Rammig (Eds.), Embedded and Ubiquitous Computing – EUC 2005. XXIII, 1204 pages. 2005.

Vol. 3823: T. Enokido, L. Yan, B. Xiao, D. Kim, Y. Dai, L.T. Yang (Eds.), Embedded and Ubiquitous Computing – EUC 2005 Workshops. XXXII, 1317 pages. 2005.

Vol. 3822: D. Feng, D. Lin, M. Yung (Eds.), Information Security and Cryptology. XII, 420 pages. 2005.

Vol. 3821: R. Ramanujam, S. Sen (Eds.), FSTTCS 2005: Foundations of Software Technology and Theoretical Computer Science. XIV, 566 pages. 2005.

Vol. 3820: L.T. Yang, X.-s. Zhou, W. Zhao, Z. Wu, Y. Zhu, M. Lin (Eds.), Embedded Software and Systems. XXVIII, 779 pages. 2005.

Vol. 3819: P. Van Hentenryck (Ed.), Practical Aspects of Declarative Languages. X, 231 pages. 2005.

Vol. 3818: S. Grumbach, L. Sui, V. Vianu (Eds.), Advances in Computer Science – ASIAN 2005. XIII, 294 pages. 2005.

Vol. 3817: M. Faundez-Zanuy, L. Janer, A. Esposito, A. Satue-Villar, J. Roure, V. Espinosa-Duro (Eds.), Nonlinear Analyses and Algorithms for Speech Processing. XII, 380 pages. 2006. (Sublibrary LNAI).

Vol. 3816: G. Chakraborty (Ed.), Distributed Computing and Internet Technology. XXI, 606 pages. 2005.

Vol. 3815: E.A. Fox, E.J. Neuhold, P. Premsmit, V. Wu-wongse (Eds.), Digital Libraries: Implementing Strategies and Sharing Experiences. XVII, 529 pages. 2005.

Vol. 3814: M. Maybury, O. Stock, W. Wahlster (Eds.), Intelligent Technologies for Interactive Entertainment. XV, 342 pages. 2005. (Sublibrary LNAI).